HACHETTE

WINE

GUIDES

dictionary of wine

dictionary of wine

ALL THE FRENCH WINE APPELLATIONS, FROM A-Z

CASSELL
ILLUSTRATED

UNITED KINGDOM

BELGIUM

GERMANY

Channel

LUXEMBOURG

Reims

Seine

Oise

Metz

Meuse

East

Épernay

Marne

Strasbourg

Paris

Champagne

Meurthe

Toul

Alsace

Rhine

Bar-sur-Aube

Colmar

Orléans

Auxerre

Les Riceys

Loire

Vendôme

Chablis

Dijon

CÔTE-DE-NUITS

ANJOU

Tours

Sancerre

Pouilly-sur-Loire

Burgundy

Saône

Angers

TOURAINE

Beaune

Jura

Nantes

Saumur

CÔTE-DE-BEAUNE

Arbois

PAYS NANTAIS

SAUMUR REGION

Bourges

CHALON REGION

Chalon-sur-Saône

SWITZERLAND

Lake Geneva

Loire Valley

Centre

Châteaumeillant

MÂCON REGION

Poitiers

Saint-Pourçain-sur-Sioule

Mâcon

Fiefs Vendéens

Vienne

Creuse

Allier

AUVERGNE

Roanne

Beaujolais

Savoie

Chambéry

ATLANTIC

Cognac

Clermont-Ferrand

Lyon

Vienne

Pineau des Charentes

OCEAN

Loire

Rhône Valley

ITALY

MÉDOC

BLAYE REGION

Bordeaux region

Dordogne

Valence

Drôme

DIOIS

Bordeaux

LIBOURNE REGION

Bergerac

Rhône

Montélimar

ENTRE-DEUX-MERS

Lot

Cahors

AVEYRON

GRAVES

Agen

South West

Tarn

Avignon

Floc-de-Gascogne

Gaillac

Albi

Nîmes

COTEAUX DU LANGUEDOC

Aix-en-Provence

Nice

Armagnac

Toulouse

Montpellier

Bayonne

MINERVOIS

LANGUEDOC

Provence

Adour

Pau

Languedoc

Marseilles

Cassis

Irouléguy

BÉARN

Garonne

Limoux

Narbonne

Bandol

Patrimonio

SPAIN

CORBIÈRES

Perpignan

Corsica

ANDORRA

Roussillon

Banyuls-sur-Mer

Mediterranean Sea

Ajaccio

Bordeaux Wine growing region

MÉDOC Wine growing sub-region

100 Kilometres

Understanding
controlled appellations

The quality of a wine is linked to its terroir of origin and the manner in which it is produced – choice of grape varieties, methods of cultivation and winemaking practices. Vineyardists have known this for thousands of years but the concept has achieved a greater degree of refinement in France than elsewhere in the world. The hierarchical system that was established in France in 1935 has been used as a benchmark by the European Union since 1970, and by a number of other countries anxious to define the identity of their wine-growing region.

The pyramid of wines

Two categories of wine have been defined: table wines (*Vins de Table*) and VQPRD wines (*Vins de Qualité Produits dans une Région Déterminée* – quality wines produced in a limited region). Table wines in the strict sense of the term originate from member states of the European Union but do not state geographic origin. They include the *Vins de Pays*: country wines from precisely delimited but rather broad production areas (a region, department, or historical area*) where rules apply relating to grape varieties, maximum yields per hectare, etc. VQPRD wines are produced in strictly limited areas. They cover AOVDQS wines (*Appellations d'origine Vins de Qualité Supérieure* – quality wines

* *excluding departments that have given their name to all AOL.*

from certain specified areas in France) and AOC wines (*Appellations d'Origine Contrôlées* – wines of controlled origin). AOVDQS status was established in 1949 and these days applies only to some 20 or so wines, serving rather as a springboard to AOC status.

Recognising origin: a French ancestral principle

France has some 450 controlled appellations, most of which were established from 1935-1940. The notion of 'origin' however, is neither recent nor exclusively French. The Romans had delimited regions, notably Falerne in Campanie. In Burgundy in the 12th century, Cistercian monks made a point of identifying the best plots of vines in the Côte d'Or, according to the type of soil. Grapes from these plots were vinified separately.

Dealing with crises

The birth of controlled appellations is certainly linked to the identification of quality regions, but it also came in response to the need to define codes of practice in times of crisis. For example, in 1756 the Portuguese Prime Minister, the Marquis of Pombal, limited port production to the terraces of the Douro in order to control a market at the mercy of fraudulent practices and over-production.

In France in the 19th and 20th centuries, a series of crises motivated legislators to act. The first came in 1851 with the arrival of powdery mildew, followed in 1860 by the death-dealing phylloxera insect, then mildew in 1878. With its vineyards in tatters, France was soon unable to meet demand and facing mounting cases of fraudulent practice, including the production of ersatz wines.

United around a collective property

In 1905 a law on the repression of fraud was passed, followed two years' later by a strict definition of wine as a product 'produced exclusively from the alcoholic fermentation of fresh grapes or fresh grape juice'.

In 1908, legislators agreed on the delimitation of wine-growing areas. The first such region was Champagne, where the limits imposed by the authorities sparked riots. In 1919, legislators tried to reach a consensus with wine-growers by identifying appellation as 'collective property'. Finally in 1935 a draft bill was adopted setting out guidelines for the appointment of a committee of wine professionals who would be responsible for drawing up texts regulating wine-growing practices. The Comité National des Appellations d'Origine (National Committee for Controlled Appellations) became an official institute in 1947 (INAO). The first decrees were published in the official Journal as early as 1936, regulating production in the following appellations of controlled origin: Arbois, Cassis, Châteauneuf-du-Pape and Monbazillac. All such legislation is continually improved to take account of progress made in the fields of wine growing and oenology. The purpose of legislation is as follows: to define the limits of plots of vines within geographical areas; to establish a list of authorised grape varieties; to describe methods of vine-training (pruning, tying up, number of feet per hectare); to fix yields, minimum and maximum degrees of alcohol and oenological practices in general. The recent introduction of compulsory tastings means that a wine cannot be granted Appellation d'Origine status without having been analysed and approved by a committee of experts.

Appellations… and crus

An appellation may be regional (Bordeaux, Burgundy), sub-regional (Entre-deux-Mers, Burgundy-Hautes Côtes de Beaune) or communal (Pauillac, Volnay). Viticultural France is divided into four regions that are distinguished by a more complex classification system within the appellation system – in some cases, it pre-dates the creation of the AOC. This is the concept of *crus* or growths, that vary in definition depending on the region. As early as 1855, Napoleon III instructed the chamber of commerce in the Bordeaux region to identify the best regional crus. Brokers analysed the price of wines produced by the leading châteaux and established a classification based on price as an indication of quality. At the top of the range are the Premier Cru Classés (the most expensive) with the Fifth Crus Classés at the other end of the scale. Thus were classified 60 crus in the Médoc region, one red cru from the Graves region (Haut-Brion), and the great wine-growing estates of the Sauternes-Barsac region. St Emilion had to wait for another 100 years (1955), Graves (now the Pessac-Léognan AOC) slightly longer (1959). The Bordeaux classification system is based on estates, whereas the Burgundy classification system took its lead from the Cistercian monks who made a selection of best-quality plots in villages (*lieux-dits* or *climats* as they are called in Burgundy). This system distinguishes between the Grands Crus (such as Chambertin), which are appellations in their own right, and the Premiers Crus that attach their names to a communal appellation.

A detailed survey in Alsace, in the period 1975-1992 led to the delimitation of 50 Grands Crus at the foot of the Vosges mountains and in the surrounding hillsides. The basis of selection was historic reputation and the quality of their terroir.

In Champagne, classification depends on the quality of production in each commune, using a system of evaluation dating from the end of the 19th century known as the 'Echelle des Crus'. According to this scale, 17 communes rank as Grands Crus, 43 as Premiers Crus. It is this detailed definition of the regions that has preserved the diversity of France's production. Each appellation has its own particular identity producing wines of characteristic appearance, bouquet and palate. You will discover that same diversity within these pages.

How to read this dictionary

The appellations are classified in strict alphabetical order and include all regions.

Name of the region

Date of official recognition of appellation

Situation

Name of sub-region

Appellation

Colour of wines and the proportion of production that they represent

Ideal characteristics of the wine at each stage of tasting

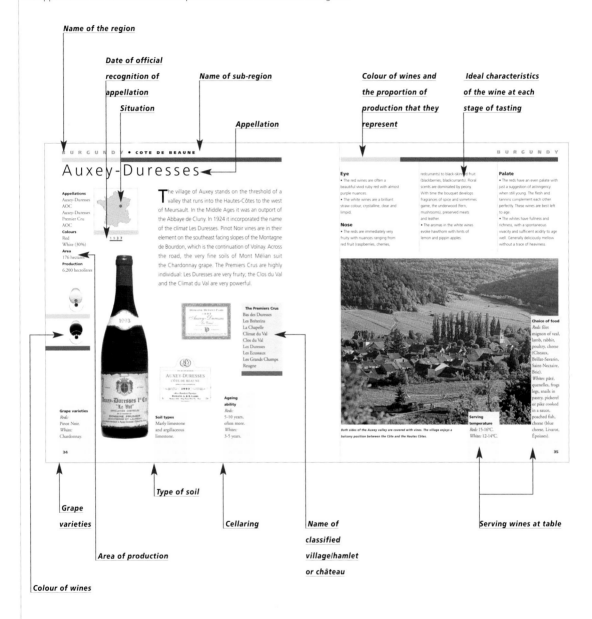

BURGUNDY • COTE DE BEAUNE

Auxey-Duresses

The village of Auxey stands on the threshold of a valley that runs into the Hautes-Côtes to the west of Meursault. In the Middle Ages it was an outpost of the Abbaye de Cluny. In 1924 it incorporated the name of the *climat* Les Duresses. Pinot Noir vines are in their element on the southeast facing slopes of the Montagne de Bourdon, which is the continuation of Volnay. Across the road, the very fine soils of Mont Mélian suit the Chardonnay grape. The Premiers Crus are highly individual: Les Duresses are very fruity; the Clos du Val and the Climat du Val are very powerful.

Appellations
Auxey-Duresses AOC
Auxey-Duresses Premier Cru AOC

Colours
Red
White (30%)

Area
176 hectares

Production
6,200 hectolitres

1937

The Premiers Crus
Bas des Duresses
Les Bréterins
La Chapelle
Climat du Val
Clos du Val
Les Duresses
Les Ecussaux
Les Grands Champs
Reugne

Grape varieties
Reds:
Pinot Noir.
Whites:
Chardonnay.

Soil types
Marly limestone and argillaceous limestone.

Ageing ability
Reds:
5-10 years, often more.
Whites:
3-5 years.

34

BURGUNDY

Eye
• The red wines are often a beautiful vivid ruby red with almost purple nuances.
• The white wines are a brilliant straw colour, crystalline, clear and limpid.

Nose
• The reds are immediately very fruity with nuances ranging from red fruit (raspberries, cherries, redcurrants) to black-skinned fruit (blackberries, blackcurrants). Floral scents are dominated by peony. With time the bouquet develops fragrances of spice and sometimes game, the underwood (fern, mushrooms), preserved meats and leather.
• The aromas in the white wines evoke hawthorn with hints of lemon and pippin apples.

Palate
• The reds have an even palate with just a suggestion of astringency when still young. The flesh and tannins complement each other perfectly. These wines are best left to age.
• The whites have fullness and richness, with a spontaneous vivacity and sufficient acidity to age well. Generally deliciously mellow without a trace of heaviness.

Choice of food
Reds: filet mignon of veal, lamb, rabbit, poultry, cheese (Cîteaux, Brillat-Savarin, Saint-Nectaire, Brie).
Whites: pâté, quenelles, frogs legs, snails in pastry, pickerel or pike cooked in a sauce, poached fish, cheese (blue cheese, Livarot, Époisses).

Serving temperature
Reds: 15-16°C.
Whites: 12-14°C.

Both sides of the Auxey valley are covered with vines. The village enjoys a balcony position between the Côte and the Hautes Côtes.

35

Grape varieties

Type of soil

Cellaring

Name of classified village/hamlet or château

Serving wines at table

Area of production

Colour of wines

Bottles, labels and estates are mentioned for editorial purposes only.

Ajaccio

Appellation
Ajaccio AOC
Colours
Red (52 %)
Rosé (37 %)
White (11 %)
Area
233 hectares
Production
103,450 hectolitres

1 9 8 4

Grape varieties
Reds and rosés:
Sciacarellu (at
least 40%),
Barbarossa.
Whites: Vermen-
tino (Malvoisie
de Corse).
*Subsidiary
varieties:* Ugni
Blanc, Grenache,
Cinsaut.

Ajaccio, the administrative centre of southern Corsica, may be justly proud of the predominantly red and rosé wines produced in its AOC. The surrounding hills are carpeted with vineyards that radiate outwards for some 10 kilometres, their leafy greenery adding to the charms of one of the most picturesque regions of the island, where golf courses, clear blue skies, lush vegetation and a jagged coastline glorify the splendour of the Mediterranean. The vines in this mountainous countryside are mainly planted around the villages, on hillsides no higher than 300-350 metres (985-1150 ft). Indeed the appellation was originally named the 'Coteaux d'Ajaccio'. Of 36 delimited communes, only 12 are included in the AOC. The region's one-and-only co-operative winery accounts for approximately 30% of total production.

*Most of the vines in
the Ajaccio AOC are
trellised and pruned* **Types of**
by the Cordon de **soil**
Royat system. Mainly granitic.

Ageing ability
Reds: up to
five years;
pleasant as a
young wine.
Rosés: drink
within the year
of production.
Whites: 1-2 years.

Eye

- The red wines are a subtle ruby-red colour.
- The rosés are bright pink with a multitude of different nuances.
- The white wines are also very bright with golden highlights.

Sciacarellu grapes planted on sunny hillsides yield fruity wines for early drinking.

Nose

- The red wines have a refined bouquet with aromas of violets and coffee and, depending on the region, hints of mineral, iodised scents.
- The rosé wines are highly aromatic, revealing fragrances of roses and cherries.
- The white wines have a floral, citrus fragrance thanks to the Vermintino grape variety. Wines made exclusively from Vermintino offer aromas of ripe fruits.

Palate

- The reds are elegant, finesse itself, enduring and fluid.
- The rosés are fresh-tasting and lively, the ideal summer wine. Generous without being aggressive.
- The whites are lively but at the same time soft with a distinctive fullness and fruitiness. The dominant impression is suppleness and roundness combined with exceptional length.

Due to its varied topography, the region enjoys many different microclimates.

Choice of food

Reds: grilled lamb, Corsican cheese.
Rosés: Corsican charcuterie, fish.
Whites: grilled fish, bouilla-baisse (fish stew), paella, mild cheese, puddings.

Serving temperature

Reds: 16-18°C.
Whites and rosés: 7-10°C .

9

Aloxe-Corton

1938

Appellations
Aloxe-Corton
AOC
Aloxe-Corton
Premier Cru
AOC

Colours
Red, white
(produced in
small quantities)

Area
Aloxe-Corton:
89.7 ha in Aloxe-
Corton
Aloxe-Corton
Premier Cru:
29.1 ha in Aloxe-
Corton and 8.4 ha
in Ladoix-Serrigny

Production
6,170 hl

Grape varieties
Reds:
Pinot Noir.
Whites:
Chardonnay.

Ageing ability
5-10 years (and
beyond,
depending on
the vintage).

The Montagne de Corton lies on the borders of the Côtes de Nuits and Beaune, forming an amphitheatre that encompasses three villages with overlapping appellations: Aloxe-Corton, Ladoix-Serrigny and Pernand-Vergelesses. The red Grands Crus and Premiers Crus are planted on limestone and marl soils on the slopes of the mountain; the vineyards of the communal AOC lie on the lower reaches on relatively shallow, pebbly soils.

Eye
Usually very deep in colour, sometimes purplish, deep ruby or intense crimson.

Nose
The young wine displays aromas of flowers (gardens in springtime) and fruit (cherry, blackcurrant, blackberry) that intensify as the wine develops with age.

Palate
Sometimes soft and fruity although it can take some years for the wine to open. The Pinot Noir grown on these deep soils on the lower slopes of the Montagne de Corton yields a full-bodied, generous wine with lasting character and good body supported by agreeable tannins and a silky, balanced texture.

The Premiers Crus
Clos des Maréchaudes
Clos du Chapitre
La Coutière
Les Chaillots
Les Fournières
Les Guérets
La Maréchaude
Les Maréchaudes
Les Moutottes
Les Paulands
Les Petites Lolières
La Toppe au Vert
Les Valozières
Les Vercots

Soil types
Reddish-brown
argillaceous
calcareous, with
an abundance of
siliceous
nodules, flint
debris and
sandstone
pebbles (*chaillots*)
and friable soils
rich in
potassium and
phosphoric acid.

**Serving
temperature**
Reds: 15-18°C.
Whites: 12-14°C.

Choice of food
Meat, roasted or
in a well-
seasoned sauce,
game (wild
rabbit) cheese
(Chaource).

Alsace Gewürztraminer

The Gewürztraminer grape variety appeared at the end of the 19th century in Alsace where it gradually replaced the Traminer. This vigorous, early-maturing grape variety is characterised by low yields (55 hectolitres/ha) and pink berries at full maturity. It is grown mainly on steeply sloping hillsides where it yields rich, full-bodied white wines with an unmistakable bouquet of great intensity.

1945

Appellation
Alsace AOC
Designation
Gewürztraminer
Area
2,538 hectares
Production
141,400 hectolitres

Eye
Fairly intense colour due to the characteristic pink pigmentation of the grapes.

Klevener de Heiligenstein: an elegant grape variety
Klevener de Heiligenstein is the same grape variety as Savagnin Rose, grown in the communes of Heiligenstein, Bourgheim, Gertwiller, Goxwiller, Heiligenstein and Obernai. Historically known as 'Traminer', this grape variety originated from Termino (Tramin) in the Haut-Adige, otherwise known as the Italian Tyrol. Like the Gewürztraminer grape variety, Klevener de Heiligenstein has fairly small clusters of thick-skinned berries that turn pink when fully ripe. It produces original, exclusively white wines that although little known are well worth discovering and ideal with foie gras.

Nose
Very aromatic with powerful aromas of flowers (roses) and tropical fruit (litchis).

Serving temperature
12°C.

Choice of food
As an apéritif with foie gras or with cheese, Kouglof or fruit tarts.

Above: view of a typical Alsace vineyard, with beautiful villages decorated with flowers and surrounded by vines.

Palate
Alsace Gewürztraminer generally combines high alcohol content, sometimes 14%/vol and more, with relatively low acidity. It reveals flavours of Muscat grapes, exotic fruit, but also quite often liquorice or smokiness. Being very sensitive to the soils where it is grown, this grape variety can acquire severe characteristics with age, displaying hints of leather. Dominantly creamy and smooth on the palate; a powerful, full-bodied, generous and well-structured wine.

Grape variety
Gewürztraminer.

Soil types
Marly limestone, shelly limestone, granitic soil.

Ageing
2-10 years.

Alsace Grand Cru

Appellation
Alsace Grand
Cru AOC
followed by
the *lieu-dit*

Colour
White

Area
15-350 hectares

Production
A few thousand
to 40,000 hl
depending on
the vintage

1975

The Hengst Grand
Cru in Alsace
(commune of
Wintzenheim).

The vineyards in Alsace extend in a long strip 1.5-3 kilometres (1-2 miles) wide and 110 kilometres (68 miles) long from north to south. The accent here is firmly on the grape variety that is nearly always stated after the appellation of origin. The Grand Cru concept may be very long standing in Alsace but the Alsace AOC Grand Cru itself was not authorised until 1975. In 1983 a decree was passed defining a first series of 25 *lieux-dits*. Then in 1992, 50 terroirs received Grand Cru status. The terroir or area is the most important production criterion in this appellation where the only authorised grape varieties are the four designated noble vine varieties: Riesling, Muscat, Pinot Gris and Gewürztraminer. These wines may only be made from grapes giving a minimum of 11% alcohol for the first two varieties and 12% alcohol for the others. The Alsace Grand Cru appellation has been a powerful driving force throughout the vineyard. At the threshold of the 21st century, significant changes to the regulations are in prospect that would enhance the individuality of each terroir and improve the management of this viticultural asset. They relate to such key factors as choice of grape variety, planting density and authorised yields.

Grape varieties
Gewürztraminer,
Pinot Gris,
Riesling,
Muscat.

**Ageing
ability**
2-10 years.

The 50 Grands Crus of Alsace
(followed by soil types and main grape varieties)

DEPARTMENT OF THE BAS-RHIN

Altenberg de Bergbieten	Dolomitic marls	Riesling, Gewürztraminer
Altenberg de Wolxheim	Limestone marls	Riesling
Bruderthal	Limestone marl	Riesling, Gewürztraminer
Engelberg	*Muschelkalk* limestone	Gewürztraminer
Frankstein	Granitic sand	Riesling
Kastelberg	Pebbly schist	Riesling
Kirchberg de Barr	Limestone	Gewürztraminer, Riesling, Pinot Gris
Moenchberg	Sandy-silty	Riesling
Muenchberg	Sandy	Riesling
Praelatenberg	Gneiss, sand	Riesling
Steinklotz	Marl covered in limestone scree	Riesling, Gewürztraminer
Wiebelsberg	Sandstone, sand	Riesling
Winzenberg	Granitic sand	Riesling
Zotzenberg	Jurassic limestone and limestone marl conglomerates	Riesling

DEPARTMENT OF THE HAUT-RHIN

Altenberg de Bergheim	Limestone marl, pebbly	Gewürztraminer
Brand	Granite	Riesling, Gewürztraminer
Eichberg	Marl mixed with limestone moraine	Gewürztraminer, Riesling, Pinot Gris
Florimont	Limestone marl	Gewürztraminer, Riesling
Froehn	Marly schist	Gewürztraminer
Furstentum	Brown calcareous	Gewürztraminer
Geisberg	Dolomitic marl	Riesling
Gloeckelberg	Sand, Vosges sandstone	Gewürztraminer, Pinot Gris
Goldert	Marl rich in limestone moraine	Gewürztraminer
Hatschbourg	Marly	Gewürztraminer, Pinot Gris, Muscat
Hengst	Limestone marl	Gewürztraminer, Pinot Gris
Kanzlerberg	Limestone marl	Riesling, Gewürztraminer
Kessler	Sand and pink sandstone on clay matrix	Gewürztraminer
Kirchberg de Ribeauvillé	Dolomitic marl	Riesling
Kitterlé	Sandstone	Riesling
Mambourg	Limestone marl	Gewürztraminer
Mandelberg	Limestone marl	Riesling, Gewürztraminer
Marckrain	Limestone marl	Gewürztraminer
Ollwiller	Pebbly marls	Riesling
Osterberg	Marls	Gewürztraminer, Riesling
Pfersigberg	Limestone/stony	Gewürztraminer, Riesling
Pfingstberg	Sandstone and limestone	Riesling
Rangen	Volcanic	Pinot Gris, Riesling
Rosacker	Marls and limestone	Riesling
Saering	Marly/sandy and moraine	Riesling
Schlossberg	Granitic sand	Riesling
Schoenenbourg	Marl overlaid with shell limestone	Riesling
Sommerberg	Granitic sand	Riesling
Sonnenglanz	Conglomerates and marls	Gewürztraminer, Pinot Gris
Spiegel	Marl and sandstone/sand	Gewürztraminer
Sporen	Marls	Gewürztraminer
Steinert	Limestone slope wash	Gewürztraminer, Pinot Gris
Steingrubler	Marls	Gewürztraminer, Riesling, Pinot Gris
Vorbourg	Limestone marl	Gewürztraminer, Riesling, Pinot Gris
Wineck-Schlossberg	Granitic	Riesling
Zinnkoepflé	Calcareous-sandy	Gewürztraminer

GEWÜRZTRAMINER flourishes in the ideal conditions provided by the vineyards of Alsace, especially on the well-exposed slopes of the Alsace Grand Cru appellation areas. The grapes achieve a high a degree of maturity, producing wines that often exceed the minimum requirement of 12% vol.

Eye

With age, the warm, golden tones of the young wines acquire a more amber hue. The wines are often sweet and fleshy with a certain smoothness that emphasises the natural warmth of the grape.

Nose

Wines produced from grapes grown on light soils (granite) are usually dominated by elegant floral aromas often mingled with scents of exotic fruit. Those from calcareous, pebbly soils are also very elegant, often with predominant aromas of flowers (roses) or hints of dried and sometimes citrus fruit. Wines from the most marly terroirs live up to the name of the grape variety – *Gewürz*, meaning spicy.

Palate

Relatively high alcohol content produces a certain warmth on the palate, balanced by a velvety sensation due to the wine's fleshiness and sometimes a certain residual sweetness. Aromatic notes are even more concentrated on the palate than on the nose, which gives the wine exceptional persistence.

MUSCAT is derived from two different grape varieties: Muscat Blanc à Petits Grains and Muscat Ottonel, which comes specifically from Alsace and ripens earlier. The two varieties are rarely present in the same cru in the sites of the Alsace AOC Grand Cru appellation because producers must select a terroir that suits each variety's speed of ripening. Plantings of Muscat grape are therefore very low in number and rarely account for more than 3% of the total. Other crus however, such as Hatschbourg and Goldert, have built their reputations on Muscat.

Eye

Limpid and brilliant, deepening in colour with age from pale yellow to golden yellow.

Nose

Young wines are dominated by natural grape aromas. Wines produced from Muscat Ottonel have a distinctive elegance. Those based on Muscat à Petits Grains are more intense with more vegetal nuances such as blackcurrant buds. Old Muscat wines deserve a special mention for the interesting aniseed nuances that they develop with age.

Palate

Alsace Muscat wines based on Muscat Blanc à Petits Grains are dry, more nervous and more solidly structured. Those based on Muscat Ottonel are elegant and subtle.

PINOT GRIS is an early-maturing grape variety that thrives on pebbly or limestone marl terroirs. In Alsace it produces a warm style of wine and is grown in most of the delimited lieux-dits, occupying 12% of the production area of the Alsace Grand Cru AOC. This grape accounts for the majority of plantings in Rangen and a significant proportion (about a third) of the area under vine in various sites including Steinert and even Sonnenglanz or Hengst.

Eye

Pale yellow, sometimes greenish-yellow in youth. With age it quickly acquires a range of golden tones that are more or less deep depending on the degree of over-ripeness in the grapes.

Nose

Depending on the terroir of origin, young wines may present hints of apricot, honey, beeswax and even cocoa. Ageing adds great class, the fruit nuances gradually giving way to smokier characteristics that are emphasised by scents of the underwood and mushrooms.

Palate

The early ripening favoured by the terroirs of the Alsace Grand Cru AOC gives these wines a characteristic opulence with plenty of structure and residual sugar. They are robust and often heady despite low levels of acidity, with a very long finish especially after a few years of ageing.

RIESLING: this major grape variety is grown in 50 sites of the Alsace Grand Cru AOC where it sometimes accounts for 100% of plantings. Being a late-ripening grape, Riesling has colonised well-exposed slopes (south-southeast) with light soils.

Eye

Riesling wines are usually dry and white with a limpid brilliance that is never too smooth. Young wines have greenish-yellow nuances that turn more golden with age.

Nose

Wines from Riesling grapes grown on light soils (granite) have predominantly floral aromas with mineral notes that grow more emphatic with age. Young wines are marked by scents of peach or lime blossom. Kastelberg wines, grown on shale soils, deserve a special mention for their floral and fruity characters. Wines from Riesling grown on limestone marl soils have distinctive floral and vegetal nuances (lemon, mint).

Palate

The wine's liveliness gives it firm structure that supports the aromas and emphasises their persistence. It has the exquisite balance of a great, aristocratic dry white wine.

Alsace Muscat

Appellation
Alsace AOC
Denomination
Muscat
Colour
White
Area
339 hectares
Production
25,870
hectolitres

1 9 4 5

Grape varieties
Muscat Blanc à
Petits Grains,
Muscat Ottonel,
Muscat Rose à
Petits Grains
(rare).

Type of soils
Mainly
limestone marl.

Muscat wines are recorded as early as the 16th century. Unlike other Alsace wines that are produced from a single grape variety, Muscat wine is a subtle blend of three. Muscat Blanc à Petits Grains (known as Muscat de Frontignan) and Muscat Ottonel are the two principal varieties, accompanied to a much lesser extent by Muscat Rose à Petits Grains. The proportion of each grape variety used depends on ripening and vineyard exposure. Alsace Muscat is generally produced from the two principal grape varieties.

Eye
Generally limpid and brilliant with youthful yellow-green nuances turning pale to golden yellow with age.

Muscat wines are characterised by their intense, elegant aromas that will suddenly change register with age to express scents of spice and aniseed.

Nose
The Muscat flavour is more or less noticeable from vegetal nuances such as blackcurrant buds and depends on the proportion of Muscat à Petits Grains. All Alsace

Palate
Quite spirited when dominated by the white Muscat grape variety, rounder when mainly based on Muscat Ottonel. Good structure, with intense aromas and persistence, often with the crisp bite of fresh grapes.

Ageing ability
1-2 years to
retain the
aromas of the
grape variety;
5 years or more
to appreciate
the aniseed
bouquet that
develops
with age.

Choice of food
As an apéritif or
with smoked
salmon,
asparagus,
oriental cuisine
or Kouglof.

**Serving
temperature**
7-10°C.

Alsace Pinot Blanc

Alsace Pinot Blanc, also known by the old Alsatian name of Klevner, may be made from two different grape varieties that give remarkable results under average conditions: Pinot Blanc and Auxerrois Blanc. The wines have a pleasing combination of freshness, body and suppleness that suits a wide variety of dishes, though not cheese or puddings.

1 9 4 5

Appellation
Alsace AOC
Denomination
Pinot Blanc
(or Klevner)
Colour
White
Area
2,983 hectares
Production
151,340
hectolitres

Eye
Very pale colour.

Nose
A rich, intense range of aromas: peaches, citrus fruit, notes of elegant white flowers and nuances of apricot.

Palate
Deliciously lively attack with a touch of spice and good balance; quite fleshy and powerful.

Serving temperature
10-12°C.
Choice of food
Seafood, quiche Lorraine, onion quiche, veal stew, *spätzle* (Alsatian pasta).

Ageing ability
1-2 years.

Soil types
Limestone marl.

Grape varieties
Pinot Blanc,
Auxerrois Blanc.

Alsace Pinot Noir

Appellation
Alsace AOC

Denomination
Pinot noir

Colours
Red
Rosé

Area
1,240 hectares

1945

P inot Noir was a major grape variety already cultivated in Burgundy in the Middle Ages, but it has almost disappeared from the Alsace vineyard where it now accounts for just 8.7% of plantings. It is an early-ripening variety well suited to limestone soils, and is the source of delightful red and rosé wines that vary in expression at each stage in their development.

Production
83,580
hectolitres

Eye

Colour can vary greatly, ranging from light pink to deep crimson. The classic Pinot Noir offers ruby-red tones of medium intensity, turning reddish-brick and lightly orange with age.

Nose

Pinot Noir is characterised by a fruity fragrance of red berries with hints of blackcurrants and raspberries. Red wines matured in wooden vats or casks retain this original fruitiness but with age acquire a touch of wood or vanilla, aromas of the underwood and gamey, animal nuances.

Palate

Despite its relatively thin colour, this is a well-macerated wine of impressive persistence and ageing ability due to its rich tannins that provide excellent structure and support for the aromas.

A distinctive grape

Pinot Noir, which was for many years planted alongside other red varieties, is now the only grape variety used to make red and rosé Alsace AOC wines. Pinot Noir may not be the preferred grape variety in Alsace but a few local wine-growers continue to exploit its distinctive qualities: Ottrott with its famous Ottrotter Rotter; also Rodern and Marlenheim.

Grape variety
Pinot Noir.

Soil types
Principally argillaceous limestone and granite soils for the production of lighter wines.

Ageing ability
2-10 years.

Serving temperature
10-14°C.

Choice of food
Grilled meat, smoked shoulder of ham, *Baeckenofe*, cheese (Comté, Brie, Gruyère, Cantal).

Alsace Riesling

his Rhine grape variety par excellence may well have been cultivated in Alsace in the days of the Roman occupation. Riesling is a late-ripening grape that is perfectly suited to the climate of the Rhine Valley where it produces regular yields. We find it on most geological formations, especially in acid soils of granitic or sandstone origin but also on the sedimentary terrain of the sub-Vosgian hillsides and the gravel soils formed by alluvial cones between the valleys. Riesling produces dry white wines that are much sought-after for their finesse and elegance.

1 9 4 5

Appellation
Alsace AOC
Denomination
Riesling
Colour
White
Area
3,338 hectares
Production
281,490
hectolitresl

Eye
Brilliantly limpid yellow colour with youthful green nuances that grow more golden with age.

Nose
Riesling is one of the aromatic grape varieties, with an agreeably terpenic fragrance that gives it great elegance: floral scents, sometimes with a hint of peach blossom or even lime blossom. Old Riesling wines acquire more mineral tones.

Serving temperature
8-12°C.

Palate
This is the perfect wine with food: lively with respectable acidity due to the late ripening grapes but also perfectly structured and uncommonly persistent when produced from grapes where the yield is strictly controlled.

Choice of Food
Seafood, fish terrine, John Dorey with sorrel, trout with blue cheese, pheasant cooked with cabbage, chicken cooked in Riesling, walnut cake.

Ageing ability
2-10 years.

Grape variety
Riesling.

Soil types
Granite or argillaceous limestone soils on well-exposed slopes.

Alsace Sélection de Grains Nobles

Appellations
Alsace AOC
Alsace Grand
Cru AOC
**Special
designation**
Sélection de
Grains Nobles
Colour
White
Area
100-1000
hectares

1 9 8 4

The term Sélection de Grains Nobles may be applied to the wines of the Alsace appellation or the Alsace Grand Cru AOC, provided that they are made exclusively from the noble grape varieties: Gewürztraminer, Pinot Gris, Riesling and Muscat. The Rhine Valley has a climate of warm, misty nights alternating with sunny days that encourages the development of a fungus called *Botrytis cinerea* (noble rot) which concentrates the juice in each grape. This in turn favours the production of wines rich in sugar – great sweet wines that combine superb aromatic intensity with an exceptionally long finish.

Sugar content (g/l) and estimated degrees of alcohol in Selection de Grains Nobles wines	
Gewürztraminer	279/16.4% vol.
Muscat	256/15.1% vol.
Pinot Gris	279/16.4% vol.
Riesling	256/15.1% vol.

Production
A few thousand
to 40,000
hectolitres,
depending on
the vintage

Grape varieties
Gewürztraminer,
Pinot Gris,
Riesling, Muscat.

Soil types
Granitic sands;
marly to
calcareous-
marly.

**Ageing
ability**
5-10 years.

**Serving
temperature**
7-10°C.
Choice of food
Asparagus,
flamiche (thin
onion pizza),
curries, delicate
apple tarts.

Eye

Whatever the grape variety, the clean, deep, golden-yellow colour is an immediate indication of great warmth. This is a fleshy wine with plenty of residual sugar: smooth, creamy and rich in tears that emphasise its warmth and opulence.

The Sommerberg Grand Cru is planted on steep, south-facing hillsides where Riesling flourishes in the sandy granitic soil.

Nose

The nature of Riesling grape skins makes them the most resistant to the development of *Botrytis cinerea*. Overripening and *passerillage* (raising) bring out floral, thoroughbred aromas that acquire mineral tones with age. Overripe Pinot Gris and Gewürztraminer grapes on the other hand develop a range of distinctly superior aromas. Smoky scents of Pinot Gris are complemented by fragrances of the underwood and mushrooms plus honey, gingerbread and sometimes cocoa or toast. Gewürztraminer develops spicy, aromatic hints of citrus skins. Botrytized Muscat grapes retain their Muscat flavours.

Palate

Residual sugar may be very high in the greatest of the Sélections de Grains Nobles wines but it is rarely excessive. Sweetness is balanced by a solid structure characterised by a wealth of factors from which the wines draw their remarkable complexity: alcohol, acidity, the grape, *Botrytis cinerea* and even fermentation. The aromas positively explode on the palate.

Alsace Sylvaner

Appellation
Alsace AOC
Denomination
Sylvaner
Colour
White
Area
2,133 hectares
Production
191,720
hectolitres

1 9 4 5

Grape variety
Sylvaner.

Originally from Austria, the Sylvaner grape variety has been recorded in Alsace since the 18th century but is now confined to the Alsace AOC, most notably the vineyards of the Lower Rhine. Sylvaner is distinguished from other grape varieties by light green leaves with very little down. This fairly late-maturing white grape variety (the grapes are white when ripe) produces surprisingly high and regular yields for such a northerly location. Alsace Sylvaner wines are light, lively and quite fruity.

**Aging
ability**
1-3 years.

Soil types
Granitic, marly,
argillaceous
limestone.

Eye

Sylvaner wines have a deliciously appealing crystalline clarity, usually distinguished by youthful yellow-green nuances except when produced from strictly limited yields or grapes grown on particularly well-exposed soils. In these cases the wines have a more golden hue.

Nose

Sylvaner is an aromatic grape variety, expressing primary grape aromas that are reinforced by its relatively late-maturing characteristics. Of medium intensity, it develops floral aromas that sometimes suggest acacia, white flowers or hints of lemon. Wines from heavier soils may offer vegetal nuances. Sylvaner is usually drunk young but it can be worthwhile to set aside a few bottles of wines from well-exposed terroirs. With age, these crystalline wines will develop those mineral aromas so typical of old Alsace wines.

Palate

The wines most typical of Sylvaner – and this is another feature of its late maturing nature – are dry, lively and refreshing. They are ideal with a meal, whether served with the entrée or with seafood (especially oysters).

Traditionally planted in the Bas-Rhin, Sylvaner has acquired a reputation in some of the terroirs of the Haut-Rhin such as Zotzenberg or Zinnkœpflé.

Serving temperature 8-12°C.
Choice of food Seafood, charcuterie, frogs' legs, *flameküche*, roast pork, sauerkraut, fruit tarts.

The role of the Chasselas grape variety in Alsace production

Chasselas is an early maturing grape variety, the berries ripening in what is known as the 'first period'. It is grown solely for the production of Alsace AOC wines – not Grand Cru wines. Used alone or blended with other grape varieties, (Alsace Chasselas and Chasselas Gutedel) Chasselas produces wines that are always dry and light. When the status of Alsace wines was first officially published in 1945, two categories of blended wines were defined:

• The Zwicker category (literally 'blend') was applied to blends of grape varieties that qualified as 'current' at that time (one of which was Chasselas). This category has since been withdrawn on the grounds that it did not do enough to enhance status.

• The Edelzwicker category (literally 'noble blend') was applied to blends of grape varieties that qualified as 'noble', among them Sylvaner which was widely cultivated in the Lower Rhine vineyard. This category has now been extended to cover all of the grape varieties authorised in the Alsace appellation.

Alsace Tokay-Pinot Gris

Appellation
Alsace AOC

Designation
Pinot Gris

Colour
White

Area
1,384 hectares

Production
98,370 hectolitres

1 9 4 5

Legend has it that Tokay or Pinot Gris came from Hungary but it most probably originated in Burgundy. Found throughout the Alsace appellation where it has been established since the 17th century, Pinot Gris does well on the tertiary soils of the Cléebourg region and on limestone and volcanic soils. It produces an exceptionally powerful, mellow wine of remarkable longevity.

Eye
Young Alsace Tokay-Pinot Gris is yellow with shades of green, changing with age to a sumptuous golden colour.

Nose
After a few years in the bottle, the wine develops a bouquet of rare complexity as the natural grape aromas are superceded by aromas of ageing: smokiness, scents of the underwood or mushrooms, a honeyed concentration.

Grape variety
Pinot Gris.

Ageing ability
3-10 years.

Soil types
Limestone or argillaceous limestone, sometimes volcanic.

Serving temperature
10-14°C.

Choice of food
Asparagus, sauerkraut, freshwater fish, poultry (goose, capon), cheese (Munster).

Palate
The wine reveals all of its strength and opulence. The acidity tends to be eclipsed by the alcohol and sugar and the sweetness is always balanced by a structure of remarkable character, giving the wine impressive aromatic persistence.

Alsace Vendanges Tardives

The sweet wines of Alsace are the product of the Rhine Valley climate which is so favourable to the development of noble rot and overripe grapes. For a long time however this style of cultivation was restricted to a few privileged estates for the production of their premium wines. Since 1984, the Vendanges Tardives designation applying to Alsace AOC and Alsace Grand Cru wines is reserved for wines made exclusively from one of the authorised grape varieties – Gewurztraminer, Pinot Gris, Riesling or Muscat – and sold under the name of that grape variety. Minimum sugar concentrations at harvest time are among the highest of all the French AOCs.

1 9 8 4

Appellations
Alsace AOC
Alsace Grand
Cru AOC
Special
Designation
Vendanges
Tardives
Colour
White
Area
100-1000
hectares

Eye
Rieslings, like Gewürztraminers and Pinot Gris, have good depth of colour – yellow-gold with brilliant green highlights. The Muscats are pale gold with green highlights.

Nose
• Riesling wines have exceptional finesse, mingling scents of citrus fruit, passion fruit, honey and acacia flower.
• Gewürztraminers offer a discreet bouquet characterised by aromas of roses, lily of the valley and crystallised fruit.
• Pinot Gris wines express aromas of violets, crystallised fruit and honey, mingled with scents of the underwood and liquorice.
• Muscats have a musky, lilac-scented fragrance.

MICHEL SCHOEPFER
Vin d'Alsace
APPELLATION ALSACE CONTROLEE
TOKAY - PINOT GRIS
13.5% Vol   **VENDANGE TARDIVE 1992**   750
Mis en bouteille par MICHEL SCHOEPFER - F 68420 EGUISHEIM - Produce of France

Production
From a few
thousand
to 40,000
hectolitres,
depending
on the vintages

Soil types
Granitic
sand; marl
to marly
limestone.

Ageing
ability
5-10 years.

**Sugar content (g/l) and
estimated degrees of alcohol in
Vendanges Tardives wines**

Gewürztraminer	243	/14.3% vol.
Muscat	220	/12.9% vol.
Pinot Gris	243	/14.3% vol.
Riesling	220	/12.9% vol.

Grape varieties
Gewürztraminer,
Muscat, Pinot
Gris, Riesling.

Palate

• Riesling wines are full-bodied, rich and generous with good aromatic persistence.

• Gewürztraminers are delightfully delicate with a velvety caress in the mouth and flavours of crystallised fruits (apricots) and honey.

• Pinot Gris wines release intensely exotic notes.

• Muscats are mellow, velvety and full-bodied.

Vineyards around Riquewhir (above) and Zellenberg (left).

Choice of food

Feathered game (pheasant, partridge, pigeon, thrush), animal game (medallions of venison with raisins), capon with truffles, leg or saddle of lamb, cheese (Epoisses, Cîteaux, Munster, Livarot, Maroilles), lemon, dark red-plum, cherry-plum or rhubarb tart.

Serving temperature 15°C.

Anjou

The Anjou region comprises two distinct geological formations: in the east is the sedimentary terrain along the southwestern border of the Paris Basin; in the west is the schistous terrain on the eastern edge of the Armorican Massif. The first zone, which is characterised by white soils on yellow tuffeau, is White Anjou, home of the Saumur appellations. The second zone is Black Anjou, producing red wines and dry or sweet white wines from Chenin grapes. These are agreeable wines, ready for drinking within six months of the harvest but with sufficient character to be laid down for three years.

1957

Appellation
Anjou AOC
Colours
Red (63%)
White (37%)
Area
2,950 hectares
Production
157,900 hectolitres

Eye
• Red Anjou wines are fresh and lively and bright ruby-red.
• The whites are yellow with green highlights, acquiring a more golden hue when they come from a very ripe vintage.

Nose
• The red wines reveal primary grape aromas, combining floral scents with red fruits and sometimes spicy tones. There are never any vegetal aromas.
• Anjou whites evoke a variety of white flowers typical of the Chardonnay, plus hints of lemon, fruit notes characteristic of Chenin (vine peaches, pears) and mineral overtones. Grapes that have been slow to mature impart aromas of crystallised fruit, quince and yellow plums.

Palate
• Red Anjou wines have a distinctive freshness with well-balanced alcohol and acidity and a structure that is finesse itself. The finish is long and lingering and characteristically fruity.
• White Anjou wines are rounded and mouth-filling with a structure built on fine elegant tannins.

Grape varieties
Reds: Cabernet Franc (Breton), with Cabernet-Sauvignon as a subsidiary variety.
Whites: Chenin Blanc (or Pineau de la Loire), Chardonnay and Sauvignon (at least 20%).

Choice of food
Reds: red or white meat, jugged hare, fish (pickerel, pike).
Whites: asparagus, fish.

Serving temperature
Rouge: 15°C.
Blanc: 8-10°C.

Ageing ability
Drink young or within 3 years.

Soil types
Soils from the hard, dark rocks of the Armorican Massif.

27

Anjou-Coteaux de la Loire

Appellation
Anjou-Coteaux
de la Loire AOC

Colour
White

Area
48 hectares

Production
1,050 hectolitres

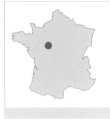

1 9 4 6

The Anjou-Coteaux de la Loire appellation lies on both sides of the Loire river to the west of the Savennières AOC, and specialises in the production of small quantities of sweet white wines made exclusively from Chenin Blanc. The grapes are carefully harvested in batches and grown only on the schist and limestone of Montjean where shallow, easily warmed soils encourage maturation in this semi late-ripening grape variety.

Eye
Pale yellow-gold with more distinctive green highlights than a Coteaux du Layon, Anjou Coteaux de la Loire is lightness itself with all the qualities of a delicate sweet wine.

Nose
A delicate bouquet of exotic fruits (litchi) and ripe fruit flavours (apricot compote, peach).

Palate
Agreeably fresh but mellow with honeyed notes that linger at the finish.

Chenin is the star grape variety in the production of the sweet Coteaux de la Loire wines. The quantities produced are extremely limited however as the Anjou region gradually moves over to red wines.

Grape variety
Chenin Blanc
(or Pineau de
la Loire).

Soil types
Schist and
limestone from
Montjean.

Ageing ability
5-20 years.

Serving temperature
8-10°C.

Choice of food
Chicken
vol-au-vent, fish.

Anjou-Gamay

One of the many Anjou wines is the Anjou-Gamay AOC, a red wine produced from black Gamay grapes grown on the most schistous soils in the AOC production area. This is an excellent carafe wine – charming as a young wine with a pleasant, lingering fruitiness.

1957

Appellation
Anjou-Gamay
AOC
Colour
Rouge
Area
316 hectares
Production
16,780
hectolitres

The Anjou vineyards are punctuated by windmills, like this one at Montsoreau.

Eye
Anjou-Gamay is an attractive deep red with purple highlights. It is made for drinking within the year of the harvest.

Nose
Aromas of flowers and red berries, sometimes developing more animal nuances and grilled fruit flavours.

Palate
Rich with good, mouth-filling substance sustained by tannins that are quick to mellow. There is a ricochet of fruit at the finish.

1999

Domaine du Fresche
ANJOU GAMAY
Appellation Anjou Gamay Contrôlée

Grape variety
Gamay Noir.

Soil types
Soils from the hard, dark rocks of the Armorican Massif.

Choice of food	Serving temperature	Ageing ability
Charcuterie, white meat.	12-13°C.	1 year.

29

Anjou-Villages

Appellation
Anjou-Villages
AOC
Colour
Red
Area
300 hectares
Production
8,740 hectolitres

1 9 8 7

The Anjou-Villages AOC covers selected areas in 46 communes, all with healthy soils (predominantly from schist) and a favourable aspect that encourages early ripening. Anjou red wines are traditionally made from the Cabernet Franc grape, known as Breton because it was first imported through the gates of Brittany back in the days of the Plantagenets. Used alone or blended with Cabernet-Sauvignon (also from South West France), it produces wines of medium longevity.

Eye
Anjou-Villages is a dark, deep, intense red, similar to a very ripe cherry.

Nose
Complex, with aromas of liquorice, underwood and black-skinned fruit.

Palate
Anjou-Villages wines are noted for their attack and full, fleshy character. They are full-bodied and harmonious, with well-balanced alcohol and tannins that give them smooth structure – good wines for laying down.

Grape varieties
Cabernet Franc (Breton), Cabernet-Sauvignon (subsidiary).

Ageing potential
2-3 years (10 years for good vintages).

Soil types
Rather shallow soils on weathered schist.

Serving temperature
15°C.

Choice of food
Red or white meat, jugged hare, river fish (pike-perch, pike).

Anjou-Villages Brissac

The 10 communes of the Anjou-Villages Brissac AOC occupy a plateau that slopes gently towards the Loire River. Bordered to the north by the river and to the south by the steep hillsides of the Layon valley, the terroir is composed of the dark, schistous, stony soils of the Armorican Massif in Black Anjou. This terrain yields sinewy red wines resembling the land of their birth.

1 9 9 8

Appellation
Anjou-Villages Brissac AOC

Colour
Red

Area
103 hectares

Production
4,770 hectolitres

Eye
Deep, dark, intense red, similar to a very ripe Burlat cherry.

Nose
A complex bouquet generally dominated by hints of very ripe red and black-skinned fruits. This fruity sensation is accompanied by a range of aromas, especially odours of empyreuma (smokiness and grilled flavours), nuances of the underwood, peat, humus, touches of spice and liquorice and heady floral scents (peony).

Palate
The palate is characteristic of a wine of medium longevity: fleshy at first, finishing in the case of very young wines with marked tannic structure.

La Croix de Mission
DOMAINE DES ROCHELLES
1997
ANJOU-VILLAGES BRISSAC
J.-Y. A. LEBRETON
49320 SAINT-JEAN-DES-MAUVRETS
FRANCE
MIS EN BOUTEILLE AU DOMAINE

Grape varieties
Cabernet Franc (Breton); Cabernet-Sauvignon as a subsidiary variety.

Soil types
Shallow soils on weathered schist.

Serving temperature
17°C.

Choice of food
Game, meat in a sauce, grilled meats.

Ageing ability
2-10 years.

Arbois

Appellation
Arbois AOC

Colours
Red
Rosé
White (50%)

Area
920 hectares

Production
50,940 hectolitres

1 9 3 6

The Arbois AOC is in the north of the Jura and is most famous for its *vins jaunes* and *vins de paille*. Today however it produces more red and rosé wines than whites. The vineyard embraces 13 communes around the town of Arbois and produces a wide range of wines. Poulsard, vinified as a red wine, is in fact a clairet (very dark pink) and often mistaken for a rosé. The *vins jaunes* are produced from the Savagnin grape matured six years *sous voile* (under a film of yeast that forms on the surface of the wine). The highly distinctive *vins de paille* are made from early-harvested red or white grapes that are then dried on racks. Other wines include white Chardonnays, reds based on the Trousseau grape, and sparkling *Méthode Traditionnelle* wines. These are highland wines of inimitable character and well worth discovering.

VIN JAUNE : SEE CHATEAU-CHALON, PAGE 102.

Main grape varieties
Reds and rosés: Poulsard, Trousseau, Pinot Noir.
Whites: Chardonnay, Savagnin.

Soil types
Liassic and Triassic clay with some limestone slope wash from the plateau.

Ageing ability
White Chardonnay wines: 3 years.
Red Poulsards: 3-5 years.
Vins jaunes: 50 years.
Vins de paille: more than 10 years.
Sparkling wines: for early drinking.

Eye

• Red Arbois wine from the Poulsard grape is pale coloured, ranging from light pink to ruby red when young to pale rosé with age.
• White Savagnin wine is golden, with pretty green highlights added by the Chardonnay.

Nose

• Red Arbois is predominantly fruity with hints of red berries that often have a deliciously 'wild' fragrance.
• White Arbois evokes walnuts and green apples.

Palate

• Red Arbois has a fruity palate, like the nose. It is low in tannins and more or less light depending on the length of fermentation. A hint of acidity is not unusual and the finish is dependably persistent.
• White Savagnin is opulent and well balanced, with flavours of walnuts and orange (peel) and already very long.

Pupillin

On 12 June 1970 it was decreed that the name Pupillin could be added to the Arbois AOC for the wines produced within the Pupillin delimited area – a tribute to the long-established reputation of its wines. A dozen or so wine-growers bottle their own production, others take their grapes to the co-operative winery. The Poulsard grape is in its element in the Arbois terroir and gives of its best.

Serving temperature
Reds: 15°C.
Whites: 12°C.
Vins jaunes: lightly chambré.
Vins de paille and sparkling wines: 8°C.

Right: harvest time in the Arbois vineyard.
Above: a cellar (chais) in Sorbief.

Mets et vins
Vins jaunes and white Savagnins: white meat, Comté cheese.
White wines: fish, white meat in a creamy sauce.
Red Poulsard wines: roasted red meat, cheese.
Red Trousseau wines: red meat with a sauce, game.
Vins de paille: puddings.
Vins jaunes: grilled lobster, chicken cooked in *vin jaune.*

Auxey-Duresses

Appellations
Auxey-Duresses
AOC
Auxey-Duresses
Premier Cru
AOC

Colours
Red
White (30%)

Area
176 hectares

Production
6,200 hectolitres

1937

The village of Auxey stands on the threshold of a valley that runs into the Hautes-Côtes to the west of Meursault. In the Middle Ages it was an outport of the Abbaye de Cluny. In 1924 it incorporated the name of the *climat* Les Duresses. Pinot Noir vines are in their element on the southeast facing slopes of the Montagne de Bourdon, which is the continuation of Volnay. Across the road, the very fine soils of Mont Mélian suit the Chardonnay grape. The Premiers Crus are highly individual: Les Duresses are very fruity; the Clos du Val and the Climat du Val are very powerful.

The Premiers Crus
Bas des Duresses
Les Bréterins
La Chapelle
Climat du Val
Clos du Val
Les Duresses
Les Ecussaux
Les Grands Champs
Reugne

Grape varieties
Reds:
Pinot Noir.
Whites:
Chardonnay.

Soil types
Marly limestone
and argillaceous
limestone.

**Ageing
ability**
Reds:
5-10 years,
often more.
Whites:
3-5 years.

Eye

• The red wines are often a beautiful vivid ruby red with almost purple nuances.

• The white wines are a brilliant straw colour, crystalline, clear and limpid.

Nose

• The reds are immediately very fruity with nuances ranging from red fruit (raspberries, cherries, redcurrants) to black-skinned fruit (blackberries, blackcurrants). Floral scents are dominated by peony. With time the bouquet develops fragrances of spice and sometimes game, the underwood (fern, mushrooms), preserved meats and leather.

• The aromas in the white wines evoke hawthorn with hints of lemon and pippin apples.

Palate

• The reds have an even palate with just a suggestion of astringency when still young. The flesh and tannins complement each other perfectly. These wines are best left to age.

• The whites have fullness and richness, with a spontaneous vivacity and sufficient acidity to age well. Generally deliciously mellow without a trace of heaviness.

Both sides of the Auxey valley are covered with vines. The village enjoys a balcony position between the Côte and the Hautes Côtes.

Choice of food
Reds: filet mignon of veal, lamb, rabbit, poultry, cheese (Cîteaux, Brillat-Savarin, Saint-Nectaire, Brie).
Whites: pâté, quenelles, frogs legs, snails in pastry, pickerel or pike cooked in a sauce, poached fish, cheese (blue cheese, Livarot, Époisses).

Serving temperature
Reds: 15-16°C.
Whites: 12-14°C.

35

Bandol

Appellation
Bandol AOC

Colours
Red (35%)
Rosé (60%)
White (5%)

Area
1,410 hectares

Production
47,460 hectolitres

1941

Soil types
Skeletal soils on calcified sandstone and sandy marls or on rendzinous slope wash.

The Bandol appellation area backs onto a vast amphitheatre of hills and spreads across eight communes on the outskirts of Toulon (Bandol, Le Beausset, La Cadière-d'Azur, Le Castellet, Evenos, Ollioules, Saint-Cyr-sur-Mer and Sanary). A hot climate with maritime influences and the meagre, calcareous soils together create an ecological niche for a demanding grape variety, Mourvèdre. Wines from this terroir take time to reveal their secrets. Bandol's majestic full-bodied powerful red wines have considerable ageing potential. Rosés occupy an ever-increasing share of the market; the production of white wines is more limited.

Eye

• When young, the red wines are a crimson colour, developing ruby and dark red tints as they age in the bottle.

• The rosé wines are generally a pale eglantine or salmon colour.

• The white wines are light straw-yellow.

Main grape varieties

Reds: Mourvèdre, Grenache, Cinsaut (at least 85% of plantings, of which at least 50% is Mourvèdre); Syrah, Carignan.

Rosés: Mourvèdre, Grenache, Cinsaut (at least 80% of plantings); Syrah, Carignan and other authorised white grape.

Whites: Clairette, Ugni Blanc, Bourboulenc (at least 60% of plantings); Sauvignon.

Left: Château de Pibarnon, one of the 58 estates of the Bandol vineyard.

Nose

• The red wines are at first characterised by rustic aromas – blackcurrant, raspberry, blackberry, peony, heliotrope. After four or five years in the bottle they acquire characteristic aromas of truffles and the underwood, liquorice, cinnamon or musk.

• The aromas of the rosés are centred on red fruits or the peach-apricot partnership, with nuances of pineapple, fennel or mint depending on the terroir.

• The white wines may evoke a range of fruity fragrances (grapefruit or dried fruit, or a bouquet of aromas in the floral series) or floral scents of white flowers (linden blossom) or yellow flowers (broom).

Ageing ability

Reds: more than 10 years.

Rosés: 1-3 years.

Palate

• The tannic structure of the Mourvèdre in red wines grows rounder and more refined with age. Truffle is the distinguishing character, expressed over fine, velvety tannins on a background of liquorice or cinnamon.

• Rosé wines are light and fresh on the palate, their structure and longevity improved by the presence of Mourvèdre.

• The white wines may be fresh and lively, their structure occasionally enhanced by creamy food flavours. Such wines are perfect with elaborate, gourmet dishes.

Choice of food

Reds: game, stews, grilled lamb, chocolate puddings.

Rosés: bouillabaisse, fish soup, grilled king prawns and red mullet, garlic tomatoes; as an apéritif with olives, anchovy paste.

Whites: fish, cheese.

Serving temperature

Reds: 16-18°C.

Rosés: 8-10°C.

Banyuls and Banyuls Grand Cru

Appellations
Banyuls AOC
Banyuls Grand
Cru AOC

Colours
Red (90%)
White (10%)

Area
1,291 hectares

Production
Banyuls: 20,946
hectolitres
Banyuls Grand
Cru: 1,471
hectolitres

1972

Soil types
Primary schist.

The Banyuls appellation area covers the coastal but mountainous communes of the Côte Vermeille (Collioure, Port-Vendres, Banyuls, Cerbère) that are bordered by Spain to the south, the Mediterranean to the east and the Pyrenees to the west. The vineyard is planted on schistous soils and yields are very low (an average of 20 hectolitres per hectare). Banyuls *vin doux naturel* is a powerful, smooth wine of exceptional length that is equally good as a *rimage* wine (produced from a single vintage that is bottled early to preserve the fruit aromas) or a blend or an old vintage. Banyuls is matured for 12 months, Banyuls Grand Cru for 30 months.

Grape varieties
Grenache Noir
(at least 50%
in Banyuls: at
least 75% in
Banyuls Grand
Cru); Grenache
Gris; Grenache
Blanc, Carignan
and Macabeu
(rarely); Muscat
and Malvoisie
(for the record).

Right: Barrels of Banyuls maturing in the open air.

Ageing ability
Several decades.

Eye

A Banyuls *rimage* wine is a deep ruby-red colour. Matured wines range from terracotta to mahogany brown, the colour gradually deteriorating on contact with the air, a process accelerated by increasing temperature. Highly oxidised wines will occasionally acquire coffee tones or green highlights indicating the development of *rancio* characteristics. Rich in alcohol and glycerol, these sweet, mellow wines leave thick tears on the walls of the glass when swirled.

Nose

One of the distinguishing features of the *vins doux naturels* is their intense, powerful nose. *Rimage* wines have characteristic scents of ripe grape, cherry, kirsch, blackberry or red fruit. The spectrum of aromas may range from stewed fruit to dried fruit with toasted, spicy notes, depending on the amount of oxidation and length of maturation. With age the wines acquire aromas of roasted coffee, leather and walnuts. Banyuls and Banyuls-Grand Cru are rarely of a common character, each wine developing its own individual bouquet.

Palate

Banyuls *rimage* wines combine youthful energy with the solid structure of wines in development. Fruity fleshiness is accompanied by powerful tannins and an underlying hint of alcohol that produce a very fresh finish. Matured wines shift to an altogether different register, their impressive structure supporting aromas that range from prunes in brandy to roasted coffee, not forgetting dried fruit, cocoa, figs, tobacco, etc. Wrapped in a harmony of alcohol and tannins, the sugar mellows and amplifies the wine's volume to create a sensation of velvety power.

Serving temperature
Young wines: 12-14°C.
Older wines: 15-17°C.

Choice of food
Reds: grilled wood pigeon.
Rosés: charcuterie, grilled meat.
Whites: poultry, fish.

Barsac

Appellation
Barsac AOC
Colour
White
(rich sweet wines)
Area
625 hectares
Production
14,268
hectolitres

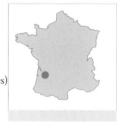

1936

The Barsac appellation, on the left bank of the river Ciron that separates it from Sauternes, enjoys a specific microclimate: damp misty autumn mornings and warm sunny afternoons brought about by the confluence of the cold waters of the Ciron and the warmer waters of the Garonne. These conditions are very favourable to the development of *Botrytis cinerea* (Noble Rot), the magical fungus that concentrates the sugar in the grape and is the key to the great sweet wines for which this appellation is famous. Barsac wines are voluptuous and thoroughbred and full of surprises as they develop, especially in great vintage years. Note that all Barsac AOC wines are entitled to the Sauternes appellation. Like Sauternes, many of the Barsac crus were classified in 1855.

Eye
Young Barsac wines are a strong golden colour, gradually acquiring more amber hues that turn to the colour of tea after a few decades.

Nose
Hints of honey, hazelnuts and flowers are mingled with aromas of candied orange, dried apricot or vanilla. Wines that have aged in the bottle for a few years develop subtle aromas of toast, spices, coconut, aniseed, beeswax, cognac or *rancio*.

Palate
Young Barsac wines are rich, creamy and generous, fresh tasting, fruity, nervous and elegant. The great old sweet wines are surprisingly fleshy, rich and powerful with an elegance, finesse and class that are more astonishing still. The aromas echo the sensations on the tongue to create perfect balance.

Grape varieties
Sémillon,
Sauvignon,
Muscadelle.

Soil types
Calcareous,
gravelly, argilla-
ceous limestone
and red sand.

Choice of food
Foie gras,
delicate fish
(monkfish with
saffron and
orange), white
meat in a cream
sauce, poultry,
Roquefort and
blue cheese,
fruit salad.

**Serving
temperature**
8-9°C.

**Ageing
ability**
20 years (up
to 100 years
for certain crus).

Bâtard-Montrachet

The Bâtard Montrachet Grand Cru is located within the communes of Puligny and Chassagne, in the south of the Côte de Beaune, running alongside the road on gently sloping terrain. Here no estate exceeds one hectare. Most are no larger than 15 ares (1,794 square yards) and planted on brown limestone soils rich in clay over ancient alluviums. The vineyard produces intensely fragrant, powerful, full-bodied wines of remarkable longevity.

1937

Appellation
Bâtard-Montrachet AOC

Classification
Grand Cru

Colour
White

Area
12 hectares

Production
545 hectolitres

Eye

A classic Bâtard-Montrachet is brilliant light gold, with glittering emerald highlights. Older wines turn a strong, golden-yellow colour.

Nose

Puligny wines reveal fern nuances; Chassagne wines have hints of butter and warm croissants. Additional aromas may include citronella, dried fruit, bitter almonds, a suggestion of minerals, spices, honey and occasional hints of orange.

Palate

A young Batard-Montrachet has all the acidity it needs, being creamy yet dry, firm and caressing, cushiony and deep. Neither too rich nor too powerful – simply highly refined.

Choice of food
Pike quenelles, chicken and mushroom vol-au-vents, boned roast duck, Morvan ham à la crème, poularde à la crème with morels.

Serving temperature
12-14°C.

The ancient name of Bâtard-Montrachet is of unknown origin but probably relates to Le Montrachet, formerly known as Montrachet aîné (the elder).

Soil types
Brown limestone, increasingly clayey and deep towards the east.

Grape variety
Chardonnay.

Ageing ability
10-15 years (up to 30 years for the great vintages).

Les Baux de Provence

Appellation
Les Baux de
Provence AOC
Colour
Red (80%)
Rosé
Area
320 hectares
Production
8,648 hectolitres

1995

The spectacular citadel of Les Baux, founded on the ruins of a Celtic stronghold at the foot of the Alpilles, watches over vines and olive trees in this terroir to the south of Saint-Rémy-de-Provence. The vineyard lies mainly at the base of slopes covered with spread and colluvial slope deposits. It produces structured reds and rosés that combine good body with finesse.

Eye
- After the required minimum period of 12 months' maturation, the red wines acquire dark red ruby hues.
- The rosés (produced by the *saignée* process) range from salmon pink to peony.

Nose
- The red wines reveal vegetal notes (rosemary, thyme, tobacco) with developing scents of black-skinned fruits and hints of animal odours (amber, game, belly of hare).
- The rosés release a bouquet that is fruity (red fruit), floral (fennel, dill) and smoky (flint).

Palate
- The red wines are robust and full-bodied with a good reserve of fine tannins that grow more refined with maturation.
- The rosé wines are usually well structured with a certain rusticity and fleshiness. Notes of dried fruit (hazelnuts) are not uncommon.

Soil types
Spread and colluvial slope deposits; erosional slopes and alluvial fans; slope wash and head; reddish brown to yellow brown stony soils, with an argillaceous-sandy matrix from brownish silty head.

Choice of food
Reds: animal game, leg of lamb, beef daube.
Rosés: as an apéritif with olives, courgettes flower fritters, grilled meats.

Main grape varieties
Grenache, Syrah, Mour-vèdre, Cinsaut, Carignan, Cabernet-Sauvignon.

Ageing ability
Reds:
5-10 years.
Rosés:
2-3 years.

Serving temperature
12-14°C.

Béarn and Béarn-Bellocq

The regional Béarn appellation extends into the following regions downstream from Orthez: around Salies-Bellocq, in the Jurançon, Madiran, the Atlantic Pyrenees, the Upper Pyrenees and the department of Gers. Béarn-Bellocq is produced in the communes surrounding Orthez and Salies-de-Béarn. The vineyard is planted on the slopes of the pre-Pyrenees and the gravels of the Gave valley, producing full-bodied red wines, rosés that are aromatic, lively and delicate, and light white wines.

1975
1990

Appellations
Béarn AOC (1975)
Béarn-Bellocq AOC
(1990)
Colours
Red
Rosé
White (limited
production)

Eye
• The reds are an intense dark red with garnet highlights.
• The rosés are recognisable by a brilliant sheen verging on yellow.
• The whites shimmer with green highlights.

Nose
• The red wines are expressive and dense with a range of aromas evoking very ripe stewed fruit (red and black-skinned), spices and liquorice.
• The rosés are packed with fruit, revealing fine Cabernet aromas.
• The whites release vegetal scents (mentholated) and floral and fruity notes (lemon and grapefruit).

Palate
• The red wines have a distinctive fruitiness that persists from the moment of crisp attack to the rich, substantial finish.
• The rosés are lively and delicate but with plenty of firm structure.
• The whites are frisky at first, becoming rounder and more persistently fruity.

Main grape varieties
Reds and rosés: Tannat, Cabernet-Sauvignon, Cabernet Franc (Bouchy), Manseng Noir, Courbu Rouge, Fer Servadou.
Whites: Petit and Gros Manseng, Courbu, Ruffiat, Sauvignon, Camaralet.

Soil types
Agillaceous-limestone and gravelly terraces of Gave de Pau.

Serving temperature
Reds:
15-16°C.
Whites and rosés:
8-10°C.

Choice of food
Reds: Garbure (cabbage soup), Pyrenean sheep's cheese.
Rosés: charcuterie, white meat, Mediterranean food.
Whites: as an apéritif (straight or as a Kir) or with poultry or salmon.

Area
160 hectares
Production
Béarn: 1,720 hectolitres
Béarn-Bellocq: 2,630 hectolitres

Ageing ability
Reds: 2-5 years.
Whites and rosés: drink in the year of production.

Beaujolais

Appellation
Beaujolais AOC
Colours
Red (98%)
Rosé
White
Area
23,000 hectares

1 9 3 7

Production
1.4 million
hectolitres

Grape varieties
Reds and rosés:
Gamay Noir.
Whites:
Chardonnay.

Beaujolais, which officially falls within the Burgundy wine-growing region, extends 50 kilometres (31 miles) from Burgundy south of Mâcon to the Coteaux du Lyonnais. The region, which owes its name to the Dukes of Beaujeu who owned it until 1400, has the beginnings of a southern feeling. The dominant grape variety is Gamay, vinified according to a special process using whole grapes to produce mainly red wines with rich flower and fruit aromas. The 10 crus of the Beaujolais and Beaujolais-Villages appellations occupy a privileged location on the ancient rounded mountain slopes in the northwest of the area. The Beaujolais AOC vineyard is planted on sedimentary terrain on a wedge of hills up to 500 metres high (1,640 feet) bordering the Massif Central.

Soil types
Mainly
limestone and
argillaceous lime-
stone; crystalline
rock in the upper
valley of the
Azergues (west).

**Ageing
ability**
1-2 years.

Eye

The ideal Beaujolais is bright red and brilliantly intense, reflecting every shade of ruby: crimson, carmine, cherry, even vermilion. It can also be garnet-red but never very dark. Violet highlights are a sign of youth.

Nose

The charm of a Beaujolais is the intense fruit that is apparent on the first nose. There may be aromas of raspberries, blackcurrants, redcurrants or strawberries, either alone or together. More subtle wines acquire floral and vegetal nuances that mingle with the fruit to create a wonderfully fresh bouquet. Beaujolais Nouveau wines are distinguished by their amyl notes – ripe bananas or pear drops.

Palate

The fruit aromas are echoed on the palate, showing great persistence in the better wines. Beaujolais is generally lively and soft, though when vinification is especially successful it can be very fleshy, with an impression of biting into fresh fruit. Such instant gratification has a price: Beaujolais wines are relatively short-lived (1-2 years). Primeur wines should be drunk within three months and before the end of the Spring following the harvest.

Beaujolais Nouveau

A few weeks after the vintage in mid-November, 50-60% of the Beaujolais and Beaujolais-Village crop is turned into Beaujolais Nouveau, a Primeur wine. This is a red, quaffable wine produced by short periods of fermentation on skins and a process known as semi-carbonic maceration that brings out the fruit aromas.

Serving temperature
11-12°C.

Choice of food
Charcuterie, roast pork, pot-au-feu, cheese.

Gamay, which accounts for 99% of all plantings in the Beaujolais AOC, is prone to droop and so for the first 10 years of its life it must be supported on poles.

45

Beaujolais-Villages

Appellation
Beaujolais-
Villages AOC
(1950)
or Beaujolais
followed by the
name of the
commune of
origin (1937)

1937
1950

Colours
Red
Rosé
White (very
limited
production)

Area
6,120 hectares

Production
367,330 hl

Grape variety
Gamay Noir.

This appellation represents a selection of the best crus of the Beaujolais region and covers 38 communes from the northern part of the vineyard. Its boundary marks the transition between the limestone marls of south Beaujolais and the exclusively granitic soils of the crus. These are structured, fruity red wines based on Gamay Noir, plus a very small number of white wines made from the Chardonnay grape grown in the appellation villages.

Eye

Wines produced from granitic sands and vinified as Primeur wines are light in colour. Darker-coloured wines are produced by longer periods of vinification and grapes from old vines planted on schistous soils that contain a slightly higher proportion of clay.

Left:

Château Corcelles, one of numerous family estates in the Beaujolais region.

Nose

Depending on the blends, the bouquet modulates all the scents of red fruits or wild flowers. The fruity fragrance often recalls blackcurrants, wild strawberries and raspberries. Amyl components evoke more exotic fruit such as bananas. The floral scents (jennet, violet) are generally characteristic of grapes grown on higher soils.

Palate

Suppleness, finesse and fruitiness are the qualities generally expected of a Beaujolais-Villages. Low tannins ensure that all of the fruitiness perceived on the nose persists well on the palate. Low acidity makes these wines eminently quaffable.

Opposite: Saint-Laurent-d'Oing in the heart of the vineyards.

Beaujolais Supérieur

This very limited appellation does not cover a specific delimited territory: a selection of vine plots is made each year and declared before the summer. The yield amounts to 62 hectolitres per hectare (12.5% vol.). The AOC produces 1,500-3,000 hectolitres of structured red wines for laying down; also white wines.

Soil types
Granitic sands, schist, gneiss.

Ageing ability
2-4 years.

Choice of food
Charcuterie, gratin, white meats.

Serving temperature
13°C.

Beaune

Appellations
Beaune AOC
Beaune Premier
Cru AOC

Colours
Red (91%)
White

1 9 3 6

Area
405 hectares
(including about
25 hectares of
white wine
production)

Production
29,300 hectolitres

Grape varieties
Reds:
Pinot Noir.
Whites:
Chardonnay.

Beaune with its Hôtel Dieu and 'Montagne' is the symbol of Burgundy and the capital of the region's wine. The appellation produces mainly red wines from Pinot Noir grown in an area with a distinctive geological profile – limestone and marls. Exposure varies from east or southeast to full south-facing slopes. Beaune wines were once reputed for their light, partridge-eye colour and youthful nature. Today they are known for their generosity, body, vigour, spirit and ageing ability. The Premiers Crus from Les Grèves tend to be quite light; those from the Clos des Mouches are fleshier.

**Ageing
ability**
Reds: 5-10 years
(sometimes
up to 20 years).
Whites:
3-5 years.

Soil types
Upper slope:
brown limestone
soils and black
rendzina in slope
wash, white and
yellow marls.
Further down:
ferruginous,
gravelly moraine;
In the piedmont:
limestone and
yellow and
reddish clays .

Choice of food
Reds: roasted
poultry, game,
cheese (Reblo-
chon, Brie).
Whites: shellfish,
warm meat
pastries and
pies, delicate
charcuterie, fish.

**Serving
temperature**
Reds:
16-18°C.
Whites: 12-14°C.

Eye

• Red Beaune Premier Cru wines are a brilliant, luminous scarlet – not the more sombre crimson.
• The white wines when young are a discreet light golden colour.

The Premiers Crus

A l'Ecu
Aux Coucherias
Aux Cras
Belissand
Blanches Fleurs
Champs Pimont
Clos de la Féguine
Clos de la Mousse
Clos de l'Ecu
Clos des Avaux
Clos des Ursules
Clos du Roi
Clos Saint-Landry
En Genêt
En l'Orme
La Mignotte
Le Bas des Teurons
Le Clos des Mouches
Les Aigrots
Les Avaux
Les Boucherotes
Les Bressandes
Les Cent Vignes
Les Chouacheux
Les Epenotes
Les Fèves
Les Grèves
Les Marconnets
Les Montrevenots
Les Perrières
Les Reversés
Les Sceaux
Les Seurey
Les Sizies
Les Teurons
Les Toussaints
Les Tuvilains
Les Vignes Franches
Montée Rouge
Pertuisots
Sur les Grèves
Sur les Grèves-Clos Sainte-Anne

Nose

• Beaune red wines evoke different nuances depending on the cru: black-skinned fruit (blackcurrants, blackberries), red fruit (cherries, redcurrants) and, with age, notes of the underwood, humus, truffle, leather, fur and spices.
• The white wines reveal a bouquet centred on bitter almonds, dried fruit, fern and classical white flowers. Vegetal aromas are frequent, together with buttery accents and sometimes a hint of honey, even the spiciness of cinnamon.

Palate

• The young red wines have a crisp, fresh, adolescent charm – like biting into a bunch of grapes. They are mostly robust, often full-bodied and spicy, sensual and fruity but neither too lean nor too heady. Wines from the slopes of Savigny tend to be powerful, intense, deep and firm; those from Pommard are rounder and more supple, delicately nuanced and earlier to mature.
• The white wines are relatively rare and, with a few notable exceptions such as the Clos des Mouches, should be drunk quite young while the fruit lasts.

On the Pommard side, the Clos des Mouches produces rounded, mellow wines from Chardonnay vines planted at the top of the slope. The name comes from the bees ('honey flies') that once flew around the beehives at the top of the Côte.

Bellet

Appellation
Bellet AOC

Colours
Red (40%)
Rosé (30%)
White (30%)

Area
32 hectares

Production
1,220 hectolitres

1 9 4 1

Main grape varieties
Reds and rosés:
Braquet, Fuella
Nera, Cinsaut,
Grenache.
Whites: Rolle,
Roussane
(Ugni Blanc),
Chardonnay.

Château de Bellet
BELLET
APPELLATION BELLET CONTROLEE

This miniscule appellation is located on the left bank of the Var facing the Mercantour Massif and the Baie des Anges. Production is so small that Bellet wines are virtually impossible to find anywhere except in Nice. The sloping coastal vineyard is planted on gravel terraces and cultivates a selection of original grape varieties. The wines produced range from very aromatic whites to silky fresh rosés and fleshy reds.

Eye
• The reds are ruby or dark garnet in colour.
• The rosés range from salmon pink to the pink of a peony.
• The whites are light yellow with green highlights, verging on straw-yellow.

Nose
• The red wines offer a bouquet of cherries over notes of plum and apricot.
• The rosés reveal notes of red fruits and floral characteristics (broom).
• The whites deliver citrus aromas, developing on a floral theme (lime blossom).

Palate
• The reds are robust and solid, with a good reserve of tannins that become well blended after maturation.
• The rosés are round and fresh, usually well structured with plenty of flesh.
• The whites have well-balanced, rounded, fresh structure, revealing notes of dried fruits (fresh hazelnuts) as they age.

Soil types
Upper Pliocene terraces of pudding stone and water rounded pebbles.

Ageing ability
Reds:
10-15 years.
Whites and rosés:
2-10 years.

Choice of food
Reds: lamb, beef daube, ravioli.
Rosés: grilled meat, vegetable tian, pissaladière, strawberries.
Whites: as an apéritif with olive paste canapés, or with fish cooked the Provençale way or goats' cheese.

Serving temperature
12-14°C.

Bergerac and Bergerac Sec

The Bergerac appellation is actually the continuation of the Bordeaux vineyard, planted with the same grape varieties. This very hilly, well-drained region comprises a mosaic of soils that are almost as varied as those of its illustrious neighbour in the Gironde. Varied soils and the Aquitaine grape varieties combine to give structured red wines, rosés both sweet and dry, and dry whites. The Bergerac vineyard straddles the Dordogne Valley and forms part of the magnificent culinary tableau of the Périgord region, alongside truffles, ceps, mushrooms and foie gras.

1936

Appellations
Bergerac AOC
Bergerac Sec AOC
Bergerac Rosé AOC
Colours
Red
Rosé
White (23%)

Main grape varieties
Reds and rosés: Merlot, Cabernet-Sauvignon, Cabernet Franc, Malbec (Côt), Mérille (subsidiary). *Whites:* Sémillon, Sauvignon, Muscadelle, Ugni Blanc (subsidiary in dry whites).

Soil types
Sands (north of the Dordogne); molasse, marl and limestone (south); clayey limestone.

Area
7,935 hectares
Production
439,170 hectolitres

Eye

• The reds are clear and brilliant with good depth of colour.
• The rosés vary from steely pink to light red.
• The dry whites are pale and limpid with lime-green highlights when young.

Nose

• The reds offer a warm, uncomplicated bouquet, with richer, sometimes fruitier nuances in the better wines (redcurrants, blackcurrants, morello cherries).
• The rosés have characteristic aromas of blackcurrants, raspberries, grenadine and violets.
• The whites vary widely in aroma according to the proportion of Sauvignon used: citrus fruit, dried flowers, wood, spices.

Palate

• Red Bergerac is above all a supple wine that develops fairly quickly. The increasing practice of maturation in barrels has led to more structured wines with toasty aromas.
• The rosé wines are agreeable, supple and aromatic.
• The dry whites tend to be quite lively and aromatic, though the diversity of soils and methods of vinification make it impossible to define a typical white Bergerac.

The Maison du Vin in Bergerac, established in the ancient 16th century cloister of the Récollets. Bergerac production is fairly stable from year to year, a sign of well-controlled yields.

Ageing ability	Serving temperature	Choice of food
Reds: 3-5 years.	*Reds:* 14-15°C.	*Reds:* grills, roasted poultry.
Rosés: 2 years.	*Whites and rosés:* 10-12°C.	*Rosés:* entrées, charcuterie.
Whites: up to 3 years.		*Dry whites:* seafood, fish.

Bienvenues-Bâtard-Montrachet

This Grand Cru in the south of the Côte de Beaune runs along the road to the north of Bâtard-Montrachet in the commune of Puligny-Montrachet. The vineyard is planted at the foot of the Côte on soils from slope wash soils containing a high proportion of clay, silt and pebbly debris. These are richly aromatic wines that take at least five years to develop their bouquet.

1 9 3 7

Eye
Light gold with green highlights.

Nose
Floral and mineral aromas of acacia, citrus fruit, verbena and honey, plus characteristic scents of Chardonnay (a hint of lime-blossom and indulgent scents of warm brioche).

Palate
Ample and rich, with a perfectly balanced body that is the essence of finesse.

Appellation
Bienvenues-Bâtard-Montrachet AOC

Classification
Grand Cru

Colour
White

Area
3 hectares 68 ares 60 centiares

Production
183 hectolitres

Chardonnay

Choice of food
Large shellfish in broth, pike quenelles, poached fish with cream Bresse poularde with cream and morels, cheese (Munster, blue cheese, matured Comté).

Serving temperature
12-14°C.

Ageing ability
10-15 years (up to 30 years for great vintages).

Grape variety
Chardonnay.

Soil types
Brown lime-stone soils, deeper, more clayey to the east.

Blagny

1937

The vineyard in this hamlet of the Côte de Beaune straddles Meursault and Puligny-Montrachet, running along the slope on marl soils covered in slope wash. The wines are known by different names depending on whether they are red or white. White wines are entitled to the communal Puligny-Montrachet AOC or the communal Meursault AOC depending on the commune of production, plus the name of the Premier Cru. Red wines are called Blagny and Blagny Premier Cru.

Appellations
Blagny AOC
Blagny Premier Cru AOC

Colour
Red

Area
In Puligny-Montrachet: 29 ha, including 21 ha of Premier Cru.
In Meursault: 25 ha, including 23 ha of Premier Cru
Total area: 54 ha, including 44 ha of Premier Cru.

In production:
7.20 hectares

Production
280 hectolitres

Grape variety
Pinot Noir.

Ageing ability
4-10 years.

Eye
Usually intense red or purple with glints of mauve, the overall colour ranging from a twilight glow to black cherry and deep ruby.

Nose
Very fruity, ranging from red berries (strawberries, raspberries) to blackcurrants and blackberries. Mature wines combine aromas of fruit macerated in brandy, leather, pepper, cocoa and liquorice. Floral scents are rare.

Palate
Blagny wine is full-bodied, concentrated and structured with a meaty consistency that needs time to soften. This is an exceptionally fragrant wine.

The Premiers Crus
Hameau de Blagny
La Garenne or Sur la Garenne
La Jeunelotte
La Pièce sous le Bois
Sous Blagny
Sous le Dos d'Âne
Sous le Puits

Soil types
Marls overlaid with slope wash. Bottom: clayey-calcareous. Top: brown limestone.

The Blagny vineyard, an island of Pinot Noir between two vineyards that produce great white wines.

Choice of food
Animal game (hare, boar), beef bourguignon, strong cheese (Soumaintrain, Epoisses, Langres, Ami du Chambertin, Munster).

Serving temperature
14-16°C.

Blanquette de Limoux

Limoux wine is represented by four AOCs. The appellation area is situated to the west of Corbières and the south of La Malepère, crossed from north to south by the Aude river and cut through by a network of streams. Perpendicular to the Aude, it dives into two very distinct zones: in the north, a gently rolling landscape with no hills higher than 400 metres (1,312 feet); to the south, steeper, more rugged terrain. Blanquette Méthode Ancestrale is made entirely from Mauzac grapes; Blanquette wines made by the *Méthode Traditionnelle* (Traditional Method) are a blend of Mauzac with Chenin and Chardonnay. Local wine growers maintain that the monks of the Abbey of Saint-Hilaire 'invented' effervescence' long before Dom Pérignon in Champagne.

1975

The Pauligne vineyard.

Appellations
Blanquette de Limoux AOC (dry, medium dry, sweet) Blanquette Méthode Ancestrale AOC

Colour
White

Area
878 ha

Production
Blanquette de Limoux: 37,407 hl
Blanquette Méthode Ancestrale: 3,213 hl

Grape varieties
Blanquette de Limoux:
Mauzac (90%), Chardonnay, Chenin.
Blanquette Méthode Ancestrale:
100% Mauzac.

Soil types
A few terraces; soils from weathering of marly limestone, and sandstone and pudding stone cemented with clay.

Ageing ability
Several years but also pleasant to drink on the day of purchase.

55

Eye

Usually brilliant pale yellow with green highlights, sometimes with a delicate golden hue. Fine persistent bubbles are a sign of quality. A fine persistent cordon enhances the visual effect.

Nose

Blanquette wines are apple-scented with delightful floral notes (acacia, hawthorn). Older wines develop hints of ripe fruits, honey or aromas of lightly toasted bread.

Palate

Limoux sparkling wines are distinguished by an aromatic consistency that endures from the nose to the palate. Fresh fruit aromas, delicate floral notes and hints of toastiness mingle with the unique flavours of particular cuvees or vintages, ranging from apple to apricot with occasional notes of more exotic fruits. Hawthorn and acacia are the white-flower scents as hints of toast and aromas of hazelnuts and golden-baked bread complete the aromatic harmony.

Mauzac, known as Blanquette, has given its name to the hilly terroir of Les Blanquettières.

Choice of food

Blanquette de Limoux: as an apéritif (straight or in a kir) or with fish, white meat or dessert (crêpes Suzette). *Sparkling wines:* puddings.

Serving temperature 8°C.

A delicate wine-making process

• *Blanquette de Limoux:* some 150kg (330.5lbs) of grapes are necessary to obtain one hectolitre of must which, after racking, is fermented at low temperatures. Clarification, blending and the addition of the *liqueur de tirage* are followed by a second fermentation in the bottle. The wine is then stored on its side and left to mature until the time comes for disgorgement and the addition of the *liqueur d'expédition.* Only then does Blanquette de Limoux become the popular wine of celebration, characterised by the fragrance and especially the mellowness and richness of Chardonnay.

• *Blanquette Méthode Ancestrale:* this is produced by secondary bottle fermentation using residual grape sugars. Fermentation occurs because the yeasts in the fermenting musts are gradually reduced by repeated rackings. This delicate process uses exclusively Mauzac grapes and no added liqueur, producing an original wine that is barely 6% proof.

Blaye, Côtes and Premières Côtes

The symbol of Blaye is the citadel built by Vauban to protect Bordeaux from the English and Dutch naval invasions. The town lies on the north bank of the Gironde at the edge of the Charente region. Together with Saint-Savin and Saint-Ciers, Blaie produces red, or dry white Vins de Côtes. The reds (Premières Côtes de Blaye) are powerful and fruity. The whites are highly aromatic (Premières Côtes de Blaye, or Côtes de Blaye).

1936

Appellations
Blaye or Blayais AOC
Côtes de Blaye AOC
Premières Côtes de Blaye AOC

Colours
Red (80%)
Dry white (only white in Côtes de Blaye AOC)

Eye
• Red Premières Côtes de Blaye is purple with tinges of black.
• White Côtes de Blaye is deep yellow, almost lemon coloured.
• White Premières Côtes is light yellow with green highlights.

Nose
• The reds have ripe red-fruit notes with spice, game and chocolate aromas. Ageing in barrels adds woody vanilla flavours.
• White Premières Côtes de Blaye have notes of lemon, grapefruit, tangerine and roasted almonds. White Côtes de Blaye are less complex but with attractive floral and fruity characteristics.

Palate
• The reds are supple, rounded and well balanced, with firm tannins and a solid structure that provides the backbone for maturation.
• White Premières Côtes de Blaye are rich and elegant, with a lively bouquet that opens up to a very pretty finish. The whites are less distinguished but not without flavour or nervousness.

Choice of food
Reds:
braised veal, pot-au-feu, stewed beef, grilled tuna with peppers.
Whites:
seafood, salmon, shellfish risotto, chicken à la crème.

Serving temperature
Reds: 16-17°C.
Whites: 10-12°C.

Vieilli en Barriques Neuves

CHATEAU
HAUT-TERRIER
PREMIÈRES CÔTES DE BLAYE
APPELLATION PREMIÈRES CÔTES DE BLAYE CONTRÔLÉE
1993
12%vol.   Bernard DENÉCHAUD   75cl
PROPRIÉTAIRE À ST-MARIENS - GIRONDE - FRANCE
TÉL. 57.68.64.94
MIS EN BOUTEILLE AU CHATEAU

Soil types
Limestone, sand, clayey-limestone.

Main grape varieties
Reds: Merlot, Cabernet-Sauvignon, Cabernet Franc.
Whites: Sémillon, Sauvignon, Muscadelle, plus Colombard in the Côtes de Blaye AOC.

Area
4,700 hectares
Production
262,000 hectolitres

Ageing ability
Reds: 3-7 years.
Whites: drink in the year of production or within 2-3 years for certain wines.

Bonnes-Mares

1936

Appellation
Bonnes-Mares
AOC

Classification
Grand Cru

Colour
Red

Area
15 ha 5 a 72 c,
including 13 ha
54 a 17 c in
Chambolle-
Musigny and
1 ha 51 a 55 c
in Morey-Saint-
Denis.

Production
610 hl

B onnes-Mares, on the border of Morey-Saint-Denis and Chambolle-Musigny, is the continuation of Clos de Tart and one of Burgundy's most reputed Grands Crus. The wines produced here are the most accomplished expression of Pinot Noir. Bonnes-Mares probably derives its name from *marer*, Old French for to cultivate – in this case, sites that are easy to cultivate or well kept.

Eye
Beautifully clear and sharp ruby-red in colour, with nuances of dark purple or deep garnet and mauve highlights.

Nose
A violet-scented bouquet with hints of the underwood, moss, mushrooms, wet earth and a few animal notes. Age brings touches of leather, musk, fur and spices. The wine also becomes more flowery than fruity (lilac and rose buds dominating over blackberry and blueberry).

Palate
This very thoroughbred wine needs several years to open up. Tannic by nature, with a robust and sometimes rather wild personality, it gradually mellows to become rich and meaty with a lovely texture and solid structure. Bonnes-Mares wine has extraordinary ageing potential – as much as 30 or even 50 years.

Grape variety
Pinot Noir.

Soil types
Brown and reddish, fairly light and gravely argillaceous-siliceous soil on limestone slabs.

Ageing ability
10-20 years.

Serving temperature
14-16°C.

Choice of food
Duck, Bresse chicken with baby vegetables, game, cheese (Epoisses, Ami du Chambertin, Soumaintrain, Langres).

Bonnezeaux

Bonnezeaux is one of the most famous growths of the Coteaux du Layon, located in the village of Thouarcé on the left bank of the Loire not far from Brissac. The vineyard is planted in shallow, schistose soils on steep slopes with a southwesterly aspect where the vines are exposed to prevailing winds that dessicate the berries on the vine. This, coupled with low rainfall, concentrates the sugars, so producing the overripe berries that gives this cru its originality. The wines have great finesse and wonderful complexity.

1951

Appellation
Bonnezeaux AOC
Colour
White
Area
106 hectares
Production
2,360 hectolitres

Eye
Bonnezeaux is golden-yellow with green highlights (in contrast to the orange tones of a concentrated wine produced from nobly rotted berries).

Palate
There is the same complexity on the palate but with an added impression of intensity and power. The aromatic persistence lasts for several caudalies (or seconds).

Nose
The bouquet is composed of distinctive aromatic notes that are never overwhelming, with modulated nuances of dried fruit (apricots, figs, sultanas), ripe fruit (pears and plums) and white flowers (acacia, hawthorn, etc).

Choice of food
As an apéritif or with foie gras, fish, white meat in a sauce, fruit tarts, fruit salad.

Soil types
Superficial, stony soils on schist.

Serving temperature
7-9°C.

Grape variety
Chenin Blanc (or Pineau de la Loire).

Ageing ability
5-20 years for average vintages, infinitely longer for great ones.

59

Bordeaux, Bordeaux Supérieur

Appellations
Bordeaux AOC
Bordeaux
Supérieur AOC

Colours
Bordeaux: red
Bordeaux
Supérieur: red
and sweet white
(rare)

Area
Bordeaux:
38,551 ha

1936

Bordeaux is the largest vineyard appellation in the world. Bordeaux and Bordeaux Supérieur are predominantly blended from Merlot or Cabernet-Sauvignon grapes with varying proportions of the other regional varieties. The wines are generally fruity and fairly light and meant for early drinking. In recent years, however, a few well-known producers have been making more structured wines that are aged in wooden casks.

Bordeaux
Supérieur:
9,095 ha
(including 50 ha
of whites)

Production
Bordeaux:
2,421,912 hl
Bordeaux
Supérieur:
546,491 hl

Bordeaux Supérieur
There is a difference in the alcohol content of Bordeaux Supérieur and Bordeaux. Bordeaux Supérieur wines do not relate to a specific terroir but to a certain selection of Bordeaux wines, and a lower authorised yield (50 hl/ha for Bordeaux Supérieur versus 60 for Bordeaux). In wine tastings they are often distinguished by stronger tannins that make them more ageworthy (up to 10 years) and good with foods such as game or mushrooms.

Main grape varieties
Merlot, Cabernet Franc, Cabernet-Sauvignon, Petit Verdot, Carmenère, Malbec.

Soil types
Argillaceous limestone, sandy silt, limestone.

Ageing ability
Bordeaux:
2-5 years.
Bordeaux Supérieur:
5-10 years.

Eye

One of the most typical features of Bordeaux wine is the colour… Bordeaux red! Specific characteristics are hints of light garnet red with brilliant highlights.

Nose

The bouquet varies depending on the blend and especially the predominant grape variety, which can be quite different from one growth to another. Some wines have a blackcurrant fragrance (a sign of Cabernet). Others are more violet-scented, indicating the presence of Merlot.

Palate

Bordeaux wines are delicate and supple, often supported by beautiful tannins. They have a suave, rounded body that is more powerful in Bordeaux Supérieur. Young Bordeaux wines are sufficiently accessible for early drinking – within a year or two of production depending on the vintage. Bordeaux Supérieur wines need more time but have improved ageing potential due to rich tannins, especially when produced from Cabernet-Sauvignon.

Choice of food

Bordeaux: charcuterie, white or red meat, cheese. *Bordeaux Supérieur:* game, marinated meat, lampreys Bordeaux-style, mushrooms.

The vineyards dedicated to Bordeaux wines are located in the region of Saint-André-de-Cubzac, in the area around the Gironde, and in the Entre-Deux-Mers appellation (above). Pictured on the left is the abbey of Sauve-Majeure.

Serving temperature

16°C.

Bordeaux Clairet and Rosé

Appellations
Bordeaux Rosé AOC
Bordeaux Clairet AOC
Colour
Rosé

1 9 3 6

All of the rosés in the Gironde are produced under the Bordeaux regional appellation. Bordeaux Rosés and Clairets may therefore come from any one of the 503 communes in this department. Clairet wine, made by macerating red wine grapes for short periods, is the descendant of the 'French Claret' that was already popular with the English back in the Middle Ages.

Area
Bordeaux Rosé:
1,658 ha
Bordeaux Clairet:
421 ha
Production
Bordeaux Rosé:
105,645 hl
Bordeaux Clairet:
26,370 hl

Eye
• The rosés are usually strong to deep pink with a wide variety of nuances – sometimes verging on salmon pink.
• Clairets are vivid in colour, ranging from crimson pink to dark red, with occasional nuances of deep purple. They usually have deeper colour than the rosés.

Nose
• The rosés are characterised by their fine, elegant floral bouquet, dominated by primary grape aromas.
• Clairets have more intense notes of red fruits: strawberries, blackcurrants or even grenadine, promising rounded, fleshy qualities.

Palate
• The rosés are supple and very quaffable with a charm that comes from a perfect balance of acidity, alcohol and tannins. The aromas are light, fresh and elegant but persistent.
• Clairets are typical of light reds – supple, fairly full-bodied and packed with aromas. The tannins are soft.

Main grape varieties
Cabernet-Sauvignon, Cabernet Franc, Merlot.

Soil types
Mud flats, gravel, clayey limestone, *boulbènes* (silty).

Ageing ability
For early drinking, within 2-3 years.

Serving temperature
8°C.

Choice of food
Charcuterie, stuffed tomatoes, grilled foods, exotic cuisine.

Bordeaux Côtes de Francs

his appellation which lies to the east of the Libournais is the most continental of all the Bordeaux areas, located on some of the highest argillaceous limestone and marl slopes in the department of the Gironde. Côtes de Francs reds are full-bodied, rich and tannic – good wines for cellaring. The appellation also produces a limited quantity of good quality, agreeable dry white wines.

1936

Appellation
Bordeaux Côtes de Francs AOC

Colours
Red
White (limited production)

Area
459 hectares

Production
27,667 hectolitres

Eye
• The reds are limpid and deep – a sign of their solid constitution.
• The whites are a pretty yellow colour with green highlights.

Nose
• The reds have an elegant, complex bouquet revealing scents of vanilla, notes of lush ripe fruits, venison, toast and hints of prunes, blueberries, leather, truffles and the underwood.
• The whites are intense and complex with scents ranging from fruit aromas to toasty notes. The main impression is of broom, boxwood, dried fruit, figs, pears, citrus fruit, vanilla, dried flowers and honey.

Palate
• The robustness and substance of the reds is evident from the attack, which is followed by good tannic development.
• The whites have a vigorous attack, followed by richness and elegance and, in the best wines, a full meaty structure sustained by a certain woodiness.

Château
Les Charmes-Godard

BORDEAUX CÔTES DE FRANCS

Choice of food
Reds: roasted red meat, poultry, game.
White: as an apéritif or with seafood, fish.

Serving temperature
Reds: 16-17°C.
Whites: 10-12°C.

Ageing ability
Reds: 3-8 years.
Whites: drink within the year.

Main grape varieties
Reds: Merlot, Cabernet Franc, Cabernet-Sauvignon, Malbec.
Whites: Sémillon, Sauvignon, Muscadelle.

Soil types
Argillaceous limestone, marls.

Bordeaux Sec

1 9 3 6

Appellation
Bordeaux Sec
AOC
Colour
White
Area
9,918 hectares
Production
539,377
hectolitres

A ny dry white appellation wine from within the Gironde is entitled to the Bordeaux Sec regional appellation. These fruity, nervous wines have gained enormously from improved vinification techniques, though there is more to Bordeaux whites than technology. Many producers look to express the personality of the terroir in their wines. Others place emphasis on skin maceration and ageing in wood to obtain full-bodied, aromatic wines.

**Main grape
varieties**
Sémillon,
Sauvignon,
Muscadelle.

Soil types
Argillaceous
limestone, clayey-
siliceous, gravel,
sand and silt.

Eye
Many Bordeaux whites are pale gold with green highlights but a few are virtually colourless, and some are a deep, eye-catching yellow.

Nose
Dry Bordeaux whites are very fragrant and develop elegant fruity and floral perfumes. Their diversity comes from the variable proportions of grape varieties used in the blends and the different methods of vinification. Maceration on skins for example produces a wide range of nuances: lemon aromas, tangerine, grapefruit, toasted almonds and vanilla, not forgetting exotic fruits.

Palate
Traditional crus are seductively fresh, lively and fruity – the perfect accompaniment to seafood, shellfish, grilled fish and hors d'oeuvres. Some whites have a more complex character, with a fleshier, fuller structure that makes them suitable partners for white meat, fish in a sauce or gourmet shellfish.

**Ageing
ability**
2-3 years.

**Serving
temperature**
10-12°C.

Choice of food
Quiche
Lorraine, pike
quenelles,
seafood, fish
(grilled or in a
sauce), poultry.

Burgundy

The Burgundy wine-growing region extends some 300 kilometres (186 miles) from a point north of the department of Yonne (Joigny) to south of the department of Saône-et-Loire (Pouilly-Fuissé, Saint-Vérand). It includes departments in the region of Burgundy itself plus a few districts in the Rhône valley, which is mainly Beaujolais country. Pinot Noir is the Burgundian grape variety par excellence and the source of red wines that include such illustrious Grands Crus as Romanée-Conti, Chambertin and Corton, as well as rosé wines. White Burgundy is produced from the Chardonnay grape that is grown throughout the region in strictly delimited production areas. The Burgundy appellation may include the name of the locality or *climat* of origin.

1 9 3 7

Appellation
Bourgogne AOC
Colours
Red
Rosé
White (40%)
Area
2,100 hectares
Production
198,000 hectolitres

> **Bourgogne Grand Ordinaire**
> The Bourgogne Grand Ordinaire regional AOC (from 'Grand Ordinaire', the bottle drunk on Sundays in the 1930s) is gradually disappearing (1.2 million bottles produced mainly in the Côte-d'Or) due to its rather unedifying name. The range of wines is too broad to fit any typical description but includes reds, rosés and whites, mainly from César, Tressot and Gamay Noir. Bourgogne Ordinaire is also now a thing of the past.

Ageing ability
2-5 years
(up to 10 years
for whites).

Soil types
Limestone
mixed with
marls and clays.

Main grape varieties
Reds and rosés:
Pinot Noir
and, very
exceptionally,
César and
Tressot (Yonne).
Whites:
Chardonnay.

Eye

• Young red Burgundy wine is crimson, maturing to a deeper ruby red that with time turns to an intense cherry black and even deep purple. The colour is usually bright, shimmering and vivid. Classic Burgundy reds have a strong, moderately deep colour.

• The rosés are a fairly intense candy pink.

• The whites are a limpid, crystalline, pale yellow-gold with green highlights.

BOURGOGNE
ÉPINEUIL
APPELLATION BOURGOGNE CONTRÔLÉE
Mis en bouteille à Épineuil par
Alain et Patricia MATHIAS
Propriétaires-récoltants à 89700 Épineuil - France
Tél. 86 54 43 90
PRODUIT DE
FRANCE

Nose

• The reds usually open with a basket of red and black fruit: on the one side, strawberries, raspberries, redcurrants and cherries; on the other side, blackberries, blueberries and blackcurrants. But they can also tend towards stewed fruit (prunes) and even candied fruit. Spicy, peppery nuances are not uncommon along with animal scents, fragrances of moss and the underwood, mushrooms and, with age, leather too.

• Rosés bring to mind wild strawberries, redcurrants and exotic fruits.

• The aromas in white Burgundies are typical of Chardonnay: white flowers, hawthorn, citronella and fern, mushrooms (St George's mushrooms, field mushrooms), almonds and hazelnuts, spices, butter, lightly toasted bread and sometimes honey.

Palate

• A good red Burgundy is full of life and passion with a supple, rounded structure. The tannins and the fruit need time to come together, but after four or five years of ageing the wine becomes fleshy and mouth-filling. This is a vinous wine with excellent ageing ability, up to eight or ten years as a general rule, although some Burgundies may be positively radiant after 15 years of cellaring.

• The rosés are vivid and fruity.

• The whites are rich without being cloying, fine but not too light. They are aromatic, fruity and not very robust, although the best of them have good aromatic persistence.

Choice of food

Reds: red meat (thick Charollais beefsteak, rib steak with mushrooms), duck with green peppercorns, game, *andouillette* sausage, cheese (Epoisses, Soumaintrain, Camembert).
Rosés: warm red mullet salad.
Whites: hot meat pie, gourmet fish, shellfish, poultry and white meat.

Serving temperature
12-14°C.

Bourgogne Aligoté

There are as many types of Aligoté as there are Aligoté production areas in Burgundy: supple and fruity in Pernand, fresh and vivacious in Les Hautes-Côtes. Bouzeron Aligotés have been granted their own appellation. This is a dry white, carafe wine to be drunk young – ideal for Kir, which is an apéritif made with crème de cassis and any crisp fresh white wine.

1 9 3 7

Appellation
Bourgogne Aligoté AOC

Colour
White

Area
1,556 hectares

Production
98,800 hectolitres

Eye
Generally a pale mineral gold, but it can also be straw-coloured.

Nose
Good depth with a flowery then fruity bouquet influenced by the terroir: Aligotés from Pernand have a fruity nose; those from Saint-Bris in the Yonne department are distinguished by notes of elderberry.

Palate
A soft, smooth wine with plenty of personality – elegant and light. Hints of lemon and a touch of acidity at the finish.

In the Côte, the Aligoté grape has been replaced by the Chardonnay. Where once it was grown on the slopes, it is found today mainly on the plain.

Choice of food
As an apéritif or with *gougères* (cheesy choux pastry puffs), snails à la Bourguignonne, terrine, shellfish, fried fish, goats' cheese, Comté.

Serving temperature
10-12°C.

Ageing ability
1-3 years.

Grape variety
Aligoté.

Soil types
Limestone mixed with marl and clays.

Bourgogne Côte Chalonnaise

Appellation
Bourgogne Côte
Chalonnaise
AOC

Colours
Red
Rosé
White (25%)

1990

T his appellation stretches across 44 communes in the northern part of the Saône-et-Loire department. It is approximately 40 kilometres (25 miles) long and 5-8 kilometres (3-5 miles) wide, running from Chagny to Saint-Gengoux-le-National. The Bourgogne Côte Chalonnaise area has real identity, with nuances that vary from terroir to terroir, and distinctions between north and south. Having the right conditions for Pinot Noir makes this good red wine country – not forgetting the white wines that are often very nicely balanced.

Eye
• The reds are a strong, lustrous crimson or brilliant ruby red, sometimes verging on deep garnet or purple.
• The whites are a clear pale yellow shimmering with gold and silver highlights.

Nose
• The red wines are a glorious celebration of red and black berries (raspberries, redcurrants, blackcurrants, blackberries), soft fruit and sometimes cherries. Also quite typical are animal scents and fragrances of the underwood and mushrooms.
• The whites evoke white flowers (hawthorn, acacia) and dried fruit over notes of lemon or aniseed, with suggestions of brioche, warm croissants and honey.

Palate
• The reds have a firm, resistant texture that is rather austere in youth but they age well, developing a pleasing roundness.
• The whites are rich and well behaved. Not overly powerful or persistent, with a clean attack, youthful enthusiasm and a lively, bracing palate.
• The fruity, warmly spontaneous rosés are quite rare but well-made by a rigorously controlled *saignée* process.

Area
3,665 hectares
delimited area
513 hectares
of plantings

Production
33,320 hectolitres

Grape varieties
Reds and rosés:
Pinot Noir.
Whites:
Chardonnay.

Soil types
South: marls,
sand and clays
with flint and
sandstone
pebbles, with
sandstone out-
crops; north:
limestone.

Ageing ability
Reds: 3-6 years.
Whites:
2-4 years.

Choice of food
Reds: poached
eggs in red wine,
meat grilled or
in a sauce,
cheese (Epoisses,
Soumaintrain).
Whites: trout,
cheese
(Cîteaux).

**Serving
temperature**
Reds: 14-16°C.
Whites:
12-14°C.

Bourgogne Hautes-Côtes de Beaune

The Hautes-Côtes de Beaune stretch from Beaune to the outskirts of Autun, across an area 30 kilometres (18.6 miles) long and 10 kilometres (6 miles) wide. Vines cover the hillsides everywhere in this part of the Burgundy regional AOC, producing wines packed with fruit that have improved greatly in quality while remaining reasonably priced.

1 9 3 7

Appellation
Bourgogne
Hautes-Côtes de
Beaune AOC

Colours
Red
White (19%)

Area
666 hectares

Production
36,880
hectolitres

Eye
• The reds are a deep purplish colour.
• The whites are a light straw colour with a delicate golden hue and occasional green highlights.

Nose
• The red wines in their youth are marked by scents of red fruit (raspberries, morello cherries). Older wines tend towards crystallised fruit, animal scents and aromas of the underwood, often with a spicy, peppery note.
• The whites have aromas of white flowers (hawthorn) and fern plus occasional notes of hazelnuts, toast, butter and honey.

Palate
• The reds are full-bodied, generous and quite round, and always true to their terroir. A certain nervousness is not uncommon in young wines as the tannins gradually mellow and the balance becomes established.
• The whites are well balanced with all the characteristic freshness of the Chardonnay but neither too lively nor too sweet.

Choice of food
Reds: poached eggs in red wine, petit salé (salted pork) with lentils, lamb, poultry, cheese (Brillat Savarin, Cîteaux).
Whites: snails, poached fish or fish in a sauce, white meat, cheese (Bleu de Bresse).

BOURGOGNE
HAUTES-COTES DE BEAUNE
APPELLATION CONTRÔLÉE

DOMAINE PARIGOT
PÈRE & FILS

Serving temperature
Reds: 15-16°C.
Whites: 12-14°C.

Ageing ability
Usually
3-5 years,
8-10 years
for very good
vintages.

Soil types
Argillaceous
pebbly lime-
stone on fairly
steep slopes.

Grape varieties
Reds:
Pinot Noir.
Whites:
Chardonnay
(very rarely
Pinot Blanc).

69

Bourgogne Hautes-Côtes de Nuits

Appellation
Bourgogne
Hautes-Côtes
de Nuits AOC

Colours
Red
Rosé
White (20%)

1937

The Hautes-Côtes de Nuits and the Hautes-Côtes de Beaune form a plateau some 12 kilometres (7.5 miles) wide between the Côte itself and the valley of the river Ouche. The AOC extends some 40 kilometres (25 miles) from the heights of Dijon to Maranges, producing vigorous, fiery wines from vines planted in hilly countryside around the historic site of Vergy.

Eye
• The reds are crimson or a dark ruby colour, often with a raspberry hue, sometimes with bluish highlights.
• The whites are a light golden colour, white gold to pale gold, occasionally more straw-coloured.

Nose
• The reds have characteristic notes of Pinot Noir – cherries, liquorice, sometimes violets – that after a few years develop to more mature notes of crystallised fruit and musk (animal, leather, the underwood, humus, moss).
• The whites offer notes of Chardonnay: white flowers (hawthorn, honeysuckle) mingled with pippin apples, lemons, white dead-nettles, hazelnuts and sometimes toast and beeswax.

Palate
• The reds are well structured with good acidity and palpable, pleasant tannins. Plenty of body, but not over-zealous.
• The whites have sufficient complexity, richness and solidity to hold their own at the dining table.

Area
656 hectares

Production
28,980
hectolitres

Grape varieties
Reds and rosés:
Pinot Noir.
Whites:
Chardonnay.

Soil types
Top of the slope:
hard limestone;
going down the
slope: clays and
marl, limestone
with sandstone
pebbles, gravelly
moraine and
pearly flagstone.

**Ageing
ability**
Reds:
3-10 years.
Whites:
2-8 years.

**Serving
temperature**
Reds: 14-16°C.
Whites: 10-12°C.

Choice of food
Reds: terrine,
red meat,
feathered game,
cheese
(Cîteaux).
Whites:
seafood,
avocado with
crab, *tourte
bourguignonne,*
fish, cheese
(Bresse Blue,
Roquefort).

Bourgogne Passetoutgrain

Bourgogne Passetoutgrain is a regional AOC that, apart from the occasional rosé, only produces red wine. The grapes are Pinot Noir (at least a third) and Gamay Noir, mixed together in the vat. This is therefore not a blended wine in the normal sense, rather the product of different grapes vinified together. Bourgogne Passetoutgrain is produced mainly in Saône-et-Loire (approximately two thirds), the remainder being produced in the Côte d'Or and the Yonne Valley. The wines are light and delicate and intended for early drinking.

__1 9 3 7__

Appellation
Bourgogne
Passetoutgrain
AOC

Colours
Red
Rosé (rare)

Area
1,242 hectares

Eye
The reds are a rich, deep crimson.

Nose
Bourgogne Passetoutgrain is berry-scented (blackcurrants, raspberries, redcurrants) underpinned by animal notes.

Palate
Distinctly Gamay, with a definite taste of the terroir. A harmonious, agreeable wine, notable for its richness and fruit that literally explodes on the palate. The best quality wines have a higher proportion of Pinot Noir and, although more refined, are also for drinking young.

Production
69,000
hectolitres

Choice of food
Charcuterie, grilled or roasted red meat, duck with cherries, cheese (Brie, Epoisses).

Serving temperature
12-14°C.

Soil types
Limestone mixed with marls and clays.

Ageing ability
2-3 years.

Grape varieties
Pinot Noir, Gamay Noir.

71

Bourgueil

Appellation
Bourgueil AOC
Colours
Red
Rosé (3%)
Area
1,285 hectares
Production
71,186
hectolitres

1937

V ine-growing may date back to Roman times, but it was in the Middle Ages that it really took off thanks largely to the pioneering efforts of the Abbaye de Bourgueil. Most of the production is in the Indre-et-Loire department, in Benais, Bourgueil, Ingrandes, Saint-Patrice and Restigné, on a high alluvial terrace on the right bank of the Loire. There are two types of terroir here: tuffeau, producing structured wines for laying down; and gravel terraces yielding aromatic, elegant wines that are accessible from an early age (*gravières* wines).

Eye

• Young red Bourgueil wines are brilliant cherry, crimson or dark red, developing amber highlights with age.

• The rosés are obtained by *saignée* (partial maceration of red wines at the start of fermentation). They have good depth of colour.

Nose

• Bourgueil is a very aromatic wine, revealing scents of cherries (morello), strawberries and blackcurrants followed by notes of raspberries. There may often be a suggestion of liquorice or green peppers, in which case the wines are said to *bretonner* – 'Breton' being the local name for Cabernet Franc. After a few years, the red fruit aromas tend more towards cooked fruit and spices. Wines at their peak release animal aromas such as leather or fur mingled with scents of the underwood. Mature wines are characterised by gamey notes.

• The rosés have the fragrance of fresh fruits.

Palate

• *Gravières* wines offer flavours that recall the aromas on the nose. The touch of acidity at the finish reminds us that we are in the Val de Loire and gives an impression of lightness. Wines from the tuffeau express thick, fleshy tannins.

• Rosé wines are structured and fresh. They may not have the opulence of the red wines but they are ideal with a summer meal.

Choice of food
Young reds and rosés:
charcuterie, white meat, cheese (Sainte-Maure), red fruit salad. *More mature reds:* red meat, game, cheese.

Grape varieties
Cabernet Franc or Breton, with maximum 10% Cabernet-Sauvignon also allowed.

Soil types
Tuffeau (argillaceous limestone); gravel terraces (siliceous-clayey or siliceous).

Ageing ability
5-10 years.

Serving temperature
Reds: depending on age, 14-16°C.
Rosés: 8-10°C.

Bouzeron

The Bouzeron area is located in the north of the Saône-et-Loire department between Chagny and Rully. The climate is continental with fairly cold winters and often hot summers. The vineyard follows a north-south-facing valley and is dedicated to the Aligoté that thrives here on Bathonian limestone terrain, producing a dry, fruity white wine, sharp as flint and delightful as an aperitif. Certain *climats* such as Les Clous, have justifiably acquired Premier Cru reputation. Bouzeron is the only communal appellation to authorise the use of Aligoté grapes.

Appellation
Bouzeron AOC
Colour
White
Area
56 hectares
Production
3,300 hectolitres

1 9 9 9

Eye
Pale gold, with a sea-green hue but should not verge on yellow.

Nose
Bouzeron evokes scents of acacia, white flowers and country lanes bordered by hazelnuts. Mineral aromas (flint, gunflint) complete the bouquet. If there is a hint of honey, it should be very discreet and accompanied by notes of warm croissant.

Palate
This is a wine to prepare the palate, occasionally with a touch of Chardonnay about it but never too much – it should remain true to its origins. Satisfyingly opulent, interestingly complex, with a dreamy unique charm that the Burgundians call 'pointed roundness'.

Choice of food
As an aperitif with *gougères*, snails à la bourguignonne, shellfish, fried fish, fried kidneys, goats' cheese, Comté.

Serving temperature
10-13°C.

Ageing ability
3-5 years.

Grape variety
Aligoté.

Soil types
Brown and marly Bathonian limestone on the slopes.

73

Brouilly, Côte de Brouilly

Appellations
Brouilly AOC
Côte de Brouilly AOC

Colour
Red

Area
Brouilly: 1,305 hectares
Côte de Brouilly: 315 hectares

Production
Brouilly: 75,800 hectolitres
Côte de Brouilly: 18,700 hectolitres

1938

Grape variety
Gamay Noir.

Ageing ability
Brouilly:
2-3 years.
Côte de Brouilly:
3-6 years.

Côte de Brouilly AOC is located to the west of Belleville-sur-Saône and confined to the schistous slopes. By contrast, the Brouilly appellation, which is the largest and most southerly of all the Beaujolais crus, is planted on a wide variety of soils: granite soils to the west, hard compact rock in the centre, and soils sometimes covered with alluvial deposits to the east of Mont Brouilly. This same diversity is reflected in the wines.

Eye
• Brouilly is ruby red, more purplish when produced from granite soils (La Chaize, Saburin) and darker when grown on the eastern slopes (Pierreux, Buisantes).
• Côte de Brouilly may be deeper – deep garnet red rather than ruby.

Nose
• Brouilly releases fruity aromas dominated by strawberry and raspberry.
• Côte de Brouilly has added floral aromas, such as violet and peony, combined with mineral and peppery notes.

Palate
• Brouilly combines suppleness, fleshiness and finesse. The wines from granite soils mature early and are ready for drinking in the spring following the vintage.
• Côte de Brouilly has the taste of fresh grapes. It is more robust with tannins that give it real ageing potential.

Soil types
Brouilly: granitic sands (50%), argillaceous-siliceous and argillaceous limestone alluviums.
Côte de Brouilly: schist, porphyries (*pierre bleue*).

Serving temperature
14°C.

Choice of food
White meat, poultry, calves' liver, game birds, pasta, cheese.

Bugey

The Bugey vineyard is located in the Ain department, occupying the lower slopes of the Jura mountains, from Bourg-en-Bresse to Ambérieu-en-Bugey. The soils vary widely, sometimes marl and clay, sometimes limestone. A number of different wine growing regions come together at this point, hence the number of grape varieties grown here. Note for instance Poulsard Jurassien, used in the Cerdon region for the production of sparkling rosés by the *Méthode Ancestrale*. One great champion of Bugey wines was Anthelme Brillat-Savarin, the famous master epicure born in Belley in 1755.

1 9 3 8

Appellation
Bugey AOVDQS
Colours
Red (45%)
Rosé (still
or sparkling)
White (still
or sparkling)
Area
445 hectares

Production
28,610
hectolitres

Eye
• The red wines are a lustrous crimson colour.
• The whites are a pretty shade of amber.
• Sparkling wines from Cerdon sparkle with delicate bubbles.

Nose
• Bugey reds offer notes of red fruit and wild berries plus fragrances of leather and cocoa.
• The white wines are fresh and open, with a few grilled notes and a touch of menthol.
• The sparkling wines have a delightful fragrance of white fruits with a hint of brioche.

Palate
• The red wines display extraordinary presence, on a spicy framework that tends towards liquorice.
• The whites are fairly lively and long with toasty aromas.
• Sparkling wines from Cerdon are rounded with a modest alcohol content (8%).

**Choice
of food**
Red or white
meat, cheese
(Reblochon,
Mont d'Or,
Tomme de
Savoie).

VIN DU BUGEY
Cerdon
Méthode Ancestrale

**Serving
temperature**
10-12°C.

**Ageing
ability**
2 years.

**Main grape
varieties**
Reds: Poulsard,
Mondeuse,
Pinot Noir,
Gamay Noir.
Whites: Jacquère,
Altesse,
Chardonnay,
Aligoté, Molette.

Soil types
Morainic
knolls and slope
wash at the foot
of the Jurassic
limestone
ranges.

Buzet

Appellation
Buzet AOC

Colours
Red (85%)
Rosé (10%)
White (5%)

Area
Red and Rosé:
1,750 hectares
White: 100 hectares

1973

T he Buzet vineyard, famous since the Middle Ages, lies halfway between Agen and Marmande, between the left bank of the Garonne and the Landes forest. Thanks to the work of a few independent producers and the Buzet co-operative (that accounts for 97% of production), Buzet today is renowned as an interesting region producing wines of character.

Eye
• The red wines have good depth of colour: ruby red when young, garnet in wines for laying down.
• Rosés range from blush pink to dark pink.
• Young whites are pale yellow with green highlights, becoming more straw-coloured with age.

Nose
• The reds reveal scents of red fruit (blackcurrant, blackberry) and sometimes crystallised fruit (prunes) plus notes of green peppers. Vanilla aromas dominate in the barrel-matured cuvées with hints of cocoa and roasted coffee. Animal notes develop with age.
• The rosés disclose powerful aromas of budding blackcurrant and mint.
• The whites acquire a touch of freshness from the Sauvignon that adds broom and elderberry aromas – sometimes with a hint of amyl – alongside floral scents and aromas of toasted almonds.

Palate
• Fleshy at first with a characteristically tannic finish in the case of very young wines – what you would expect of a wine of medium ageing ability.

Production
116,658
hectolitres

Main grape varieties
Reds and rosés:
Merlot, Cabernet Franc, Cabernet-Sauvignon.
Whites: Sémillon, Sauvignon.

Soil types
Gravel, argillaceous limestone and *boulbènes*.

Ageing ability
Reds:
5 years and more.
Whites and rosés:
1-3 years.

Serving temperature
Reds: 15-17°C.
Whites and rosés:
8-10°C.

Choice of food
Reds: game, roasted lamb, duck (magret or confit), osso bucco.
Rosés: as an apéritif or with charcuterie.
Whites: seafood, grilled crayfish, squid, young eels, pissaladière.

Cabardès

The Cabardès vineyard to the northwest of Carcassonne is the most westerly in the Languedoc. This historic land, where every fortress seems to echo to the sounds of the Albigensian Crusade, is also where the digging of the Canal du Midi commenced in 1666. Oceanic influences define the distribution of different grapes, Mediterranean varieties in one place, Atlantic varieties elsewhere. Grenache and Syrah grow on the drier soils, Cabernet-Sauvignon and Merlot on the deepest.

1998

Appellation
Cabardès AOC
Colours
Red
Rosé
Area
330 hectares
Production
19,040 hectolitres

Eye
Cabardès usually has good depth of colour, crimson at first, developing orange nuances after two or three years' ageing, especially when there is a high proportion of Grenache.

Nose
• Red Cabardès has a strawberry fragrance punctuated with hints of crystallised fruit or prunes. Wines for laying down offer aromas of venison and spices, plus vanilla when aged in barrels.
• The rosés are a subtle alliance of strawberry, citrus fruit and flowers.

Palate
Combining Syrah and Merlot with a small percentage of Grenache makes a very elegant wine, balancing the smoothness of the Merlot with the powerful tannins of the Syrah.

Choice of food
Reds: red meat, game, cassoulet.
Rosés: as an apéritif or with grilled meat, exotic cuisine.

Serving temperature
Reds: 16-18°C.
Rosés: 12°C.

Ageing ability
2-5 years (up to 10 years for great vintages).

Grape varieties
Grenache Noir, Syrah, Merlot, Cabernet-Sauvignon.

Soil types
From north to south, gneiss and schist, limestone, sandstone marls and ancient terraces.

Cabernet d'anjou et de Saumur

Appellations
Cabernet
d'Anjou AOC
Cabernet de
Saumur AOC
Colour
Rosé

1 9 6 4

Anjou and Saumur rosé wines come from Cabernet grapes, and are typical of this northern climatic region. The wines are sold under the name of the main appellation, Cabernet d'Anjou, or under the name of an appellation that is secondary in terms of production, Cabernet de Saumur, confined to the white chalky soils of Saumur. Cabernet d'Anjou is a fresh fruity wine that is traditionally lightly coloured because it is produced by direct pressing. Notable for its finesse, it is suitable for laying down in good vintage years.

Area
Cabernet
d'Anjou: 2,722
hectares
Cabernet de
Saumur: 91
hectares
Production
Cabernet
d'Anjou: 142,568
hectolitres
Cabernet de
Saumur: 6,298
hectolitres

Grape varieties
Cabernet Franc,
Cabernet-
Sauvignon.

Soil types
*Cabernet
d'Anjou:* any of
the terroirs that
come under the
Anjou AOC.
*Cabernet de
Saumur:* argilla-
ceous limestone
on slopes of
tuffeau chalk.

Eye
• Cabernet d'Anjou is a delightful shade of pink, turning to a striking orange colour in older wines.
• Cabernet de Saumur is the colour of rose petals.

Nose
• Cabernet d'Anjou is distinguished by its aromas of red, white and yellow fruits (peaches, pears). Exotic fruits add a pleasant touch to a rich variety of aromas that also includes vegetal nuances (peppers) with spicy and floral notes.
• Cabernet de Saumur wines reveal soft notes of red fruits.

**Ageing
ability**
*Cabernet
d'Anjou:*
1-2 years.
*Cabernet de
Saumur:*
5-10 years.

Palate
• Cabernet d'Anjou is deliciously refreshing and notable for its aromatic intensity and balance.
• Cabernet de Saumur is thirst-quenching, well balanced and discreet.

**Serving
temperature**
*Cabernet
d'Anjou:* 8-10°C.
*Cabernet de
Saumur:* 12°C.

Choice of food
Cabernet d'Anjou:
charcuterie,
duck à l'orange,
red fruit salad.
*Cabernet de
Saumur:* as an
apéritif or with
fish.

Cadillac

The walled town of Cadillac, dominated by its 16th century castle, is regarded as the capital of the hillsides that border the right-bank of the Garonne River upstream from Bordeaux. Here the limestone gravel slopes are ideally suited to the production of sweet white wines. The Cadillac appellation extends across 22 communes from Baurech to Saint-Maixent, embracing Loupiac and Sainte-Croix-du-Mont.

1 9 7 3

Appellation
Cadillac AOC
Colour
White (sweet, rich wines)
Area
274 hectares
Production
6,885 hectolitres

Eye
The golden yellow or topaz tones characteristic of sweet wines darken in the course of ageing - which is easy to observe through the clear glass bottle.

Nose
A complex bouquet of honey, acacia, honeysuckle, vanilla, citrus fruit and apricot. Many Cadillac wines are marked by a touch of toastiness, a sign of nobly rotted grapes.

Palate
Young Cadillac wines are fruity and nervous, becoming creamy, smooth and full-bodied with age. In either case, there is good solid substance. A hint of toastiness reveals the sweet character of the wine, which tends to go from strength to strength with each successive vintage.

Choice of food
As an apéritif or with foie gras, white meat, poultry, fish in sauce, cheese (Roquefort, blue cheese), sorbets, tarts.

Serving temperature
8-9°C.

Ageing ability
10 years (more for certain crus in the best vintage years).

Main grape varieties
Sémillon, Sauvignon and Muscadelle.

Soil types
Clayey lime-stone, gravel.

79

Cahors

Appellation
Cahors AOC
Colour
Red
Area
4,200 hectares
Production
248,336
hectolitres

1971

The Cahors vineyard follows the meanderings of the Lot River, nestling into terraces halfway up the slopes on thin soils rich in pebble and gravel. One distinctive feature of this vineyard is its commitment to the local grape variety, the Auxerrois or Côt, which reinforces the colour of the wines with its powerful pigments. Cahors wines are solid and tannic with good ageing ability although they are also accessible as young wines.

Eye
Young wines are very dark, somewhere between ruby red, crimson and dark red with purplish highlights.

Nose
Cahors is a fragrant wine with great aromatic complexity. Behind dominant aromas of red and black-skinned fruit (plums, ripe blackcurrant) are notes of jam, spices (cinnamon, pepper), cocoa and a hint of truffles.

Palate
Powerful and tannic, with an agreeable combination of concentration and elegance. Well balanced, rich and long, opening up to a finish punctuated by notes of liquorice, roasted aromas or violets. This is a solid, fleshy wine, relatively austere for the first two or three years after which it emerges as more rounded and harmonious, with aromas of underwood and spices.

Main grape varieties
Auxerrois (Malbec or Côt), Merlot, Tannat, Jurançon Noir.

Soil types
Quartz pebbles, red clay, ferruginous sands, slope wash, limestone.

Ageing ability
4-8 years (10 and over for certain estates and vintages).

Serving temperature
17-18°C.

Choice of food
Charcuterie, duck confit, game, cassoulet, mushrooms, cheese (Bleu d'Auvergne, Roquefort).

Canon-Fronsac

The 20th century has seen a complete replanting of the Fronsac and Canon-Fronsac appellations that in 1900 were dominated by the Malbec. Today, this frost-sensitive grape variety is in decline, currently accounting for barely 1% of the area under vine whereas plantings of Merlot have risen from 20% to 75%. Canon-Fronsac, together with Fronsac, is one of the most interesting communal appellations in the Bordeaux region.

1939

Appellation
Canon-Fronsac AOC

Colour
Red

Area
303 hectares

Production
16,881 hectolitres

Eye

The colour ranges from dark red with purplish highlights to deep ruby or crimson.

Nose

Intense, with a wide range of aromas, from red fruit with pronounced spicy notes to scents of game and woodiness in wines that have been matured in barrels.

Palate

Canon-Fronsac displays all the characteristics that are essential in Fronsac wines: remarkable consistency with an even balance of tannins and fruit; power offset by a very agreeable crunchiness on the attack, later giving way to great richness. Their sappiness and velvety flavours give them a uniquely seductive personality not unlike that of some Pomerol wines.

Château Cassagne-Haut-Canon dominates the view from the Canon-Fronsac hilltop.

Choice of food
Lampreys Bordeaux-style, red meat (rib steak), *confit*, *cassoulet*, fricassee of mushrooms, cheese.

Serving temperature
8°C.

Soil types
Limestones, argillaceous limestone on beds of starfish limestone, sandy molasse.

Main grape varieties
Merlot, Cabernet Franc, Cabernet-Sauvignon and Malbec.

Ageing ability
4-9 years (up to 20 years for certain vintages).

81

Cassis

Appellation
Cassis AOC

Colours
White (70%)
Rosé (25%)
Red (5%)

Area
168 hectares

Production
5,587 hectolitres

1 9 3 6

Main grape varieties
Whites: Ugni Blanc, Clairette, Marsanne, Doucillon (Bourboulenc), Sauvignon, Pascal Blanc.
Reds: Grenache, Cinsaut, Barbaroux, Carignan, Mourvèdre.

The sheer, jagged coastline between Marseilles and Toulon is riven with deep cuts – the famous *calanques*. Vines have been cultivated here since Roman times. The limits of the appellation today coincide with those of the commune of Cassis. The area is famous for its dry, white, heady wine with a very fragrant bouquet.

Eye
• White Cassis wines are clear and brilliant, evolving from green to straw-yellow in the course of maturation.
• The rosés are a brilliant rose-petal.
• The red wines are a beautiful shade of ruby red.

Nose
• White Cassis wines offer a range of aromas that are finesse itself, with dominant scents of fruit (citrus, quince, lemon) and balsam (pine resin).
• The rosés explode with floral notes (hyacinth, peach blossom) and fruity aromas (vanilla and bilberry).
• Young Cassis red wines are marked by vegetal tones (bay, thyme) that develop floral or spicy nuances (liquorice).

Soil types
Erosional soils and shallow, very pebbly brown soils.

Ageing ability
Whites: up to 10 years.
Rosés: drink early.
Reds: 3-5 years.

Palate
• The white wines are distinguished by their creaminess, roundness, richness and length. Retro-olfaction confirms the fruity and balsamic notes perceived on the nose.
• Cassis rosés are light and supple on the palate.
• Red wines are solid and powerful, with a generous and rustic nature.

Serving temperature
Whites and rosés: 8-10°C .
Reds: 16-18°C.

Choice of food
Whites: fish, anchoïade (anchovy and garlic toast), bouillabaisse, exotic cuisine.
Rosés: grilled fish, white meat.
Reds: meat in a sauce, game, strong cheese.

Cérons

The Cérons appellation lies northwest of Barsac within the limits of the Graves AOC. It stretches across three communes where the soil is typical of the whole of this sector of the left bank of the Garonne: gravel terraces and sands. Cérons produces a fairly limited quantity of an original white wine, ranging from sweet to rich sweet wines with good ageing ability and distinctive sappiness.

1936

Appellation
Cérons AOC

Colour
White
(rich, sweet)

Area
98 hectares

Production
2,421 hectolitres

Eye
A lustrous golden colour maturing to straw-yellow or antique gold.

Nose
Dominant notes of apricot followed by citrus and developing scents of exotic fruit. Very sweet wines have powerful aromas of crystallised fruit and 'roasted' fragrances. The more complex wines evoke honey, caramel, orange marmalade, vanilla and acacia flowers.

Palate
Young Cérons sweet wines have appealing suppleness and roundness. The rich sweet wines have a liveliness that distinguishes them from Barsac wines. Those from great vintages have excellent ageing ability, growing more powerful and more mature but also more refined.

Choice of food
Foie gras,
delicate fish
in a sauce,
poultry, tarts.

**Serving
temperature**
8°C.

**Ageing
ability**
8-10 years
(25 years
and over for
certain crus).

**Main grape
varieties**
Sémillon,
Sauvignon,
Muscadelle.

Soil types
Gravel and
clayey limestone.

83

Chablis

Appellation
Chablis AOC
Colour
White
Area
2,782 hectares
Production
166,550
hectolitres

1 9 3 8

Chablis represents the principal vineyards of the Yonne department, planted in the northernmost region of Burgundy on south-southeast-facing slopes along the Serein River, a favourable location for good ripening. The region has a long-standing policy of quality production based exclusively on Chardonnay grapes, to the point where the name Chablis is now universally associated with distinctive, dry white wines. There are four appellations covering some 20 villages: Chablis Grand Cru, Chablis Premier Cru, Chablis and Petit Chablis.

Eye

The colour is a discreet white-green or pale gold (pale yellow) with emerald or blush pink highlights.

Nose

Chablis wine has a very fresh, mineral bouquet, evoking green apples, lemons and grapefruit. As it develops it acquires notes of the underwood and mushrooms (meadow mushrooms) together with scents of mint, white flowers (acacia), lime blossom or violets. Maturity gives the palate a spicy dimension.

Palate

Chablis has an aftertaste of gunflint or mushrooms. It is bone dry, with admirable finesse and distinctive personality.

Grape variety
Chardonnay
(known locally
as Beaunois).

Soil types
Brown lime-
stone soils, hard
limestone and
marly, partly
Kimmeridgian
limestone.

**Ageing
ability**
3-5 years.

**Serving
temperature**
8-9°C.

Choice of food
Seafood,
*andouillette
chablisienne*
(a local sausage),
snails, white
meat in a sauce,
lamb (sautéed or
curried),
asparagus, fish
with sorrel, goats'
cheese or Comté.

Chablis Grand Cru

The Chablis Grand Cru appellation is reserved for the most prestigious terroirs covering some 100 hectares nearly all planted in the commune of Chablis. They are situated on the right bank of the Serein on very favourable, well-exposed soils enriched by argillaceous-stony colluviums. The Chablis Grand Cru appellation is divided into seven *climats* (localities) that constitute the very finest that Chablis has to offer.

1938

Appellation
Chablis AOC
Classification
Grand Cru
Colour
White
Area
100 hectares
Production
5,500 hectolitres

The *climats*

Les Blanchots
Bougros
Les Clos
Grenouilles
Les Preuses
Valmur
Vaudésir

The soils of Chablis are characterised by tiny fossil oysters, exogyra virgula.

Chablis, the wine capital of the department of the Yonne.

Grape variety
Chardonnay.

Soil types
Upper Jurassic bedrock with small fossil oysters; Kimmeridgian marl.

Ageing ability
10-15 years.

Eye

Chablis wines have those discreet golden green tones that are a sign of perfection in this appellation.

Nose

The classic aromas are distinguished by buttery notes (warm croissant). Chablis has a mineral quality (flint, gunflint) with touches of lime blossom – some will say jujube – dried fruit, honey and roasted almonds from maturation in casks. St George's mushrooms are a typically Chablisian touch.

Palate

Chablis Grand Cru naturally has the taste of Burgundian Chardonnay, but the honey is more discreet, yielding to the more powerful mineral sensations. The charm and originality of this inimitable yet frequently imitated wine reside in the perfect balance of acidity and richness.

The Kimmeridgian

The Yonne vineyard rests on Upper Jurassic strata: Kimmeridgian marl facies with layers of marl some 50-100 metres (164-328 ft) deep interspersed with small benches of limestone. The landscape presents gently rolling hills with no real plateaux or steep cliffs. The vines are planted on well-exposed slopes, often topped by clumps of trees. The viticultural zone of Chablis coincides with the outcrop of the Kimmeridgian. There is also hard limestone in the surrounding area. The best vineyards lie on brown limestone soils on southwest-facing slopes at altitudes of 130-250 metres (430-825 ft).

Leaving Chablis, the Grand Cru slope runs along rounded hilltops of marl full of Exogyra virgula (small fossil oysters).

Choice of food
Seafood, fish in sauce, trout and almonds, white meat, poultry (poularde à la crème), frogs' legs, Burgundy snails.

Serving temperature
12-14°C.

Chablis Premier Cru

Here as everywhere else in Chablis, the original growers of the vines were the Cistercian monks of Pontigny Abbey. The Premiers Crus are located on both sides of the Serein river, either bordering the Grands Crus (right bank) or facing them (left bank), on argillaceous limestone terrain and Kimmeridgian marl, and on the limestone slopes, at an altitude of 150-190 metres (492-623 feet). The appellation extends across eight communes: Chablis, Fontenay, Maligny, Chichée, La Chapelle-Vautelpeigne, Courgis, Fleys and Beines. The most reputed *climats* are La Montée de Tonnerre, Mont de Milieu, Forêts, Fourchaume and Vaillons.

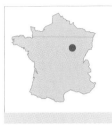

1 9 3 8

Appellation
Chablis
Premier Cru
Colour
White
Area
734 hectares
Production
45,000
hectolitres

The Chablis Premiers Crus are established in the northernmost region of the Burgundy vineyard. Together with the Grands Crus they form the basis of the Chablis region's historic wine-growing reputation.

Ageing ability
10-15 years.

Grape variety
Chardonnay.

Soil types
Argillaceous
limestone and
marl with upper
and middle
Kimmeridgian,
Exogyra virgula.
Portlandian
limestone
further up
the slopes.

Eye

Chablis was once appreciated for its light limpid colour. Today the colour is deeper, pale to darker gold with greenish highlights – the celebrated green-gold that is never quite yellow.

VENDANGES MANUELLES

PRODUCE OF FRANCE

CHABLIS 1ᵉʳ CRU

MONTS DE MILIEU

APPELLATION CONTROLEE

MIS EN BOUTEILLE A LA PROPRIETE

DOMAINE DE LA MEULIÈRE

RECOLTANT A FLEYS F 89800 CHABLIS

750 ml   13% vol

The Premiers Crus

Les Beauregards
Berdiot
Beauroy
Beugnons
Butteaux
Chapelot
Chatains
Chaume de Talvat
Côte de Bréchain
Côte de Cuissy
Côte de Fontenay
Côte de Jouan
Côte de Léchet
Côte des Prés Girots
Côte de Savant
Côte de Vaubarousse
Les Epinottes
Forêts
Fourchaume
Les Fourneaux
L'Homme Mort
Les Landes et Verjuts
Les Lys
Mélinots
Mont de Milieu
Montée de Tonnerre
Montmains
Morein
Pied d'Aloup
Roncières
Sécher
Troesmes
Vaillons
Vaucoupin
Vaugiraut
Vau Ligneau
Vau de Vey
Vaulorent
Vaupulent
Vaux Ragons
Vosgros

The church of Sainte-Claire in Préhy in the heart of the vineyards.

Nose

An original range of aromas dominated by notes of iodine and minerals (gunflint, flint) on a background of St George's mushrooms and scents of the underwood. Other frequent scents are lemon, dried fruit, almonds, blackcurrant leaves and a nutty fragrance of fruit kernels.

Palate

Chablis Premier Cru is dry, vivid and light, with a roundness and distinction that it shares with all Premiers Crus. The temperament is usually crisp but generous, and the harmony between body and acidity is quite remarkable: a glint of minerals wrapped in richness. This is a long, and very up-front wine.

Serving temperature
12-14°C.

Choice of food
Seafood, frogs' legs, roasted capon, Bresse poularde, river fish in a sauce or with sorrel, cheese (Bleu de Bresse, Crottin de Chavignol).

Chambertin

Chambertin made its entrance in the 13th century. By the 17th century it was already considered one of the very best red wines in Europe and ranked as the king of wines. The Chambertin terroir was the property of the canons of Langres and until the French Revolution followed the same path as its neighbour, Clos de Bèze. Today it is one of the nine Grands Crus in Gevrey-Chambertin, the foremost wine-growing village on the Route des Grands Crus in the direction of Beaune. The vineyard occupies the major part of the slope up to an elevation of 300 metres (186 feet). It produces powerful, structured wines with impressive ageing ability.

1 9 3 7

Appellation
Chambertin AOC
Classification
Grand Cru
Colour
Red
Area
12 hectares 90 ares 31 centiares

Production
480 hectolitres

Chambertin. En griotte. La Chapelle. Clos de Bèze. Ruchottes dessus. les Géneraux. Maris haut.

COMMUNE DE GEVREY CHAMBERTIN

Lithograph from **Histoire et statistique de la vigne et des grands vins de la Côte d'Or** *by Jules Lavalle (1855). This work was used as a basis for the classification of the Burgundy Crus.*

Grape variety
Pinot Noir.

Soil types
Shallow topsoil covering limestone rock; erosional pockets of gravelly slope wash brought down from the mountain; steep slopes with high levels of active limestone.

Ageing ability
10-20 years (30-50 years for great vintages).

89

Eye

Chambertin is a vivid colour with nuances ranging from dark ruby to black cherry.

Nose

The range of aromas may open with blackcurrant, followed by redcurrant then raspberry on the finish. Other scents often include cherries in brandy, fruit-kernels, spices and liquorice plus a few floral hints (rose, jasmine or reseda) with notes of moss, the underwood and game.

Palate

Body, finesse and bouquet – Chambertin oozes sappiness and mellowness. This is a complete, concentrated wine, assured and quite forceful, with a wonderful harmony of flesh and structure. It becomes sumptuous with age.

MAZOYÈRES
Chambertin

LATRICIÈRES
Chambertin

CHAMBERTIN

CHARMES
Chambertin

CHAMBERTIN
Clos de Bèze

GRIOTTES
Chambertin

MAZIS
Chambertin

CHAPELLE
Chambertin

RUCHOTTES
Chambertin

GEVREY·
CHAMBERTIN
1er Cru

GEVREY·
CHAMBERTIN
1er Cru

GEVREY·CHAMBERTIN

A royal family of wines

Next to Chambertin and Chambertin Clos de Bèze are seven historic *climats* linked to this royal family of wines. Other crus are called after families, but here it is the *climats* that gave their name to the man who made them famous, Claude Jobert (1701-1768). Employed as a lay vineyard worker by the canons of Langres, he eventually turned them out of their property, becoming a shipper-grower and selling his wines to the German courts. His business acumen secured him a small fortune plus a coat of arms and a title. We also know from *Mémorial de Sainte-Hélène* by Las Cases that Napoleon remained faithful to Chambertin all his life.

CHAMBERTIN
GRAND CRU
APPELLATION CHAMBERTIN CONTRÔLÉE
RED BURGUNDY WINE
1998
DOMAINE ROSSIGNOL-TRAPET
MIS EN BOUTEILLE AU DOMAINE

Choice of food

Poached trout or pike cooked in Chambertin, casseroles, coq au Chambertin, game (venison, hare, boar), cheese with character (Ami du Chambertin).

Serving temperature
Young wines: 12-14°C.
Older wines: 15-16°C.

Chambertin-Clos de Bèze

The Clos de Bèze is the most senior clos in Burgundy and has become quite a symbol over the years. Originally the Abbey of Bèze, it was given lands and vines in Gevrey by the Duke of Burgundy in 640 AD. The Clos then belonged to the canons in Langres until the French Revolution. The cru is situated at the top of the slope between Chambertin and Mazis-Chambertin on shallow soils where the vines yield complex, thoroughbred wines.

1 9 3 7

Appellation
Chambertin-Clos de Bèze
Classification
Grand Cru
Colour
Red
Area
15 hectares 38 ares 87 centiares
Production
480 hectolitres

Eye
Chambertin-Clos de Bèze is limpid with good depth of colour.

Nose
Tender, liquorice-scented and fruity (blackcurrants, blackberries), opening with morello cherries and raspberries

Palate
Chambertin Clos de Bèze is powerful and long. Strength, opulence and elegance are there in force and the flesh is voluptuous. Leave untouched for a good ten years.

Outcrops of limestone bedrock are found throughout the vineyards.

Choice of food
Haunch of venison, pigeon with spices.

Grape variety
Pinot Noir.

Soil types
Limestone and gravelly slope wash.

Serving temperature
Young wines: 12-14°C.
Older wines: 15-16°C.

Ageing ability
10-20 years (up to 30 and 50 years in great vintage years).

Chambolle-Musigny

Appellation
Chambolle-Musigny AOC
Chambolle-Musigny Premier Cru AOC

Colour
Red

Area
Chambolle-Musigny: 146 ha
Chambolle-Musigny Premier Cru: 61.16 ha

Production
6,500 hl

1936

This hamlet with its tight rows of houses is entirely dedicated to wine. The 200 hectare vineyard produces a silky, lacy wine that is the most 'feminine' of all the Côte de Nuits. Les Amoureuses produces the flagship of the Chambertin Premiers Crus, equal in reputation to a Grand Cru.

Eye
Chambolle-Musigny sometimes has red brick or ruby nuances, often very vivid, with a halo of brilliant, luminous highlights.

Nose
These wines frequently have aromas of violets and red berries (especially strawberries and raspberries). Wines of a certain age express spicy ripe fruits, prunes and sometimes 'wilder' notes, scents of truffles, the underwood and animal odours.

Palate
Rich, fragrant and complex – Chambolle Musigny wines have a distinctive personality, the Premiers Crus in particular. Silk and lace come to mind, although their plump finesse retains a solid structure capable of withstanding the effects of age.

Choice of food
Poultry and tender meat (tournedos chasseur, braised duck in red wine or à l'orange, sautéed lamb), cheese (Brillat-Savarin, Cîteaux).

Serving temperature
17°C.

Grape variety
Pinot Noir.

Soil types
Limestone and pebbles; very shallow soils on the slopes; deeper, marly soils at the foot of the slope.

1992

Ageing ability
3-15 years (more for vintages with ageing ability and the best of the Premiers Crus).

The Premiers Crus
Les Amoureuses
Les Baudes
Aux Beaux Bruns
Les Borniques
Les Carrières
Les Chabiots
Les Charmes
Les Chatelots
La Combe d'Orveau
Aux Combottes
Les Combottes
Les Cras
Derrière la Grange
Aux Echanges
Les Feusselottes
Les Fuées
Les Groseilles
Les Gruenchers
Les Hauts Doix
Les Lavrottes
Les Noirots
Les Plantes
Les Sentiers
Les Véroilles

Champagne

The Champagne region is the most northern vineyard in France. It is chiefly located in the departments of the Marne and the Aube, with modest plantings in the Aisne, Seine-et-Marne and Haute-Marne. The vines are planted on permeable chalky bedrock rich in minerals from which Champagne wines derive their finesse. The undulating countryside is divided into four main regions: the Montagne de Reims, the Côte des Blancs, the Vallée de la Marne and the Aube vineyard. The appellation may be unique, but it produces an infinite variety of Champagne wines – white or rosé sparkling wines of course, but also Blanc de Blancs (produced exclusively from the Chardonnay grape), Blanc de Noirs (from Pinot Meunier, Pinot Noir or the two together) and white wines produced from a blend of all three grape varieties. Dosage moreover differentiates the extra-dry *bruts zéro* from *bruts*, *demi-secs* and *doux*. There are also non-vintage wines and vintages. The Champenois use the terms *brut sans année* (BSA – brut non- vintage), or *millésimé* (vintage). Then there are the prestige cuvées, or special cuvées, that occur in all categories. They are sold in specially designed bottles and priced at the premium prices you would expect of top-ranking wines.

1936

Artists deploy their talent on behalf of the major champagne houses – Savignac, for instance, and Alain Gauthier for De Castellane Champagne.

Appellation
Champagne AOC
Colours
White
Rosé
Area
30,685 hectares

Production
2,443,011 hectolitres

Grape varieties
Whites: Chardonnay (100% in Blanc de Blancs Champagnes).
Reds: Pinot Noir, Pinot Meunier.

93

BRUT SANS ANNÉE

Brut non-vintage (NV) is the most representative of all Champagne wines. Due to the northern situation of the vineyard, not all years achieve the quality of harvest necessary to produce a vintage, which must be blended from wines of a single year. To make up for weak years, the Champenois have created a 'bank' of reserve wines from previous years on which the Cellar Master can draw to balance the blend. Such champagnes will classify as non-vintage although in principle the vinification of vintage champagne does not differ from that of brut non-vintage. The key factor is the blend that each house keeps a closely guarded secret. Brut non-vintage champagnes are the most widely produced and the cheapest of all the champagnes and can be blended from variable proportions of Chardonnay, Pinot Noir and Pinot Meunier. They can also be Blanc de Blancs or Blanc de Noirs.

The Méthode Champenoise (Champagne Method)

Other vineyards call this the *Méthode Traditionnelle* because the term *Méthode Champenoise* is reserved by law for the wines of Champagne. It refers to the process of making a white wine sparkling by putting it through a second fermentation after bottling. To do so, a *liqueur de tirage*, composed of sugar dissolved in wine and yeasts, is added to the wine at the time of bottling. After the second fermentation, a *liqueur de dosage* is added to eliminate the sediment formed by the yeasts and replace any wine that has been lost. Brut champagne contains less *liqueur de dosage* than a *demi-sec* or *sec*. The dosage is measured in grams per litre. *Brut Zero* or *Brut Absolu* champagnes have no added sugar whatsoever – the bottle is topped up with pure wine. This is rare and ideally applies only to champagnes which have aged for long periods *sur pointe* (upside down). This exception apart, a champagne is said to be *brut* when it contains 0-15g of sugar per litre. Average dosage is around 10g/l.

Soil types
Limestone chalky.

Ageing ability
For immediate drinking.

Choice of food
As an apéritif or with fish (smoked salmon), foie gras, white meat.

Oil burners are installed in the vineyards of Champagne to combat frosts.

Eye

Brut Champagne with a higher proportion of Chardonnay is straw-gold or tinged with brilliant green highlights. Wines made predominantly from black grapes are white gold, sometimes with the slightest suggestion of pink. The golden colour soon becomes more yellow with age.

Nose

The bouquet is boosted by Carbon dioxide. Depending on the proportions of the Pinot varieties or Chardonnay in the blend, the aromas are more or less marked by fruit (Pinot) or notes of citrus, flowers and toast (Chardonnay). Additional aromas may include butter, brioche, lemon, citronella, quince jelly, apple, apricot, peach, pear, white flowers, violet, blackcurrant blossom, hawthorn, hyacinth and honey.

Palate

Those wines based on black grapes are fruity; those based on white grapes are refined and nervous. The art of the Cellar Master lies in creating a harmonious, balanced blend.

Serving temperature 8°C.

For the second fermentation, the bottles are placed on racks and turned regularly so that the sediment formed by the yeasts slides into the neck. This deposit will be expelled before shipment.

CHAMPAGNE BLANC DE BLANCS

Appellation
Champagne
AOC

Denomination
Blanc de Blancs

Colour
White

Area
27%
Chardonnay out
of 30,000
hectares

1936

The Blanc de Blancs denomination refers to champagnes produced exclusively from the white Chardonnay grape variety. They are distinguishable from other champagnes by subtle characteristics detectable to the eye, nose and palate. Note that the Côte des Blancs is exclusively planted with the Chardonnay grape.

Eye

Chardonnay wines are distinguished from Blanc de Noirs Champagnes by their golden colour, glittering with green highlights.

Nose

Blanc de Blancs have a fairly characteristic bouquet of delicate, empyreumatic aromas: toast, butter, brioche, almonds, hazelnuts (fresh or roasted), straw or hay. Wines at their peak evoke white fruits: white peaches, apples, pears and sometimes apricots, quinces and honey, always on a background of lemony citrus flavours.

Palate

These champagnes are a triumph of finesse, freshness and vivacity due to the sharper acidity of the Chardonnay that is usually more acid than the Pinot varieties.

Grape variety
Chardonnay.

Soil types
Chalk.

Ageing ability
4-10 years.

Serving temperature
8°C.

Choice of food
As an apéritif or with entrées, crustaceans, fish, white meat.

CUVÉES SPÉCIALES

A Special Cuvée is the jewel of a particular brand that is blended from specially selected top-quality wines. White or rosé, they are presented in distinctive, original bottles and command a high price. The first special cuvée was created by Eugène Mercier for Emperor Napoleon III, and the second by Louis Roederer for Alexander II, Tsar of all the Russias. The third special cuvée, labelled Dom Pérignon, was launched in 1936 and sailed with the SS Normandie on her inaugural trip.

1 9 3 6

Appellation
Champagne AOC
Colours
White
Rosé
Area
Variable each year
Production
Variable each year

Eye
The gold colour may be more or less light but it should be absolutely limpid and dazzling. Chardonnay adds a touch of emerald green; Pinot Noir and Meunier bring out paler gold tones. There is no trace of that pinkish hue that is occasionally noticeable in other champagnes.

Nose
Spécial Cuvées are richer, stronger, more complex and more refined than the classic cuvées and magnify their aromas. The bouquet, which depends on the proportion of grape varieties used in the blend, offers a wealth of citrus aromas, fragrances of dried hay, hazelnuts and brioche and a touch of empyreuma. Floral and green leafy scents of acacia, violets and ferns suggest the fruitiness in store on the palate.

Palate
Depending on the blend, the fruity scents – which do not stand out but are interwoven with the other aromas – suggest white, yellow or red fruit. Spécial Cuvées are rich, full-bodied and long and supported by impressive structure and balance.

Serving temperature
8-9°C.

Choice of food
As an apéritif or with crustaceans, fish, white meat or poultry.

Grape varieties
Chardonnay,
Pinot Noir,
Pinot Meunier.

Soil types
Chalk.

Ageing ability
Up to
10 years.

Chapelle-Chambertin

1937

Appellation
Chapelle-Chambertin AOC

Classification
Grand Cru

Colour
Red

Area
5 hectares 48 ares 53 centiares

Production
193 hectolitres

Chapelle-Chambertin, to the east of the Route des Grands Crus, owes its name to the Notre-Dame chapel built in Bèze in 1155 but demolished towards 1830. The appellation is divided into 20 vineyard plots with a dozen different owners. This is a terroir of fragmented rock and tiny stones in an intermediate dip that enjoys a very favourable micro-climate. The wines of Chapelle-Chambertin are similar in fragrance to those of Clos de Bèze and although the finish may not always have quite the same flourish, the delicacy of emotion is indescribable.

Eye
Dark tones that eventually acquire a crepuscular hue.

Nose
Predominantly empyreumatic but retaining scents of red fruits and vegetal aromas. The bouquet also offers notes of spice and roasting followed by fragrances of raspberry and cinnamon.

Palate
Clean attack, powerful tannins, persistent palate. Chapelle-Chambertin should be allowed to age for at least 10 years.

Grape varieties
Pinot Noir.

Soil types
Limestone, slope wash.

Ageing ability
10-15 years (up to 30 and 50 years in great years).

Serving temperature
Young wines: 12-14°C.
Older wines: 15-16°C.

Choice of food
Rabbit with Chasselas grapes, roasted wood pigeon, pigeon or duck with spices.

Charmes-Chambertin

The name of this Gevrey-Chambertin Grand Cru in the south of the appellation comes from *chaume* meaning an abandoned vineyard plot. Charmes-Chambertin includes a lower section beside the main road and is adjacent to Mazoyères-Chambertin for which it is often mistaken under the name of Charmes-Chambertin. The vines are planted on pebbly soils producing an elegant wine with a very rounded palate.

1 9 3 7

Appellation
Charmes-Chambertin AOC

Classification
Grand Cru

Colour
Red

Area
12 hectares
33 ares

Production
1,230 hectolitres

Eye
Limpid garnet red with purplish highlights.

Nose
A bouquet of violets and liquorice with vanilla or grilled nuances that owe nothing to ageing in wood.

Palate
Rich, concentrated and passionate – all the signs of an aromatic palate. Characteristically silky.

Choice of food
Poultry with truffles, haunch of venison, filet of doe, pigeon with spices.

Serving temperature
Young wines: 12-14°C.
More mature wines: 15-16°C.

Ageing ability
10-15 years (up to 30 and 50 years in great vintage years).

Soil types
High levels of active limestone, pebbly soils.

Grape variety
Pinot Noir.

Chassagne-Montrachet

Appellations
Chassagne-
Montrachet AOC
Chassagne-
Montrachet
Premier Cru
AOC

1937

Colours
Red (45%)
White

Area
300 hectares
including 7
hectares in
Remigny

Production
15,700
hectolitres

Grape varieties
Reds:
Pinot Noir.
Whites:
Chardonnay.

The Chassagne-Montrachet vineyard lies south of the Côte de Beaune, planted on east-southeast-facing slopes between Puligny, Montrachet and Santenay. This appellation successfully unites the two great Burgundian grape varieties that may sometimes even be planted in alternate rows. Clos Saint-Jean, Champs Gain, Boudriotte and Morgeot are among the most famous First Growths. Vide-Bourse is a neighbour of Bâtard-Montrachet.

Soil types
Ranges from
limestone and
pebbles to marl
and sandier
terrain.
Soil-type from
top to bottom
of slope: steep
Rauracian oolite,
Callovian lime-
stone talus and
Argovian marl
facies, Bathonian
limestone.

*Only The route
nationale 6
separates the
villages of
Chassagne and
Puligny that
both produce
the fabulous
Montrachet.*

**Ageing
ability**
Reds:
5-15 years.
Whites:
3-12 years.

The Premiers Crus
Abbaye de Morgeot
Blanchot-Dessus
Bois de Chassagne
La Boudriotte
Les Brussonnes
Cailleret
Les Champs Gain
Les Chaumées
Les Chevenottes
Clos Saint-Jean
Dent de Chien
En Cailleret
En Remilly
La Grande Montagne
La Maltroie
Les Macherelles
Tonton Marcel
Les Vergers
Vide-Bourse

Eye

• The reds are vivid with violet reflections and good depth of colour verging on black from the Pinot Noir.
• The whites have the distinctive gold-lamé hue of Chardonnay, shimmering with green highlights.

Nose

• The reds are characterised by fragrances of Morello cherries, cherry-stones, raspberries, wild strawberries and redcurrants plus touches of animal scents and spices.
• The whites, as you would expect of wines based on Chardonnay, reveal aromas of white flowers (honeysuckle), verbena and hazelnuts. These are accompanied by mineral notes (flint) and a toasty bouquet due to the cask and the fresh, buttery character of the wine. Scents of honey and sometimes ripe pears are also present.

Palate

• The reds have a fleshy generosity over tannins that may seem rather austere in young wines. The overall impression is of a concentrated wine of agreeable complexity.
• The whites have no shortage of liveliness on the attack but a few years of ageing brings appropriate richness to an agreeably fresh palate. Chassagne-Montrachet Premier Cru is deliciously curvaceous and often opulent.

The 19 Premiers Crus in the Montrachet AOC represent a third of the area under vine.

Choice of food

Reds: meat (shoulder of mutton, tournedos with béarnaise, coq au vin, jugged hare), cheese (Epoisses, Soumaintrain, Morbier).
White: vol-au-vent, fish, scallops, Bresse poultry with cream; goats' cheese, Comté.

Serving temperature
Reds: 14-16°C.
Blanc: 13-15°C

Château-Chalon

Appellation
Château-Chalon
AOC

Colour
White (*vin jaune*)

Area
45 hectares

Production
2,054 hectolitres
(widely variable
from vintage to
vintage)

1 9 3 6

This prestigious appellation is confined to four communes in the Jura: Château-Chalon, Menétru-le-Vignoble, Nevy-sur-Seille and Domblans. Leaving the remote village of Baume-les-Messieurs, the road winds through the vineyards to the edge of the first Jurassic plateau and the village of Château-Chalon. This most famous of all the *vins jaunes* is not to be tasted lightly. A white wine by birth, Château-Chalon ranks almost equal to a red wine as the accompaniment to refined cuisine. It is better suited to white meats than fish, pairs well with cheese and should be served chambré. This is an excellent wine for laying down, and a fine reward for those who appreciate its particular nature.

1989   1989

CHATEAU-CHALON

14% vol   Appellation d'Origine Contrôlée   62 cl

Mis en bouteille au domaine par JEAN BERTHET-BONDET
Propriétaire Récoltant à Château-Chalon, Jura - France

Grape variety
Savagnin.

Soil types
Liassic blue
or grey marls;
layers of
limestone
slope wash.

**Ageing
ability**
50-100 years.

**Serving
temperature**
Lightly
chambré.

Choice of food
American-style
lobster, trout,
coq au *vin jaune*
with morels,
white meat,
cheese (Gruyère,
Comté),
chocolate
cake and
walnut cake.

Eye

Château-Chalon is a deep yellow, sometimes turning amber with age.

Nose

A surprising, inimitable 'yellow nose', chiefly reminiscent of walnuts and mainly derived from ethanal. Green apple, hazelnut and almond add a touch of freshness.

The vineyard is dominated by the village of Château-Chalon, perched high on the Jurassic plateau.

Palate

Remarkably rich, with scents of walnuts often enhanced by spices such as nutmeg or cinnamon. But beware – Château-Chalon is a dry wine, with a certain vivacity that is tempered by fairly high alcohol content. It is a *vin jaune* not to be mistaken for a *vin de paille*. Although it is not to be recommended, an open bottle of Château-Chalon can be left for quite some time without losing any of its quality. It may be used in cooking, particularly to make the celebrated coq au *vin jaune* with morels.

Vin de Voile

The Jura is virtually the only vineyard in France that uses the *vin jaune* method of vinification. First, well-ripened Savagnin grapes are vinified in the classic fashion, as for any dry white wine. Alcoholic fermentation, which is often slow due to the natural richness of sugars and musts, is followed by malo-lactic fermentation. The wines are then transferred to casks for a minimum of six years. During this period, a film or *voile* of yeasts forms on the surface of the wine protecting it from over-rapid oxidation, maderisation and acescence. At the same time, the controlled oxidation of the alcohol stimulates the production of ethanal and other constituents responsible for the famous *goût de jaune* or 'yellow taste'. The film will only form however, provided the temperature and humidity of the cellar create the right conditions for the development of the yeasts. The wine is bottled in special squat-shaped bottles called *clavelins* which each hold 62 cl. This corresponds to one litre of the wine placed in casks six years earlier.

Château-Grillet

Appellation
Château-Grillet
Colour
White
Area
3.4 hectares
Production
93 hectolitres

1936

The Château-Grillet appellation, the south of Vienne on the right bank of the Rhône, is produced by a single estate – rare in France – from a single grape variety, the Viognier, planted on narrow terraces. This is a wine that needs to air properly before it releases its full range of fragrances – take your time to appreciate its bouquet. It may be drunk young, but will acquire further aromas with age, making it an ideal wine to drink with fish.

VIN BLANC
CHATEAU-GRILLET
APPELLATION CONTROLÉE
1994
MIS EN BOUTEILLE AU CHATEAU
NEYRET-GACHET
PROPRIÉTAIRE DE CHATEAU-GRILLET VERIN (LOIRE) FRANCE
FRANCE

Eye
Golden, with a multitude of highlights.

Nose
Youthful Château-Grillet is bursting with fresh fruit fragrances (apricot, peach, litchi), camomile and especially violets and wild flowers.

Palate
Rich in alcohol, low on acidity. Very fragrant on the palate with surprising finesse. The rather weak acidity of the Viognier adds richness and roundness.

The wholly owned Château-Grillet AOC is located in the heart of the Condrieu appellation area.

Serving temperature
12-14°C.

Choice of food
Fish (raw marinated salmon), crayfish, scallops, asparagus with a fine mousse sauce, goats' cheese.

Grape variety
Viognier.

Soil types
Sandy argillaceous.

Ageing ability
2-10 years.

Châteaumeillant

The vines of Châteaumeillant are planted to the south of Bourges, not far from La Châtre on a series of slopes at altitudes of 250-300 metres (820-984 feet). The soils have been fashioned by the waterways that rise in the first stratum of the Massif Central: Triassic sands, largely overlaid by Tertiary formations, or schists containing both black and white mica to the east of the vineyard. The appellation is renowned for its *vin gris*, a delicately flavoured rosé obtained by direct pressing of Gamay, Pinot Noir and Pinot Gris grapes. The red wines are also deliciously quaffable.

1965

Appellation
Châteaumeillant AOVDQS
Colour
Red
Rosé
Area
73 hectares
Production
4,046 hectolitres

Eye
• The reds are ruby or garnet, shimmering with purplish highlights when young.
• The rosés and *vins gris* have hints of pale rosé.

Nose
• The reds develop notes of pepper and spice together with aromas of red fruits.
• The rosés express very fresh, floral and fruity aromas (violets, citrus fruit, cherry).

Palate
• The reds have a light, fresh structure with very discreet tannins.
• The rosés are lively and elegant, with remarkable texture and fruitiness. They should be served cool and drunk when young.

Grape varieties
Gamay Noir,
Pinot Noir,
Pinot Gris.

Choice of food
Reds: red meat grilled or roasted, cheese.
Rosés: charcuterie.

Serving temperature
Reds: 15°C.
Rosés: 10°C.

Ageing ability
2-5 years.

Soil types
Argillaceous limestone, granite, gravel terraces.

Châteauneuf-du-Pape

Appellation
Châteauneuf-du-Pape AOC

Colours
Red
White (7%)

Area
3,200 hectares

Production
110,146 hectolitres

1936

This prestigious appellation to the north of Avignon dominates the plain of the Comtat Venaissin, extending over the communes of Châteauneuf-du-Pape, Orange, de Courthézon, Bédarrides and Sorgues. It is located on a hill on the left bank of the Rhône, overlooked by the former residence of the Popes of Avignon. The vineyards appear as a succession of pebbly, Villefranchian terraces that are very resistant to the dry Mediterranean climate and the Mistral. Since 1929, the appellation has been entitled to grow 13 grape varieties for red and white wine production. To judge from the scale of output, the red wines have largely established their reputation; but the white Châteauneuf-du-Pape is also regarded by connoisseurs to rival the greatest.

Main grape varieties
Reds: Grenache Noir, Syrah, Mourvèdre, Cinsaut, Terret Noir, Muscardin, Vaccarèse.
Whites: Grenache Blanc, Clairette, Roussane, Picpoul, Picardan, Bourboulenc.

Soil types
Red clay, pebbles.

Ageing ability
Reds:
5-20 years.
Whites:
1-10 years.

Choice of food
Reds: beef daube, steak au poivre, jugged hare, haunch of venison, wild mushroom risotto, cheese.
Whites: crustaceans, grilled salmon, salt cod brandade, veal chop with chanterelles, pigeon with petits pois.

106

Eye

• The reds are always very intense in colour due to their concentrated substance. Young wines are brilliant ruby. Old vintages acquire orange nuances.

• The whites are crisp and brilliant, ranging from light to darker yellow.

Nose

• The reds are powerful, fine and complex, dominated by rich, ripe red fruit and aromas of truffle, mushrooms and the underwood – also spicy, wild notes of the Provencal *garrigue*.

• The white wines in their youth reveal a delicately floral nose (mainly white flowers) often accompanied by fruity notes (citrus, apricot, pear) plus a hint of exotic fruits (mango, passion fruit). Once they reach five years of age, they develop nuances of honey and beeswax.

Palate

• Power and strength are the terms that first spring to mind when describing the reds. Retro-olfaction confirms the notes of spice (liquorice, pepper, cinnamon), fruit (blackcurrant, fruit in brandy, quince jelly, cooked fruit) with wild and sometimes empyreumatic or animal aromas. A good, long palate.

• The whites have a structure characterised by fullness and roundness. The dominant notes are floral and fruity with an occasional touch of dried fruit (roasted almonds) and perhaps a discreet signature of wood.

The ancient Palais des Papes, a historic landmark in the Châteauneuf-du-Pape region.

Serving temperature
Reds: 16-18°C.
Young whites: 8-10°C.
Older whites: 12-14°C.

Following the success of the wines produced and first exported by the popes in 1768, the commune of Châteauneuf-Calcernier changed its name to Châteauneuf-du-Pape.

Chénas

Appellations
Chénas AOC
Chénas and
climat of
origin AOC

Colour
Red

Area
283 hectares

Production
16,000
hectolitres

1 9 3 6

Chénas, meaning 'area planted with oak trees', is the smallest of the Beaujolais appellations. It extends over the communes of Chénas and La Chapelle-de-Guinchay, hugging the slopes to either side of the Mauvaise River, facing the Saône Valley and dominating the Moulin-à-Vent area from east to west. Here, very poor sandy soils on granite slopes produce a very limited yield of exceptional quality.

Eye
Thanks to a period on skins often exceeding 10 days, Gamay Noir produces that deep, purplish red colour that is so typical of Beaujolais Grands Crus. With age the colour acquires nuances of dark garnet red.

Nose
Fruity and floral aromas join with vanilla and spicy fragrances inherited from the oak casks. Rose and peony in particular are often characteristic aromas in the first years.

Palate
The attack is clean, with little acidity and the tannins are sturdy without masking the meaty, fruity character of the Chénas. The Burgundy note really asserts itself with age, giving a thoroughbred Chénas a life expectancy of 8-10 years.

Soil types
Granitic sands in the Chénas commune; granitic sands and ancient argillaceous-siliceous alluvial deposits in La Chapelle-de-Guinchay.

Grape variety
Gamay Noir.

Ageing ability
4-8 years (more for great vintages).

Serving temperature
14-15°C.

Choice of food
Hot saucisson, poultry, salted pork, veal stew in a white sauce.

Chevalier-Montrachet

The name of Chevalier-Montrachet goes back to the 18th century. The vineyard is located south of the Côte de Beaune in Puligny-Montrachet, higher up the slope than Montrachet at altitudes of 265-290 m (869-951 ft). Here the eastwards and southwards aspect suits the Chardonnay which is planted on a steep regular gradient on shallow soils. It produces a solidly-built wine of admirable aromatic finesse for laying down.

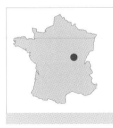

1 9 3 7

Appellation
Chevalier-Montrachet AOC
Classification
Grand Cru
Colour
White
Area
7 hectares 58 ares 89 centiares
Production
350 hectolitres

Eye
A classic brilliant light gold colour, sparkling with emerald highlights, turning vivid yellow gold with age.

Nose
Elegantly mineral, combined with notes of fresh bread and vegetal aromas (verbena, fern). Floral aromas (hyacinth) emerge at an early age.

Palate
Great aromatic finesse on the nose is echoed in a beautifully constituted palate of great persistence.

Choice of food
Grilled rock lobster and regular lobster, scallops, crayfish in their shell, pike mousse, char.

Serving temperature
12-14°C.

Ageing ability
10-15 years (up to 30 years for great vintages).

Soil type
Shallow, stony soils.

Grape variety
Chardonnay.

Cheverny

Appellation
Cheverny AOC

Colours
Red
Rosé
White (42%)

Area
380 hectares

Production
21,338 hectolitres

1 9 9 3

The Cheverny AOC is situated to the south of Blois within the Sologne region. Its symbol is the castle of Cheverny, built in the style of Louis XIII and used by Hergé as the model for Moulinsart's castle. The predominantly sandy terroir runs along the left bank of the river as far as the Orléans region. It produces Gamay and Pinot Noir-based red wines that are fruity in their youth; dry, fragrant rosés based on Gamay; and delicate whites based on Sauvignon and Chardonnay.

Soil types
Siliceous-argillaceous and sometimes argillaceous limestone.

Ageing ability
Whites and rosés: 2-4 years.
Reds: 2-8 years, depending on the grape variety.

Grape varieties
Reds:
Gamay Noir,
Pinot Noir,
Cabernet Franc,
Côt.
Rosés:
Same as reds, plus Chenin or Pineau d'Aunis.
Whites:
Sauvignon, Chardonnay.

Eye
• The reds are a lovely, brilliant cherry red.
• The rosés have a salmon hue.
• The whites are often pale with greenish highlights.

Nose
• The reds evoke red fruits, with an animal touch when Pinot Noir is prominent, together with a clove-like hint of spice.
• The rosés bring to mind red berries with an occasional touch of spice.
• The whites are fragrant with Sauvignon aromas of gooseberries and blackcurrant buds. Spicy nuances may also be present.

Palate
• The reds have discreet tannins, with very imposing fruit and freshness. Wines with a high proportion of Pinot Noir are robust and characteristically spicy. Liquorice is often detected on the finish. This is a wine that can age for many years.
• The rosés are fresh and thirst quenching, with a rich and spicy palate – very agreeable in summer.
• The whites have a noticeable fragrance of blackcurrant buds with agreeable touches of exotic fruit. Their liveliness is tempered by the roundness of the Chardonnay.

Serving temperature
Reds: 12-14°C.
Whites and rosés: 8-10°C.

Choice of food
Reds: red or white meat, cheese.
Rosés: white meat, charcuterie, North African cuisine.
Whites: quiche, grilled salmon, grilled *andouillette* sausage, semi-hard goats' cheese.

Chinon

The Chinon appellation lies in a triangle between the Vienne and Loire departments. Famous for its red wines, the vineyard is planted on tuffeau, a chalky bedrock of variable hardness. The town of Chinon was the favourite residence of the Plantagenet King Henry II, and it was in the Great Hall of the château during the Hundred Years' War in 1429 that Joan of Arc acknowledged the future King Charles VII. The great French humanist Rabelais was born within the Chinon terroir at La Devinière in 1494.

1 9 3 7

Appellation
Chinon AOC
Colour
Red (93%)
Rosé (6%)
White (1%)
Area
2,070 hectares
Production
103,083 hectolitres

Eye
• The reds are not so light as some Primeur wines, but never very dark – deep ruby more than purplish or crimson.
• The rosés are a light ruby colour.
• The whites are a light straw-yellow.

Nose
• The reds and rosés are invariably fruity with dominant aromas of red and pitted fruit: usually blackcurrant, raspberry, cherry, prune and sometimes redcurrant, blackberry and wild strawberry.
• The whites have modulated tones of citrus with occasional touches of gillyflowers and hints of honey and quince.

Palate
• The reds are as aromatic on the palate as they are on the nose, with a foundation of elegant tannins.
• The rosés are fruity, with a good structure and persistent floral aromas.
• The whites are supple and fresh with a certain roundness.

Choice of food
Reds: red meat, game, cheese.
Rosés: charcuterie, white meat, goats' cheese (Sainte-Maure-de-Touraine).
Whites: river fish.

Serving temperature
Young reds: 13-14°C.
Older reds: 16°C.
Whites and rosés: 12°C.

Ageing ability
Reds: five years average, 10 years and longer for good vintages.
Whites and rosés: five years.

Soil types
Chalk (tuffeau) in the vineyards on the slopes; ancient alluviums from the Loire and the Vienne; sand (on the plateau to the north of Chinon).

Grape varieties
Reds and rosés: almost exclusively Cabernet Franc (10% Cabernet-Sauvignon authorised).
Whites: Chenin Blanc (or Pineau de la Loire).

Chiroubles

Appellation
Chiroubles AOC

Colour
Red

Area
373 hectares

Production
21,482
hectolitres

1936

The Chiroubles appellation is located 10 kilometres (6.2 miles) to the west of Romanèche-Thorins and the Saône Valley, between Villié-Morgon to the south and Fleurie to the northeast. The terroir is planted on soils of granitic sands in a natural amphitheatre within the boundaries of the Chiroubles commune – a spectacular site to match the quality of the wines which are without doubt some of the finest and fruitiest of the Beaujolais region.

Eye

Chiroubles is a light, ruby red colour. Sandy, meagre, arid soils combined with an average altitude of 400 metres (1,312 feet) create a terroir that produces wines that are more spirited than rich in matter.

Nose

The floral aromas of violets and irises are not unlike those of the Fleurie cru. The red berry fragrance, such as wild strawberries and especially raspberries, serves to emphasise the Grand Cru qualities.

Palate

Lightly tannic, tender and very delicate. Delicate fruity flavours develop and linger on the palate. These feminine traits do not interfere with the wine's ageing potential. Depending on the method of vinification and the vineyard plot, some Chiroubles wines are capable of being kept for ten years. Three years is enough however to bring out all their charms.

**Grape
variety**
Gamay Noir.

Soil types
Granitic sands.

**Ageing
ability**
2-5 years.

**Serving
temperature**
13°C.

Choice of food
Charcuterie,
calves' liver,
pigs' trotters,
chicken.

Chorey-lès-Beaune

Chorey-lès-Beaune is close to Savigny-lès-Beaune and Aloxe-Corton, its vines spread across the plain in the direction of the Côte on soils mainly composed of slopewash. Wines from this communal area are sold under various appellations: Chorey, Chorey-lès-Beaune or Chorey-Côte-de-Beaune (for reds). Tender and quaffable, these are excellent wines to drink as an introduction to red Burgundies.

1970

Appellation
Chorey-lès-Beaune AOC
Colours
Red
White (3%)
Area
132 hectares in production
Production
6,490 hectolitres

Eye
• The reds are fairly vivid in colour, often dark crimson with purplish highlights.
• The whites are light gold, occasionally verging on light yellow.

Nose
• The reds are dominated by red berries (raspberry, Morello cherry) and black berries (blackcurrant) with secondary aromas of liquorice and the underwood. Complementary aromas include very ripe plum, crystallised fruit, strawberry jam, gingerbread, animal scents and leather.
• The whites offer a range of aromas including white flowers, hawthorn and acacia, pleasantly accompanied by hazelnuts, almonds, citronella, white fruit (pear) and maybe a discreet hint of honey.

Palate
• The reds have impeccable structure, with elegant and assertive tannins that reflect their status. They leave a sensation of youth on the palate but with no shortage of roundness and meatiness. Deliciously fruity.
• The whites are fruity and rather vivacious in their youth, growing rich and supple with age.

Choice of food
Reds: poached eggs in red wine, rabbit, fish (pike-perch, red mullet), cheese (Cîteaux, Reblochon, Brillat-Savarin).
Whites: vol-au-vents, *andouillette* sausage, fish, cheese.

Serving temperature
Reds: 14-16°C.
Whites: 12-14°C.

Soil types
Alluvia over stone, ferruginous in places, near terrain with oolitic subsoil. Sandy, very dry bedrock. On the Savigny-lès-Beaune side, argillaceous material and pebbly limestone. On the Aloxe-Corton side, siltier soils, rich in *chailles* (sandstone pebbles).

Grape varieties
Reds: Pinot Noir.
Whites: Chardonnay.

Ageing ability
Reds: 3-10 years.
Whites: 3-8 years.

Clairette de Bellegarde

Appellation
Clairette de Bellegarde AOC

Colour
White

Area
40 hectares

Production
2,357 hectolitres

1 9 4 9

The Clairette de Bellegarde AOC lies within the boundaries of the Bellegarde commune, between Beaucaire and Saint-Gilles in the Gard department. One part is planted on slopes and terraces in the south-eastern part of Costière de Nîmes. The other part is situated in the low-lying plains on the border of the Rhône, close to the Camargue, between Arles and Nîmes.

Eye
Light yellow with green highlights.

Nose
Notes of citrus peel and dried fruit punctuate a range of aromas rich with scents of white flowers.

Palate
A good balance of roundness with mild acidity, developing a hint of noble bitterness.

Clairette is a vigorous grape variety that has adapted to the region's poor soils of Villefranchian scree and pebbly terraces.

Soil types
Villefranchian scree.

Grape variety
Clairette.

Ageing ability
1-2 years.

Serving temperature
8-10°C.

Choice of food
Fish in a sauce.

114

Clairette de Die

Diois is the hard-to-pronounce geographical name for the wines that are produced on the two sides of the Drôme Valley: Clairette de Die AOC (sparkling wines) and Châtillon-en-Diois. The Diois region falls within the most northerly fringe of the southern sub-Alpine ranges, bordered to the north by the high cliffs of the Vercors and to the west by the Rhône basin. The climate is uncompromisingly sunny and Mediterranean.

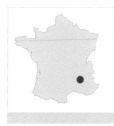

1942

Appellations
Clairette de Die
AOC
Colour
White (*Méthode Traditionnelle*)
Area
1,232 hectares
Production
71,644
hectolitres

Châtillons-en-Diois: mountain wines

The nine-hectare vineyard is planted at an average altitude of 550 metres (1,804 feet) with an extremely favourable south-facing aspect. It backs onto the Massif du Glandasse that peaks at more than 2,000 metres (6,562 feet) dominating the valley of the River Bez, a tributary of the Drôme. Here fruity, quaffable reds are made predominantly from Gamay Noir; light, fresh whites from Aligoté and Chardonnay. Total production is up to 3,230 hectolitres.

Eye

Fairly pale with light green highlights and very fine bubbles forming a persistent mousse on the disc.

Nose

Rich, elegant and delicate with the characteristic fragrance of Muscat as you would expect. Close analysis reveals a fresh and elegant aromatic richness: rose, lemon, citrus fruit and honey. Clairette de Die should not be kept too long because its subtle fragrances are soon replaced by less pleasant ones such as dried fig.

Palate

The first impression is like biting into lush, golden Muscat grapes, before the bubbles commence to caress the taste buds. This lightness is accompanied by a sensation of softness, due to the non-fermented sugar in the wine. Incomplete fermentation means a relatively low alcohol content (7-8% vol). A light and elegant wine.

Choice of food	Serving temperature	Ageing ability	Soil types	Grape variety
Apéritif; desserts.	6-8°C.	For early drinking.	Clayey limestone.	Muscat Blanc à Petits Grains.

Clairette du Languedoc

Appellation
Clairette du
Languedoc AOC
Colour
White
Area
90 hectares
Production
3,362 hectolitres

1 9 6 5

The Clairette du Languedoc AOC lies in the heart of the Hérault department at the foot of the Pic de Vissou, extending across 11 communes to the north of Pézenas. Being 30 kilometres from the sea, the climate is Mediterranean (hot, dry summers). The first foothills of the Cévennes mountains serve as a buttress against the prevailing winds from the north. The vineyard produces dry white wines and also a few sweet *rancio* and rich sweet wines.

Three original styles of wine
• Sweet (*blonde*) Clairette du Languedoc is low in sweetness and generally intended for early drinking.
• *Rancio* wines have been aged for three years and are at least 14% proof.
• Clairette de Languedoc rich sweet wines are obtained by *mutage* (chemical sterilisation) where fermentation is arrested by the addition of grape spirit. Sugar content should be in the range 9-40 g/l. These wines are only sold direct from the property.

Eye
The young dry whites are a limpid, brilliant light yellow with green highlights, turning golden yellow with age.

Nose
Clairette grapes vinified as dry white wines produce characteristic aromas of apple, sometimes accompanied by scents of grapefruit and white flowers.

Palate
Although low in acidity, young Clairette has a slight bitterness on the finish which makes it a match for hors d'oeuvres.

1997

CLAIRETTE

ADISSAN

750ml   M   75cl

APPELLATION CLAIRETTE DU LANGUEDOC CONTROLEE
MIS EN BOUTEILLE A LA PROPRIÉTÉ
S.C.V. LA CLAIRETTE D'ADISSAN 34230 ADISSAN - FRANCE
PRODUIT DE FRANCE

Soil types
Terraces of
Quaternary
gravel, covered
with ancient
alluviums
from the
Hérault.

Grape variety
Clairette.

Ageing ability
Dry whites:
2-3 years.
Other types:
10 years and
longer.

**Serving
temperature**
8-10°C.

Choice of food
Dry whites:
hors d'oeuvres.
Sweet wines:
foie gras,
chocolate cake.

Clos de la Roche

This Grand Cru borders on Gevrey-Chambertin in the northern part of Morey-Saint Denis, continuing on from Latricières-Chambertin and Combottes, planted some 250-300 metres (820-984 feet) up the slope. Now a Grand Cru comprised of several *climats* and *lieux-dits*, Clos de la Roche takes its name from the distinctly limestone, rocky slope on which it is situated, source of robust, solidly textured wines.

1 9 3 6

Appellation
Clos de la Roche
Classification
Grand Cru
Colour
Red
Area
16 hectares 90 ares 27 centiares
Production
600 hectolitres

Eye
Clear ruby, bordering on raspberry with occasional dusky, dark, purplish nuances.

Nose
The most common aromas fall into several categories. There are scents of fruit (wild cherry, cranberry) and flowers (especially violet) plus notes of humus, the underwood and wet earth. Other common aromas are truffles and liquorice.

Palate
Rich, robust, chewy and surprisingly powerful. Great vintages linger endlessly on the palate.

Choice of food
Ham in wine sauce, saddle of hare, haunch of boar, venison, wood pigeon, veal chop with mushrooms, cheese (Vacherin, Mont-d'Or, Saint-Nectaire, Cîteaux).

Serving temperature
14-16°C.

Ageing ability
10-15 years (up to 30 or 50 years for great vintages).

Grape variety
Pinot Noir.

Soil types
Mostly shallow, very calcareous soils with few pebbles but abundant rocks.

117

Clos des Lambrays

Appellation
Clos des
Lambrays AOC

Classification
Grand Cru

Colour
Red

Area
8 hectares 83 ares
94 centiares

Production
315 hectolitres

1981

The Clos des Lambrays vineyard is situated in the southern part of Morey-Saint-Denis, at an elevation of 250-320 metres (820-1,050 feet) between the Grands Crus of Clos Saint-Denis and Clos de Tart. It was created by the re-grouping of some 75 plots in the mid-19th century. Located in a central area of the village, the upper part of the Clos lies on marl soils and the lower part on argillaceous limestone. The estate has its headquarters in a beautiful property built in 1630 surrounded by grounds. With the exception of one tiny plot, it belongs to a single owner. The Clos des Lambrays has not been recognised for long as application was not made until the 1930s.

Grape variety
Pinot Noir.

Soil types
Fairly marly in
the upper part,
distinctly
argillaceous
calcareous in
the lower part.

Eye
Clear ruby red, verging on raspberry with occasional dark purplish nuances.

Nose
Complex aromas of leather, baked fruit, dead leaves and the underwood. Animal characteristics appear in wines that have been laid down.

Ageing ability
10-15 years
(up to 30 years
for great
vintages).

Palate
Clos des Lambrays is a full-bodied wine that is both rugged and supple – an iron fist in a velvet glove. Scents of red and black berries are rare.

Choice of food
Feathered game
(wood pigeon,
pheasant,
thrush), animal
game (venison,
hare, young
wild boar),
soft cheese.

Serving temperature
14-16°C.

Clos de Tart

Only three owners since the Middle Ages! The Clos de Tart is located at an elevation of 250-300 metres (820-984 feet) between the Clos des Lambrays and Les Bonnes-Mares to the south of Morey-Saint-Denis. Its vineyard, consisting of adjoining hectares alongside the production facilities, belonged to the nuns of Tart from 1250 until the French Revolution. It then passed to the Marey-Monge family and finally in 1932 to the Mommessins. Like the Premiers Crus of Morey-Saint-Denis, wine from young vines is sold under the name of La Forge, like the second wine from a Bordeaux Grand Cru. Clos de Tart is blended as a single cuvée just before bottling (25,000 to 30,000 bottles per year).

1939

Appellation
Clos de Tart AOC

Classification
Grand Cru

Colour
Red

Area
7 hectares 53 ares 28 centiares

Production
235 hectolitres

Eye
Dense ruby red.

Nose
Young Clos de Tart has strawberry and violet aromas. After about ten years it becomes very fragrant, with scents of venison, spices, leather and ripe fruit.

Palate
Rather tannic in youth, Clos de Tart softens with age to become a very great wine, elegant and structured.

Choice of food
Ham with cream, animal game (hare, boar, venison), cheese (Vacherin, Mont-d'Or, Saint-Nectaire, Cîteaux).

Serving temperature
14-16°C.

Ageing ability
10-15 years (as much as 30-50 years for great vintages).

Soil types
Thin soils with limestone and slope wash.

Grape variety
Pinot Noir.

Clos de Vougeot

Appellation
Clos de Vougeot
AOC

Classification
Grand Cru

Colour
Red

Area
50 hectares
59 ares
10 centiares

Production
1,880 hectolitres

1 9 3 7

A vineyard, a wine and a castle – the Clos de Vougeot was founded around 1110 by the Abbey of Cîteaux and has been enclosed by the same walls for centuries. Situated between Chambolle-Musigny and Flagey-Echézeaux in the Côte de Nuits, this Grand Cru covers 50 hectares (not including the castle) divided into a hundred or so plots belonging to 80 different owners. From this diversity of plots comes a wealth of characteristics and wines that have certain traits in common but defy any single description.

Eye
From raspberry red to intense garnet, depending on age and the method of vinification.

Soil types
Deep brown soil over marl (bottom section); brown argillaceous soil over pebbly limestone (middle section); shallow, grainy, less argillaceous but more gravelly soils on Bajocian limestone slabs (upper section).

Nose
A suave bouquet with the fragrance of springtime – freshly opened rose buds, dew-covered violets, wet reseda, dog rose. Other characteristic aromas are blackberry, raspberry, liquorice, wild mint and truffle.

Choice of food
Animal game (venison wild boar), feathered game (partridge, woodcock, thrush), roast beef, ham in a pastry crust, warm pâté, cheese (Epoisses, Langres, Ami du Chambertin, Saint-Florentin, Soumaintrain).

Palate
Clos de Vougeot is sappy and mellow with great finesse – a royal taste. Full and fleshy, it occasionally explodes on the palate. It is remarkable for its great ageing ability and extraordinary persistence on the palate where, once settled, it lingers forever.

Grape variety
Pinot Noir.

Ageing ability
10-30 years (more for good vintages).

Serving temperature
16-18°C.

Clos Saint-Denis

Clos Saint-Denis is situated in Morey-Saint-Denis between Clos de la Roche and Clos des Lambrays, and dates back to the 11th century. The vineyard is planted halfway up the hillside at an elevation of 280-320 metres (820-1,050 feet), producing a full-bodied red wine with good ageing ability. From an initial area of two hectares, the vineyard grew by stages to incorporate the neighbouring *climats* of Maison Brûlée, Calouère and a part of Chaffots. It now covers 40 or so plots producing 20,000-25,000 bottles per year.

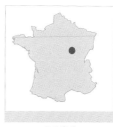

1936

Appellation
Clos Saint-Denis
AOC
Classification
Grand Cru
Colour
Red
Area
6 hectares 62 ares
60 centiares
Production
240 hectolitres

Eye
Dark garnet red with distinctive purplish highlights.

Nose
A subtle, complex weaving of fragrances: blackcurrant, blackberry and gingerbread mingled with prunes, musk, violets and coffee.

Palate
Clos Saint-Denis often has a tender fruitiness coupled with captivating charm. More notable for its nuances than its fullness, it is warmer in character when it comes from the southern part of the appellation.

Choice of food
Ham with cream or with wine lees, game (saddle of hare, haunch of boar, venison), cheese (Vacherin, Mont-d'Or, Saint-Nectaire, Cîteaux).

Serving temperature
16-18°C.

Ageing ability
10-15 years (up to 30-50 years for great vintages).

Soil types
Liassic and Triassic limetone with limestone slope wash from the plateau.

Grape variety
Pinot Noir.

Collioure

Appellation
Collioure AOC

Colours
Red
Rosé (30%)

Area
412 hectares

Production
15,710 hectolitres

1 9 7 1

This world-famous little port nestling in a Mediterranean creek is also a tiny appellation area alongside Banyuls in the communes of Banyuls-sur-Mer, Cerbère, Collioure and Port-Vendres. Collioure produces a powerful, velvety red wine and an elegant, generous rosé. The vineyard thrives on schistous soils in a sunny climate influenced by the Tramontane and sea winds.

Eye

• The reds are a deep garnet colour, often with a brick-red hue.
• The rosés are a delicate salmon-pink, more rarely blush pink.

Nose

• The reds are very fruity, the young wines revealing red berry aromas and amyl notes while mature wines have spicy tones and leather scents. Notes of roasting signal the presence of Mourvèdre.
• The rosés have a red-berry fragrance with a trace of amyl, occasionally with surprising scents of violets in blends where Syrah dominates.

Palate

• The reds are powerful, warm and rich in ripe fruit: cherry, pomegranate, blackcurrant. Age brings notes of baked fruit. These wines are distinguished by their supple tannins and velvety, creamy palate, accompanied by flavours of spice and toast.
• The rosés, beneath a first delicate impression of freshness, reveal a surprising power and creaminess, with no loss of that nervousness that is all their charm.

Main grape varieties
Grenache Noir, Mourvèdre, Syrah, Carignan and Cinsaut, with Grenache Gris for the rosé (up to 30%).

Soil types
Primary schists.

Ageing ability
Five years and more.

Serving temperature
Reds: 16-18°C.
Rosés: 10-12°C.

Choice of food
Reds: grilled meat, game.
Rosés: Catalan charcuterie, *pissaladière*, paella.

Condrieu

Historically speaking, the Condrieu vineyard is the continuation of the Côte-Rôtie. It is located some 10 kilometres to the south of Vienne, along the edge of the Massif Central on very steep hillsides that slope down to the right-bank of the Rhône. Its vines produce delicate, unctuous white wines made from the single authorised grape variety, Viognier. The old city of Condrieu itself has the look of a small Mediterranean fishing town.

1940

Appellation
Condrieu AOC
Colour
White
Area
101 hectares
Production
2,550 hectolitres

Eye
The colour is more or less intense depending on maturity and ranges from straw to golden with light green highlights.

Nose
Young Condrieu wines are bursting with fragrance. The dominant aroma is fresh fruit (apricot or peach) enhanced by floral notes such as violet. Wines from very ripe harvests are marked by notes of honey, sometimes with roasted, mineral nuances. In slightly older wines, the fresh fruit aromas fade in favour of dried fruit.

Palate
Acidity is dominated by other taste sensations, giving Condrieu a very original style that is difficult to imitate. The overriding sensation is suave, with a marked richness and roundness.

Choice of food
Frogs' legs, river fish, fried scampi, pike quenelles, asparagus with mousse sauce, apricot tart.

Serving temperature
12-14°C.

Ageing ability
1-5 years (depending on terroir and vintage).

Soil type
Sandy-clayey.

Grape variety
Viognier.

Corbières

Appellation
Corbières AOC

Colours
Red
Rosé
White (7%)

Area
12,192 hectares

Production
553,365 hectolitres

1 9 8 5

Grape varieties
Reds: Carignan
(max. 60%),
Grenache Noir,
Syrah, Cinsaut
and Mourvèdre
(for the rosé).
Whites:
Grenache,
Maccabéo,
Bourboulenc,
Marsanne,
Roussanne and
Vermentino.

The Corbières range is an arid mountainous massif, bordered to the east by the Mediterranean coast and to the south by a striking limestone barrier that separates them from Roussillon. The boundary to the north is the main Carcassonne-Narbonne autoroute, and to the west a series of heights that includes for instance the Pech de Bugarach. This is a dominantly red-wine region, that relies on the Syrah grape variety for richness and fruit, especially in the west of the area where the vines are slower to mature. In the east it is Mourvèdre, Carignan and Grenache Noir that give the vineyard its identity. The rich and unctuous white wines are definitely Mediterranean in character. The quality of this appellation is continually improving, with promotion focused on the best terroirs, notably Boutenac, Durban, Lagrasse and Sigean.

Soil types
From north to
south: vast
pebbly terrraces,
sandstone and
marls; limestone
and schists
in the upper
sector.

**Ageing
ability**
2-5 years
(more than
10 years for
great vintages).

Eye

• The reds are deep and dark in youth, blackish-red when blended from Syrah and mature Carignan. Great vintages acquire amber tints with age.

• The whites when young are pale yellow with green highlights; wines matured in barrels are golden yellow.

• The rosés have deep purple tones when produced by the *saignée* process.

Nose

• The reds of average ageing ability display fruit aromas with notes of blackcurrant and blackberry; wines with good ageing ability are often closed and even austere for the first few months, with aromas of spice, pepper and liquorice appearing towards late spring. Notes of thyme and rosemary add a hint of the *garrigue*.

Choice of food

Reds: grilled beef, fricassee of ceps, cheese (Livarot).
Rosés: charcuterie, artichokes with ham and garlic, *pissaladière*.
Whites: stuffed mussels, squid, grilled fish, chicken with lemon, fresh goats' cheese.

The Corbières terroir is very varied in geological and viticultural terms, ranging from inland vineyards such as those around Opoul (below) to coastal, Mediterranean terrain.

Serving temperature

Reds: 14-18°C.
Whites and rosés: 12-14°C.

Maturation introduces notes of seasoned leather (especially when Mourvèdre is present), coffee and cocoa. The greatest wines develop aromas of the underwood and game.

• The rosés are marked by their intense fruit.

• The whites combine aromas of white flowers with exotic fruits – never too intense, and all finesse.

Palate

• The reds are generally powerful and robust, reflecting the bio-diversity of the appellation's terroirs. Wines from the argillaceous limestone and pebbly terraces of the Mediterranean sector are warm with solid tannins. Those from the sandstone of the Fontfroide region are softer and those from the schists of the Durban Basin have outstand-ing finesse. Wines from the higher sector are of a different nature altogether with elegant tannins and a light vivaciousness. The finer cuvées are generally based on Carignan and are quite distinctive when they come from the Boutenac terroir.

• The rosés have the characteristic qualities of the black grape varieties on which they are usually based (Grenache Noir, Cinsaut and Syrah): velvety smoothness, finesse and aromatic strength.

• The whites are lightly acidic, rich and unctuous – a perfect match for fish.

Cornas

Appellation
Cornas AOC
Colour
Red
Area
94 hectares
Production
6,300 hectolitres

1938

The village of Cornas is situated to the northwest of Valence in a grandiose natural amphitheatre with steep sloping terraces. The vineyard is planted on a slope of weathered argillaceous-sandy soils from granite outcrops. Cornas like the Côte-Rôtie AOC produces red wines only. It is distinguished from the other great red wine appellations of the Upper Rhône Valley by the use of a single grape variety – Syrah – and the precocity of the vines in this terroir. The result is a powerful, robust *vin noir* or black wine of excellent structure with tannins that soften over the years.

Grape variety
Syrah.

Soil types
Granitic sand, with patches of limestone.

Ageing ability
5-20 years (depending on terroir, vintage and method of vinification).

The name Cornas probably derives from a Celtic word meaning 'burned soil'. Screened from the Mistral by the Massif des Arlettes, this terroir is indeed very hot.

Eye

A very deep, dark colour, as you might expect of a wine that is sometimes referred to as a *vin noir*.

Nose

Young wines are reserved, with a characteristic bouquet of red or black-skinned fruit (blackberry, cherry) combining with notes of the underwood, spices and pepper. They only come into their own after five or six years' ageing, typically revealing animal nuances (leather), scents of the underwood, tobacco and in some cases more original, wild notes such as truffle.

Palate

A subtle balance of strength and body. Syrah here takes on an almost southern expression, marked by strength and warmth, the latter often masked by tannins. Wildly rustic in youth, the tannins only attain their famous finesse after many years of ageing in wood.

This delicious *vin noir*

Cornas shares its ancient history with the wines of other Rhône appellations. The Romans are said to have built chalets or *chaillées* (vineyards terraces) close to the sources of the Colombier, La Fontaine and Chemin de Pied de la Vigne. Evidence of ecclesiastical influence is found as early as the 10th century in an obedience brief from the canons of Viviers that mentioned the vines *in Cornatico*. A similar mention appears in a cartulary from the Abbey of Saint-Chaffre-de-Monastier.

Choice of food
Hare à la Royale, haunch of venison, beef casserole, rib of beef, cheese (Bleu des Causses).

Serving temperature 16-18°C.

127

Corton

Appellation
Corton AOC
Classification
Grand Cru
Colours
Red
White (4%)
Area
160 hectares 19
ares 39 centiares
in production
Production
3,670 hectolitres

1 9 3 7

The villages of Aloxe-Corton, Ladoix-Serrigny and Pernand-Vergelesses share this Grand Cru at the foot of the Montagne de Corton where Côte de Beaune takes over from Côte de Nuits. Especially famous for its rich, powerful and generous Pinot Noir red wine, Corton also produces a fragrant white wine from the Chardonnay grape. This vast appellation area is composed of many different *climats* and produces wines that vary widely in character.

Eye

• The reds are predominantly deep crimson or dark red with purplish density.
• The whites are usually a fairly pale yellow or light gold with green highlights.

Nose

• The reds have a full and generous bouquet with fruity (bilberry, blackcurrant, cherry, kirsch) or floral notes (violets) maturing into nuances of the underwood, tanned leather, fur and animal odours. Stewed apricot sometimes adds an original note. Other frequent aromas are pepper, liquorice and fruit stones.
• The whites combine mineral nuances (flint) with buttery notes (butter, baked apple), scents of plants (fern, juniper), spice (cinnamon) and honeyed aromas (honey, mead).

Soil types
Limestone, stony, red with ferruginous oolite, inter-bedded with potassium-rich marl, sometimes marly (Le Clos du Roi), some-times argillaceous (La Vigne au Saint) in places.

Grape varieties
Reds:
Pinot Noir.
Whites:
Chardonnay.

Ageing ability
Reds:
8-15 years.
Whites:
4-12 years.

The Montagne de Corton is surrounded by vines on three sides.

Choice of food

Reds: feathered game (duck à l'orange, quails with grapes, partridge), animal game (hare, venison), cheese (Cîteaux, Munster, Tamié).
Whites: prepared crustaceans (crayfish, lobster, spiny lobster), fish, white meat or poultry à la crème.

Serving temperature

Reds: 14-16°C.
Whites: 12-14°C.

Palate

• Red Corton is an openly demonstrative wine – big, solid, powerful and structured. Wonderfully chewy with great body, finishing on a tannic note. Some *climats* yield softer, finer, more delicate wines, and modern methods of vinification are also producing less austere wines that are ready for drinking after two or three years. Generally speaking though, young Corton appears hard and sharp with a firm, sound character that needs time to express itself.
• The whites are supple and round, elegant and thoroughbred – an original style on the Chardonnay scene.

The name of the *climat* may appear after the Corton AOC

From Aloxe-Corton comes the Clos du Roi, often regarded as the most Corton of Cortons – a powerful, well-balanced and velvety wine. Les Renardes wines have a rugged, aggressive, animal temperament, as do Les Paulands. Les Perrières are quite feminine and delicate. Les Bressandes have a smooth, meaty texture. Les Pougets are deeply rich and very round. The Clos des Meix are jewels of subtlety and finesse. Les Languettes are fairly supple and highly successful as white wines. Les Charmes are elegant and full. The Vigne au Saint produces a very delicate wine from clay soils. Among the *climats* of Ladoix-Serrigny, the Hautes Mourottes are light and delicate in temperament. Les Grandes Lolières are rather firm, robust and rustic. Les Vergennes is notable for Corton white wine. The wines of Le Rognet-et-Corton are very similar to Bressandes. Aux Renardes offers solid, powerful wines. Côté Ladoix has floral accents with firm and vigorous flesh beneath. Côté Pernand is more supple, elegant and fruity. Others are: Les Grèves, Les Maréchaudes, Les Moutottes, La Toppe au Vert, Les Carrières, Les Fiètres and Les Combes.

Corton-Charlemagne

Appellation
Corton-Charlemagne
AOC

Classification
Grand Cru

Colour
White

Area
51 hectares in
production

Production
2,280 hectolitres

1 9 3 7

The Corton-Charlemagne vineyards occupy the upper reaches of the Montagne de Corton in the north of Beaune. At an elevation of 280-330 metres (919-1,083 feet), this is the highest of the Burgundy Grands Crus. Its magnificent white wine is produced in the *climats* of Le Charlemagne (Aloxe-Corton), En Charlemagne (Pernand-Vergelesses) and in other *climats* that are partly or wholly covered by this appellation (Les Pougets, Le Corton, Les Languettes). The label never indicates the climat of origin, however. Corton-Charlemagne should not be drunk too early – this is a wine for cellaring that reaches its apogee after 10 years or so, and can generally be kept for 20-25 years.

Eye
The young wine is pale gold, often with the celebrated green highlights of Chardonnay. With age the gold sometimes takes on amber yellow nuances.

Soil types
Argillaceous marl on a fairly steep slope in the highest part of the Montagne de Corton.

Grape variety
Chardonnay.

Nose
An extremely delicate bouquet, with buttery tones of baked apple and touches of citrus fruit (pineapple), flint, lime blossom, fern, juniper and cinnamon. There may also be notes of honey, even mead. Leather and truffle scents are present in older vintages.

Choice of food
Roasted spiny lobster with saffron, sole with lemon butter, pike mousse, crayfish in the shell, fish with cream or sorrel, poultry with morels.

Ageing ability
5-25 years.

Palate
Corton-Charlemagne packs a powerful punch. Remarkably rich and surprisingly concentrated, it is seductively elegant and thoroughbred. Rarely are the qualities of a grape variety so perfectly integrated with a terroir. A very well-balanced structure gives the wine lingering persistence.

Serving temperature
12-14°C.

Costières de Nîmes

The Costières de Nîmes vineyard is planted on sunny slopes to the north of the Camargue, in an area 40 kilometres (25 miles) long between Meynes and Vauvert, and 10 kilometres (6.2 miles) wide between Saint-Gilles and Beaucaire. It is the most easterly appellation of the Languedoc region. The soils are characterised by Villefranchian moraine: pebbles, gravel and sand alluvia deposited by the Rhône. Situated at low altitude and close to the sea, Costière enjoys a temperate Mediterranean climate. Wines produced from the seaward-facing slopes in the southern part of the region are powerful and full-bodied. Those from the northern slopes facing the *garrigue* around Nîmes are supple, quaffable and fruity.

1986

Appellation
Costières de
Nîmes AOC

Colours
Red (75%)
Rosé (20%)
White (5%)

Area
3,373 hectares

Choice of food
Reds: grilled
meat, Camargue
beef stew
(*Gardianne*),
cheese
(Laguiole).
Rosés: Cévennes
charcuterie.
Whites: seafood,
Mediterranean
fish.

**Serving
temperature**
Reds: 14-18°C.
Whites and rosés:
12-14°C.

Grape varieties
Reds: Carignan,
Cinsaut,
Grenache Noir,
Syrah,
Mourvèdre.
Whites:
Grenache,
Clairette,
Marsanne and
Roussanne
with Rolle as
a subsidiary
variety.

Production
225,635 hectolitres

Soil types
Villefranchian
gravelly moraine.

Ageing ability
Reds: 4-5 years.
Whites and rosés:
for early
drinking.

Eye

• The reds are intense and brilliant with frequent violet nuances in young wines.

• The rosés range from pale pink to deeper pink with purple highlights in young wines, becoming more salmon-coloured. Syrah adds brighter tones.

• The whites are a brilliant light yellow.

Soils from Villefranchian moraine define the character of the Costières-de-Nîmes AOC, which was called Costières-du-Gard until 1989.

Nose

• The reds have a characteristic fragrance of red berries and pitted fruits, followed by developing notes of crystallised fruit and spices. Syrah supplies aromas of red fruit and violet scents, while Grenache adds spicy notes.

• The rosés in their youth are floral and fruity (cherry, strawberry, raspberry) with occasional notes of ripe banana.

• The whites express floral aromas (white flowers, acacia) with occasional hints of citrus or exotic fruit.

Palate

• The reds have quality tannins thanks to the Syrah, and roundness and warmth from the Grenache Noir. Carignan and Cinsaut sometimes add to the overall complexity.

• The rosés display a perfect balance of roundness and acidity. These are delicate wines that are generally made by the *saignée* method.

• The whites are round and rich, with fresh aromas that make up for their low acidity.

Coteaux Champenois

Coteaux Champenois are still wines which may be produced anywhere inside the boundaries of the Champagne appellation. The name of the commune often figures on the label, one of the best known being Bouzy, a Pinot Noir Grand Cru. But Vertus, Sillery and Aÿ also produce well-known Coteaux Champenois. The vast majority of these wines are non-vintage, being produced from a blend of wines from different years. Coteaux Champenois are rare because their production is limited. In years when yields are small, the entire harvest may be reserved for sparkling champagnes.

1974

Appellation
Coteaux
Champenois
AOC

Couleurs
Red
White
Rosé (rare)

Eye
• The reds are moderately coloured.
• The whites are ideally pale gold with green highlights. Blanc de Noirs wines are white gold or silver gold.

Nose
• Red Coteaux Champenois wines are said to *pinoter*, meaning that they reflect the characteristic raspberry and cherry aromas of Pinot grapes. Woodiness is never overwhelming. Tertiary leathery aromas may develop in exceptionally good years.
• No one disputes the supremacy of the Blanc de Blancs wines with their aromas of buttery brioche, toast and light hints of hazelnuts mingled with citrus flavours.

Palate
• The reds have a refined, elegant, precise structure.
• The whites have a light, delicate structure, in perfect harmony with the lively acidity that gives them their freshness.

Choice of food
Reds: white meat, poultry.
Whites: seafood, grilled fish.

Serving temperature
Reds: 11°C.
Whites and rosés: 8-9°C.

Soil type
Chalky limestone.

Ageing ability
Up to 10 years.

Area
The whole of the Champagne wine-growing area

Production
720 hectolitres

Grape varieties
Reds: Pinot Noir, Pinot Meunier.
Whites: Chardonnay.

133

Coteaux d'Aix-en-Provence

Appellation
Coteaux d'Aix-en-Provence AOC

Colours
Red (25%)
Rosé (70%)
White (5%)

Area
3,452 hectares

1 9 8 5

Main grape varieties
Reds: Grenache, Cinsaut, Syrah, Counoise, Mourvèdre (each limited to 40% maximum); Carignan, Cabernet-Sauvignon (each limited to 30% maximum).
Whites: Bourboulenc, Clairette, Grenache, Rolle, Ugni Blanc (each limited to 40% maximum); Sémillon and Sauvignon (each limited to 30% maximum).

Production
82,080 hectolitres

Soil types
Stony, argillaceous limestone; stony with silt-sand matrix; sandy/ gravelly on molasse and sandstone; colluvial slope deposits.

Ageing ability
Reds: 10-15 years.
Whites and rosés: 2-5 years.

The Coteaux d'Aix-en-Provence AOC is in the eastern section of limestone Provence, surrounding the Etang de Berre. It is bordered by the Durance River to the north, the Mediterranean to the south, the plains of the Rhône to the west and Provence to the east. Grenache, Cinsaut and Syrah are the main grape varieties, producing agreeable red and rosé wines plus limited quantities of white wines that are worth discovering.

Eye
• The reds are crimson, gradually developing a ruby hue.
• The colour of the rosés ranges from translucent pink to vivid, salmon or coral pink.
• The whites are a brilliant, pale yellow colour with green highlights.

Nose
• The reds offer note of flowers (violets) or plants (hay, mint, bay leaf, tobacco) that give way to more developed nuances (cinnamon, fur) after a few years of ageing.
• The rosés are marked by fruity aromas (strawberry, peach) with floral scents (lime blossom, broom) and balsamic notes (pine bark).
• The whites are fragrant with scents of acacia, broom and citrus fruit.

Palate
• The reds are light and supple but need time to refine their tannins.
• The rosés are supple and fresh on the attack.
• The whites are generous, although with a fresh finish.

Serving temperature
Reds: 16-18°C.
Whites and rosés: 8-10°C.

Choice of food
Reds: Provençale cuisine.
Rosés: as an apéritif or with scallops, fish, oriental cuisine.
Whites: Provençale entrée, fish, goats' cheese.

Coteaux d'Ancenis

The Coteaux d'Ancenis vineyard lies to the east of Nantes on either side of the River Loire, spreading across 27 communes and adjoining the terroirs of Muscadet. The soils are schists and gneiss and the climate is temperate – less windy and sunnier than Brittany. Coteaux d'Ancenis produces reds, rosés and whites, each based on a single grape variety: Gamay, Cabernet Franc, Chenin or Malvoisie.

1973

Appellation
Coteaux d'Ancenis AOVDQS
Colours
Red
Rosé
White (sweet, produced in limited quantities)

Eye
• The reds should be elegant with purplish highlights.
• The rosés have a pleasing clarity.
• The whites are pale yellow, verging on gold in the sweet wines.

Nose
• The reds and rosés are aromatic wines with an elegant nose of cherry, strawberry and raspberry.
• Honey and beeswax are the characteristic aromas of great, sweet, perfectly mature whites .

Palate
• The reds develop flavours of crystallised fruit.
• The rosés are light, lively and fruity.
• The whites achieve a perfect balance of residual sugars and welcome acidity.

Choice of food
Reds: white meat and poultry, Camembert and Mont-d'Or cheese.
Rosés: entrée, charcuterie, Beaufort cheese.
Sweet whites: foie gras.
Serving temperature
Reds: 12-13°C.
Rosés: 10°C.
Whites: 8°C.

Ageing ability
Reds and rosés: 2-3 years.
Whites: 2-5 years.

Soil types
Northern Loire: red schists from the Ancenis syncline, mica schist. Southern Loire: green schist and gneiss.

Area
262 hectares
Production
17,000 hectolitres

Grape varieties
Reds: Gamay Noir (main variety), Cabernet Franc (subsidiary variety).
Whites: Chenin, Malvoisie (Pinot Gris).

135

Coteaux de l'Aubance

Appellation
Coteaux de
l'Aubance AOC

Colour
White

Area
204 hectares

Production
4,660 hectolitres

1950

The wine-growing region of Coteaux de l'Aubance is bordered to the west by the confluence of the Aubance and Loire rivers, and to the north by the Loire Valley. Part of the Anjou wine-growing region, this is an area low in rainfall and sheltered from oceanic influence by the Mauges hills and peaks around Cholet. It produces sweet, rich wines.

Eye

Golden highlights turning orangey with age are signs of concentrated grapes nobly rotted by the action of *Botrytis cinerea*. Lemon-yellow and green nuances indicate grapes that have dried naturally on the vine by the action of sun and wind (*passerillage*, or raisining).

Nose

The main impression is one of lightness (airy aromas) and finesse with mineral notes, floral scents (citronella, lime blossom, white flowers, acacia), toastiness and fruit (apricot, citrus, vine peach, quince).

Palate

A sensation of balance and freshness and a thirst-quenching quality even in wines from the richest grapes – there is no trace of heaviness about a Coteaux de l'Aubance. Those revealing a multitude of aromatic notes are very great wines to be treasured.

Grape variety
Chenin Blanc
(or Pineau de
la Loire).

Soil types
Shallow
soils on
schist.

Ageing ability
5-20 years
for average
years
(infinitely
longer great
vintages).

Choice of food
Rich wines: apéritif; foie gras.
Lighter wines:
fish, white meat
in a sauce,
puddings.

Serving temperature
7-9°C.

Coteaux de Pierrevert

A OC status has been granted to the medieval village of Pierrevert and 10 communes, located not far from Manosque in the hottest part of the Alpes-de-Haute-Provence (a region dear to the 20th century writer Jean Giono). The red, rosé and white wines have relatively low alcohol content and good liveliness, making them a perfect match for local produce such as lamb and goats' cheese from Banon.

1998

Appellation
Coteaux de
Pierrevert AOC
Colours
Red (55%)
Rosé (30%)
White (15%)
Area
378 hectares

Eye
• The reds are limpid with good depth of colour.
• The rosés range from light pink to a clear, light red.
• The whites are usually a very pale, brilliant yellow.

Nose
• The reds are dominated by aromas of blackcurrant, fresh butter and toast.
• The rosés offer aromas of red berries, sometimes with scents of fruit drops and a hint of toast.
• The whites are straightforward with lemony notes.

Palate
• The reds reveal admirable tannins with a good balance of richness and acidity. Fruity aromas are sometimes underscored by a hint of wood.
• The rosés display good acidity balanced by great richness, as is typical of the terroir.
• The whites are supported by good acidity softened by the Grenache Blanc and enhanced by the fruity aromas (citrus) of the Vermentino.

Production
14,160 hectolitres

**Serving
temperature**
Reds: 15°C.
Rosés and whites:
10°C.

Choice of food
Reds: asparagus, grilled lamb.
Rosés: as an apéritif or with anchoïade.
Whites: lamb, goats' cheese.

Ageing ability
Reds:
2-5 years.
Rosés and whites:
1-3 years.

**Principaux
cépages**
Reds and rosés :
grenache noir, syrah, cinsaut, carignan.
Whites: ugni blanc, vermentino, grenache blanc, clairette, roussanne.

Soil types
Ancient alluvia from the Durance River; conglomerate from the Valensole plateau; sandy-calcareous.

Coteaux du Giennois

Appellation
Coteaux du
Giennois AOC

Colours
Red
Rosé
White (35%)

Area
140 hectares

1 9 9 8

T he Coteaux du Giennois appellation area, next door to the Sancerre and Pouilly-Fumé AOCs, is the most northerly vineyard in the Nevers region of the Loire. The vines run from the ancient terraces of the Loire at Gien towards Cosne-sur-Loire on argillaceous limestone soils. Originally the hillsides of the Gien region produced red and rosé wines from a blend of Gamay and Pinot Noir, but are now gradually switching to Sauvignon.

Production
8,220 hectolitres

Grape varieties
Sauvignon,
Pinot Noir,
Gamay Noir.

Soil types
Limestone
marl rich
in shells,
flinty clay.

**Ageing
ability**
2-5 years.

Eye
• The reds are an intense red with purplish highlights.
• The rosés are very lightly orange or salmon coloured.
• The whites are a pale, brilliant gold.

Nose
• The reds reveal notes of morello cherry, cherry stalks or very ripe bigarreau cherry and venison.
• The rosés are intensely fruity and marked by peach aromas.
• The whites combine notes of citrus with scents of acacia or fern, peach, pear and apricot.

Vineyards on the slopes of the Gien region, in the vicinity of Saint-Père.

Palate
• The reds have supple structure, well-blended tannins and flavours that recall the cherry and violet scents detected on the nose.
• The rosés are lively, elegant and deliciously rounded.
• The whites are light and fruity, with a softness and roundness that lingers in perfect balance, revealing aromas of passion fruit.

**Serving
temperature**
Reds: 15°C.
Whites and rosés:
10°C.

Choice of food
Reds: grilled
red meat,
cheese.
Rosés: charcuterie.
Whites: seafood,
fish.

Coteaux du Languedoc

This is France's oldest wine-growing region, situated between Narbonne and Nîmes, along the southern slopes of the Massif Central at the foot of the Montagne Noire and the Cévennes. The land is an amphitheatre open to the Mediterranean, with Mistral and Tramontane winds to each side. The ancient Greeks had already planted vines around Agde as early as the 5th century BC. Six grape varieties dominate the production of red and rosé wines. Carignan and Cinsaut are limited to 40%, with the exception of Cabrières rosé which is made exclusively from Cinsaut. White wine production is much smaller and based on Grenache Blanc, Clairette and Bourboulenc. The variety of soils from Quatourze to Vérarques makes it impossible to describe a typical Coteaux du Languedoc wine.

1985

Appellation
Coteaux du Languedoc AOC, which may or may not be followed by a designation

Colours
Red (75%)
Rosé (13%)
White (12%)

Soil types
Quaternary terrain of rounded pebbles; slope wash on the edge of the limestone *causses*; schist; more or less hard limestone.

Grape varieties
Reds and rosés:
Grenache Noir, Syrah, Mourvèdre, Carignan, Cinsaut, Lladoner.
Whites: Clairette, Grenache Blanc, Bourboulenc, Picpoul, Marsanne, Roussanne.

Ageing ability
2-4 years (4-8 years for great vintages).

Area
10,000 hectares
Production
428,150 hectolitres

Eye

• The reds are usually crimson, often deep in colour when the wines have undergone long periods of maceration. Soils capable of slightly higher yields produce lighter wines.

• The rosés are a bright, pale pink.

• The whites are a brilliant golden straw-yellow.

Nose

• Young reds are dominated by red fruit aromas (raspberry, blackcurrant) joined by spice and pepper when Carignan and Syrah have been vinified by carbonic maceration. Scents of leather, dried fruit and roasted almond develop after 3-4 years. Wines from the borders of the *garrigue* take on accents of bay leaf.

• The rosés are distinguished by their intense floral notes (acacia) and scents of red fruit (burlat cherry).

• The whites offer scents of apricot and citrus fruit, with an infusion of *garrigue* herbs, spices and honey.

Palate

• The reds are powerful but rather closed in their early years, eventually opening out to reveal beautiful structure. The wines from schistous soils offer more mineral aromas and finer tannins.

• The rosés are round, full, supple and soft.

• The whites are flavoursome and fresh, with a dominant impression of fullness and silkiness.

Designations of the Coteaux du Languedoc AOC

RED AND ROSÉ WINES

IN THE AUDE DEPARTMENT:

La Clape Quatourze

IN THE HERAULT DEPARTMENT:

Cabrières
Coteaux de la Méjanelle
Montpeyroux
Pic-Saint-Loup
Saint-Christol
Saint-Drézéry
Saint-Georges-d'Orques
Saint-Saturnin
Coteaux de Vérargues

WHITE WINES

IN THE AUDE DEPARTMENT:

La Clape

IN THE HERAULT DEPARTMENT:

Picpoul-de-Pinet

The mountains of Pic-Saint-Loup and Hertus.

Serving temperature
Reds: 15-17°C.
Whites: 10-12°C.

Choice of food
Reds: red or white meat.
Rosés: charcuterie, stuffed tomatoes, squid, artichokes *à la barigoule*, North African cuisine.
Whites: fish (*brandade de Morue*, sautéed fillets of mullet, bouillabaisse, *bourride*).

Coteaux du Layon

The Layon River is an affluent of the Loire that rises in the south of the Maine-et-Loire department on the border of Deux-Sèvres. There are 27 communes in the geographical area of the Coteaux du Layon AOC, of which six are well known and their names sometimes follow the appellation (Faye-d'Anjou, Beaulieu-sur-Layon, Rochefort-sur-Loire, Saint-Aubin-de-Luigné, Saint-Lambert-du-Lattay and Rablay-sur-Layon). The famous Coteaux du Layon Chaume is produced in Rochefort-sur-Loire. Layon is sheltered from ocean humidity by the Mauges and Cholet hills. The vines are planted on shallow stony soils which are quick to warm up, producing sugar-rich harvests of concentrated, sometimes nobly rotted grapes that are picked manually in batches. Coteaux du Layon are sweet, rich wines.

1 9 5 0

Appellation
Coteaux du Layon AOC
Coteaux du Layon AOC (followed by the name of the commune)
Coteaux du Layon Chaume AOC

Colour
White (sweet, rich wines)

Area
Coteaux du Layon: 1,787 hectares
Coteaux du Layon Chaume: 81 hectares

Production
Coteaux du Layon: 52,770 hectolitres
Coteaux du Layon Chaume: 2,380 hectolitres

Soil types
Slope of Carboniferons or Briovrian schists with seams of eruptive rock (phtanite, spilite) and Carboniferous pudding stone in places (Chaume).

Ageing ability
More than 40 years for great vintages.

Grape variety
Chenin Blanc (or Pineau de la Loire).

Eye

The ideal Coteaux du Layon is a lustrous gold with green highlights. When dominated by nobly rotted grapes, it ages to a sumptuous amber colour with orange-bronze highlights – always an impressive sight. A venerable Coteaux du Layon leaves a rich legacy of tears on the walls of the glass from concentrated grapes that have slowly overripened in the autumn sunshine.

Above: old 16th century wine-growers' houses in Saint-Aubin-de-Luigné.

Nose

For the first 5-10 years, the bouquet is dominated by aromas of white flowers (rose, mock orange, hawthorn) and white fruits (pear, peach) powerfully enriched by scents of citrus (grapefruit peel, orange wood), exotic fruit (mango, corossol, guava) or dried fruit (apricot, fig) depending on vintage, soil type and topography. In certain cases there may also be mineral touches (iodine, mineral oil) that may be excessive. Once the wines reach maturity, the floral nuances fade in favour of much rarer aromas: scents of precious woods used in marquetry (citrus wood, exotic wood, resinous wood from Asia Minor), dried and crystallised fruit and bergamot, with nuances of honey and almonds. The mineral aromas frequently grow stronger, punctuating the pleasures of exoticism with an agreeable hint of severity.

Palate

Coteaux du Layon wines reveal a good balance of acid and sweet flavours, with notes of mint or liquorice complementing the aromas detected on the nose.

Serving temperature
Reds: 16-18°C.
Whites:
8-10°C.

Choice of food
Young wines:
fish, white meat in a sauce, veined cheese, fruit puddings.
Older wines:
apéritif;
foie gras, veined cheese, puddings.

Coteaux du Loir

The vineyards of the Coteaux du Loir AOC cling to the slopes overlooking the River Loir, between Vendôme and Château-du-Loir. The river flows east to west in a valley that is 2 kilometres (1.2 miles) wide and sometimes almost 80 metres (262 feet) deep. It is sheltered from north winds by the forest of Turkey oaks in Bercé but the vines still enjoy maritime influences from the Atlantic.

1 9 4 8

Appellation
Coteaux du Loir
AOC
Colours
Red
Rosé
White (40%)
Area
71 hectares

Eye
• The reds are a rather light shade of ruby.
• The rosés are lightly coloured but brilliant.
• The whites are a fairly pale straw-yellow.

Nose
• The reds and rosés combine aromas of red fruit and spices with a delicate peppery touch.
• The whites reveal primary grape aromas of acacia, citrus fruit, apricot and hawthorn. After a few years' ageing, they develop the Chenin nose dominated by aromas of quince and honey in great years.

Palate
• Pineau d'Aunis reds are light in tannins and marked by spices (cloves). Red fruit notes appear with age, especially morello cherry. Cherry aromas are more pronounced in wines produced from Gamay, which are for early drinking.
• The rosés are refreshing and enhanced by a delicately spicy bouquet.
• The dry whites have a straightforward attack followed by an impression of freshness and a delicate finish punctuated by fruit. A lingering impression of gunflint is more or less pronounced, depending on the vintage.

Choice of food
Reds: red or white meat, cheese.
Rosés: charcuterie, white meat, North African cuisine.
Whites: charcuterie, seafood, fish.

Serving temperature
Reds: 12-14°C.
Whites and rosés: 8-10°C.

Soil types
Clayey-limestone.

Ageing ability
Reds: 5-10 years.
Rosés: 4 years.
Whites: 20 years and more.

Production
2,570 hectolitres

Grape varieties
Reds: Pineau d'Aunis, Cabernet Franc, Gamay Noir.
Rosés: Côt, Groslot.
Whites: Chenin Blanc (or Pineau de la Loire).

143

Coteaux du Lyonnais

Appellation
Coteaux du
Lyonnais AOC

Colours
Red
Rosé
White (8%)

Area
320 hectares

1 9 8 4

Production
20,950
hectolitres

Grape varieties
Reds:
Gamay Noir.
Whites:
Chardonnay,
Aligoté.

Ageing ability
1-3 years.

This very fragmented vineyard extends across the Rhône department, from the river Azergues to the Gier valley. It is bordered to the west by the Rhône, and to the east by the Saône and the slopes of the Monts du Lyonnais. The AOC today is a far cry from the 12,000 hectare vineyard of the pre-phylloxera era in the 19th century. All that remains are 320 hectares of vines, producing a fruity, floral wine mainly served in the *bouchons*, the typical restaurants of the Gaul capital Lyon.

Eye
• The reds are vivid with occasional nuances of dark purple in the more structured wines.
• The whites are a lustrous straw colour, with green reflections.

Nose
• The reds release aromas of red and black berries such as blackcurrant, wild blackberry, strawberry and raspberry.
• The whites have aromas of pineapple and grapefruit in the first months, later acquiring perfumes of white peach.

Soil types
Granitic
sand, schist
plus
argillaceous
limestone
and moraine.

Palate
• The reds combine lightness and balance and confirm the dominant fruitiness of the nose. Certain cuvées have mineral touches and richer tannins that make them good for a few years' cellaring.
• The whites are supple and round and sometimes quite lively due to a soupçon of the crisper, more nervous Aligoté.

Choice of food
Reds and rosés:
andouillette
sausage,
Lyon saucisson,
white meat.
Whites:
fish, goats'
cheese.

**Serving
temperature**
13°C.

Coteaux du Quercy

The Coteaux du Quercy appellation area lies between the appellations of Cahors and Gaillac, embracing 33 communes in the Lot and Tarn-et-Garonne departments in the south of the region of Quercy. The main grape variety is Cabernet Franc which thrives on the molasse-based soils and limestone plateaux of the area. Coteaux du Quercy produces mostly fleshy, generous red wines with a complex bouquet. The fruity, lively rosés are made from the same grape varieties as the reds.

1 9 9 9

Appellation
Coteaux du
Quercy AOVDQS

Colours
Red
Rosé

Area
Nearly 500
hectares

Eye
- The reds are deep crimson.
- The rosés are crystalline.

Nose
- Red Coteaux du Quercy reveals a complex bouquet: scents of ripe fruit, blackcurrant, raspberry, leather and the underwood.
- The rosés are fruity, and lightly acidulous.

Palate
- The reds are fleshy, generous and long. Their youthful tannins mature well, blending with notes of red fruit and blackcurrant. These are good wines for laying down.
- The rosés are sometimes vivacious on the attack, developing a pleasing roundness and fruitiness.

Production
23,000
hectolitres

Choice of food
Magret (cutlet)
and *confit* of
duck, *cassoulet*,
cheese
(Cantal, Salers,
Laguiole).

**Serving
temperature**
12-14°C.

**Ageing
ability**
2-4 years.

Soil types
Molasse, Tertiary
limestone.

Grape varieties
Cabernet Franc
(60%), Tannat,
Côt, Gamay,
Merlot (a
maximum of
20% each for
each of these
three varieties).

Coteaux du Tricastin

Appellation
Coteaux du
Tricastin AOC

Colours
Red (94%)
Rosé (4%)
White (2%)

Area
2,630 hectares

1973

Production
112,220
hectolitres

Grape varieties
Grenache Noir,
Syrah, Carignan,
Cinsaut,
Grenache Blanc,
Clairette,
Marsanne,
Roussanne,
Viognier.

The limestone hillsides of Coteaux du Tricastin to the south of Montélimar continue down to the river terraces on the left bank of the Rhône. Vines occupy only a small part of this land of plenty, rich in lavender, lamb and black truffles. Being close to the Côtes du Rhône AOC, many people imagine that Coteaux du Tricastin is part of the same area. In reality, it is a very separate appellation with its own unique identity.

Eye
More or less light in colour depending on the quantity of Syrah in the blend. The more intense the wine, the better its ageing ability.

Nose
A characteristic fruitiness is more emphatic in the Primeur wines that are produced here in small amounts. Blends marked by Syrah from the more powerful terroirs reveal original notes of the underwood, spices or well-ripened fruit.

Palate
Most of the red wines are characterised by their easy-going tannins, and most are for early drinking. Blends with a higher proportion of Syrah from warmer, more powerful terroirs are more structured and capable of a few years' cellaring.

Soil types
Marly,
argillaceous
sands;
Quaternary
alluvial terraces.

Ageing ability
1-3 years.

Serving temperature
Reds 14-16°C
Whites and rosés:
12°C.

Choice of food
Reds:
red meat, grilled or in a sauce.
Rosés:
charcuterie, salad and crudités.
Whites:
white meat.

Coteaux du Vendômois

The Coteaux du Vendômois vineyards are planted on limestone slopes up the Loire Valley, on either side of the river between Vendôme and Montoire. The main grape varieties are Chenin Blanc, Gamay and Pineau d'Aunis, the latter often vinified as a *vin gris* or blush wine. Consumer demand in recent years has led to a rise in the production of red wines.

1 9 6 8

Appellation
Coteaux du
Vendômois AOC
Colours
Red
Rosé (*vin gris*)
White (12%)
Area
137 hectares

Eye
• The reds are crimson with violet highlights.
• The *vins gris* are a surprising pale bronze colour.
• The whites are a glistening golden yellow.

In the Middle Ages the Vendômois region was a busy thoroughfare widely used by pilgrims on their way to Santiago to Compostella. Today it is a haven of peace.

Nose
• The reds have a complex nose of spices, cherries and blackcurrants.
• The *vins gris* have a remarkably fresh, powerful, peppery bouquet.
• The whites produced from the Chenin grape are dry and fruity with scents of honey and lime blossom.

Palate
• The reds have an agreeable structure: supple, smooth and well blended.
• The *vins gris* are well balanced, intense and beautifully long.
• The whites are fresh and mouth-filling, with good aromatic intensity.

Production
8,630 hectolitres

Choice of food
Reds: charcuterie (*rillettes*),
red meat.
Whites: seafood,
fish.

Serving temperature
Reds: 15°C.
Whites and rosés: 10°C.

Ageing ability
1-2 years.

Soil types
Brown soils over flinty clay.

Grape varieties
Reds: Pineau d'Aunis, Gamay, Cabernet Franc, Pinot Noir.
Whites: Chenin Blanc (otherwise known as Pineau de la Loire).

147

Coteaux Varois

Appellation
Coteaux Varois
AOC

Colours
Red (25%)
Rosé (70%)
White (5%)

Area
1,865 hectares

1993

The Coteaux Varois AOC nestles at the foot of the Sainte-Baume range around Brignoles, once the summer residence of the Comtes de Provence. The vineyards, spread between 28 communes interrupted by wooded limestone massifs, are subject to very varied weather conditions. Coteaux Varois produces appealing, lively and tender wines with an individuality that sets them apart from the Côtes de Provence and Coteaux d'Aix of the surrounding area.

Eye

• The reds are crimson with violet highlights, developing a ruby hue.
• The rosés are a delicate shade of rose petal, ranging from salmon to plain pink.
• The whites are a clear brilliant yellow with green or grey highlights.

Nose

• The reds open with floral (violet) or vegetal notes (hay, mint) that gradually yield to more developed nuances (liquorice, venison, leather).
• The rosés are predominantly fruity (peach, raspberry, strawberry).
• The whites have a finesse expressed in floral or fruity notes (citrus peel, pineapple).

Palate

• The reds are rustic, full of character on the attack and solidly structured. They need time to refine their tannins.
• The rosés are characterised by a delicate attack, good structure, freshness and balance.
• The whites are harmonious and fresh.

Production
31,620
hectolitres

Ageing ability
Reds:
3-5 years
(up to 10 years).
Rosés: for early
drinking.
Whites:
2-3 years.

**Main grape
varieties**
Reds: Syrah,
Grenache, Mour-
vèdre, Carignan,
Cinsaut, Caber-
net-Sauvignon.
Rosés: Grenache,
Cinsaut, Syrah,
Mourvèdre, Cari-
gnan, Tibouren.
Whites: Clairette,
Grenache,
Rolle, Sémillon,
Ugni Blanc.

Soil types
Decalcified
clay beds
with angular
limestone
debris; brown
soils on marls;
soils from
colluvial deposits
or ancient stony,
alluvia, deep
around the
edges of the
basins.

**Serving
temperature**
Reds: 16-18°C
Rosés and whites:
8-10°C.

Choice of food
Reds: poultry
in a sauce,
scrambled
eggs with
truffles.
Rosés:
Provençale
entrées, exotic
cuisine, grilled
fish, grilled
red meat.
Whites: grilled
fish, white meat,
cheese.

Côte de Beaune

This sub-regional appellation is restricted to a few *lieux-dits* (vineyard plots) in the Montagne de Beaune, excluding Premiers Crus. It produces either white (Chardonnay) or red wines (Pinot Noir). The name of the *climat* may or may not follow the name of Côte de Beaune on the label.

1936

Appellation
Côte de Beaune AOC
Colours
Red
White (40%)
Area
52 hectares
Production
1,160 hectolitres

Eye
• The reds are crimson or even garnet.
• The whites are an intense golden yellow.

Nose
• The reds are steeped in humus and blackcurrant.
• The whites are floral, buttery, toasty and mineral.

Palate
• The reds are tannic in their youth, developing notes of fruit (blackcurrant) and the underwood with a pleasantly balanced texture.
• The whites are floral and toasty and seductively round and mellow when carefully aged in wood.

Côte de Beaune-Villages
The Côte de Beaune-Villages appellation applies exclusively to Pinot Noir red wines produced in the communal AOCs of Auxey-Duresses, Blagny, Chassagne-Montrachet, Chorey-lès-Beaune, Ladoix, Maranges, Meursault, Monthélie, Pernand-Vergelesses, Puligny-Montrachet, Saint-Aubin, Saint-Romain, Santenay and Savigny-lès-Beaune, excluding the Premiers Crus. It is therefore a variation of these communal appellations. The same wine may be labelled, for example: Auxey-Duresses, Auxey-Duresses-Côte de Beaune or Côte de Beaune-Villages. The wines are generally supple and light in the northern part of the AOC, more reserved with greater depth of colour in the south.

Soil types
Upper slope: brown limestone soils and black rendzina in slope wash; further down: white and yellow marls and ferruginous gravelly moraine; in the piedmont: yellow and reddish limestone and clays .

Choice of food
Reds: red meat, roasted poultry, cheese (Reblochon, Brie).
Whites: seafood, fish, charcuterie.

Serving temperature
Reds: 14-16°C.
Whites: 12-13°C.

Ageing ability
3-5 years.

Grape varieties
Reds: Pinot Noir.
Whites: Chardonnay.

Côte de Nuits-Villages

Appellation
Côte de Nuits-Villages AOC

Colours
Red
White (limited production)

Area
160 hectares

Production
6, 230 hectolitres

1 9 6 4

T he Côte de Nuits-Villages appellation is reserved for the production of five communes at the two extremities of the Côte de Nuits. To the north there is Fixin, which can choose between its own AOC or this alternative appellation; and Brochon, a section of which is classified as Gevrey-Chambertin AOC. To the south, the AOC embraces part of Prissey, Comblanchien and Corgoloin. Côte de Nuits-Villages is essentially a red wine made from Pinot Noir but these days whites are also starting to appear.

Eye

• The reds verge on garnet or purplish ruby, taking on an amber nuance with age. Young wines are a brilliant cherry colour.
• The whites should be pale, lightly golden and limpid.

Nose

• The reds have a background fragrance of blackcurrant, redcurrant, cherry and strawberry overlaid by aromas of the underwood, mushrooms and cinnamon.
• The whites bring to mind aromas of white flowers (acacia, hawthorn). With age they acquire notes of plums, ripe apples, figs, pears and quince – also spicy notes.

Palate

• The reds are powerful wines that need a few years' ageing to reach their full potential. Richness accompanies well-blended tannins.
• The whites are vivacious and clear-cut but always very pleasant.

Soil types
Slopes of *calcaire à entroques* (crinoidal limestone) in the north; Comblanchien granulose limestone in the south.

Ageing ability
3-5 years.

Grape varieties
Reds:
Pinot Noir.
Whites:
Chardonnay.

Choice of food
Reds: grilled red meat, poultry, cheese.
Whites: fish.

Serving temperature
Reds: 14-16°C.
Whites: 12-13°C.

Côte Roannaise

The Côte Roannaise vineyard backs onto the eastern slope of the Monts de la Madeleine in the heart of the Massif Central. It is exclusively planted on the best hillsides to the west of Roanne where the soils lie over granite. This is Gamay country, producing fruity, original red wines and agreeable rosés that are also entitled to the Côte Roannaise AOC.

1994

Appellation
Côte Roannaise
AOC
Colours
Red
Rosé
Area
171 hectares
Production
8,890 hectolitres

Eye
• The reds are a beautiful cherry red with purplish highlights. Cuvées from mature vines develop darker, deeper tones.
• The rosés obtained by the *saignée* method are often a light salmon pink.

Nose
• The reds release a multitude of aromas dominated by berry fragrances (blackcurrant, raspberry, cherry, wild blackberry or wild strawberry).
• The rosés may combine notes of exotic fruits with fruit scents of the terroir (apples, pears, etc).

Palate
• Red Côte Roannaise wines are a harmony of lightness, balance and fruitiness. Characteristics vary depending on the length of fermentation, the origin of the grapes and the age of the vines. Some wines are light and fruity, some are robust, occasionally with mineral overtones and a rustic touch that underscores the unique nature of the terroir.
• The rosés are nervous and fruity.

Choice of food
Reds:
charcuterie,
white meat,
cheese (Fourme
de Montbrison).
Rosés: as an
apéritif or with
grilled foods.

Serving
temperature
13°C.

Grape variety
Gamay Noir.

Soil type
Granitic
sands.

**Ageing
ability**
1-3 years.

Côte-Rôtie

Appellation
Côte-Rôtie AOC

Colour
Red

Area
197 hectares

Production
6,930 hectolitres

1 9 4 0

This is the oldest vineyard in the Rhône Valley, and it is probably here that vines were first planted in the days of Gaul. The vines cling to the sheer south-southeasterly- facing slopes of the Côte Brune and Côte Blonde on the right bank of the Rhône, a few kilometres to the south of Vienne. The appellation extends across the communes of Ampuis, Saint-Cyr-sur-Rhône and Rupins-Sémons, and produces exclusively red wines mainly from Syrah. Côte Rôtie wines are the epitome of this 'roasted slope' scorched by the summer sun, and they become exceptionally full-bodied with age.

Soil types
Weathered crystalline rocks from gneiss or mica schists.

Grape varieties
Syrah and Viognier (20% maximum).

Ageing ability
5-15 years depending on terroir and vintage.

Serving temperature
16-18°C.

Choice of food
Terrine, small game (pheasant, duck), mutton stew, pigeon with spices, turkey with chestnuts, cheese (Munster, Livarot).

Eye

Côte-Rôtie red wines are quite deeply coloured, with a garnet nuance in their youth that turns more orangey with age.

Côte Brune and Côte Blonde

Legend has it that these two hillsides were named in memory of the two daughters of the Lord of Ampuis, one brunette and one blond. More important is the distinctive nature of the geological substrata into which the vines sink their roots. The soils of the Côte Blonde are mainly from gneiss bedrock, weathered to form siliceous, greyish soils, often 'seasoned' by deposits of loess from the plateau. The Côte Brune on the other hand lies on mica-rich schist. The rock weathers to a dark brown (which gave the Côte its name) that is more ferruginous and clayey but less flinty.

Nose

Very elegant and rich, distinguished in their youth by dominant aromas of fresh red fruit (blackberry, myrtle, blackcurrant) and also sweet spices. Floral notes similar to violets are the mark of wines that include a small quantity of Viognier. Age adds more distinctive notes of empyreuma and especially nuances of baked or crystallised fruit such as morello cherry or cherries in brandy.

Palate

The Syrah in this AOC produces a somewhat finer palate than is expected from other northern appellations, giving the wines an unusual elegance. They are not however short of tannins that develop a delicate texture after a few years of ageing when the wines have reached peak maturity. This finesse may be magnified by richness and roundness in wines from very ripe harvests, all the more so when the Syrah has been blended with a small proportion of Viognier (less than 20%) in the course of vinification. As is conventional for great Syrah wines, these wines are matured in the wood to refine their bouquet and palate.

Syrah vines – the main grape variety of the Côte-Rôtie AOC – are trained up an army of poles.

Côtes d'Auvergne

Appellation
Côtes d'Auvergne
AOVDQS

Colours
Red
Rosé
White (7%)

Area
332 hectares

1 9 7 7

Production
17 100 hl

The Auvergne vineyards lie in the Puy-de-Dôme, between Riom to the north and Issoire to the south, spread across 52 communes. The appellation is located on the hillsides at the edge of the Limagne plain and up the sides of the *puys* (volcanic peaks of the Auvergne region) at altitudes of 350-500 metres (1,148-1,640 feet). The principal grape stock is Gamay. Depending on aspect and type of soil, it is vinified either as red wine, principally in Chateaugay, or as rosé in Corent. Pinot Noir (known locally as 'Auvernat') and Chardonnay are also grown here.

Eye
• The reds have a purplish hue.
• The whites have a platinum tinge that reflects their youth and vivaciousness.
• The rosés have nuances of very pale pink.

Nose
• The reds evoke a marinade of lush, ripe bigarreau cherries and lightly acidulous red fruit.
• The whites offer a bouquet of very ripe fruit and white flowers.
• Côtes d'Auvergne rosés are fresh and floral, with subtler, more generous aromatic characteristics when produced in Corent, Chateaugay and Boudes.

Palate
• The reds are especially fleshy and powerful when they come from the slopes of Boudes, Madargues, Chateaugay and Chanturgues. Their rather tannic structure makes them a perfect match for the regional cuisine.
• The whites are young and fresh, for drinking within two years of the harvest.
• The rosés are lively and elegant.

Choice of food
Reds: charcuterie, roasted or grilled red meat, cheese (Cantal, Fourme d'Ambert).
Rosés: charcuterie.
Whites: crustaceans, fish.

Serving temperature
Reds: 15°C.
Whites and rosés: 10°C.

Grape varieties	Soil types	Ageing ability		
Gamay Noir, Pinot Noir and Chardonnay.	Clayey limestone with volcanic slope wash.	2-5 years.		

Côtes de Bergerac

Recognition for Côtes de Bergerac (as reds) and Côtes de Bergerac Moelleux (as whites) was sought as a means to establish a category superior to the Bergerac AOC. They are produced on the same terroirs as Bergerac wines, and are much sought-after for their concentration, obtained by very strict harvesting conditions – no Ugni Blanc in the sweet wines, in particular.

1 9 3 6

Appellations
Côtes de Bergerac AOC
Côtes de Bergerac Moelleux AOC

Colours
Red (22%)
White (sweet)

Area
1,389 hectares

Production
104,920 hectolitres

Eye
• The reds are dark, deep and intense, the colour of very ripe burlat cherries.
• Bergerac Moelleux is a pale yellow.

Nose
• The reds have a complex bouquet dominated by ripe red and black-skinned fruit but including a wealth of other aromas: empyreuma (smoke and toast), the underwood, peat, humus, spices and liquorice, with wafts of heady floral fragrances (peony).
• Bergerac Moelleux offers 'roasted' scents and aromas of beeswax and honey typical of overripe grapes.

Palate
• The reds have the characteristic qualities of wines of moderate ageing ability: fleshy at first but with a finish in very young wines that reveals their tannic structure. Côte de Bergerac reds are 11% proof compared with 10% proof for Bergerac.
• Bergerac Moelleux is fruity with plenty of liveliness at the finish. Alcohol content is 11.5% vol.

CHATEAU TOUR DE GRANGEMONT
CÔTES DE BERGERAC
1995

Main grape varieties
Reds: Merlot, Cabernet-Sauvignon, Cabernet Franc, Malbec, Mérille (subsidiary).
Whites: Sémillon, Sauvignon, Muscadelle.

Soil types
Sand (north of the Dordogne); molasse, marl and limestone (south); argillaceous limestone.

Ageing ability
Reds: 3-5 years.
Bergerac Moelleux: up to 5 years.

Choice of food
Reds: grills, roasted poultry.
Bergerac Moelleux: as an apéritif.

Serving temperature
Reds: 14-15°C.
Bergerac Moelleux: 10-12°C.

Côtes de Bourg

Appellation
Côtes de Bourg
AOC
Colour
Red
White (0.5%)
Area
3,741 hectares
Production
228,260
hectolitres

1 9 3 6

The Côtes de Bourg vineyards border the Gironde, the estuary of the Dordogne and the Garonne, planted on three rows of hills parallel to the riverbanks surrounding the citadel of Bourg. The red wines are rich in colour, fruity and fleshy, with good ageing ability. The dry whites are in very limited production, but their high quality makes them very interesting.

**Main grape
varieties**
Reds: Merlot,
Cabernet Franc,
Cabernet-Sauvi-
gnon, Malbec.
Whites: Sémi-
llon, Sauvignon,
Muscadelle,
Colombard.

Eye
• The reds have deep, dark tones promising a wine of solid constitution.
• The whites are a lustrous yellow with green highlights.

Nose
• The reds are characterised by fragrances of red fruits and, in great vintages, black-skinned fruit such as dark plums. In both cases, there are also notes of spice and woodiness (vanilla).
• The whites have a very identifiable bouquet with floral notes.

Soil types
Argillaceous
limestone,
sandy-silty
soils and
gravel spread.

Ageing ability
Reds: 3-8 years.
Whites: 3-4 years.

Palate
• The reds are supported by silky tannins which are especially agreeable in the young wines. Malbec gives the wines roundness, and soil type determines the character. Those produced on the first row of hills are robust with rich tannins that can be somewhat coarse in the first years. Those from the middle row are identified by rounder tannins and a chocolaty sensation. Wines from the eastern slopes are less robust but elegant.
• The whites have a rich and harmonious palate that echoes the floral notes of the nose.

**Serving
temperature**
Reds: 16-17°C.
Whites: 10-12°C.

Choice of food
Reds:
charcuterie,
red meat, game,
cooked cheese.
Whites:
seafood, fish
in a sauce,
gizzard salad,
white meat,
tarts.

Côtes de Castillon

It was near Castillon in 1453 that English troops led by John Talbot were defeated, so ending the Hundred Years' War. Côtes de Castillon is located to the east of the Saint-Emilion AOC, 50 kilometres (31 miles) from Bordeaux and 40 kilometres (25 miles) from Bergerac, on the edge of the Périgord. The area boasts a large number of old vines capable of yielding concentrated grapes. There are two different types of terroir: on the one hand, the sites on the plain that produce warm, supple wines; on the other hand, the hillside and plateau sites that produce more robust wines with better ageing ability.

1 9 8 9

Appellation
Côtes de Castillon AOC
Colour
Red
Area
2,900 hectares
Production
172,300 hectolitres

Eye
A very strong colour somewhere between ruby and topaz, with a pronounced garnet hue. The depth of colour reflects the solidity, strength and concentration of the wine.

Nose
Côtes de Castillon wines develop an expressive bouquet that reveals the influence of Merlot, with well-marked perfumes of ripe red fruit and notes of fruit stones. Aromas vary according to growths and vintages: from spices, ripe grapes and dark plum to liquorice or smoky notes, toast and ivy. Notes of vanilla reflect the time spent in wood.

Palate
Elegant, full-bodied and solidly constituted, with powerful tannins surrounding smooth, ripe, generous and delicate substance – these are wines for cellaring.

Main grape varieties
Merlot, Cabernet Franc, Cabernet-Sauvignon.

Soil types
Argillaceous limestone, sandy gravel, silty sand and limestone.

Choice of food
Red or white meat, game, cheese.

Serving temperature
16-18°C.

Ageing ability
4-9 years.

Côtes de Duras

Appellation
Côtes de Duras
AOC

Colours
Red
Rosé
White (dry and
sweet, 43%)

Area
1,758 hectares

1937

This appellation is planted at the foot of a superb 17th century castle, between the vineyards of Bordeaux to the west, Bergerac to the north and the Côtes du Marmandais to the south. The appellation merges with the canton of Duras which is part of the Bordeaux region but acquired recognition in its own right in 1937 – the Bordeaux appellation having been reserved since 1919 for wines from the Gironde department. The limestone soils of the hilltops carved by the Dropt and Dourdèze rivers are planted with white grape varieties. The stony, argillaceous limestone slopes meanwhile are more suited to Cabernet, Merlot and Malbec. The white wines are dry, nervous and thoroughbred, or sweet. The reds are supple and fruity or very tannic and good for ageing. The rosés are fruity and fresh.

Production
117,480
hectolitres

Ageing ability
Reds:
5-10 years.
*Dry whites
and rosés:*
1-3 years.
Sweet whites:
up to 5 years.

**Main grape
varieties**
Reds: Merlot,
Cabernet-Sauvignon, Cabernet
Franc, Côt.
Whites: Sauvignon, Sémillon,
Ugni Blanc,
Muscadelle.
Subsidiary:
Mauzac, Ondenc, Chenin.

Soil types
Molasse and
boulbènes (see
page 62) on the
plateaux and
hilltops suitable
for white grapes;
argillaceous
limestone on the
slopes suitable
for red grapes.

**Serving
temperature**
Traditional reds:
14-15°C.
*Rosés and light
reds:* 10°C.
Dry whites:
8-10°C.
Sweet whites:
8°C.

Eye

• The reds vary in colour depending on the method of vinification. Wines produced by carbonic maceration are lighter with a more violet hue and intended for early drinking. Wines that have spent longer periods on skins are darker.

• The rosés obtained by the *saignée* process (from vats of red wine) have the characteristics of the vintage. The intensity of colour reflects aromatic concentration and the length of fermentation on skins.

• The dry whites are very light in colour with metallic highlights and green nuances.

• The sweet whites are yellow-gold.

Nose

• The reds produced by carbonic maceration develop fragrances of red fruit; others are more classical, in the manner of Bordeaux.

• The rosés are very fine and fruity.

• The dry whites are distinguished by floral aromas, especially when the blend includes a high proportion of Sauvignon.

• The sweet whites offer fruity aromas.

Palate

• The reds produced by carbonic maceration are light. The traditional reds are fruity but also tannic and take longer to soften.

• The rosés, like the reds produced by carbonic maceration, are light, vivacious and fruity, and delicious when chilled.

• The dry whites are lively, light and fruity.

• The sweet whites are delicate, developing ripe fruit flavours.

The Duras vineyard enjoyed a revival in the 1980s thanks to the development of red wines.

The castle of Duras, on the crest of the hill where the town was established.

Choice of food
Traditional reds: regional dishes (duck confit, roasted or grilled red meat, veal with ceps, lampreys). *Rosés and light reds:* charcuterie, exotic cuisine. *Dry whites:* seafood, freshwater fish. *Sweet whites:* as an apéritif or with foie gras.

159

Côtes de la Malepère

Appellation
Côtes de la Malepère
AOVDQS

Colours
Red
Rosé

Area
515 hectares

1983

Production
41,060 hectolitres

Main grape varieties
Merlot, Cabernet-Sauvignon, Côt, Grenache Noir and Cinsaut (for the rosés).

Soil types
Sandstone molasse, Quaternary terraces.

The Côtes de la Malepère AOVDQS covers 31 communes to the southwest of Carcassonne between the Limouxin and the Canal du Midi, spread over the slopes of the Massif de la Malepère which peaks at the Mont Naut at 442 metres (1,450 feet). The vines are planted only on the poorest terrain, mainly on sandstone slopes in an area where the climate varies from Mediterranean on the southern slopes to markedly Atlantic on the western side. The wines are robust and fruity.

Eye

• Young reds have great depth of colour with dark purple highlights, the colour evolving with time but always remaining very intense.

• The rosés are a delicate salmon pink, especially when produced from the Cinsaut grape.

Nose

• The reds are rich and powerful, predominantly fruity when young, turning with time to more mature scents of baked fruit mingled with notes of the underwood.

• The rosés have the same fruitiness (often with notes of citrus).

Palate

• The reds are powerful and spicy, with marked tannins if the blend includes Cabernet-Sauvignon. Some may be drunk young, others are for keeping a few years, depending on the length of maturation.

• The rosés are full and vivacious with a long finish overlaying aromas of redcurrant.

Serving temperature
Reds: 16-18°C.
Rosés: 12°C.

Choice of food
Reds: red meat, game.
Rosés: as an apéritif or with entrées, grills, exotic cuisine.

Ageing ability
2-5 years (up to 10 years for great vintages).

Côtes de Millau

The history of the Côtes de Millau, in the Tarn valley in the Aveyron department, is very old indeed, as proved by the discovery of an antique press in Montjux. The vines are planted on slopes of sedimentary terrain where the climate enjoys Mediterranean influences. Côtes de Millau produces tannic red wines, mainly from Gamay and Syrah; also crisp whites and rosés made by the *saignée* method.

1994

Appellation
Côtes de Millau
AOVDQS
Colours
Red (60%)
Rosé (32%)
White (8%)
Area
38 hectares

Eye
• The reds range from deep red to ruby red with vivid highlights.
• The rosés are a brilliant pink of medium intensity.
• The whites are very pale and limpid with brilliant highlights.

Nose
• The reds offer progressive aromas of violets, grape marc and very ripe or even baked fruit, with an additional spicy touch.
• The rosés have a discreet, fresh, pleasant fragrance reminiscent of strawberry syrup.
• The whites have a subtle bouquet of white flowers with an occasional hint of hazelnuts.

Palate
• The balance of the reds varies according to the vintage, with slightly vegetal tannins. The palate reveals spicy aromas.
• The rosés have a distinctively fresh structure that lasts right through to the finish.
• The whites have a straightforward attack and predominantly lively balance.

Choice of food
Reds: grilled meat.
Rosés: charcuterie.
Whites: : fish, crustaceans, seafood.

Serving temperature
14-17°C.

Ageing ability
1-2 years.

Soil types
Argillaceous limestone over slope wash (east), Triassic sandstone (west).

Production
1,500 hectolitres

Main grape varieties
Reds: Syrah, Gamay Noir, Cabernet-Sauvignon, Fer-Servadou.
Whites: Chenin, Mauzac.

Seigneurs de
Peyreviel

CÔTES DE MILLAU
Appellation d'Origine
Vin Délimité de Qualité Supérieure
1997

MIS EN BOUTEILLE À LA PROPRIÉTÉ PAR
S.C.V. Les Vignerons des Gorges du Tarn
12520 Aguessac

75cl
12%vol.
PRODUIT DE FRANCE

161

Côtes de Provence

Appellation
Côtes de
Provence AOC

Colours
Rosé (80%)
Red (15%)
White (5%)

Area
19,160 hectares

1977

Production
870,590 hectolitres

**Main grape
varieties**
Reds: Grenache,
Cinsaut, Syrah,
Mourvèdre,
Tibouren, Cari-
gnan, Cabernet-
Sauvignon.
Whites: Rolle,
Ugni Blanc, Clai-
rette, Sémillon.

Vines are the mark of the Provençal countryside, clustered around the *calanques* (rocky inlets) and beaches between Marseilles and Nice, scrambling up the valleys of the Arc and the Argens, gorging on scents of thyme and rosemary. The appellation as a whole extends into three departments (Var, Bouches-du-Rhône, Alpes-Maritimes). The climate in general is Mediterranean, with numerous microclimates produced by the uneven terrain and variable maritime influences. The geology and soils are also very diversified: crystalline Provence in Maures and Estérel, limestone Provence to the west. A rich variety of vine stock yields predominantly rosé wines plus smaller quantities of red and white.

Soil types
Red
Mediteranean
soils on compact
limestone,
marl and
sandstone;
skeletal or
erosional soils
on metamorphic
rocks, phyllite,
marls,
limestone,
sandstone
and ancient
alluvia;
rendzina on
limestone
slope wash.

Pine forests with the Mediterranean in the background, hillsides and plateaux – the wines of the Côtes de Provence appellation originate from very varied terroirs with weakening maritime influences from south to north.

Above:
The Fouques estate in Hyères.

Opposite:
The Clos Mireille in La Londe-les-Maures.

Eye

- The reds are crimson with violet highlights in their youth, developing ruby tints as they mature.
- The rosés are limpid and fluid, ranging from pale to clear pink, light orange, salmon pink, peony.
- The whites are pale brilliant yellow with green highlights.

Nose

- Young reds offer notes of fruit (red fruit) or plants (bay leaf, rosemary, thyme, tobacco); more forceful wines that have aged for a few years reveal notes of black-skinned fruit mingled with animal or spicy nuances (liquorice, cinnamon).
- The rosés may be intense or discreet, powerful or delicately tender. The nose can be fruity (red fruit, black-skinned fruit) floral (fennel, lime blossom, thyme, broom, dill), vegetal

(mint, tobacco, herbal tea), empyreumatic (gunflint) or balsamic (pine tree bark).

• The whites have a discrete bouquet with subtle scents of flowers (fennel, acacia, broom), fruit (lemon, grapefruit), spice (pepper) or balsam (resin).

Palate

• The reds may be light and supple, or more rustic and a good match for strong-tasting dishes. Some of today's red wines have beautiful structure, real power and good ageing ability.

• The rosés are dry, round and structured but always crisp and quaffable with a delicate balance of acidity, alcohol and tannins.

• The whites are well structured and fresh on the finish.

The history of the vineyard pre-dates the Christian era, Provence having been settled by the Etruscans, Phocaeans and Ligureans.

One notable contributor to the vineyard was the 15th century monarch King René who took an interest in the preservation of regional grape varieties.

Ageing ability
Reds: up to 10 years.
Whites and rosés: drink within the year (though certain vintages are suitable for cellaring).

Serving temperature
Reds: 12-14°C.
Whites and rosés: 14-16°C.

Choice of food
Reds: casseroles, stews, sautéed lamb, grilled foods with herbs.
Rosés: as an apéritif or with charcuterie, entrées (tomatoes and mozzarella, courgette flowers), fish (red mullet, bouillabaisse), red or white meat (grilled), cheese, puddings (crème brûlée, strawberries).
Whites: cold Provençale entrées, fish (grilled or à la crème), goats' cheese.

Côtes de Saint-Mont

The Côtes de Saint-Mont vineyard is a continuation of the Madiran, planted on alluvial terraces and gravelly hillsides on the banks of the Adour River. The famous Armagnac vineyard lies on its southwest and northeast flanks. The local wine co-operative – the Producteurs de Plaimont – has played a very important role here. The Côtes de Saint-Mont AOC produces tannic red wines, nervous, elegant whites and vivacious, fairly robust and aromatic rosés.

1 9 8 1

Appellation
Côtes de Saint-Mont
AOVDQS
Colours
Red
Rosé
White (15%)
Area: 785 hectares
Production
53,000 hectolitres

Eye
• The reds range from dark crimson to garnet – almost black.
• The whites are a very distinctive light straw-yellow.
• The roses are pale coloured.

Nose
• Young reds release fragrances of red fruits, developing more mature notes of dark plum, game and old leather.
• The whites evoke white fruit, verbena and lime blossom.

• The rosés develop fruit aromas of great finesse.

Palate
• Red Côtes de Saint-Mont are robust wines supported by goodly tannins, becoming smoother with a few years ageing.
• The whites are dry without too much acidity, supple, fresh and vivacious.
• The rosés are fresh with characteristic mineral notes (gunflint).

Choice of food
Reds: grills, confit, duck cutlet, *garbure.*
Rosés: charcuterie, grilled foods.
Whites: fish (grilled or in a sauce), white meat in a sauce.

Serving temperature
Reds: 15-17°C.
Whites and rosés: 8-10°C.

Ageing ability
Reds: 4-8 years.
Whites and rosés: for early drinking.

Soil types
Gravel, marl and limestone.

Main grape varieties
Reds: Tannat, Cabernet-Sauvignon, Cabernet Franc, Merlot.
Whites: Clairette, Arrufiac, Courbu, Manseng.

165

Côtes de Toul

Appellation
Côtes de Toul
AOC

Designation
Vin gris in most cases, or the name of the grape variety.

1998

T he Côtes de Toul production area covers eight communes around the town of Toul on the Côte de Meuse, a hillside terrroir characterised by sedimentary soils. The appellation produces white wines (made mainly with Auxerrois grapes) and red wines (usually based solely on Pinot Noir), but it is especially famous for its original *vins gris*. These are produced from red-skinned grapes with colourless pulp – Gamay or Pinot Noir, for instance – that are vinified as white wines.

Eye
• The *vins gris* are grey more than pink, except in years of peak maturity when the colour tends to assert itself very rapidly.
• The reds made from Pinot Noir always have good depth of colour, tending towards garnet. They are only produced in the best vintage years.
• The whites have a yellow-green nuance in their youth, becoming golden with age.

Nose
• The *vins gris* have a classic nose that is generally elegant and very fruity, combining floral fragrances (violets) and fruit (morello cherry, redcurrant, cranberry).
• The reds are often partially aged in casks, giving them a harmony of fruit notes (blackcurrant) and woody or vanilla nuances.
• The whites have floral aromas.

Palate
• The *vins gris* have greatly improved thanks to increased blending with Gamay and Pinot Noir. As lively as ever, they are now longer and more complex and beautifully harmonious.
• The reds are generally fleshy and powerful.
• The whites are dry, crisp and fruity with a hint of bitterness on the finish.

Colours
Rosé (blush)
White
Red

Area
102 hectares

Production
5,400 hectolitres

Main grape varieties
Gamay, Pinot Noir, Auxerrois.

Soil types
Mainly argillaceous limestone with strips of Triassic terrain to the north.

Ageing ability
2 years.

Serving temperature
8-10°C.

Choice of food
Entrées, charcuterie, Quiche Lorraine.

Côtes du Brulhois

The Comté of Brulhois is in Armagnac, on the banks of the Garonne river, on hillsides that are continuations of the hillsides of Moissac and Gascony to the south. The appellation produces predominantly red wines from Bordeaux grape varieties plus Tannat and Côt. They are well balanced with a generous bouquet of mushroom and spices and should be drunk young with regional dishes such as *confits* or *magrets de canard* (preserved duck or duck breast fillet).

<u>1 9 8 4</u>

Appellation
Côtes du Brulhois
AOVDQS
Colours
Red
Rosé
Area
250 hectares
Production
10,825 hectolitres

Eye
• The reds should be dark in colour – as you would expect of a wine that used to be known as *vin noir* (black wine).
• The rosés are light but bright.

Nose
• The reds combine fragrances of blackcurrant and cherry, often accompanied by notes of spice and cocoa.
• The rosés have delicate, powerful aromas marked by scents of red fruits.

Palate
• The reds are structured, tannic and balanced from the outset.
• The rosés are light, very slightly effervescent and fruity.

Choice of food
Reds: game, confit of duck, cassoulet, stews, ceps, red meat, cheese.
Rosés: charcuterie, grilled foods.

Serving temperature
Reds: 15-17°C.
Rosés: 8-10°C.

Lavilledieu
The 62 ha Lavilledieu vineyard is situated in the north of the Fronton region between Montauban and Castelsarrasin on terraces extending from the Tarn to the Garonne. Here soils from siliceous, sometimes gravelly silt yield rounded, velvety, well-balanced reds and fruity, aromatic rosés. Output is relatively limited (2,280hl).

Ageing ability
Reds: 2-4 years.
Rosés: for early drinking.

Main grape varieties
Cabernet-Sauvignon, Cabernet Franc, Merlot, Tannat,
Soil types
Gravel, limestone clay and *boulbènes* (p. 62).

167

Côtes du Forez

Appellation
Côtes du Forez
AOC

Colours
Red
Rosé

Area
193 hectares

Production
7,625 hectolitres

2000

In 1956, the Marcilly vineyard became part of the Côtes du Forez appellation (then an AOVDQS).

Grape variety
Gamay Noir.

Soil types
Granitic sands and basaltic sands in places.

Ageing ability
2-3 years.

Choice of food
Reds: boudin (white sausage), poultry, cheese (Fourme).
Rosés: grilled fish.

The Côtes du Forez vineyard is located between Clermont-Ferrand and Saint-Etienne, on magnificently exposed terrain. The vines are planted at altitudes of 400-600 metres (1,312-1,968 feet) shielded from unfavourable weather by the Monts du Forez. The only vine stock is Gamay, planted on granitic soils over basaltic knolls of volcanic origin. The wines inherit distinctive character and have all the prerequisites of a sound structure.

Eye
• The reds are generally a fairly light, vivid cherry red. Wines produced from basaltic soils are darker.
• The rosés are pale salmon and limpid.

Nose
• The reds, vinified from whole black Gamay grapes, develop a fruity bouquet dominated by red berries such as redcurrants and especially raspberries. Certain blends acquire original mineral notes.
• The rosés release delicate scents of apricot, pineapple and grapefruit.

Serving temperature
Reds: 13°C.
Rosés: 10°C.

Palate
• The reds are supple, fresh, fruity and quaffable. Blends from basaltic soils are more tannic and thoroughbred, with better ageing potential.
• The rosés are supple and delicate and much less widely produced than the reds. They are usually made by the *saignée* method and express the freshness of the grape variety.

The *saignée* method
Rosé wines made by partial maceration are obtained by *saignée* ('bleeding'). The vat is filled with de-stalked, sorted grapes and fermentation causes the marc to rise. When enough colour has been extracted, after 12-24 hours, some of the juice is run off and fermented separately.

Côtes du Frontonnais

The terraces of the Côtes du Frontonnais are located between the Tarn and Garonne rivers to the north of Toulouse, a perfect location for Négrette, a grape variety with characteristic aromas of violets. This is the source of the traditional wines of Toulouse – vivacious, fruity rosés, and reds which may be either light, fruity and aromatic or powerful and tannic.

1975

Appellations
Côtes du
Frontonnais AOC
Côtes du
Frontonnais
Fronton AOC
Côtes du
Frontonnais
Villaudric AOC

Colours
Red
Rosé (20%)

Area
1,827 hectares
Production
116,660 hectolitres

Main grape varieties
Négrette,
Cabernet Franc,
Cabernet-
Sauvignon, Côt,
Mérille, Syrah.

Eye
• Négrette grapes produce red wines that may be recognised by their deep ruby tones.
• The rosés are also deeply coloured.

Nose
• One of the distinctive features of Côtes du Frontonnais reds is their very diverse bouquet ranging from violet-scented to spicy, with aromas of red fruit, liquorice, blackcurrant or raspberry.
• The rosés are very expressive, with aromas of red fruit, exotic fruit and white flowers (acacia).

Palate
• Reds with a high proportion of Cabernet, Gamay or Syrah are supple, aromatic and elegant, and intended for early drinking. Those containing a high proportion of Négrette are more powerful with a perfume marked by the terroir and greater ageing potential.
• The rosés are agreeably round, and for early drinking.

Choice of food
Reds: grilled foods, poultry, game, cheese.
Rosés: charcuterie, fish, white meat.

Serving temperature
Reds: 15-17°C.
Rosés: 8-10°C.

Soil types
Red soil, gravel and *boulbènes* (see page 62).

Ageing ability
Reds: 4-5 years.
Rosés: for early drinking.

169

Côtes du Jura

Appellation
Côtes du Jura
AOC
Colours
Red
Rosé
White (78%)
Area
639 hectares

1 9 3 7

Production
33,360
hectolitres

**Main grape
varieties**
Reds: Poulsard,
Trousseau, Pinot
Noir.
Whites: Chard-
onnay, Savagnin.

The Côtes du Jura AOC in the Franche-Comté region extends from west to east between the Bressane plain and the first Jura plateau, and from north to south from Salins-les-Bains to Saint-Amour. The vines are planted on hillsides at altitudes of 220-380 metres (722-1,247 feet). The appellation represents the complete spectrum of Jura wine: whites, rosés, reds, *vins jaunes*, *vins de paille* and sparkling. Of these, the most important in terms of volume are the whites, produced from Chardonnay, or from blends of Chardonnay and Savagnin, or from pure Savagnin. The latter are relatively rare, Savagnin usually being reserved for the production of *vin jaune*.

Soil types
Liassic and
Triassic clay,
some limestone
slope wash from
the plateau.

**Ageing
ability**
*Chardonnay
whites:* 3 years.
Poulsard reds:
3-5 years.
Vins jaunes:
50 years.
Vins de paille:
more than
10 years.
Sparkling wines:
for early
drinking.

Eye

- The reds are cherry red with purplish highlights in youth. Age adds terracotta tints typical of the Jura grape varieties.
- Young whites are pale yellow, golden when from a Chardonnay-Savagnin blend.
- The *vins jaunes* are lustrous gold with a characteristic Savagnin appearance.
- The *vins de paille* have seductive straw gold tones.

Nose

- The reds offer a basket of red fruit and blackcurrants.
- Young whites based on Chardonnay are fresh and floral, with notes of honey, hazelnut and roasted almonds from the wood. Mature wines often have an additional aromatic touch from the Savagnin.
- The *vins jaunes* have a spicy range of aromas dominated by unmistakable scents of walnuts and dried apricots.
- The *vins de paille* reveal exotic fruit fragrances mingled with dried fruit.

Palate

- The reds are tannic and aromatic.
- Young whites based on Chardonnay are fruity and rather lively with a rounded palate and even more surprising background flavours of walnuts and almonds when Savagnin is present – a typical feature that grows more pronounced as the proportion of Savagnin increases.
- The *vins jaunes* are rich and beautifully structured, with exquisite aromas that are seductive from the outset although it takes many years for the wine to develop.
- The *vins de paille* are round, with a good balance of sugar and alcohol. Notes of quince mingle with apricot and there is sometimes a hint of beeswax on the finish.

Choice of food

Poulsard reds: red meat, cheese (Bleu de Gex). *Trousseau reds:* game. *Chardonnay whites:* fish, dishes à la crème. *Sparkling wines and vins de paille:* puddings. *Vins jaunes and Savagnin whites:* white meat à la crème, coq au *vin jaune,* cheese (Comté, Mont-d'Or).

The Jura has a continental climate with severe winters and unpredictable summers. The vines are trained up stakes to keep the grapes off the ground, protecting them from occasionally harmful levels of autumn humidity.

Serving temperature

Reds: 15°C. *Whites:* 12°C. *Sparkling and vins de paille:* 6°C. *Vins jaunes:* lightly chambré.

Côtes du Luberon

Appellation
Côtes du
Luberon AOC
Colour
Red (50%)
Rosé (28%)
White (22%)
Area
3,700 hectares

1988

CHÂTEAU LA CANORGUE
1995

CÔTES DU LUBERON
Appellation Côtes du Luberon Contrôlée
Mis en bouteille au Château
Alc. 12.5% vol.
EARL MARGAN J.P. ET M. - PROPRIÉTAIRE-RÉCOLTANT - F 84480 BONNIEUX FRANCE

Production
180,930
hectolitres

**Main grape
varieties**
Reds: Grenache
Noir, Cinsaut,
Syrah,
Mourvèdre.
Whites: Grenache
Blanc, Clairette,
Vermentino,
Roussanne.

Soil types
Soils from
debris shed
by the massif;
sandy soils
on Miocene
molasse;
stony soils
on ancient
terraces.

Ageing ability
Reds: 5 years
(10 years for
certain
vintages).
Rosés: 2 years.
Whites: 3 years.

**Serving
temperature**
Reds: 15°C.
Whites and rosé:
10°C.

T his appellation is located on the left bank of the Rhône, defined by the natural geographical limits of the Massif du Luberon. Bordered to the north by the Calavon Valley (Apt) and to the south by the valley of the Durance (Cavaillon, Pertuis, Manosque), the appellation covers 36 communes in the Vaucluse department. Culture, Mediterranean climate and rosé wines make this a typically Provençal viticultural region, although somewhat relieved by Alpine influences that give it cooler temperatures than the Rhône Valley – hence the rather high proportion of white wines.

Eye
• The reds are a brilliant and fairly deep ruby-red.
• The rosés are lively with cherry highlights.
• The whites are pale, limpid and brilliant.

Nose
• The reds are dominated by fruity aromas (blackcurrant, raspberry) with spicy and sometimes toasty nuances.
• The rosés are fresh and fruity, sometimes with hints of toast.
• The whites offer fresh, floral aromas often mingled with fruity notes, mainly citrus (lemon, grapefruit).

Choice of food
Reds: lamb, beef daube, game (boar).
Rosés: charcuterie, snails, grilled foods.
Whites: shellfish, fish cooked with fennel.

Palate
• The reds are full-bodied, often with silky tannins, growing more complex in aroma after 3-5 years.
• The rosés are well balanced, fresh and quaffable, with all the fragrance of Provence.
• The whites achieve a fine balance of acidity and richness.

Côtes du Marmandais

he Marmandais region is an area of hillsides and small valleys between Agen and Bordeaux bordered to the south by the forested massif of the Landes. It lies in a transitional zone, between the slopes of Entre-Deux-Mers to the west and those of the Agen region to the east. The AOC produces fresh, fruity white wines and supple, fragrant rosés and reds.

1 9 9 0

Appellation
Côtes du Marmandais AOC

Colour
Red (91%)
Rosé (5%)
White (4%)

Area
1,462 hectares

Eye
• The reds are deep in colour.
• The rosés are beautifully clear, neither too pale nor too deep.
• The dry whites are pale yellow with green highlights.

Nose
• The reds have a bouquet of red fruits with just a hint of spice.
• The rosés are dominated by notes of red fruits.
• The whites have characteristic varietal Sauvignon aromas (white fruits).

Palate
• The reds have rounded, full-bodied but not excessive substance, and well-balanced tannins.
• The rosés have a lightly tannic structure with a hint of vivaciousness that makes them ideal accompaniments for the first course.
• The whites are crisp and fruity

Production
92,800 hectolitres

Main grape varieties
Reds and rosés:
Merlot (31%), Cabernet Franc (24%), Cabernet-Sauvignon (17%), Côt (12%), Abouriou (11%), Syrah, Gamay.
Whites:
Sauvignon (86%), Sémillon (13%), Muscadelle, Ugni Blanc.

Cuvée de l'Oratoire
1994
CHATEAU DE BEAULIEU
CÔTES DU MARMANDAIS
Appellation Côtes du Marmandais Contrôlée

Choice of food
Reds: red meat, confit or *magret* of goose or duck.
Rosés: as an apéritif or with charcuterie.
Whites: fish from the Garonne (pike, shad with sorrel).

Serving temperature
Reds: 15-17°C
Whites and rosés: 8-10°C.

Ageing ability
Reds:
5-10 years.
Whites and rosés:
1-3 years.

Soil types
Brown soils on molasse and *boulbènes* (p. 62); gravelly soils on the terraces.

Côtes du Rhône

Appellation
Côtes du Rhône
AOC

Colours
Red (75%)
Rosé (23%)
White (2%)

Area
42,000 hectares

1 9 3 7

The Rhône Valley appellation runs 200 kilometres (124 miles) from Vienne to Avignon. This is the second largest regional appellation after Bordeaux, covering 163 communes and six departments (Rhône, Loire, Drôme, Ardèche, Gard and Vaucluse). It is also one of the oldest of the AOCs. The vineyards in the north are devoted to communal appellations (Côte-Rôtie, Condrieu…). Côtes du Rhônes, which are not wines for cellaring, are mainly produced in the southern part between Bollène and Avignon. The pebble and red sandy-clay soils on the left bank of the Rhône provide excellent terroirs for the vines. Red wines are by far the most important category, and are as diverse as the soils and microclimates from which they originate.

Production
2,255,000
hectolitres

Grape varieties
Reds and rosés:
Grenache, Syrah, Cinsaut, Mourvèdre, Carignan, Counoise.
Whites:
Grenache Blanc, Clairette, Bourboulenc, Marsanne, Roussanne, Viognier.

Soil types
Limestone, rounded pebbles, Miocene molasse.

Ageing ability
1-3 years.

Eye

- The reds are light ruby-red – darker when Syrah dominates.
- The rosés are a delicate colour with violet highlights.
- The whites are a limpid, brilliant yellow.

The rounded pebbles of the Southern Côtes du Rhône (below) play a vital role in storing daytime heat which is returned to the roots at night.

Nose

- The reds are discreetly fruity, with a fragrance red berries, but some have the intensity of a great wine, with animal or spicy notes or ripe-fruit aromas.
- The rosés have intense aromas of fruit drops, red berries and floral scents dominated by violets.
- The whites offer a very delicate, floral bouquet.

Palate

- The reds reveal flavours that echo the aromas detected on the nose. Those from the light soils of Puymeras, Nyons, Sabran and Bourg-Saint-Andéol are tender and quaffable; those from warmer areas like Domazan, Courthézon and Orange, and terroirs of ancient alluvia, offer well-structured but supple tannins.
- The rosés finish on a lingering note of red fruits.
- The whites are agreeable, round and full, well balanced with elegant aromatic persistence.

Opposite: Syrah is one of the Rhône's star grape varieties.

Choice of food
Reds: grilled beef, grilled lamb chops, cheese (Neufchâtel, Bleu de Gex, Picodon). *Rosés:* salade Niçoise, charcuterie. *Whites:* sea fish à la crème.

Serving temperature
Reds: 14-16°C.
Whites and rosés: 12°C.

Côtes du Rhône-Villages

Appellation
Côtes du Rhône-Villages AOC (sometimes followed by the name of the commune)

1966

Colours
Red (98%)
Rosé (1%)
White (1%)

Area
6,740 hectares

Production
273,380 hectolitres

Soil types
Terraces of rounded pebbles; stony slopes.

The communes of the Côtes du Rhône-Villages are located in the southern part of the Côtes du Rhône area, in four departments: the Ardèche, the Drôme, the Gard and the Vaucluse. The Mediterranean climate here is particularly arid, in summer and winter alike, and the land is lashed by the Mistral, a violent wind that sometimes blows for more than 200 days a year. The soils are mainly limestone but vary widely in texture, hydric regime, fertility and microclimatic conditions related to their exposure. These differences combine to explain the particular nuances of each sub-region. Côtes du Rhône Villages wines are distinguished from those of the Côtes du Rhône AOC by their characteristically generous nature and superior ageing potential.

Main grape varieties
Reds and rosés: Grenache Noir, Syrah, Cinsaut, Mourvèdre, Carignan, Counoise.
Whites: Grenache Blanc, Clairette, Bourboulenc, Marsanne, Roussanne, Viognier.

Ageing ability
1-5 years.

Right: Vinsobres, one of the villages in the Côtes du Rhone, produces fruity, full-bodied red wines and floral whites.

Gard wines

- **Chusclan:** red wines characterised by rich colour, balance and fragrances of fruit and bay leaf; rosés that combine fairly good depth of colour with a smooth palate.
- **Laudun:** rich and floral white wines; rare but distinguished rosés; supple and delicate reds.
- **Saint-Gervais:** rich, tannic reds with aromas of red fruit and spice; fresh, floral whites.

Drôme wines

- **Rochegude:** the red wines are fairly light and warm – drink them within the first few years to get the full benefit of their fruity aromas.
- **Rousset-les-Vignes:** red wines dominated by red berry fragrances.
- **Saint-Maurice:** elegant, tannic red wines with good ageing potential; crisp, refreshing rosés.
- **Saint-Pantaléon-les-Vignes:** the reds are firm, quite tannic and capable of ageing.
- **Vinsobres:** red wines with fruit fragrances, balanced body and good tannic structure – certain to age well. Also fresh, floral whites for early drinking.

Vaucluse wines

- **Beaume-de-Venise:** the reds are among the best balanced of any, with aromas of red fruit and almonds and a beautifully rounded palate. The rosés are rich, fruity and fresh.
- **Rasteau:** solid, spicy red wines that mature to perfection, and heady rosés.
- **Cairanne:** powerfully structured reds, dominated by aromas of pitted fruit and leather; remarkably rounded whites.
- **Roaix:** reasonably supple and fruity reds; fresh, quaffable rosés.
- **Sablet:** red wines with a fragrance of ripe fruit and dried fruit; fruity, powerful rosés.
- **Séguret:** red wines with delicate nuances of almond; fresh and aromatic rosés.
- **Valréas:** well-balanced reds, not very tannic, with aromas of fruit and aniseed; harmonious, delicate whites and rosés.
- **Visan:** reds with a fragrance of fruit and leather, sometimes with an added mineral touch – impressively full on the palate.

Choice of food

Reds: grilled red meat, lamb.
Rosés: grilled sea fish.
Whites: as an apéritif or with freshwater fish.

Serving temperature

Reds: 14-16°C.
Whites and rosés: 12°C.

Côtes du Roussillon

Appellation
Côtes du
Roussillon AOC

Colours
Red (85%)
Rosé (9%)
White (6%)

Area
5,380 hectares

1977

It was close to the Spanish border, between Corbières and the Pyrenees, that the Greeks planted the first vines in the 7th century BC. Today Côtes du Roussillon wines are produced in 118 communes of the Pyrénées-Orientales. The vines, pruned in the goblet fashion, are well adapted to the dry climate, wind and variable soils. The vinification of whole grapes produces excellent results in the red wine category. The rosé wines are made by the *saignée* method and are approximately 12% proof. The white wines are perfect with seafood.

Eye
• The reds are ruby-red or quite intense garnet, with a reddish-brown hue.
• The rosés are an exquisite, very pale pink.
• The whites are pale gold with green highlights.

Grape varieties
Reds and rosés:
Carignan (60%),
Grenache Noir,
Syrah, Mourv-
èdre, Lladoner.
Whites:
Macabeu,
Grenache Blanc,
Malvoisie,
Marsanne,
Roussanne,
Vermentino
Blanc.

Nose
• The reds have the fruitiness of Grenache (morello cherry and blackberry) with aromas of blackcurrant and violets from the Syrah and touches of toast and spice from the Carignan. Next to follow are notes of leather, dark plum, cistus flowers and crystallised fruits.
• The rosés have an amyl fragrance combined with aromas of red berries.
• The whites reveal elegant floral aromas (vine blossom) enhanced by wooded notes.

Palate
• Red wines from argillaceous limestone soils are powerful and generous with solid structure and good ageing potential.
• The rosés make a robust impression.
• The whites are light.

Production
236,040
hectolitres

Soil types
Limestone,
schist, granite,
gneiss, sands.

**Ageing
ability**
1-4 years.

Choice of food
Reds: feathered game, grilled meat.
Rosés: charcuterie, chicken Catalane-style.
Whites: seafood, fish.

**Serving
temperature**
14-17°C.

Côtes du Roussillon-Villages

Vines are everywhere in this part of Roussillon between the Massif des Corbières and the river Têt. This is a region of great geological diversity where pebbly terraces, schists and granitic sands have given rise to four distinctive terroirs identified with four Village appellations – Caramany, Latour-de-France, Tautavel and Lesquerde. They produce very robust red wines.

1977

Appellation
Côtes du Roussillon-Villages AOC
Colour
Red
Area
2,975 hectares
Production
109,420 hectolitres

Eye
The wines of Côtes du Roussillon-Villages are strong in colour.

Nose
Intense and complex, suggesting roasted fruit and fruit macerated in brandy, with touches of vanilla.

Palate
Delicate tannins seductively coated with smooth flavours; a gorgeous, lingering finish.

The Château de Jau, founded in 1900 near an ancient 12th century monastery.

Choice of food
Game (hare, young wild boar), grilled beef, saddle of lamb Catalane-style.

Serving temperature
14-17°C.

Soil types
Limestone, schists, granitic sands, pebbly terraces, gneiss, sands.

Grape varieties
Carignan, Grenache Noir, Syrah, Mourvèdre, Lladoner.

Ageing ability
3-10 years.

Côtes du Ventoux

Appellation
Côtes du
Ventoux AOC
Colours
Red (80%)
Rosé (15%)
White (5%)
Area
7,700 hectares

1973

This appellation is located to the east of the Rhône Valley, in an area sheltered from the Mistral wind by the mountain range of the Dentelles de Montmirail and the foothills of the Mont Ventoux and the Monts du Vaucluse. The Côtes du Ventoux AOC extends through 51 communes between Vaison-la-Romaine to the north and Apt to the south. It produces very fruity wines characterised by a careful balance of freshness and elegance.

Eye

• The reds are a clear, brilliant ruby-red colour.
• The rosés range from very pale pink to light ruby.
• The whites are limpid and brilliant with attractive green or yellow highlights.

Nose

• The red wines have characteristic aromas of red fruit and spice, occasionally complemented by notes of liquorice, woodiness, truffles and leather.
• The rosés reveal floral accents (rose, broom) in counterpoint to cherry and raspberry nuances.
• The whites offer a bouquet of floral fragrances (narcissus, iris) and fruit (pear, green apple, almond, citrus fruit).

Palate

• The reds are quaffable, with rather more finesse than body. Fruity, spicy aromas are followed by notes of leather and game.
• The rosés have flowing substance with dominant notes of red fruits.
• The whites echo the floral and fruity aromas on the nose.

Production
330,000
hectolitres

Main grape varieties
Reds: Grenache, Cinsaut, Syrah, Mourvèdre.
Whites: Clairette, Grenache Blanc, Bourboulenc, Roussanne.

Soil types
Mediterranean red soils; stone on calcareous substratum; sand overlaying molasse; pebbly, ancient alluvial soils.

Ageing ability
Reds: 3-5 years.
Whites and rosés: 1-2 years.
Primeur wines: drink within six months of the harvest.

Serving temperature
Reds: 15°C.
Rosés: 10°C.
Whites: 8-10°C.
Primeur: 12°C.

Choice of food
Red primeur wines: grilled meat.
Aged reds: meat in a sauce, feathered game, strong cheese.
Rosés: charcuterie.
Whites: apéritif.

Côtes du Vivarais

The Côtes du Vivarais vineyards straddle the Ardèche and Gard departments on the northwest limit of the southern Rhône Valley. The vines are planted on white chalky rubble on the plateaux surrounding the Gorges de l'Ardèche. Grenache and Syrah grapes produce red and rosé wines of exceptional finesse, dominated by aromas of little fruit.

1999

Appellation
AOC Côtes
du vivarais
Couleurs
Rouge (78 %)
Rosé (17 %)
Blanc (5 %)
Area
650 hectares

Eye
- The reds are characterised by their deep red tones with a purplish or crimson nuance.
- The rosés are an attractive salmon colour.
- The whites are light and brilliant.

Choice of food
Reds and rosés:
charcuterie,
grilled meat,
game, sweets
with zabaglione.
Rosés: good with
any meal.
Whites: fish.

**Serving
temperature**
Reds: 15-18°C.
Rosés and whites:
10-12°C.

Nose
- The reds create an immediate of impression of fruit, with frequent touches of spice, pepper and liquorice.
- The rosés have a very fruity nose (pineapple, grapefruit, redcurrant, blackcurrant).
- The whites have an intense, complex and expressive bouquet, that includes scents of lime blossom, jasmine, peach, apricot, pineapple and grapefruit.

Palate
- The reds display fairly soft tannins with a lightness and freshness that comes from the late maturation of Grenache and Syrah in this particular weather zone.
- The rosés are crisp, lively and long.
- The whites have rounded substance, steeped in the aromas detected on the nose.

**Ageing
ability**
1-3 years.

Production
21,240
hectolitres

**Main grape
varieties**
Reds: Grenache,
Syrah.
Whites: Grenache, Clairette,
Marsanne.

Soil types
Clayey limestone.

181

Cour-Cheverny

Appellation
Cour-Cheverny
AOC

Colour
White

Area
46 hectares

Production
1,980 hectolitres

1993

The Cour-Cheverny AOC is located to the south east of Blois in the heart of the Sologne viticultural region, extending from the Loire to the Grande Sologne on a terroir that is cut by three valleys, the Beuvron, the Cosson and the Bièvre. The area has a wine-growing history that goes back to François I. White wines that undergo long periods of fermentation are produced exclusively from Romorantin that thrives here on selected terrain.

Eye
Cour-Cheverny wine is a fairly deep straw-yellow, sometimes golden.

Nose
The aromas bring to mind apples, pears and acacia flowers. Honey aromas appear after a few years' ageing.

Palate
The attack is finesse itself, with hints of empyreuma and mineral aromas. The wine has respectable acidity and surprising length, with a hint of elegance on the finish.

Grape variety
Romorantin.

Soil types
Siliceous-clayey; sometimes clayey limestone.

Ageing ability
10 years.

Serving temperature
8-10°C.

Choice of food
Charcuterie, seafood, fish, grilled cockerel.

The Château de Cheverny, emblem of the Sologne vineyard.

Crémant

Crémant meaning 'effervescent' is the term used by appellations producing sparkling wines by the *Méthode Traditionnelle* (traditional method): Alsace, Burgundy, Bordeaux, Limoux, Jura, Die and the Loire. The wines are uncomplicated and elegant with a stream of tiny bubbles and characteristic aromas. The vineyards are generally planted on sandy-clayey soils.

CRÉMANT D'ALSACE (1976)
Light and fine.
Colours
White, rosé.
Area
1,690 ha
Production: 170,800hl
Grapevines
Pinot Blanc, Auxerrois, Riesling, Pinot Gris, Pinot Noir, Chardonnay

CRÉMANT DE BOURGOGNE (1975)
The closest to Champagne – of great finesse as a Blanc de Blancs, vigorous as a Blanc de Noirs.
Colours
White, rosé.
Area
550 ha
Production: 37,510hl
Grapevines
Pinot Noir, Chardonnay, Sacy, Aligoté, Gamay

CRÉMANT DU JURA (1995)
Strongly characteristic of the Jura terroirs.
Colours
White, rosé.
Area
157 ha
Production
15,080hl
Grapevines
Chardonnay, Poulsard, Pinot Noir, Pinot Gris, Trousseau, Savagnin

CRÉMANT DE BORDEAUX (1990)
Well-blended acidity on the palate.
Colours
White, rosé.
Area
101 ha
Production
5,752hl
Grapevines
Sémillon, Sauvignon, Muscadelle, Ugni Blanc, Colombard

CRÉMANT DE DIE (1993)
A fine, light mousse with aromas of green fruit.
Colour
White
Area
69 ha
Production
4,870 hl
Grapevine
Clairette.

CRÉMANT DE LOIRE (1975)
Many different grape varieties create a broad range of characteristics.
Colours
White, rosé
Area
497 ha
Production
37,020 hl
Grapevines
Whites: Chenin (Pineau de la Loire), Chardonnay.
Rosés: Cabernet Franc, Cabernet-Sauvignon, Pinot Noir, Pineau d'Aunis, Grolleau Noir and Gris

CRÉMANT DE LIMOUX (1990)
Elegance and roundness from Chardonnay and Chenin, freshness and finesse from Mauzac.
Colour
White
Area
1000 ha (approx)
Production
19,525 hl
Grapevines
Mauzac, Chenin, Chardonnay

Ageing ability
For early drinking.

Choice of food
Apéritif, entrées, fish, puddings.

Serving temperature
6-8°C

Crépy

Appellation
Crépy AOC

Colour
White

Area
72 hectares

Production
2,200 hectolitres

1 9 4 8

The Crépy appellation on the southern side of Lake Geneva features just one grape variety, the Chasselas, also found in the Valais region under the name of Fendant. The AOC produces a light dry, white wine with floral fragrances that often give way to a very particular hazelnut aftertaste.

Eye
This is a light, golden-brown wine.

Nose
Floral at first, followed by notes of fresh walnuts, hazelnuts and sweet almonds.

Palate
An overriding impression of power and fleshiness, with a touch of crystallised fruit on the finish that underscores the roundness of the wine.

Grape variety
Chasselas.

Soil types
Glacial moraine soils.

Ageing ability
2 years.

Serving temperature
10-12°C.

Choice of food
River fish, *raclette*, cheese (Reblochon, Mont-d'Or).

Criots-Bâtard-Montrachet

This Burgundy Grand Cru in the south of the Côte de Beaune occupies the south-southeast flank of a hillside adjoining Bâtard-Montrachet, planted at an elevation of 240 metres (787 feet). The wines are drier than those of Bienvenues and they age well. The idea of a Criots-Bâtard-Montrachet appellation came in 1939, at the same time as the area of Bienvenues-Bâtard-Montrachet was defined. The aim was to settle numerous claims relating to the vaguely defined Bâtard-Montrachet area. The Criots AOC lies in Chassagne whereas the Bienvenues AOC lies in Puligny.

1937

Appellation
Criots-Bâtard-Montrachet AOC

Classification
Grand Cru

Colour
White

Area
1 hectares 57 ares 21 centiares

Production
75 hectolitres

Eye
Criots-Bâtard-Montrachet is a crystalline green gold with a brilliant, limpid quality.

Nose
Extremely complex floral aromas of hawthorn, lime blossom and white fruit are expressed on a background of vanilla, sometimes tending towards flint and gunflint.

Palate
Generous texture, clean, persistent and enormously elegant.

Choice of food
Boned roast duck, quenelles of pike, Bresse poulard with cream and morels.

Serving temperature
12-14°C.

Ageing ability
10-15 years (up to 30 years for great vintages).

Soil types
Shallow brown limestone soils, warmer than those of Montrachet.

Grape variety
Chardonnay.

185

Crozes-Hermitage

Appellation
Crozes-
Hermitage AOC

Colours
Red
White (10%)

Area
1,200 hectares

Production
57,150
hectolitres

1937

The vines of Crozes-Hermitage surround the Hermitage appellation to the north and south of Tain-l'Hermitage. The area of vineyard in this vast, relatively flat region virtually equals the area of the peach orchards, and it is still expanding. A variety of geological outcrops produces wines of some diversity. Syrah reigns supreme for the production of fruity red wines, while the great white grape Marsanne produces crisp, quaffable whites.

Eye
• The reds have a lush purplish hue recalling plump, ripe burlat cherries.
• The whites are light in colour.

Nose
• The reds have a complex bouquet featuring ripe red and black-skinned fruit accompanied by a whole range of aromas: empyreuma (smoke, toast), the underwood, peat, humus, spices and liquorice, together with heady floral scents (peony).
• The whites reveal notes of almonds, passion fruit and white flowers.

Palate
• The reds have smooth, rounded tannins, finesse, substance, elegance and reserve. Of moderate ageing potential, they have less powerful tannins than Hermitage wines but they are more supple in their youth.
• Whites for early drinking may occasionally lack freshness but they are not generally marked by acidity. Good balance and agreeable persistence develop with time.

Grape varieties	**Soil types**	**Ageing ability**	**Serving temperature**	**Choice of food**
Syrah, Marsanne, Roussanne.	Granitic sand, more or less calcareous gravelly soils.	2-5 years (depending on the terroir and the vintage).	*Reds and certain very rich whites:* 16-18°C. *Whites:* 12-14°C.	*Reds:* charcuterie, relatively spicy foods. *Whites:* crudités, freshwater fish.

Échézeaux

The Echézeaux appellation is one of the greatest of the Burgundy Grands Crus. It is located in the centre of the Côte de Nuits, between Chambolle-Musigny and Vosne-Romanée, overlooking the Clos de Vougeot. The vineyard was created nine centuries ago by the Cîteaux monks, and takes its name from the word *chezeaux* meaning a group of houses or a hamlet. Les Echézeaux covers a much larger area than Grands-Echézeaux. Different *climats* with different aptitudes produce solid, robust, sappy wines of impressive ageing potential.

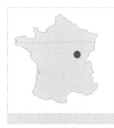

1937

Appellation
Echézeaux AOC

Classification
Grand Cru

Colour
Red

Area
36 hectares 25 ares 83 centiares

Production
1,200 hectolitres

Eye

A clear, vivid, limpid ruby-red, with nuances usually verging on fairly dark garnet or purplish-crimson.

Nose

With age the nose becomes peppery with aromas of musk, fur, leather, spices and dark plum, alongside scents of the underwood, moss, mushrooms, wet earth and game. Fruit in brandy and blackberry complete the aromatic range. Young wines offer aromas of pine, dog rose, rose, violet and fresh cherries.

Palate

Echézeaux is perfect at 2-3 years old, after which it closes to reopen at 5-10 years of age. The attack is spirited, the balance agreeably supported by fairly supple tannins, the roundness full of flavour and often raspberry-tasting.

Choice of food

Leg of lamb, red meat, game, cheese (Cîteaux, Saint-Nectaire, Coulommiers, Brillat-Savarin, Reblochon).

Serving temperature
15-16°C.

Ageing ability
10-15 years (15-20 years for great vintages).

Grape variety
Pinot Noir.

Soil types
Bajocian marl covered in pebbles.

Entre-Deux-Mers

Appellations
Entre-Deux-Mers
AOC
Entre-Deux-
Mers-Haut-
Benauge AOC

Colour
White

Area
1,778 hecctares

Production
110,240
hectolitres

1 9 3 7

GRAND VIN SEC DE BORDEAUX

CHATEAU BONNET
ENTRE-DEUX-MERS
Appellation Entre-Deux-Mers Contrôlée
1993
11.2%vol ANDRÉ LURTON 750 ml
MIS EN BOUTEILLE AU CHATEAU
PRODUIT DE FRANCE

T he term *entre-deux-mers* appeared in the Middle Ages, referring to this region's particular situation between two tidal rivers, the Garonne and the Dordogne. The appellation consists of a predominantly argillaceous limestone plateau and excludes the hillsides overlooking the Garonne and the communes of Vayres and Arveyres. It is sufficiently vast however to account for a positive mosaic of terroirs. The most important grape variety is Sauvignon, source of a highly distinctive aroma that is especially appreciated in young wines. Entre-Deux-Mers is dry, crisp and fruity with a markedly sappy personality.

Main grape varieties
Sémillon,
Sauvignon,
Muscadelle.

Soil types
Argillaceous
limestone,
argillaceous-
siliceous, gravel
and silt.

Ageing ability
2-3 years.

Entre-Deux-Mers-Haut-Benauge

Nine communes around Targon have the right to add Haut-Benauge to the Entre-Deux-Mers appellation: Arbis, Cantois, Escoussans, Gornac, Ladaux, Mourens, Soulignac, Saint-Pierre-de-Bar and Targon. The wines come from the same area as those of the Bordeaux-Haut-Benauge AOC. Both AOCs take their name from the old viscounty that was ruled over by the Château de Benauge in Arbis.

Eye
Entre-Deux-Mers comes in a wide variety of shades, although it is typically pale gold.

Nose
Very fragrant, with elegant fruity and floral fragrances, from the Sémillon and Sauvignon grapes respectively. Wines from certain crus have an extraordinary wealth of aromas encompassing floral notes and scents of citrus fruit and exotic fruit.

Serving temperature
8-10°C.

Choice of food
Hors d'oeuvres,
seafood,
grilled fish.

Palate
Like all dry white wines, the character of an Entre-Deux-Mer varies with the terroir. Predominantly argillaceous limestone soils produce some of the best wines, with a distinctive balance and texture on the palate matched by the finesse of their bouquet. Siliceous clay soils give the wines a full-bodied, quaffable quality that could be described as 'more palate than nose'. Wines from *boulbènes* on the other hand (the silty soils characteristic of this area) have a delicate, light palate that contrasts with the intensity of their markedly fresh and floral bouquet.

Faugères

This terroir is in the north of the Hérault department, backing onto the first foothills of the Montagne Noire, between the Orb Valley and the Béziers plain. The vegetation on these schistous hillsides is quite distinct from the neighbouring limestone *garrigue*, a typical example being the very fragrant cistus. This is rugged countryside, very much like the Cévennes, with a Mediterranean climate characterised by hot summers and dry, mild winters. Rainfall is very irregular from one year to the next, in the range 800-1000 mm (12-15 inches). The AOC produces red wines and a few rosés. As with most southerly vineyards, the most complete wines are obtained from blends of several grape varieties.

1 9 8 2

Appellation
Faugères AOC
Colours
Red
Rosé (15%)
Area
1,778 hectares
Production
75,560
hectolitres

Eye
• Red Faugères wines are rich in colour with purplish highlights in their youth, developing more crimson nuances.
• The rosés are light and bright.

Choice of food
Light and fruity reds:
white meat.
Full-bodied reds:
meat in a sauce, game.
Rosés: some shellfish, charcuterie, snails.

Nose
• The reds are marked by empyreumatic fragrances (toast, roasted coffee, smoke) combined with aromas of red berries and spices. They reach peak maturity at 2-3 years, after which leathery, animal notes start to appear.
• The rosés have a fine floral nose, sometimes with hints of peach skin.

Palate
• The reds are full-bodied, rounded and powerful. With age, they acquire well-blended tannins of great finesse that give them broader aromatic expression and surprising persistence.
• The rosés have a balance of flavours built on roundness.

Serving temperature
Reds: 16-18°C.
Rosés: 11-13°C.

Ageing ability
Reds: 4-5 years.
Rosés: for early drinking.

Soil types
Schist.

Grape varieties
Grenache Noir, Syrah, Mourvèdre, Carignan, Cinsaut.

189

Fiefs Vendéens

Appellation
Fiefs Vendéens
AOVDQS
(followed by
the name of the
production area:
Brem-sur-Mer,
Mareuil, Vix or
Pissotte).

1 9 8 4

There are four distinct categories to this appellation. Brem-sur-Mer, on the Atlantic coast to the north and south of Sables-d'Olonne, is an area of dry iodised white wine. Mareuil, to the southeast of La Roche-sur-Yon, produces reds and rosés of great finesse. Meatier wines come from Pissotte and Vix, the first to the north of and the second to the south of Fontenay-le-Comte. These terroirs far from the Loire produce wines with the spirit, lightness and natural fruit of Loire wines.

Colour
Red (40%)
Rosé (45%)
White (15%)
Area
392 hectares
Production
20,790 hectolitres

Soil types
Clay on
schist or
limestone.

Eye
• The reds are a vivid ruby-red colour.
• Pinot Noir vinified as rosé wine yields light, eye-of-partridge coloured wines. Rosés based on Gamay or Cabernet are more purplish.

Grape varieties
Reds: Gamay Noir or Pinot Noir (50% minimum), Cabernet Franc or Sauvignon, Négrette.
Whites: Chenin (50% minimum), Chardonnay, Sauvignon (Vix), Melon de Bourgogne (Pissotte), Grolleau Gris (Brem).

• The whites are distinguished by their pale gold tones with green highlights.

Ageing ability
1-2 years.

Nose
• The reds have an animal side to them with notes of red fruit and green pepper. Wines produced from Pinot Noir have a cherry theme, while those produced from Négrette are wonderfully light.
• The rosés are built around red fruit (redcurrant, strawberry, raspberry).
• White wines based on Chenin have aromas of green apple, lemon and quince, with sustained acidity. Wines blended with Chardonnay offer aromas of exotic fruit and toast, while Sauvignon plays on notes of boxwood and broom and Brem is associated with iodised accents.

Palate
• The red wines are light, delicate and not very tannic.
• The rosés are lively.
• The whites have distinctively supple body.

Serving temperature
Reds: 16-17°C.
Whites and rosés: 12°C.

Choice of food
Reds: ham with *mogettes* (large haricot beans), green cabbage with bacon, red meat, local snails.
Rosés: shrimps.
Whites: seafood, fish (mackerel).

Fitou

The Fitou vineyard boasts the best terroirs of the Massif des Corbières. The location is very original. To the east is maritime Fitou skirting the lagoon of Leucate – a place of stones, dryness and wind. To the west is the inland sector, sheltered by the Mont Tauch and divided into two basins. Fitou was the first officially recognised Languedoc appellation. Today it only produces red wine, from the Carignan grape, which is originally from Spain and so in its element here. Provided yields can be kept low, mature Carignan vines can give superb results. Such is the case in Fitou.

1948

Appellation
Fitou AOC
Colour
Red
Area
2,565 hectares
Production
93,580 hectolitres

Eye
An intense ruby-red colour, sometimes dark in young wines, maturing into orange then amber nuances. Great Fitou wines need time to age.

Nose
Aromas of red fruits (blackberry, raspberry, cherry), possibly discreet in the young wine but growing dominant after a period in the cellar. Fruit is accompanied by spicy scents like pepper, with occasional woody notes of vanilla that are typical of Carignan wines at peak maturity, whether or not they have aged in wood. Age also brings on notes of very ripe fruit or prunes, combined with aromas of toast, roasted almonds and sometimes leather.

Palate
Somewhat closed and wild in the first months, these wines need at least one year's ageing to open up and express their power and full-bodied fleshiness. Maturity brings warm aromas of ripe fruit and roasted dried fruit that echo the scents on the nose. Fitou wines are rich in tannins, the mark of Carignan. They may be a little rustic in the first months but they grow progressively rounder over the years, helped by the Grenache Noir that contributes fat, roundness and warmth.

Choice of food
Charcuterie, red meat, game (boar, partridge, hare).

Serving temperature
16-17°C.

Soil types
Argillaceous limestone in the maritime sector and the Bassin de Tuchan-Paziols; schistous soil in the Bassin de Villeneuve and in Cascastel; a few stony terraces at the bottom of the Bassin de Tuchan-Paziols.

Grape varieties
Carignan (60-70%), Grenache Noir, Mourvèdre, Syrah.

Ageing ability
3-10 years.

Fixin

Appellations
Fixin AOC
Fixin Premier
Cru AOC
Colours
Red
White (limited
production)
Area
107 hectares 40
ares 28 centiares
Production
3,870 hectolitres

1938

The Premiers Crus
Arvelets
Clos de la Perrière
Clos du Chapitre
Clos Napoléon
Hervelets

Grape varieties
Reds:
Pinot Noir.
Whites:
Chardonnay.

Ageing ability
Reds:
5-10 years.
Whites:
3-6 years.

Soil types
Brown
limestone, more
marly in some
climats (such as
Les Hervelets)
in the Premier
Cru. Marly-
limestone in the
Villages
appellations.

The Fixin Premiers Crus lie to the south of the Marsannay area in the Côte de Nuits, on the upper part of the hillside on brown limestone soils. The most outstanding *climats* are Les Arvelets, Les Hervelets and Le Chapitre. The Villages appellation is located somewhat lower down on limestone and marl soils. Fixin wines are powerful and structured, and they age well.

Eye
• The reds are a strong dark purple, limpid and brilliant, enhanced by purplish highlights. Some wines are softer in colour. Others by contrast are close to cherry black.
• The whites are golden straw-yellow.

Nose
• The reds have a bouquet divided between floral aromas (violet, peony), fruity scents (morello cherry, blackcurrant, blackberry, sometimes quince) and animal, musky or peppery aromas. Notes of cherry stones and liquorice are common and there may sometimes be a hint of baked peach and brambles.
• The whites are dominated by a bouquet of dog roses on a mineral background with a lightly Muscat fragrance.

Serving temperature
Reds: 14-16°C.
Whites: de 12-14°C.

Palate
• Often tannic and a little hard in youth, the reds need a few years to reach maturity. The attack is then round and spirited, and the structure is solid. These are very persistent wines in good years, remarkably fat with a fine delicate texture. Good acidity promises good ageing. Fixin is regarded as a winter wine because it needs time to mature. Each Premier Cru has its own particular characteristics: firm and distinguished from the Clos de la Perrière; often harsh in youth from the Clos du Chapitre, but then remarkably radiant; appealing and tender from Les Hervelets and Les Arvelets.
• The whites are clean and pleasant-tasting.

Choice of food
Reds: poached eggs in red wine, Bresse chicken with morels.
Whites: gourmet fish (monkfish).

Fleurie

The Fleurie area is one of the most prestigious of the Beaujolais vineyards, with Moulin-à-Vent to the north, Morgon to the south and Chiroubles to the west. The vines are planted on very steep granite slopes or shingle soils of crystalline or volcanic origin. Fleurie wines, made from Gamay, are vivacious and fruity, often considered to be the most 'feminine' of the Beaujolais crus.

1 9 3 6

Appellations
Fleurie AOC
Fleurie AOC
(followed by
the name of the
climat of origin)

Colour
Red

Area
864 hectares

Production
49,690
hectolitres

Eye

Young Fleurie wines are a beautiful purplish-red, characteristic of granite soils. Mature wines acquire a carmine, ruby hue. Intensity of colour is linked to the *climat* of origin: brighter on shallow soils, darker from the deeper terrain.

Nose

Delicate at first with floral notes such as violet and iris, followed by fragrances of red berries (raspberries). Certain blends express fragrances of wild blackberry or blackcurrant.

Palate

The attack is straightforward but not aggressive thanks to discreet acidity and tannins of great finesse. The fragrances line the palate as fleshiness, roundness and velvetiness combine to create a lingering fruity sensation with no loss of lightness or elegance. Grapes from particularly hard granite plots, such as Les Moriers or La Roilette, produce surprisingly concentrated wines.

Choice of food
White meats, leg of lamb, *andouil-lette* sausage.

Serving temperature
13-15°C.

Ageing ability
2-5 years.

Grape variety
Gamay Noir.

Soil types
Granitic sand.

Floc de Gascogne

Appellation
Floc de Gascogne
AOC

Colours
Rosé
White

Area
15,000 hectares

1990

Grape varieties
Rosés: Cabernet
Franc, Cabernet-
Sauvignon, Côt,
Fer-Servadou or
Pinenc, Merlot
and Tannat (the
latter no more
than 50% of
total plantings).
Whites:
Colombard,
Folle Blanche
and Ugni Blanc
(these three
grape varieties
must represent
at least 70% and
no single variety
can exceed
50%); subsidiary
varieties are Gros
Manseng, Petit
Manseng,
Mauzac, Sauvig-
non, Sémillon.

Production
Up to 60
hectolitres per
hectare (hl/ha)

Soil types
Boulbènes
(see page 62),
gravels.

Ageing ability
Drink within
the year.

F loc de Gascogne is a liqueur wine (16-18% proof) made by chemical sterilisation with Armagnac (see page 116). It is produced in the geographical area of the Armagnac AOC, a viticultural region in the Pyrenean foothills that covers three departments: Gers, Les Landes and Lot-et-Garonne. Wine-growers here have established a system based not on registered plots like wines, nor on a simple geographical area like brandies or eaux-de-vie in general. The definition of this appellation is based on lists of plots which are approved annually by the INAO (*Institut National des Appellations d'Origine*).

Eye
• Floc de Gascogne rosés are often dark ruby-red.
• The whites are a brilliant straw-yellow.

Nose
• The rosés reveal aromas of red fruits (blackcurrant, strawberry) and flowers (violets).
• The whites are floral, light and lively, making this a crisp, agreeable wine to drink as an apéritif. Notes of fresh grapes often mingle with notes of honey, dried fruit and peach.

Palate
The impression is of a rounded, rich, persistent wine with a good balance of sweetness and freshness. Overall harmony depends on the quality of the Armagnac used in the chemical sterilisation.

Serving temperature
Chilled.

Choice of food
Apéritif; foie gras, patisserie, ice cream, fresh fruit salad.

Fronsac

On the Fronsac bluff, overlooking the confluence of the Dordogne and the Isle rivers, is a fortress built by Charlemagne to control navigation and the land route to Bordeaux. The Fronsac region today is famous for its hillside terroir that lies tucked away from main thoroughfares, spreading over six communes. Two communes within the Fronsac AOC are entitled to a specific appellation: Fronsac and Saint-Michel-de-Fronsac, which is the domain of Canon-Fronsac.

1 9 3 7

Appellation
Fronsac AOC
Colour
Red
Area
828 hectares
Production
46,570
hectolitres

Eye
Dense colour, varying from dark red with purplish highlights to dark ruby-red or crimson. Either way, this is sure to be a very powerful wine.

Nose
Very intense and varied fragrances ranging from red fruit to spices. Closer inspection reveals hints of black-skinned fruit, coffee and toast.

Palate
Fronsac's most typical characteristics are often expressed by its tannins, which are as dense as they are powerful but always elegant and usually with a well-rounded, beautifully ripe quality.

Château La Rivière.

Choice of food
Lampreys
Bordeaux-style, red meat, game, cheese.

Serving temperature
16-17°C.

Soil types
Limestone, argillaceous limestone, sandstone molasse.

Main grape varieties
Merlot, Cabernet Franc, Cabernet-Sauvignon and Malbec.

Ageing ability
4-9 years.

195

Gaillac

Appellations
Gaillac AOC
(red, rosé and
white)
Gaillac Doux
AOC (sweet)
Gaillac Mousseux
AOC (sparkling)

1 9 3 8

The Gaillac vineyard extends across 73 communes on either side of the Tarn river, some 50 kilometres (31 miles) to the northwest of Toulouse and to the west of Albi. Here, a diversity of different terroirs – terraces, hillside and plain – produce a wide range of wines: reds, dry or sweet whites, rosés, sparkling and slightly sparkling (Gaillac Perlé). Part of this appellation's originality is due to local grape varieties such as Mauzac, Ondenc, Len de l'El and Duras.

Gaillac Perlé AOC
(lightly sparkling)
Gaillac Premières
Côtes AOC

Colours

Red

Rosé

White (28%)

Area

2,687 hectares

Production

163,300 hectolitres

Main grape varieties

Reds: Ruras, Braucol, Gamay, Syrah, Cabernet-Sauvignon, Cabernet Franc, Merlot.

Whites: Mauzac, Len de l'El, Ondenc, Muscadelle, Sémillon, Sauvignon.

Soil types

Gravelly clay, molasse, argillaceous limestone, limestone.

Ageing ability

Reds: 4-5 years.

Whites and rosés: for early drinking

Choice of food

Reds: roasted meat, casserole (daube), cheese (Bleu d'Auvergne).

Whites: river fish, crayfish.

Perlé wines: as an apéritif.

Sweet whites: cheese (Roquefort).

Eye

- The reds are a rich dark ruby, sign of their warm character.
- The rosés have a salmon hue.
- The dry whites are golden. The sparkling wines, especially those made by the *Méthode Gaillacoise*, have abundant mousse. The slightly sparkling, Gaillac Perlé wines twinkle with delicate bubbles on a pale background.

Nose

- The reds develop an extremely rich pallet of aromas dominated by fruit and notes of spice.
- The rosés combine red fruit aromas with scents of acid drops.
- The whites, especially the lightly sparkling or sparkling wines made by the *Méthode Gaillacoise*, have a distinctive bouquet marked by aromas such as white peach or baked apple, William pears and spicy or honeyed notes.

Palate

- Red Primeur wines produced from Gamay are supple, round, quaffable and fruity. Gaillac wines intended for ageing on the other hand have solid structure built on rounded, spicy tannins. The result is a warm, fleshy wine.
- The rosés are fresh and fruity, light and easy to drink. Like the whites, they are intended for early drinking.
- The white wines, especially when produced from Mauzac, have typical characteristics that vary according to style. Dry whites are lively with a respectable hint of acidity; sweet whites are rich and suave; the sparkling wines are fruity in nature; the ideal Perlé wine is as fragrant on the palate as on the nose, with a light touch of welcome bitterness that adds a refreshing quality.

Serving temperature

Reds: 16°C.
Whites: 8-10°C.

The abbey of Saint-Michel in Gaillac, on the right-bank of the Tarn, was built under Carolingian rule and established the reputation of the Gaillac vineyard.

The Méthode Gaillacoise

Sparkling Gaillac wines may be made by the *Méthode Traditionnelle* or the *Méthode Gaillacoise*, (artisanal): fermentation is restarted by allowing residual sugar to ferment in the bottle, fermentation in the tank having ended of its own accord. These wines contain no *liqueur de tirage*.

Gevrey-Chambertin

Appellations
Gevrey-
Chambertin
AOC
Gevrey-
Chambertin
Premier Cru
AOC

1 9 3 6

Colour
Red

Area
410 ha (in Gevrey-
Chambertin and
Brochon), including
50 ha of Premier Cru
(in Gevrey-Chambertin).

Production
16,700 hl, including
2,500 hl of Premier Cru.

Grape variety
Pinot Noir.

Soil types
Rich in
limestone and
pebbles,
becoming more
argillaceous
further down
the slope.

Gevrey-Chambertin lies at the foot of the Combe de Lavaux, some 12 kilometres (7.5 miles) south of Dijon. It is one of the premier wine producing villages of the Côte, representing the whole spectrum of Burgundy appellations. The slopes to the south of the Combe de Lavaux are home to the seven Grands Crus that carry the name of Chambertin: Ruchottes, Mazis, Clos de Bèze, Chapelle, Latricières, Chambertin and Charmes. To the north are the gravelly soils of the Premiers Crus. The Gevrey-Chambertin appellation lies mainly at the foot of the hills. These shallow, brownish-red soils mixed with pebbles and limestone are home to Pinot Noir that yields concentrated wines with sublime overtones.

**Ageing
ability**
3-15 years.

**Serving
temperature**
Young wines:
12-14°C.
*More mature
wines:* 16°C.

Choice of food
Coq au vin,
beef daube,
zander in red
wine, cheese
(Chaource).

Eye

Highly coloured with a youthful radiance (vivacious ruby-red) that often darkens to become almost black with reddish highlights.

Left: Château Gevrey-Chambertin

Below: individual vine-plots are marked out by low walls.

Nose

Young Gevrey-Chambertin wines have aromas of strawberry, blackcurrant, violet and reseda. Age brings fragrances of leather, fur and liquorice. Certain *climats* and methods of vinification produce wines with aromas of earth or animal burrows, humus and venison, often with foxy notes – Les Cazetiers is a good example.

Palate

Foursquare and powerful – a great Burgundy. Good strong body, well-balanced by the nature of the terroir which is one of the most gravelly on the Côte de Nuits. Current methods of vinification however tend to produce more spontaneous, less austere wines, richer in fruit and very agreeable within just two or three years of the harvest.

The Premiers Crus

Au Closeau
Aux Combottes
Bel Air
La Bossière
Les Cazetiers
Champeaux
Champonnet
Cherbaudes
Clos des Varoilles
Clos du Chapitre
Clos Prieur
Clos Saint-Jacques
Combe au Moine
Les Corbeaux
Craipillot
En Ergot
Estournelles-Saint-Jacques
Fonteny
Les Goulots
Issarts
Lavaut Saint-Jacques
Petite Chapelle
Petits Cazetiers
La Perrière
Poissenot
La Romanée

Gigondas

Appellation
Gigondas AOC

Colours
Red
Rosé (4%)

Area
1,312 hectares

Production
44,000
hectolitres

1971

Grape varieties
Grenache Noir,
Syrah,
Mourvèdre,
Cinsaut.

Soil types
Sandy soils on
molasse; soils of
water rounded
stones from
alluvial deposits.

The village of Gigondas backs onto one of the loveliest beauty spots in the valley: the massif of the Dentelles de Montmirail. This terroir had to wait patiently for several centuries before conquering the old olive groves and asserting its viticultural personality. Today, thanks to a policy that favours plantings of Grenache Noir and strictly limited yields, Gigondas has acquired a reputation for solid, full-bodied and very structured red wines that have excellent ageing potential. Red Gigondas wines together with Châteauneuf-du-Pape are the lords of the lower Rhône Valley.

Ageing ability
Reds:
8-10 years.
Rosés:
2-3 years.

The Gigondas vineyard between the Mont Ventoux (above) and the Dentelles de Montmirail (on the right) enjoys a dry Mediterranean climate.

Eye

• The red wines are often deep, dark, even austere in colour, acquiring a delightfully delicate brick-red hue with age. Their dense substance as they flow into the glass is a sign of concentrated, carefully selected grapes.

• The rosés have the same depth of colour as the reds.

Nose

• The red wines have initially fruity aromas (red fruit, such as blackberries, blackcurrants, soft fruits, kirsch) followed by scents of roasting (coffee, cocoa), spices, liquorice and crystallised fruit. Older vintages have hints of animal notes – leather, fur and game – that make them the ideal accompaniment to warming, winter dishes.

• The rosés are distinguished by their scents of baked fruit and roasted almonds.

Palate

• The reds, especially the young wines, are very full-bodied with a tannic side to them that needs to age slowly to allow these wines to come into their own. This strong structure combined with rich alcohol content makes up for weak acidity and provides good ageing support.

• The rosés are heady and elegant, the ideal wine to sharpen the apetite at summer parties.

Serving temperature
Reds: 15-16°C.
Rosés: 10°C.

Choice of food
Reds: game (hare, young boar, duck), beef daube.
Rosés: charcuterie, grilled foods.

Givry

Appellations
Givry AOC
Givry Premier
Cru AOC

Colours
Red
White (17%)

Area
282 hectares

Production
11,110
hectolitres

1946

T he village of Givry has given its name to one of the five appellations of the Côte Chalonnaise in Saône-et-Loire that continues on the same line of hills as the celebrated Côte d'Or. It was the monks of Cluny and then the Cistercians who developed viticulture along these hills that border the eastern face of the northern Massif Central. Givry produces predominantly red wine from Pinot Noir.

Eye
• Givry red is bright red with carmine or crimson nuances, often with attractive purple highlights.
• The whites are limpid and lively and light gold in colour, without being yellow which is more a sign of maturity.

The Premiers Crus
Les Bois Chevaux
Cellier aux Moines
Clos Charlé
Clos de la Barraude
Clos du Cras Long
Clos du Vernoy
Clos Jus
Clos Marceaux
Clos Marole
Clos Saint-Paul
Clos Saint-Pierre
Clos Salomon
Les Grands Prétans
Les Grandes Vignes
Petit Marole
Servoisine

Nose
• The reds have a bouquet of violets, strawberries or blackberries plus shades of liquorice and animal notes (wild cats) with sometimes a hint of spice (cloves).
• The whites may be honeyed and lemony, recalling lime blossom, lilies and nuts (hazelnuts).

Palate
• The reds are spicy and quite tannic in youth, becoming supple and appealing with age. They are often best tasted after 3-5 years' cellaring.
• The whites are firm and harmonious, poised between sweetness and acidity, with plenty of grip on the palate. They have good ageing ability.

**Grape
varieties**
Reds:
Pinot Noir.
Whites:
Chardonnay.

Ageing ability
Reds: 5-8 years.
Whites:
3-6 years.

Soil types
Brown or calcic limestone from weathered Jurassic limestone, sometimes marly limestone.

**Serving
temperature**
Reds: 14-15°C.
Whites: 11-13°C.

Choice of food
Reds: charcuterie, eggs poached in red wine, game terrine, duck cooked with cherries, grilled chicken.
Whites: mussels à la crème, lobster bisque, fish with white butter sauce.

La Grande Rue

This narrow strip of land between Romanée and Romanée-Conti to the north and La Tâche to the south, is one of the flagship vineyards of the Côte d'Or and the most recent of the Vosne Grands Crus. The *lieu-dit* of La Grande Rue, first mentioned in 1450, is wholly owned by the Domaine Lamarche, producing chewy, elegant wines that are long on the palate and benefit from being decanted. They grow even better with age and are well worth waiting for.

1 9 9 2

Appellation
La Grande Rue AOC
Classification
Grand Cru
Colour
Red
Area
2 hectares
Production
57 hectolitres

Eye
Magnificent, brilliant garnet-red.

Nose
Characteristic aromas of violets, raspberries and wild berries with hints of smokiness and liquorice.

Palate
Dense and chewy with great structure and all the qualities of well-controlled ageing in the wood. La Grande Rue wines have excellent ageing potential and always develop very harmoniously.

The village of Vosne-Romanée.

Grape variety
Pinot Noir.

Soil types
Higher up: rendzina on Prémeaux marly limestone; lower down, slightly deeper brown limestone soils.

Choice of food
Game, red meat, cheese (Cîteaux, Brillat-Savarin).

Serving temperature
14-15°C.

Ageing ability
15-20 years.

Grands-Echézeaux

Appellation
Grands-
Echézeaux AOC
Classification
Grand Cru
Colour
Red
Area
9 hectares 13 ares
11 centiares
Production
250 hectolitres

1 9 3 7

Grands-Echézeaux, between Chambolle-Musigny and Vosne-Romanée, is one of the Grands Crus that have made the Côte de Nuits so famous among Côte d'Or wines. Just look at its neighbours. Immediately next door is the Clos Vougeot, separated only by a wall between the two vineyards. To the east on the upper part of the slopes is Echézeaux. To the north along the same hillside is Musigny. Grands-Echézeaux like the Clos Vougeot was founded by the Cîteaux monks in the 12th century. Its wines have power, distinction and longevity.

Eye
A rather dark shade of garnet with a violet-crimson hue.

Nose
A rich, complex bouquet reveals notes of pepper and spice, animal odours, plums and a hint of the underwood, complemented by aromas of well-controlled wood ageing.

Palate
Grands-Echézeaux is subtle and refined, with the complexity of a Burgundy and the promise of Pinot Noir from an ideal Pinot Noir terroir. This is a wine that lives up to its name: truly a great Echézeaux, with dense texture, a tight weave and that added touch of class and sensuality.

Grape variety
Pinot Noir.

Soil types
Argillaceous limestone over a slab of Bajocian limestone.

Ageing ability
10-15 years (15-20 years for great vintages).

Serving temperature
16-17°C.

Choice of food
Leg of lamb, roast beef, feathered game, cheese (Cîteaux, Saint-Nectaire, Coulommiers, Brillat-Savarin, Reblochon).

Graves, Graves Supérieures

This well-known terroir is one of the few to have given its name to an appellation. It lies on undulating pebble and gravel terraces on the left bank of the Garonne, bordered to the southwest by the forest of Les Landes. In the Middle Ages this was the Bordeaux vineyard that produced most of the claret, those light red wines that were so popular in England. Today the Graves region produces red wines and also dry and sweet white wines – the Graves Supérieures. The vast area of appellation follows the left bank of the Garonne for 60 kilometres (37 miles) as far as Langon. In 1987, the northern zone near Bordeaux was granted the Pessac-Léognan AOC.

1937

Appellations
Graves AOC
Graves Supérieures AOC

Colours
Red
White (dry and sweet)

Area
3,124 hectares

Production
Graves: 175,000 hectolitres
Graves Supérieures: 19,000 hectolitres

Soil types
Gravel and gravel terraces on a bedrock of clay and starfish limestone.

Ageing ability
7-15 years.

Main grape varieties
Reds: Merlot, Cabernet-Sauvignon and Cabernet franc.
Whites: Sémillon, Sauvignon et Muscadelle.

205

Eye

• The reds are a classic Bordeaux red, poised between ruby and crimson with dark shimmering hues that promise good ageing potential.

• The whites are a pale gold with green highlights or pale yellow with gold highlights – colour is often an indication of the wine-making process.

• The Graves Supérieures are yellow with good depth of colour.

PRODUCE OF FRANCE

CLOS FLORIDENE

GRAVES SEC

APPELLATION GRAVES CONTRÔLÉE

1994

Denis et Florence DUBOURDIEU, EARL
PROPRIÉTAIRES A 33210 PUJOLS/CIRON FRANCE
MIS EN BOUTEILLE A LA PROPRIÉTÉ
12,5 % vol. 750ml

Nose

• The reds are among the most typical of the Gironde region and many are recognisable by their violet-scented bouquet with smoky overtones. They also reveal scents of red fruits and notes ranging from game, mocha and roasted coffee to flowers.

• The aromas most characteristic of the white wines are broom, citrus and exotic fruit.

• The Graves Supérieures are supple and elegant and distinguished by their highly varied bouquet (citrus fruit, white peaches, apricots and acacia).

Palate

• This is where the reds come into their own, revealing a personality built on a balance of strength, body and roundness. The best of them are a triumph of fullness and volume, with no loss of charm. The elegance of the bouquet comes through on the palate, ending on a long velvety finish.

• The whites are full-bodied and meaty, fresh with the scent of flowers and highly aromatic. The best whites may be laid down for several years.

• The Graves Supérieures are mouth-filling, fat and well-structured.

Villa Bel Air is a typical example of an 18th century Bordeaux chartreuse (charterhouse).

Choice of food

Reds:
red meat, feathered game, cheese.

Dry whites:
seafood, fish in a sauce, white meat.

Sweet whites:
exotic cuisine, puddings, fruit salad.

Serving temperature

Reds:
16-17°C.

Dry whites:
10-12°C.

Sweet whites:
8-9°C.

Graves de Vayres

Vayres lies to the northwest of the Entre-Deux-Mers plateau on the left bank of the Dordogne. It is famous for its imposing Renaissance Château that overlooks the river. The vineyard is planted on pebbly terrace slopes formed from deposits of gravel and sand. Graves de Vayre red wines are supple and fruity. The whites used to be sweet but are now mainly dry and similar to Entre-Deux-Mers wines.

1937

Appellation
Graves de Vayres AOC

Colours
Red
White (25%)

Area
1,570 hectares

Production
33,870 hectolitres

Eye
• The reds have intense colour, glinting with ruby-red and cherry highlights.
• The whites are a pale yellow.

Nose
• The reds have a fruity bouquet characteristic of Merlot that gives them great charm and freshness.
• The whites offer elegant fragrances mingling fruit and flowers, broom and boxwood.

Palate
• The reds are supple and well-balanced with good body that tends to soften quite quickly although they can also improve with a few years' cellaring.
• The whites are crisp and fresh with good balance supported by rich, supple substance. The fruit sensations detected on the nose linger on the palate.

Serving temperature
Reds: 16-17°C.
Whites: 10-12°C.

Choice of food
Reds: white meat, poultry, cheese.
Whites: entrées, seafood.

Ageing ability
Reds: 3-7 years.
Whites: drink within the year.

Grape varieties
Reds: Merlot, Cabernet-Sauvignon, Cabernet Franc.
Whites: Sémillon, Sauvignon, Muscadelle.

Soil types
Gravel and sand.

Griotte-Chambertin

Appellation
Griotte-Chambertin AOC

Classification
Grand Cru

Colour
Red

Area
2 hectares 69 ares 18 centiares

Production
110 hectolitres

1937

This tiny cru to the north of the Côte d'Or has earned a great reputation. It is one of the seven privileged Gevrey-Chambertin *climats* entitled to bear the name of one of the greatest Burgundy wines. Griotte-Chambertin is planted in an intermediate dip to the east of the Route des Grands Crus and Chambertin. Like Chambertin, it has the advantage of an east-facing aspect. The name *Griotte* does not come from wild cherries but from the word *crais* meaning pebbly terrain. These stony soils produce wines that are well supported by tannins but nonetheless renowned for their finesse.

Eye
Deep, dark red, reminiscent of cherry.

Nose
The main impression is of lush, ripe red- and black-skinned fruit with underlying notes of liquorice.

Palate
Griotte-Chambertin combines finesse and strength with a structured body and good length.

Grape variety
Pinot Noir.

Soil types
Pebbly terrrain, stony soils on Bajocian limestone substratum.

Ageing ability
10-15 years (up to 50 years for the great vintages).

Serving temperature
Young wines: 12-14°C.
More mature wines: 15-16°C.

Choice of food
River fish (trout, poached pike, zander), coq au vin, white meat, cheese (Ami du Chambertin), vine peaches with Chambertin.

Gros-Plant du Pays Nantais

The Gros-Plant du Pays Nantais AOVDQS has a production area that almost entirely overlays that of Muscadet, extending across 92 communes situated mainly to the south of the Loire around Nantes. The grape variety is Gros Plant, originally from the Charentes region where it is known as Folle Blanche and used in Cognac production. Gros Plant here produces a dry, light white wine that is sometimes aged on lees to intensify its crispness, finesse and bouquet. It is especially delicious with oysters.

1954

Appellation
Gros-Plant du Pays Nantais AOVDQS
Colour
White
Area
2,370 hectares
Production
157,000 hectolitres

Eye
Pale with brilliant light green highlights and sometimes a slightly *perlant* quality, indicating bottling on lees in the spring following the vintage.

Nose
Dominant vegetal and floral aromas (white flowers), together with mineral notes and hints of citrus fruit (lemon, grapefruit).

Palate
Lively, nervous, and astonishingly light (approximately 11% proof) and crisp.

Soil types
Sand and Eocene gravel, Pliocene silt, brown soils on granite and metamorphic rock.

Choice of food
Seafood.

Serving temperature
8-9°C.

Ageing ability
For early drinking.

Grape variety
Gros Plant (Folle Blanche).

209

Haut-Médoc

1936

Appellation
Haut-Médoc
AOC

Colour
Red

Area
4,260 hectares

Production
250,000
hectolitres

Grape varieties
Cabernet-
Sauvignon,
Cabernet Franc,
Merlot, Petit-
Verdot, Malbec.

Soil types
Gravel and
argillaceous
limestone.

This AOC covers a fairly vast area of the Médoc to the south of the Gironde, alongside the top part of the estuary, north of Bordeaux. It includes six communal appellations boasting the most prestigious terroirs and including the majority of the Crus Classés. Here, impressive gravel mounds create ideal conditions for the Cabernet-Sauvignon. These factors, plus numerous châteaux estates and a very active wine trade account for the quality of this vineyard that includes five crus listed in the famous 1855 classification. Haut-Médoc wines are mainly for cellaring.

Eye
The colour is intense, poised between ruby, Bordeaux-red and garnet, promising a wine of solid constitution that loses none of its brightness with age.

Nose
The bouquet discloses notes of blackcurrant together with aromas of roasting and spices. Ripe red fruits merge with scents of vanilla and burning from the wood to irresistible effect.

Ageing ability
7-16 years (longer for some crus).

Palate
Young Haut-Médoc wines have a solid, tannic side to them: some wines are quite undrinkable for the first few years. With age, they grow supple and succulent, with palate aromas that echo the nose and that whatever the origin of the wine, always grow richer and more varied with age.

The Crus Classés
Quatrième Crus
Château La Lagune
Château La Tour-Carnet
Cinquième Crus
Château Belgrave
Château Camensac
Château Cantemerle

Choice of food
Red or white meat, poultry, game, cheese.

Serving temperature
17-18°C.

Haut-Poitou

The Haut-Poitou vineyards flourished in the Middle Ages when Poitou was part of Aquitaine and they remained very extensive until the end of the 19th century. Today they are reduced to a selection of enclaves between grazing meadows and arable land to the north and east of Poitiers. The wines they produce may belong to the Val de Loire family but they reflect the influence of Bordeaux. The reds are generally light and fresh but with good structure; the rosés are similar in character; the whites are lively and fragrant. All of these wines are usually intended for early drinking.

1 9 7 0

Appellation
Haut-Poitou
AOVDQS
Colours
Red
Rosé
White
Area
443 hectares

Production
33,350
hectolitres

Eye
• Typical Haut Poitou reds are light and often cherry-coloured. More robust wines verge on garnet.
• The whites are a brilliant pale yellow.

Nose
• The reds reveal notes of strawberry and morello cherry.
• The whites offer Chardonnay-type fragrances of white fruit or citrus fruit with notes ranging from yellow peach to green apple and aniseed. Whites based on Sauvignon mingle scents of white flowers with broom and budding blackcurrant.

Palate
• Haut Poitou red wine is typically fresh, refreshing and fruity, but it can also be robust, solidly structured and capable of ageing.
• The whites are crisp and light and develop with finesse.

Choice of food
Reds and roses:
charcuterie,
red meat, cheese
(Chabichou
du Poitou).
Whites:
oysters, grilled
fish.

Serving temperature
Reds:
12-14°C.
Whites and rosés:
8-10°C.

Ageing ability
Reds: 4-5 years.
Whites and rosés:
for early
drinking.

Soil types
Limestone,
clayey- limestone.

Grape varieties
Reds and rosés:
Gamay Noir,
Cabernet Franc.
Whites:
Sauvignon,
Chardonnay.

211

Hermitage

Appellation
Hermitage AOC
Colour
Red (80%)
White (20%)
Vin de Paille
Area
120 hectares
Production
4,830 hectolitres

1 9 3 7

Chante-Alouette·
HERMITAGE
APPELLATION HERMITAGE CONTRÔLÉE
M. CHAPOUTIER (MAN TAIN FRANCE)
Vin Blanc–White Wine
75 cl

The Hermitage vineyard is situated to the northeast of Tain-l'Hermitage, clinging to a magnificent escarpment inscribed with the names of such important wine traders as Jaboulet and Chapoutier. Its reputation dates back to Roman times but it is mainly famous today for a legendary knight who is said to have returned exhausted from the Crusades to retire to a hovel by the Hermitage chapel and plant vines. The AOC produces fabulous red wines for laying down, made exclusively from Syrah; also whites that are capable of ageing for several years, and limited quantities of *vin de paille*.

PRODUCT OF FRANCE

Hermitage
APPELLATION HERMITAGE CONTRÔLÉE
Mise en bouteilles à la propriété
Domaine Jean-Louis CHAVE
Propriétaire-Viticulteur - MAUVES en Ardèche - France

Eye
• Young reds are a very deep garnet colour, developing an orange hue with age.
• Young whites are light in colour with green highlights, maturing to deeper, golden tones.

Nose
• The reds combine strength and finesse. Young wines have dominant aromas of violet and red fruits before developing fragrances of cooked fruit (prunes) mingled with notes of spice, the underwood and animal scents.
• Young whites are very floral (white flowers, hawthorn) acquiring notes of toastiness, and nuances of honey and beeswax when fully mature.

Palate
• The reds have surprising tannic strength combined with very refined substance.
• The whites are rich and full-bodied but usually have little acidity to speak of – a profile that gives them a style all of their own and sets them apart from most French white wines.

Choice of food
Reds: fillet of beef à la Provençale, spicy foods.
Whites: fish in a sauce, roasted poultry.
Vins de paille: puddings.

Serving temperature
Reds and certain very rich whites: 16-18°C.
Whites: 12-14°C.

Grape varieties	**Soil types**	**Ageing ability**
Reds: Syrah. *Whites:* Marsanne with some Roussanne.	Granitic sands, more or less calcareous gravelly soils.	5-10 years (depending on terroir and vintage).

Irancy

Irancy is a picturesque ancient wine growing village nestling at the bottom of a valley that opens onto the right-bank of the Yonne River 15 kilometres (9 miles) from Auxerre. The vines are mainly planted on the marl slopes overlooking the Côte des Bars. Irancy is a robust red wine made from Pinot Noir, sometimes blended with a rustic local vine variety, the César. The *lieu-dit* sometimes appears on the label: Côte du Moutier, Les Cailles, Boudardes, Vauchassy, Les Mazelots, Les Bessys or La Palotte, a *climat* of ancient repute.

1 9 4 6

Appellation
Irancy AOC
Colour
Red
Area
250 hectares
Production
6,500 hectolitres

Eye
Ruby-red, sometimes verging on garnet, moderately intense but brilliant.

Nose
A lively, fresh range of aromas with red fruit (raspberry, cherry, nuances of morello cherry) to the fore enhanced by rather headier scents of black-skinned fruit, sometimes with floral notes of violet. With age, Irancy evokes spices, truffle, leather and the underwood.

Palate
Fairly corpulent and rich, with a distinctive balance of meatiness and liveliness. Young wines may appear austere and rather closed but they grow elegant and spirited after a few years' ageing. A good Irancy wine should combine impressive concentration with a robust framework and just enough roundness.

Choice of food
Charcuterie, parsley ham, meat in sauce, duck with olives, salted pork with lentils, beef cooked in a salt crust, cheese (Epoisses, Chaource, Soumaintrain).

Serving temperature
14 -16°C.

Ageing ability
5-12 years. Good vintages blended with the César variety can be laid down for 20-30 years.

Soil types
Best terroirs: limestone soils enriched with slope wash, on Kimmeridgian marl and beneath the limestone plateau of Barrois.

Grape varieties
Pinot Noir and occasionally César (maxium 10%).

Irouléguy

Appellation
Irouléguy AOC

Colours
Red
Rosé
White (10%)

Area
190 hectares

Production
7,000 hectolitres

1970

Irouléguy is one of the smallest viticultural districts in France, situated in the north of the Basque Country, scattered about the mountainsides between the communes of Irouléguy, Saint-Etienne-de-Baïgorry and Anhaux. This 'vineyard at the end of the world' is a place steeped in history. Close by are St-Jean-Pied-de-Port and the pass of the Col de Roncevaux through which countless pilgrims passed in the Middle Ages on their way to Santiago de Compostella. Irouléguy reds age well; the rosés are nervous and aromatic; the whites are fresh and fruity.

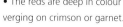

Eye
• The reds are deep in colour verging on crimson or garnet.
• The rosés shimmer with raspberry-red highlights.
• The whites are straw-gold with green highlights.

Nose
• Aromas of spice and wild flowers are part of the originality of Irouléguy reds that also release fragrances of red- and black-skinned fruit, humus and the underwood.
• The rosés are aromatic and reminiscent of wild flowers.
• The whites are distinguished by their aromas of white flowers and exotic fruit.

Palate
• The reds are fleshy and long, well-structured without a trace of heaviness.
• Solid tannins make the rosés seem rather virile in character, but they should leave a smooth, supple impression on the palate.
• The whites have good balance built on freshness and aromatic length.

Grape varieties
Reds: Tannat, Cabernet Franc and Cabernet-Sauvignon.
Whites: Courbu, Gros and Petit Manseng.

Soil types
Limestone, schist, red clay, argillaceous-gravelly and argillaceous-silty.

Ageing ability
3-6 years.

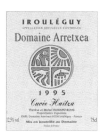

IROULÉGUY
APPELLATION IROULÉGUY CONTRÔLÉE
Domaine Arretxea
1995
Cuvée Haitza
Thérèse et Michel RIOUSPEYROUS
Propriétaires Vignerons
EARL Domaine Arretxea 64220 Irouléguy - France
12.5% vol.   Mis en bouteille au Domaine   75cl

Serving temperature
Reds: 16-17°C.
Whites and rosés: 8-10°C.

Choice of food
Reds: confit of duck, cured Bayonne ham, tuna à la Basquaise, Pyrenean sheep's cheese.
Rosés: piperade (pepper omelette), charcuterie, fish soup.
Whites: fish with Béarnaise sauce.

Jasnières

The vineyards of the Jasnières appellation in the Sarthe department are part of the Coteaux du Loir. These are the most northerly of the Loire vineyards, distributed along a single slope four kilometres (2.5 miles) wide and facing full south. Chenin Blanc is the only authorised grape variety, producing dry, fruity wines with a pronounced hint of gunflint and surprisingly good ageing potential.

Appellation
Jasnières AOC
Colour
White
Area
45 hectares
Production
2,100 hectolitres

Eye
Rather pale yellow-gold with more depth of colour in rich vintages.

Nose
Primary aromas of acacia, citrus fruit, apricot and hawthorn with hints of empyreuma.

Palate
An honest attack precedes a sensation of freshness typical of Loire wines. This first impression is balanced by a certain roundness that makes the wine accessible. The delicate finish recalls the aromas of fruit, underscored by mineral notes.

The Lhomme vineyard in the Jasnières AOC.

Choice of food
As an apéritif or with crustaceans, gourmet fish, chicken fricassee, rabbit with baby vegetables.

Serving temperature
8-10°C.

Ageing ability
20 years and more.

Grape variety
Chenin Blanc (otherwise known as Pineau de la Loire).
Soil types
Clayey limestone.

Juliénas

Appellation
Juliénas AOC

Colour
Red

Area
604 hectares

Production
34,830 hectolitres

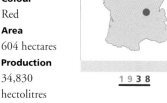

1 9 3 8

The Juliénas area covers the south and southwest facing slope of the Mont de Bessay, the northernmost slope of the Beaujolais district, peaking at 478 metres (1,568 feet). The terrior of the Juliénas appellation is restricted to the communes of Pruzilly, Emeringes, and most notably Jullié and Juliénas – names that bring to mind Julius Caesar and the Roman legions who occupied the region and may perhaps have grown vines here. Granitic and alluvial soils yield wines of distinctive character for laying down.

Eye
The purplish hue noticeable in the first few months sometimes persists, eventually growing darker after five years' ageing.

Nose
A complex range of aromas, floral fragrances (peony or violet) mingling with fruit scents (raspberry, strawberry, blackcurrant and redcurrant). Certain vintages have aromas of vine peaches.

Notes of mineral and spices complete the bouquet, adding a sign of distinction.

Palate
Rich tannins are balanced by characteristic nervousness. Juliénas wines have a somewhat rustic structure that confirms their personality. The qualities of the wine endure and greatly improve with several years of ageing.

Grape variety
Gamay Noir.

Soil types
Granitic, schists and clay seams.

Ageing ability
5-7 years.

Serving temperature
13-15°C.

Choice of food
Red meat, game, coq au vin, poultry in a sauce, cheese (Neufchâtel).

Jurançon, Jurançon Sec

Legend has it that the lips of the future King Henry IV of France were moistened with a few drops of Jurançon wine. Collette, the famous 20th century French writer, described this authentically mountainous wine as 'an imperious, passionate prince'. The Jurançon vineyards cling to a ridge facing the Pyrenees, sheltered by the Midi d'Ossau mountain. They produce sweet, rich and dry white wines characterised by the local grape varieties, Gros Manseng, Courbu and Petit Manseng.

1975

Appellation
Jurançon AOC
Jurançon Sec
AOC
Colours
White (dry, sweet or rich wines)
Area
821 hectares
Production
Jurançon:
10,430 hl
Jurançon Sec:
31,280 hl

Eye
• Sweet Jurançon wines are golden, ranging from golden yellow with green reflections in young wines to antique gold in wines that have spent many years in the cellar.
• Dry Jurançon is pale yellow gold with a greenish hue.

Nose
• Sweet Jurançon has an unmistakable honeyed fragrance, with aromas that mingle scents of spice (nutmeg, cloves), with white flowers and crystallised fruit. Petit Manseng adds nuances of ripe fruit (peach) and cinnamon.
• Dry Jurançon wines have the same spicy, honeyed fragrance as the sweet wines but the intensity of the aromas is less pronounced. This wine also has an aromatic expression of its own with scents of flowers (broom) and exotic fruit.

Palate
• Sweet Jurançon varies according to the producer but the key to a successful wine is the right balance of sweetness, residual sugar and liveliness. Though surprisingly concentrated, it should always remain delicate.
• Dry Jurançon is honest, fruity and elegant. Sprightly and lightly *perlant*, it has a rounded, sappy structure, finishing on a hint of respectable sharpness.

Choice of food
Sweet wines: as an aperitif or with foie gras, poularde à la crème, Pyrenean sheep's cheese.
Dry wines: as an aperitif or with river fish (trout, salmon, shad, pike), white meat.

Serving temperature
Sweet wines:
8-9°C.
Dry wines:
10-12°C.

Ageing ability
Sweet wines:
up to 20 years.
Dry wines:
5 years.

Grape varieties
Gros Manseng, Petit Manseng, Courbu.

Soil types
Limestone, sandy, stony, clayey soils.

Ladoix

Appellations
Ladoix AOC
Ladoix Premier
Cru AOC

Colours
Red
White (14%)

Area
Ladoix: 120 hectares
64 ares 45 centiares
Ladoix Premier Cru:
14 hectares 38 ares
06 centiares

Production
4,460 hectolitres

1970

VIN DE BOURGOGNE

Jean Guiton
viticulteur

LADOIX PREMIER CRU
LA CORVÉE
APPELLATION CONTROLÉE

Heading south from the Côte de Nuits the Montagne de Corton is a landmark set in a landscape of plains and valleys perfect for vines. The Ladoix-Serrigny vineyard is divided between Ladoix and Ladoix Premier Cru, high up the slope on fairly marly-clayey soils. Stony limestone soils halfway up the slope produce powerful, robust red wines. Lower down, the brown or reddish soils mixed with limestone, clay and flints (*chaillots*) or flinty limestone debris, yield red wines that are tender and fruity.

Eye
• The reds are similar in colour to crème de Cassis: brilliant garnet with a blackish hue and purplish highlights.
• The whites are usually gold or light straw-coloured.

Nose
• The reds have a bouquet marked by raspberry and especially crystallised cherries or cherries in brandy, and ripe fruit. The range of aromas is completed by vegetal (sorrel) and spicy scents (cloves) together with notes of coffee or cocoa.
• The whites are dominated by a fragrance of acacia underscored by a hint of butteriness. Other typical aromas are damson, ripe apple, fig, quince and spiced pears.

Palate
• The reds have a rather soft expression, lining the palate with roundness, fullness and spherical velvetiness. The tannic structure is good.
• The whites are quite firm and vivacious but reserved, with a richness and fullness that balance their freshness. Age adds a creamy sweetness.

Grape varieties
Reds:
Pinot Noir.
Whites:
Chardonnay.

Ageing ability
Reds:
5-8 years.
Whites:
3-5 years.

The Premiers Crus
Basses Mourottes
Bois Roussot
Le Clou d'Orge
La Corvée
Les Joyeuses
Hautes Mourottes
La Micaude

Soil types
Upper part:
stony, reddish
(ferruginous
oolite and marl)
calcareous soil.
Lower part:
reddish-brown
soils of
limestone and
clay with
substantial
flintstone
debris.

Serving temperature
Reds: 15-16°C.
Whites: 12°C.

Choice of food
Reds: meat pies, red meat, coq au vin, cheese (Reblochon, Vacherin).
Whites: freshwater fish, veal Orloff, cheese (Bleu de Bresse, Comté).

Lalande-de-Pomerol

The alluvial terrraces of the Lalande-de-Pomerol terroir are separated from Pomerol by the Barbanne river. The AOC embraces two communes, Lalande-de-Pomerol and Néac, in an area of varied countryside. To the west are the flat horizons of the commune of Lalande. To the east around Néac, the terrain is hilly and steeper, especially in the eastern part.

1 9 3 6

Appellation
Lalande-de-Pomerol AOC
Colour
Red
Area
1,090 hectares
Production
56,000 hectolitres

Eye
Like all great Bordeaux wines, Lalande-de-Pomerol is distinguished by its strong, deep ruby-red and garnet hues.

Nose
Very expressive, developing a powerful, rich bouquet. The range of aromas features red berries plus vanilla, toast, spices, candied fruit and prunes. Wines from great vintages may offer a broader range of aromas with notes of cocoa and animal or gamey scents.

Palate
Tannins are noticeable from the moment of attack, but the impression of warmth soon returns with the tannins becoming smooth and velvety.

Choice of food
Red meat, small game, cheese (Maroilles).

Serving temperature
17°C.

Soil types
Clayey, clayey-gravelly, gravelly and sandy.

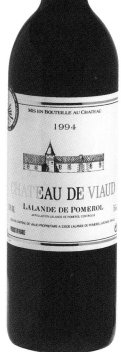

Grape varieties
Merlot (dominant), Cabernet Franc, Cabernet-Sauvignon, Malbec.

Ageing ability
5-10 years.

Latricières-Chambertin

Appellation
Latricières-
Chambertin
AOC

Classification
Grand Cru

Colour
Red

Area
7 hectares 35 ares
44 centiares

Production
300 hectolitres

1937

The vines of Latricières-Chambertin lie to the south of the Gevrey-Chambertin area towards Morey-Saint-Denis, planted on sparse soils over very hard bedrock. The name Latricières dates from 1508 and means shallow, infertile soil. Only vines thrive here, producing wines that are comparable to Chambertin in terms of richness, purity of fruit and finesse. The only difference is a barely perceptible drop in strength.

Eye
An intense, purplish garnet red.

Nose
This is a wine of enterprising nature, with noble vegetal notes and a refined woodiness. The bouquet is reminiscent of the underwood, moss and mushroom.

Palate
Full-bodied and exceptionally concentrated, with a rounded, caressing texture, plenty of sappiness and great length.

Grape variety
Pinot Noir.

Soil types
Thin soil over hard limestone substratum.

Ageing ability
10-15 years
(up to 50 years for great vintages).

Serving temperature
Young wines:
12-14°C.
More mature wines: 15-16°C.

Choice of food
Duck 'au sang', grilled duck cutlet, coq au vin, salmis of guinea fowl.

L'Etoile

L'Etoile is a small appellation in the Jura region to the northwest of Lons-le-Saunier within the Côtes du Jura district. The name may come from the five hills that form the shape of a star around the village, or it may refer to the tiny, star-shaped crinoidal fossils in the soil. Chardonnay, Savagnin and Poulsard grapes yield complex white wines, among them the uniquely traditional *vin de paille* and *vin jaune*; also a sparkling wine that will soon be known as Crémant du Jura, the only appellation reserved for sparkling Jura wines.

1 9 3 7

Appellation
L'Etoile AOC
Couleur
White (still or sparkling)
Area
79 hectares
Production
3,160 hectolitres

Eye

Wines that are predominantly based on Chardonnay are pale yellow with green highlights. Those blended from the three grape varieties develop limpid, brilliant, straw-yellow tones. Ageing in barrels can give them a more golden hue.

Nose

Remarkably complex with a notable floral side (acacia). With age, Etoile wines develop more intense notes of hazelnuts or almonds.

Palate

Extremely well behaved, with a touch of liveliness but never aggressive. Chardonnay brings freshness, Savagnin adds typical Jura characteristics, and Poulsard contributes a certain roundness. Ageing in the wood develops notes of vanilla and sometimes prunes.

Choice of food

Still wines: crustaceans, fish, white meat, cheese fondue, cheese (warm Mont-d'Or).
Vins jaunes: river fish, coq au vin, cheese (Comté).

Serving temperature

Still wines: 12°C.
White sparkling wines and vins de paille: 6°C.
Vins jaunes: lightly chambré.

Vin de Paille

Vin de paille is a naturally sweet wine produced from the very best grapes. The grapes are left to dry for at least six weeks on beds of straw or on wooden slats (*claies*) or sometimes hung to dry in well-ventilated attics. Desiccation concentrates the sugars in the grapes, which are then pressed and the musts placed in casks to ferment. A long period of ageing completes the process.

Ageing ability

Still wines: 5-10 years.
Sparkling wines: for early drinking.
Vins de paille: 10 years plus.
Vins jaunes: 50 years plus.

Grape varieties

Chardonnay, Savagnin, Poulsard.

Soil types

Liassic blue, grey or black marl, with limestone slope wash at the surface.

Limoux

Appellation
Limoux AOC
Colour
White
Area
59 hectares
Production
1,840 hectolitres

1975

The Limoux viticultural area extends along the Aude River from Campagne-sur-Aude and Espéraza as far as Pomas to the northeast of Limoux. The appellation comprises 41 communes nestling in the foothills of the Pyrenees, enclosed by the Monts des Corbières and opening onto the Carcassonne region to the north. The traditional vine variety is Mauzac, joined since 1992 by higher proportions of Chardonnay and Chenin. The AOC produces dry whites that must be vinified and matured in oak barrels until the first day of May following the vintage.

Eye
Limoux wines are light golden.

Nose
Characteristic aromas of flowers and the *garrigue*, grilled hazelnuts and liquorice on a woody background.

Grape varieties
Chardonnay, Chenin and Mauzac (at least 15%).

Palate
Well-balanced between freshness and roundness, with a harmony that persists through to a touch of liveliness at the finish.

Soil types
A few terraces; soils from weathering of hard limestone and marl, and sandstone and puddingstone of clayey cement.

Choice of food
Sea bream with fennel, chicken with lemon, fresh goats' cheese.

Ageing ability
3-6 years.

Serving temperature
10-12°C.

222

Lirac

The Lirac vineyard is located in a bend of the Rhône not far from Orange and Avignon, spread over the sun-bathed terraces and hillsides of four communes: Lirac, Roquemaure, Saint-Laurent-des-Arbres and Saint-Géniès-de-Colomas. The soils are as diversified as the grape varieties, the common factor being the Mediterranean climate.

1947

Appellation
Lirac AOC
Colours
Red (80%)
Rosé (15%)
White (5%)
Area
486 hectares
Production
23,920 hectolitres

Eye
• The reds range from deep ruby-red to garnet and seem unaffected by age.
• The rosés have a soft pink hue that sometimes verges on ruby.
• The whites have youthful yellow-green nuances that mature to golden yellow.

Choice of food
Reds: red meat, casseroles, coq au vin, cheese.
Rosés: charcuterie, crudités, grilled foods.
Whites: asparagus, seafood, fish.

Serving temperature
Reds: 14-16°C.
Whites and rosés: 10-12°C.

Nose
• Young reds are characterised by aromas of red berries or pitted fruit. More mature wines develop notes of leather, the underwood or liquorice.
• The rosés offer fragrances of red fruit combined with almond notes.
• The whites develop an intensely floral bouquet enhanced by vegetal touches.

Palate
• Lirac reds need a few years' ageing in the bottle to reach their peak. A mature wine has well-blended tannins that make it plump and rounded without being overly powerful.
• The rosés have a touch of liveliness reinforced by the effect of the tannins.
• The whites are fresh and round, with good ageing potential.

Soil types
Mainly terraces of rounded pebbles and limestone slopes.

Ageing ability
2-8 years, depending on the colour.

Grape varieties
Reds and rosés: Grenache Noir, Syrah, Mourvèdre, Cinsaut, Carignan.
Whites: Clairette, Grenache Blanc, Bourboulenc, Ugni Blanc, Piquepoul, Roussanne, Marsanne, Viognier.

Listrac-Médoc

Appellation
Listrac-Médoc
AOC
Colour
Red
Area
649 hectares
Production
38,000
hectolitres

1 9 5 7

Listrac-Médoc stands at the margin of the two Médoc areas – the wine-growing area and the forest land – and is the youngest communal appellation in the Médoc district. Like Moulis, it is situated inland, on a plateau of old gravel soils. This is a highly original appellation that once figured on the wine list of the legendary *Trains Bleus* from Paris to the Midi. It made its reputation as a powerful, vigorous wine although a great many producers these days place greater emphasis on its elegance.

Eye

Dark with a purplish tinge, indicating a wine of solid constitution.

Nose

Dominant fragrances of ripe red fruit but also a wealth of other nuances, such as balsam, leather and liquorice, plus a whole range of spicy aromas such as vanilla, or toasty scents acquired from ageing in oak.

Palate

Young wines are foursquare and powerful, but revealing a certain roundness that balances their tannic strength.

Grape varieties
Cabernet-
Sauvignon
(often
dominant),
Merlot, Petit
Verdot.

Soil types
Pyrenean and
Garonne gravel,
argillaceous
limestone.

**Ageing
ability**
7-18 years.

Choice of food
Red meat in a
sauce, game.

**Serving
temperature**
17-18°C.

Loupiac

The Loupiac appellation, like the enclaves of Cadillac to the west and Sainte-Croix-du-Mont to the east, is located on the right bank of the Garonne on south-southwest-facing slopes protected from the north winds. Research and archaeological exploration suggest that Loupiac was originally the site of a Gallo-Roman villa, perhaps the property of the 4th century Latin poet Ausone. These days, the appellation is distinguished from its neighbours by its light, airy, sweet, rich wines.

1 9 3 6

Appellation
Loupiac AOC
Couleur
White (rich, sweet wines)
Area
416 hectares
Production
14,214 hectolitres

Eye
Gold, or yellow with gold highlights.

Nose
An elegant bouquet marked by notes of roasting, crystallised or ripe fruit, figs and honey. Age brings on a much richer range of aromas that includes toast, gingerbread, flowers, citrus fruit, sultanas, nuts, raisins, dried prunes and broom.

Palate
Rich and opulent with an elegant, well-balanced structure and a sappiness that lingers at the finish, echoing the aromas on the nose. With age, the wine grows even more unctuous and voluptuous but retains sufficient body to continue ageing for more than 10 years.

Choice of food
As an apéritif or with foie gras, gourmet fish (turbot), poultry, puddings (fruit tarts, fruit salads, sorbets).

Serving temperature
8-9°C.

Ageing ability
8-10 years (longer for certain crus).

Grape varieties
Sémillon, Sauvignon, Muscadelle.

Soil types
Argillaceous limestone, clay, gravel.

225

Lussac-Saint-Emilion

1 9 3 6

Appellation
Lussac-Saint-Émilion AOC

Colour
Red

Area
1,424 hectares

Production
84,840 hectolitres

Grape varieties
Merlot (often dominant), Cabernet Franc, Cabernet-Sauvignon.

Soil types
Argillaceous limestone, clayey sand and clayey gravel.

As you would expect of an appellation in the Libourne region, this is an AOC dedicated to the production of red wines. It is also one of the areas richest in Gallo-Roman remains. Like the other appellations to the north of Saint-Emilion, the terroir is of three types – hillside, plateau and lower slopes. The plateau in the centre and to the north of the AOC is composed of Périgord sands, source of agreeable wines for early drinking. Wines with longer ageing ability come from the well-exposed argillaceous limestone slope.

Eye
A seductive dark ruby-red.

Nose
Lussac-Saint-Emilion has a characteristically Merlot bouquet, gradually revealing elegant aromas of red fruit plus a very complex array of scents that include leather, prunes, the underwood, green peppers, spices and game.

Palate
Elegant and robust with balance as the keynote. Aromas of crystallised fruit mingle with well-measured scents of wood and powerful but rounded tannins that provide good cellaring ability.

Ageing ability
4-9 years.

Serving temperature
16-18°C.

Choice of food
Red or white meat, game, cheese.

226

Mâcon

The French poet Lamartine was born in the Mâconnais, a region entirely within the Saône-et-Loire department, bordered by the Côte Chalonnaise to the north and Saint-Véran and Pouilly-Fuissé to the south. The area forms a rectangle 50 kilometres from north to south and 15 kilometres from east to west. Mâcon Blanc is produced by all of the communes of the Mâcon district; 12 other communes produce reds and rosés.

1937

Appellations
Mâcon AOC
Mâcon Supérieur AOC
Colours
Red
Rosé
White
Area
3,350 hectares

Production
Reds: 49,000 hectolitres
Whites: 11,500 hectolitres

Choice of food
Reds: charcuterie, *andouille* sausage with beans, salted pork with lentils, beef with rock salt, cheese (Reblochon, Tomme, Abondance). *Whites:* frogs' legs, snails, parsley ham, poached fish (with young wines) or prepared fish (with more mature wines), *andouillette,* Bresse chicken à la crème, goats' cheese. *Rosés:* entrées, charcuterie.

Serving temperature
Reds:
13-14°C.
Whites and rosés:
11-13°C.

The Mâconnais is well known for its vine-covered hillsides, and also for its châteaux. Shown above is the Château de Cruzille.

Ageing ability
Reds:
5-7 years.
Whites:
3-5 years.
Rosés: 2 years.

Grape varieties
Reds: Gamay or Pinot Noir (the latter in very small quantities).
Whites:
Chardonnay.

Soil types
Siliceous, argillaceous or sandy soils, often mixed with sandstone pebbles (*chailles*).

Eye

• The reds range from cherry red to dense garnet and deep ruby, accompanied by the purplish highlights typical of Gamay.

• The whites range from yellow-gold to straw-coloured, sometimes with a white or platinum gold hue. The colour is harmonious, soft, limpid, quite light and shimmering.

Nose

• Young reds have aromas of the underwood, mushrooms and fruit stones, maturing with age to modulated notes of prunes and spices (especially pepper).

• The whites offer aromas of broom, white rose, acacia, honeysuckle, fern, verbena, citronella and citrus fruit (grapefruit, orange peel, mandarin, orange).

Palate

• The reds are spirited and full of vitality, spontaneous and natural with all the characteristics of a cheerful, creamy Gamay. A vivacious yet fleshy wine, deliciously crunchy on the palate.

• Mâcon whites can reveal many different facets depending on the village and the terroir. In most cases they are fresh, quaffable and dry with a pleasing fruitiness, no shortage of roundness and good concentration.

Mâcon Supérieur

Mâcon Supérieur, or 'Mâcon' followed by the name of the particular commune, is produced in the Mâcon district and a few other communes. White Mâcon Supérieur is produced in 43 communes close to the limits of Beaujolais (for example La Chapelle-de-Guinchay, Saint-Amour-Bellevue), on the Saint-Vérain terroir (Prissé, Davayé, Leynes, etc), on the Pouilly-Fuissé terroir (Solutré-Pouilly, Fuissé, Chaintres, etc) and also on the Monts du Mâconnais (Azé, Berzé-la-Ville, Igé, Lugny, Milly-Lamartine, etc).

Top: Roman church in Igé.

Above: a wine-grower's house with gallery in the village of Azé.

Mâcon-Villages

The Monts du Mâconnais and the Côte d'Or form two chains of hills bordered by longitudinal faults running north-northeast and south-southeast, between the valleys of the Saône and the Grosne. These hills are suited to the Chardonnay for the production of early-maturing white wines. The best-known villages are Lugny, Chardonnay, Azé, Péronne, Viré and Clessé, the latter two representing a joint communal appellation.

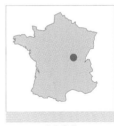

1937

Appellation
Mâcon-Villages AOC

Colour
White

Area
3,800 hectares

Production
185,540 hectolitres

Eye
Somewhere between yellow-gold and straw-coloured, occasionally verging on white gold or ash.

Nose
A floral bouquet reminiscent of broom, acacia and honeysuckle. Fern, verbena, citronella and citrus fruit complete the range.

Palate
A fresh dry wine, pleasantly fruity but with no shortage of roundness or suaveness. Good acid support gives it the quality of constitution for limited ageing.

Choice of food
Frogs' legs, snails, parsley ham, *andouillette* sausage.

Serving temperature
11-13°C.

Ageing ability
5-6 years.

Grape variety
Chardonnay.

Soil types
Brown calcareous or calcic soils, rendzinas.

Macvin du Jura

Appellation
Macvin du Jura
AOC

Colours
White
Red
Rosé

Area
36 hectares

1 9 9 1

Production
1,700
hectolitres

Grape varieties
Chardonnay,
Savagnin,
Poulsard,
Trousseau and
Pinot Noir.

Ageing ability
30 years.

Soil types
Liassic and
Triassic clay with
some limestone
slope wash from
the plateau.

Choice of food
As an apéritif or
with local dishes.

Serving temperature
10°C.

This sweet, rich wine probably originates from a recipe invented by the abbesses of the Abbey of Château-Chalon. It is made by the addition of Franche-Comté marc eau-de-vie, also produced here, that arrests the fermentation of the must almost as soon as it has begun. The eau-de-vie should be *rassise* (stale), meaning that it has been aged in oak casks for at least 18 months. The Macvin must then rest for a further year in oak casks, and cannot be marketed before the first day of October of the year following the vintage.

Eye
• Macvin red wines have a brilliant, light brick-red hue.
• The rosés are pale in colour.
• Macvin whites are pale yellow with green highlights.

Nose
• The reds have noticeable aromas of red berries and raisins.
• The rosés have a fruit nose.
• Macvin whites are very aromatic and rather exotic, with floral and fruity aromas that are accompanied by notes of walnut and caramel.

Palate
• Macvin red wines are complex and surprisingly aromatic.

The village of Château-Chalon, birthplace of Macvin du Jura.

• The rosés have a distinctive finish marked by aromas of grapes and morello cherries.
• The whites have rounded, rich substance steeped in fresh fruit.

Madiran

adiran is produced not far from the Adour River in an area that straddles the departments of the Gers, Hautes-Pyrenees and Atlantic-Pyrenees. This is a wine of ancient repute, much appreciated by pilgrims on their journey to Santiago de Compostela. Soils of siliceous or argillaceous limestone mixed with fine-particled gravel make this terroir perfectly suited to the dominant grape variety, Tannat. It yields wines of characteristic vigour with the constitution to age well, maturing to a velvety smoothness that lines the palate with silkiness.

1975

Appellation
Madiran AOC
Colour
Red
Area
1,200 hectares
Production
69,900 hectolitres

Eye

Like many wines from South West France, Madiran has very deep, dark ruby-red tones signalling a powerful wine.

Nose

The most characteristic fragrance is raspberry with accompanying notes of red- and black-skinned fruit and juniper.

Palate

With suitable vinification (such as shorter periods of maceration), this can be a supple, fresh, fragrant and fruity wine, and therefore suitable for early drinking. Most Madiran wines however are aged in the barrel and require a number of years' patient cellaring to mature and soften their tannins. They then become sensual and fleshy – big, mouth-filling wines that line the palate with aromas of spice, black-skinned fruit and toast.

Choice of food

Cassoulet, *confit*, duck cutlet, game, Pyrenean sheep's cheese, Bleu d'Auvergne.

Serving temperature

16-17°C.

Ageing ability

5-10 years.

Grape varieties
Tannat, Cabernet-Sauvignon, Cabernet Franc, Fer-Servadou.

Soil types
Clayey lime-stone, siliceous, gravelly soils.

Maranges

Appellations
Maranges AOC
Maranges
Premier Cru

Colours
Red
White (limited
quantities)

Area
152 hectares

Production
Red: 8,660
hectolitres
White: 200
hectolitres

1 9 8 9

The Maranges appellation, situated between the Côte de Beaune and the Côte Chalonnaise, is an amalgamation of Cheilly-lès-Maranges, Dezize-lès-Maranges and Sampigny-lès-Maranges. Maranges wines are similar to those of nearby Santenay although differences between the terroirs yield wines of distinctive style. Light, gravelly soils in Cheilly produce a remarkably delicate wine. Structure and firmness are typical of wines from Dezize and Sampigny. The AOC also produces a limited volume of white wines with floral characteristics.

Eye
• The reds are a dark ruby-red, sometimes verging on deep garnet. A carmine tinge is not uncommon.
• The whites are clear and luminous, a light or delicate straw colour, enhanced by emerald highlights.

Nose
• The reds have aromas of strawberry, raspberry and morello cherry, with emerging floral notes (peony, violet). Age brings on impressions of gingerbread, venison and leather.
• The whites have a fresh bouquet of hawthorn and acacia.

Palate
• The reds are firm and structured with a fat, fairly complex, expressive palate. They usually have sufficient acidity to age well for a few years.
• The whites are spirited, sappy and sometimes lively.

Grape varieties
Reds:
Pinot Noir.
Whites:
Chardonnay.

Ageing ability
Reds: 2-5 years
(up to 7-8 years
for good
vintages).
Whites:
5-6 years.

Soil types
Argillaceous
limestone
with some
granitic
material from
the distant
Morvan.

The Premiers Crus
Clos de la Boutière
Clos de la Fussière
La Fussière
Le Clos des Loyères
Le Clos des Rois
La Croix aux Moines
Le Clos Roussots

GRANDS VINS — DE BOURGOGNE
MARANGES 1ᵉʳ CRU
· LA FUSSIÈRE ·
APPELLATION MARANGES 1ᵉʳ CRU CONTRÔLÉ
13.5 % Vol. — 750 ml
Jean-Claude REGNAUDOT
Viticulteur à Dezize-les-Maranges · 71150 France
PRODUIT DE FRANCE

**Serving
temperature**
*Young reds and
whites:* 12-14°C.
*More mature
reds:* 14-16°C.

Choice of food
Reds: beef
bourguignon,
partridge with
cabbage, osso
buco, cheese
(Epoisses,
Soumaintrain).
Whites:
freshwater fish.

Marcillac

Marcillac, not far from Rodez at the base of the Aubrac plateau, is linked historically to the Abbey of Conques and is the most important appellation in the Aveyron department – the only one to have AOC status. The vineyard benefits from a favourable microclimate on very steep hills or terraces with red clay soils (*rougiers*) that are rich in ferrous oxide. The principal grape variety is Fer-Servadou, or Mansois, that produces a highly original, tannic wine.

1 9 9 0

Appellation
Marcillac AOC
Colours
Red
Rosé (rare)
Area
120 hectares
Production
5,220 hectolitres

Eye
Deep, dark crimson.

Nose
Vegetal on a background of red fruit (raspberry, blackcurrant, myrtle) and subtle spices.

Palate
Rustic character due to powerful, spicy tannins – a wine of solid constitution but moderate alcohol content.

MARCILLAC
1999
CUVÉE RÉSERVÉE

MARCILLAC
APPELLATION MARCILLAC CONTROLEE
Jean-Luc Matha
vigneron

75 cl.   Mis en bouteille à la propriété   12,5%

Choice of food
Charcuterie, grilled pork, *tripoux* (sheep's offal and trotters), *aligot* (mashed potato and cheese), cheese.

Serving temperature
Reds: 14-16°C.
Rosés: 8-10°C.

Ageing ability
1-3 years.

Soil types
Marcillac red soils (*rougiers*), limestone.

Grape varieties
Fer-Servadou (90% minimum), Cabernet Franc, Cabernet-Sauvignon, Merlot.

233

Margaux

Appellation
Margaux AOC
Colour
Red
Area
1,350 hectares
Production
70,000
hectolitres

1 9 5 4

Margaux is the only communal AOC of the Haut-Médoc to bear the name of a Premier Grand Cru Classé. It covers five communes: Margaux, Cantenac, Labarde, Soussans and Arsac. The appellation occupies the best sites and includes some of the finest gravel mounds in the whole of the Bordeaux region – source of the remarkably refined nose, harmony and ageing potential of Margaux wines.

Eye
Intense colour in the Médoc tradition, retained throughout the ageing of the wine. Young wines have strong depth of colour, between ruby-red and garnet, signalling their structure and potential for ageing.

Grape varieties
Cabernet-Sauvignon, Merlot, Cabernet Franc, Petit Merlot.

Soil types
Gravel.

Ageing ability
10-20 years.

Choice of food
Red and white meat, poultry, game, cheese.

Serving temperature
17-18°C.

The Crus Classés

Premiers Crus
Château Margaux

Deuxièmes Crus
Château Brane-Cantenac
Château Durfort-Vivens
Château Lascombes
Château Rauzan-Ségla
Château Rauzan-Gassies

Troisièmes Crus
Château Boyd-Cantenac
Château Cantenac-Brown
Château Desmirail
Château Ferrière
Château Giscours
Château d'Issan
Château Kirwan
Château Malescot-
    Saint-Exupéry
Château Marquis
    d'Alesme-Becker
Château Palmer

Quatrièmes Crus
Château Marquis de Terme
Château Pouget
Château Prieuré-Lichine

Cinquièmes Crus
Château Dauzac
Château du Tertre

Nose

A remarkably broad, complex range of aromas with vivacious, elegant overtones. Fruit is to the fore very early on (cherry, redcurrant) mingling with beckoning notes of exotic lands: cinnamon, spices, roasting coffee. With age the bouquet acquires fragrances of the underwood, mushrooms and cloves.

Palate

A rich, full-bodied, robust wine that shows signs of greatness from an early age, but with no trace of harshness or arrogance. Its suppleness and aromatic complexity recalls the experience on the nose, giving it a seductive, harmonious character. The finish is refined, flavoursome and lingering, in total keeping with a wine of this calibre. Margaux is perfectly constituted, and develops superbly with age. The tannins soften by degrees to produce wines that are round, suave and warm. The finish signs off with a harmonious impression of finesse and elegance.

Château Margaux

Château Margaux has become a legend in its own time, acclaimed in literature and cinema – not least for the majestic neoclassical château and outbuildings, built in 1802-1810 by the architect Louis Combes. The crowning glory of Château Margaux's 1855 classification as a Premier Cru is due to its exceptional terroir, blessed with an abundance of fine gravel combined with a location at the edge of the plateau and limestone bedrock. The unity of the estate is another important factor. But these would have meant nothing without the contributions of certain men. The magnificent ornamental ponds that decorate the property, for instance, were originally dug to improve the drainage of the vines. Château Margaux today is one of the most elegant Bordeaux wines.

Marsannay

Appellation
Marsannay AOC

Colours
Red (59%)
Rosé (30%)
White (11%)

Area
200 hectares

1 9 8 7

I n the north of the Côte de Nuits are three communes (Chenôve, Marsannay-la-Côte and Couchey) that produce red, rosé and white wines. This appellation is exposed to the east and partly to the south, on gently sloping hillsides at altitudes of 260-320 metres (853-1,050 feet) where dry, brown limestone soils mixed with stones and gravel provide good natural drainage. An increasing number of Marsannay wines bear the name of the village of origin in recognition of the nuances created by different microclimates, valleys and faults. The white and red wines are produced from above the Route des Grands Crus. The very elegant rosés come from a much wider area.

Production
Reds and rosés:
8,600 hectolitres
Whites: 1,400
hectolitres

Grape varieties
Reds and rosés:
Pinot Noir.
Whites: Chard-
onnay and a
little Pinot Blanc.

Soil types
Mainly brown
limestone, marly
limestone on
the piedmont.

Ageing ability
Reds: 5-10 years
(up to 15 years
for good
vintages).
Rosés: 2 years.
Whites:
2-3 years (as
much as 8-10
years for good
vintages).

**Serving
temperature**
Reds: 13-15°C.
Whites and rosés:
11-13°C.

Choice of food
Reds: red meat,
turkey with
chestnuts,
cheese
(Epoisses,
Ami du
Chambertin).
Rosés: frogs' legs,
snails, parsley
ham.
Whites: terrine
of poultry
liver, freshwater
fish, white meat,
poultry with
morel
mushrooms.

Eye

• The reds tend to be rather pale, developing a bluish-garnet hue.

• The rosés are the colour of redcurrant or tinged with orange, shimmering with delicate carmine highlights.

• The whites are pale white gold with lime-green highlights.

Marsannay-la-Côte is the first village on the Côte-de-Nuits, and unusual for its production of rosé wines.

Nose

• The reds offer a bouquet of fern, violet, blackberry, blackcurrant, dried prunes and liquorice. Age brings notes of the underwood, moss, leather and spices.

• The rosés display aromas of freshly crushed grapes and peaches, plus discreet floral scents.

• The whites open on a fragrance of citronella followed by notes of dried fruits, hawthorn and sometimes honey.

Palate

• The reds are a harmony of richness and structure. Marsannay wines are a degree severe in youth but soar to great heights with age.

• The rosés are floral, vinous and fat, with a seductive consistency.

• The whites are supple, full bodied and fat.

Maury

Appellation
Maury AOC
Colours
Red
White (3%)
Area
954 hectares
Production
26,700
hectolitres

1 9 7 2

The Maury vineyard is a quadrilateral shape, three kilometres (two miles) wide by 11 kilometres (seven miles) long, situated 30 kilometres (19 miles) from Perpignan. It starts in the plain of Estagel and ends in the west at the gates of Saint-Paul-de-Fenouillet. The vines are planted on small slopes in a basin area bordered to the north and south by spectacular limestone cliffs. To the north looms the Cathar castle of Queribus. The Maury *vin doux naturel* comes from a fairly homogeneous terroir. It is produced mainly from Grenache Noir grown almost exclusively on black schist, hence the name Maury from *Amarioles* or *Amariolas* meaning 'black earth'.

**Grape
varieties**
Mainly
Grenache Noir
(at least 50%);
Grenache Gris
and Blanc;
also Macabeu;
Malvoisie and
Muscat (for
the record).

1994

VINTAGE
Maury

MIS EN BOUTEILLE AU DOMAINE
Mas Amiel
S.C. CHARLES DUPUY - 66460 MAURY FRANCE
PROPRIETAIRE RECOLTANT

Soil types
Black schistous
marl (metamor-
phic rock).

Ageing ability
Up to 30 years
and more
(depending
on the type
of wine).

Choice of food
All Maury wines:
as an apéritif.
Young wines:
melon, fruit
puddings.
Mature wines:
Roquefort,
goats' cheese,
chocolate or
coffee cake.

**Serving
temperature**
13-16°C.

Eye

Wines bottled shortly after the vintage are a deep, concentrated ruby-red. Depending on the length of maturation and the method used, older wines take on red-brick highlights before acquiring the mahogany tones typical of Maury. The rare *rancio* wines (produced by maturation in contact with the air) are orangey with green reflections, eventually turning walnut with age.

Nose

Always intense. Young wines display a range of aromas reminiscent of morello cherry, blackberry and red berry fruit – typical of the crunchy fruitiness of Grenache Noir. Short periods in the barrel sometimes introduce a fine vanilla fragrance.

Maturation develops a range of very complex aromatic sensations: first prunes and crystallised fruits, then notes of dried fruits, beeswax, spices, roasted aromas, cocoa, coffee, leather and finally, when the wine has acquired its *rancio* personality, there is walnut. This array of aromas is generally accompanied by a suggestion of eau-de-vie.

The small Maury AOC, situated in the extreme north-east of Roussillon, is one of the region's five vin doux naturel appellations.

Palate

Young wines are warm, tannic and full bodied, with that same crunchy fruitiness that was noticed on the nose, sometimes with a hint of liquorice in wines that have spent time in wood. The craftsmanship of the wine-grower is displayed in the fine balance of alcohol and tannin, underpinned by omnipresent fruit (mainly cherry). Matured wines are remarkably complex, mingling ripe fruits and prunes in eau-de-vie with dried fruits, roasted aromas, coffee, spices, cocoa and walnuts in older wines. The overall impression is structured and rich: tannins enveloped in mellowness by the alcohol, roundness heightened by sweetness. The finish is fresh and remarkably lingering.

Vins Doux Naturels

The *vins doux naturels* are subject to the strictest production conditions.

• The grapes must contain more than 252g/l natural sugar (the equivalent of more than 14% vol.).

• The yield per hectare must never exceed 28 hectolitres (hl/ha) for certain Muscats, and 30 hl/ha for the others.

• The only authorised vine varieties are Grenache, Macabeu, Malvoisie, Muscat Blanc à Petits Grains, Muscat d'Alexandrie (only for Muscat de Rivesaltes).

• There is a compulsory maturation period of 12-30 months, except for Muscats.

The *vins doux naturels* are distinguished by the process of chemical sterilisation (*mutage*) where fermentation is arrested by the addition of neutral grape spirit (96% proof). This operation is generally performed halfway through the fermentation so that the wine retains 54-125g/l grape sugars (17g of sugar are required to produce one degree of alcohol). The wines produced are 15% proof.

Mazis-Chambertin

Appellation
Mazis-
Chambertin
AOC

Classification
Grand Cru

Colour
Red

Area
9 hectares 10 ares
34 centiares

Production
335 hectolitres

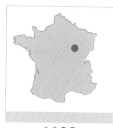

1937

Mazis-Chambertin is located to the north of Clos-de-Bèze and bears an undeniable family resemblance to its great neighbour. Its name first appeared as early as 1420, a reminder of the hovels that once lined this hillside. This is an area of sparse soil that is unrivalled for producing powerful, richly nuanced wines. The Hospices de Beaune produces a cuvée from this Grand Cru (donated by Thomas Collignon in 1976).

Eye
Mazis-Chambertin wine is a deep, dark ruby-red.

Nose
A bouquet of crystallised cherries, blackcurrants, myrtle and spices, plus a suggestion of leather and liquorice.

Palate
Power, distinction, richness and fullness are the characteristics of this memorable wine of almost infinite length.

Soil types
Thin soil over hard limestone substratum; gravelley erosional slope wash from the mountain; steep slopes with a high proportion of active limestone.

Grape variety
Pinot Noir.

Ageing ability
10-15 years
(as much as 30-50 years for great vintages).

Serving temperature
Young wines:
12-14°C.
More mature wines: 15-16°C.

Choice of food
Fish (trout, pike poached in Chambertin), game (jugged hare), beef casserole, cheese (Ami du Chambertin).

Mazoyères-Chambertin

This Grand Cru is situated in the south of the Gevrey-Chambertin district, between the Route des Vins and the main road. The appellation is characterised by a very high proportion of active limestone and stony soils and has historically been taken for Charmes-Chambertin and sold under the same label.

1 9 3 7

Appellation
Mazoyères-Chambertin AOC
Classification
Grand Cru
Colour
Red
Area
18 hectares 49 ares 87 centiares
Production
48 hectolitres declared

Eye
Vivid red with purplish highlights in youth.

Nose
Aromas of fresh or crystallised red berries (morello cherries) share the limelight with toasty notes, followed by leather nuances.

Palate
A powerful wine with a very complex fruit sensation (pitted fruits) and excellent length.

Choice of food
River fish, game, poultry with truffles, cheese (Ami du Chambertin, Epoisses).

Serving temperature
Young wines: 12-14°C.
More mature wines: 15-16°C.

Ageing ability
10-15 years (up to 30-50 years for great vintages).

Soil types
Limestone, pebbly, gravelly.

Grape variety
Pinot Noir.

Médoc

Appellation
Médoc AOC

Colour
Red

Area
4,791 hectares

Production
290,598 hectolitres

1 9 3 6

The Médoc appellation can apply to the whole of the region, but it is mainly used by the villages in the north of the Médoc peninsula. The best terroirs are the gravel mounds left behind by the former island that today lies buried with the marshes dried up by the Dutch in the 17th century. Médoc wines are well rounded with a characteristically fruity bouquet due to a higher proportion of Merlot than those of the Haut-Médoc.

Grape varieties
Cabernet-Sauvignon, Cabernet Franc, Merlot, Petit-Verdot, Malbec.

Soil types
Gravelly and argillaceous limestone.

Eye

Médoc wines have unmistakable elegance, with deep, dense ruby tones that often develop crimson or garnet nuances.

Nose

One of the great attractions of a Médoc is the sheer range of aromas: red fruits, baked fruits, crystallised and dried fruits, jam, chocolate and cocoa, spices, liquorice and the underwood. Aromas of roasting and sometimes warm toast add the finishing touches.

Palate

Wines produced from gravel soils are powerful and full-bodied, but can be tannic in youth and benefit from 5-6 years ageing or more. Those from argillaceous limestone soils are lighter and suitable for drinking from an early age (3-4 years). Fine, elegant and subtle, they also age well and may be laid down for 6-10 years.

Choice of food
Warm foie gras with apples, red or white meat, animal or feathered game, cheese (Emmenthal, Mimolette, Saint-Nectaire, Coulommiers), red fruit tart.

Ageing ability
6-15 years.

Serving temperature
17-18°C.

Menetou-Salon

The Menetou-Salon vineyard owes its existence and reputation to the nearby medieval city of Bourges to the southwest. Its wines were served at the table of Jacques Coeur, Minister of Finance to Charles VII. The vines extend across two agricultural regions: the Pays-Fort (in the Sancerre region) and Champagne (in the Berry). Sauvignon here reflects the nuances of a terroir characterised by marl and Kimmeridigian limestone, yielding fresh, fruity white wines. The delicious reds are a more recent production.

 1959

Appellation
Menetou-Salon AOC

Colours
Red
Rosé
White (70%)

Area
371 hectares

Eye
- The whites are a brilliant, pale gold.
- The reds have a ruby hue.
- The rosés produced from Pinot Noir shimmer with silver-grey highlights.

Nose
- The whites mingle notes of citrus fruit (orange or orange blossom, grapefruit, lemon) with mint, fern and acacia.
- The reds express notes of cherry and venison from the Pinot Noir.
- The rosés have a delicate peach fragrance.

Palate
- The whites line the palate with intense aromas typical of the Sauvignon: orange, orange blossom, quince, blackcurrant, fresh apple, mint, honey and spices.
- The reds are occasionally aged in barrels where they acquire supple structure after 3-4 years' cellaring, plus aromas reminiscent of cherry and violet.
- The rosés are fresh and light.

Choice of food
Reds: poultry, red meat.
Rosés: entrees, grilled foods.
Whites: asparagus, fish, calves' liver Venetian style, cheese.

Serving temperature
Reds: 14°C.
Whites and rosés: 12°C.

Ageing ability
1-5 years.

Production
22,380 hectolitres

Grape varieties
Reds and rosés: Pinot Noir.
Whites: Sauvignon.

Soil types
Calcareous marl rich in shells *(Ostrea virgula).*

La Tour Saint-Martin
1995
MENETOU-SALON
MOROGUES
Appellation Menetou-Salon Contrôlée
Mis en bouteille à la propriété

243

Mercurey

Appellations
Mercurey AOC
Mercurey
Premier Cru
AOC

Colours
Red
White (14%)

Area
530 hectares

Production
25,200
hectolitres

1 9 3 6

Grape varieties
Reds: Pinot
Noir.
Whites:
Chardonnay.

Mercurey backs onto hillsides some 12 kilometres (7.5 miles) to the south of Chagny where the best vines are to be found at altitudes of 260 metres (853 feet). This is the most extensive communal appellation of the Côte Chalonnaise stretching across three communes: Mercurey, Saint-Martin-sous-Montaigu and Bourgneuf-Val-d'Or. It produces mainly red wines. Vines planted on deep, marly subsoils produce the most robust wines (Les Crêts, Les Velley, Le Clos du Roy, Clos des Barraults). Those from stony soils derived from decomposed rock yield finer, more supple wines (Sazenay, Les Champs Martin, Les Croichots). In between the two are a wide variety of nuances. White marls, for instance, are the source of a rich, fat white based on Chardonnay (Les Velley).

Soil types
Terres blanches
and limestone;
red, argillaceous
soil; marly,
calcareous-
marly.

**Ageing
ability**
3-6 years
(up to
10 years
for some
vintages).

Choice of food
Reds: veal
with carrots,
beef
Bourguignon,
cheese
(Langres).
Whites: entrees,
seafood, pressed
cheese.

Eye

• The reds tend to be deep, almost dark in colour, often with purplish and garnet highlights. There are noticeable similarities with a Pommard or a Volnay.

• The whites reflect the golden tones of the Chardonnay. They are more or less pale and enhanced by green highlights.

Nose

• The reds always have good crunchy fruit, whether raspberry, strawberry or cherry. Age brings classical Mercurey notes: shades of the underwood, moss and even leather, fur and game.

• The whites have a floral bouquet complemented by aromas of mint, lime fresh almonds and hazelnuts.

Palate

• Red Mercurey is a complete wine with good chewy substance. An occasional touch of bitterness, due to the tannins, disappears over time leaving firm, full wines of simple, elegant structure.

• The whites have a roundness that makes them very similar to white Côte de Beaune wines.

The Premiers Crus

La Bondue
Les Byots
La Cailloute
Les Champs Martin
La Chassière
Clos de Paradis
Clos des Barraults
Clos des Grands Voyens
Clos des Montaigus
Clos des Myglands
Clos du Roy
Clos l'Évêque
Clos Marcilly
Clos Tonnerre
Clos Voyens
Grand Clos Fortoul
Les Combins
Les Crêts
Les Croichots
Les Fourneaux
Griffères
Le Levrière
La Mission
Les Montaigus
Les Naugues
Les Ruelles
Sazenay
Les Vasées
Les Velley

Mercurey is one of the four communal AOCs of the Côte Chalonnaise. The others are Rully, Montagny and Givry.

Serving temperature
Young reds: 14-15°C.
Older reds: 15-16°C.
Whites: 12-14°C.

Meursault

Appellations
Meursault AOC
Meursault
Premier Cru
AOC

Colours
White
Red (4%)

Area
375 hectares

Production
White: 18,500
hectolitres
Red: 830
hectolitres

1 9 3 7

ESTATE BOTTLED • MISE DU CHATEAU

CHATEAU DE MEURSAULT
MEURSAULT
APPELLATION MEURSAULT CONTROLÉE
SOCIÉTÉ CIVILE DU
DOMAINE DU CHATEAU DE MEURSAULT
PROPRIÉTAIRE À MEURSAULT, CÔTE-D'OR, FRANCE
DISTRIBUTION EXCLUSIVE COMTE DE MOUCHERON CHATEAU DE MEURSAULT
FRANCE   75 cl

This large village is bordered to the north by Volnay, to the west by Monthélie and Auxey-Duresses and to the south by Puligny-Montrachet. The best terroirs are situated halfway up the slope, on mainly marly soils with an oblique, east-south aspect. The image of Meursault is of a great white wine that is a tribute to the Chardonnay grape; but this appellation also produces red wines.

Eye

The classical Meursault is more or less amber-coloured gold depending on age; limpid and radiant, often with grey highlights.

Nose

The bouquet evokes ripe Chardonnay gorged on sunshine and strongly influenced by the terroir: hawthorn, apricot, lemon and exotic fruits (mango, papaya) mingling with the characteristic nuttiness of Chardonnay (hazelnuts and almonds) accompanied by notes of lime blossom and butter. Scents of truffles and toast are signs of good ageing.

Palate

Meursault tends to be rather fleshy with good length and structure. A silky texture is accompanied by flavours of fresh hazelnuts and honey that persist through to the original finish fragrant with Mirabelle plums.

The Premiers Crus
Charmes
Clos des Perrières
Genevrières
Le Porusot
Les Bouchères
Les Caillerets
Les Cras
Les Gouttes d'Or
Les Plures
Les Santenots Blancs
Les Santenots du Milieu
Perrières
Porusot
La Jeunellotte
La Pièce sous le Bois
Sous Blagny
Sous le Dos d'Ane

Grape varieties
Whites:
Chardonnay.
Reds: Pinot
Noir.

Ageing ability
Whites:
8-15 years.
Reds:
5-10 years.

Soil types
White marl in
a limestone
environment;
Bathonian,
Callovian and
Argovian strata;
occasional hints
of magnesium.

Choice of food
Whites: foie
gras, seafood,
pike quenelles,
fish, cheese
(Munster,
Epoisses,
Roquefort or
Bleu de Bresse),
tarte tatin (with
old wines).
Reds: grilled or
roasted red meat.

Serving temperature
Whites: 12-14°C.
Reds: 15°C.

Minervois

Vines have been a feature of the Minervois countryside for more than 2,000 years. The village of Minerve itself was the centre of the famous Cathar tragedy. The vineyard, on mainly limestone terrain, runs down in a series of terraces from the foot of the Montagne Noire to the river Aude. It is visible from the motorway between Narbonne and Carcassonne, resembling a disorderly chessboard of vines and *garrigue* nestling among gently rolling hills.

1985

Appellations
Minervois AOC
Minervois-la-Livinière AOC

Colours
Minervois
Red (90%)
Rosé
White

Minervois-la-Livinière
Five communes nestling in the foothills of the Montagne Noire were granted special status under the Minervois-la-Livinère appellation: Azillanet, Cesseras, Siran, La Livinière and Félines-Minervois. They produce exclusively red wines obtained from low-yielding Grenache, Syrah and Mourvèdre.

Soil types
To the north: stony slopes of mainly Eocene limestone from the piedmont of the Montagne Noire. To the south: flat expanses of water-rounded stones from Quaternary terraces; the driest soils are on Upper Eocene marl and sandstone.

Grape varieties
Reds: Carignan, Grenache Noir, Syrah, Cinsault, Lledoner, Mourvèdre, Piquepoul.
Whites: Grenache, Bourboulenc, Marsanne, Macabeu, Roussanne, Vermentino.

Ageing ability
2-4 years
(up to 8 years for great vintages).

Minervois-la-Livinière
Red

Area
Minervois: 4,285 ha
Minervois-la-Livinière: 2,600 ha

Production
Minervois: 206,300 hl
Minervois-la-Livinière: 6,870 hl

Eye

• The reds are a lustrous ruby or intense garnet-red colour, developing brick-red nuances with age.

• The rosés also have a brick-red hue.

• The whites are brilliant, light and luminous.

Nose

• The reds, especially when mainly based on Syrah, are dominated by aromas of blackcurrant and violets in their early years. These aromas are joined by scents of spice, vanilla and cinnamon.

• The rosés offer a complex range of fruit aromas – strawberry, grenadine, blackcurrant – interwoven with fragrances typical of the *garrigue*.

• The whites reveal aromas of white fruit (peach) and exotic fruit (pineapple, orange, grapefruit).

Palate

• The reds are generally powerful and full-bodied. Those from stony terraces predominantly planted with Syrah are elegant and fruity and suitable for fairly early drinking. Wines from the slopes of the Montagne Noire are more powerful and intense, often needing two years' cellaring to open up and reveal their fullness. Wines produced from the best vintage years have excellent ageing potential.

• The rosés are fresh but quite powerful, with a long, lingering finish.

• The whites have a clean attack, finishing on a note of ineffable softness as notes of vanilla, honey and a hint of Muscat blend together to reveal the secret of skilfully controlled ageing.

The Minervois vineyard.

Choice of food
Reds: beef medallions with chanterelle mushrooms, game.
Rosés: exotic cuisine, spicy dishes.
Whites: seafood, fish.

Serving temperature
Reds: 15-17°C.
Whites and rosés: 10-12°C.

Monbazillac

The Monbazillac appellation, in the heart of the Bergerac vineyard, is regarded as somewhat of an exception. This is because many of its vines are planted on a rather steep slope with a northerly aspect, opposite the town of Bergerac on the left-bank of the Dordogne. Here, cool autumn mornings create the mists that favour the spread of noble rot. Thanks to this ideal microclimate, the wine-growers of Monbazillac have been producing sweet wines since the 17th century.

1936

Appellation
Monbazillac AOC

Colour
White (rich, sweet wines)

Area
1,927 hectares

Production
43,830 hectolitres

Eye
Pure gold, with light youthful tones that deepen with age, especially in wines that have aged in barrels. Monbazillac eventually turns amber after a few decades.

Nose
Monbazillac is all honey and flowers in youth, eventually developing aromas of dried fruits, almonds and hazelnuts.

Palate
Fat and powerful but well-balanced due to a degree of liveliness, and with that inimitable 'roasted' taste that is typical of nobly rotted grapes.

Choice of food
Foie gras, poultry à la crème, Périgord strawberries, melon..

Serving temperature
8-9°C.

Ageing ability
3-10 years.

Soil types
Clayey limestone throughout, on diverse bedrock depending on the terracing along the slope: molasse alternating with limestone.

Grape varieties
Sémillon, Sauvignon, Muscadelle.

Montagne-Saint-Emilion

Appellation
Montagne-Saint-Emilion AOC
Colour
Red
Area
1,588 hectares
Production
91,350
hectolitres

1 9 3 6

The Montagne-Saint-Emilion is a region of rich architectural heritage, with Roman buildings, ancient fortresses such as the château de Tours and elegant, neo-classical properties. The vineyard is divided between a number of small producers and the wines are as varied as the terroirs. The argillaceous limestone typical of the Côtes yields robust reds; the more gravelly soils produce wines that lose in power what they gain in finesse.

Eye
Ruby-red, sometimes with dark nuances indicating sound ageing potential.

Nose
A broad range of fragrances – blackcurrant, leather, prunes, cherries, undergrowth, green pepper, blackberry, liquorice and game – accompanies notes of roasted coffee and chocolate from ageing in wood. Certain vintages have surprising aromas of crystallised fruit.

Palate
Elegant, full-bodied and supported by ripe, powerful tannins. A plump palate, revealing a fullness and complexity typical of the appellation. Gloriously seductive finish: fresh, spicy, fruity and persistent.

MONTAGNE SAINT-EMILION
Vieux Château Saint André
APPELLATION MONTAGNE SAINT EMILION CONTROLÉE
1992
MIS EN BOUTEILLE A LA PROPRIÉTÉ

Choice of food
Charcuterie, terrine, fish (salmon, mullet), duckling with cherries, *cassoulet*, rack of lamb, cheese (Brie, Pont-l'Evêque, Roquefort), chocolate soufflé.

Grape varieties
Merlot, Cabernet Franc, Cabernet-Sauvignon.

Soil types
Clayey limestone, silty-clayey and gravelly.

Ageing ability
4-9 years.

Serving temperature
16-18°C.

Montagny

The vines of Buxy, Montagny-lès-Buxy, Jully-lès-Buxy and Saint-Vallerin face east and southeast at the southern tip of the Côte Chalonnaise, at altitudes ranging from 250-400 metres (820-1,312 feet). The soils here are very different from those of the other communal appellations of the Côte Chalonnaise, producing a dry white wine with a delicate bouquet.

1936

Appellations
Montagny AOC
Montagny
Premier Cru
AOC
Colour
White
Area
263 hectares
Production
14,010
hectolitres

Eye
Limpid gold with green highlights, more buttercup-yellow in the case of older wines.

Nose
Aromas reminiscent of hawthorn, acacia, honeysuckle and fern mingle with sharper impressions of citronella and gunflint. Notes of white peach, pear and white fruit create a fruity sensation, often with a hint of hazelnut due to ageing in the wood or even a trace of honey that heightens the overall softness.

Palate
A fresh wine, young at heart, sprightly and accessible. Strong on retro-olfaction (sometimes slightly spicy) and spontaneity, with a structure that harmonises remarkably well with the finesse of the flavours.

Choice of food
Gougères
(cheese puffs),
mussels,
crayfish,
scallops,
andouillette
sausage, frogs'
legs, freshwater
fish, Bresse
poultry, goats'
cheese or
Saint-Nectaire.

The Premiers Crus
Les Coères
Montcuchot
Les Chaniots
Les Bonneveaux
Vignes sur le Cloux
Les Burnins
Le Vieux Château
Les Bordes
Les Platières

**Serving
temperature**
12-14°C.

Grape variety
Chardonnay.

Soil types
Liassic or Triassic marl or lime-stone and marl or calcareous and marly; Kimmeridgian.

Ageing ability
3-6 years.

Monthélie

Appellations
Monthélie AOC
Monthélie
Premier Cru
AOC

Colours
Red
White (6%)

Area
117 hectares

Production
Red: 5,100
hectolitres
White: 420
hectolitres

1936

The village of Monthélie lies on a ledge between the first hills of the Côte de Beaune and the Hautes-Côtes. The vineyard comprises approximately 100 hectares of communal appellation including 31 hectares of Premiers Crus. It faces south and southeast on good red soils and marls, the best *climats* being situated on the slope closest to Volnay.

Eye
• Monthélie red is often a lustrous, vivid ruby colour with almost purplish nuances.
• The whites are a brilliant straw-colour, clear and limpid.

Nose
• The reds are immediately fruity: raspberry, cherry, redcurrant, blackberry and blackcurrant. Peony is the most obvious floral scent. Maturity brings notes of spice and sometimes animal scents, notes of the underwood (fern, mushroom), preserved meats and leather.
• The whites have a lemony hawthorn fragrance and notes of pippin apples.

Palate
• The reds are harmonious with just a touch of astringency in young wines.
• White Monthélie has a delicious balance of richness and liveliness.

The Premiers Crus
Le Cas Rougeot
Les Champs Fulliots
Le Château Gaillard
Le Clos Gauthey
Les Duresses
Le Meix Bataille
Les Riottes
Sur la Velle
La Taupine
Le Village (Monthélie)
Les Vignes Rondes

Choice of food
Reds: white meat, rabbit, poultry, cheese (Cîteaux, Brillat-Savarin, Saint-Nectaire, Brie).
Whites: quenelles, pike-perch or pike in a sauce, cheese (Blue, Livarot, Epoisses).

Grape varieties
Reds: Pinot Noir.
Whites: Chardonnay.

Soil types
Limestone, marl and argillaceous limestone.

Ageing ability
Reds: 5-10 years (sometimes longer).
Whites: 3-5 years.

Serving temperature
Reds: 15-16°C.
Whites: 12-14°C.

Montlouis

The Montlouis vineyard is located between Amboise and Tours, opposite Vouvray. It links the Loire to the Cher and enjoys Atlantic weather influences that encourage good ripening. The vines are planted on stony, south-facing soils that absorb the slightest ray of sunshine. The only authorised grape variety is the Chenin, or Pineau de la Loire, source of wines of varying sweetness – dry, medium-dry or sweet – depending on the year and the time of harvest.

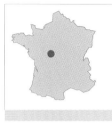

1938

Appellation
Montlouis AOC
Colours
White (sweet, dry or sparkling)
Area
384 hectares
Production
15,860 hectolitres

Eye
Young Montlouis is a fairly light straw-yellow, deepening with age and turning golden in the sweet wines. Wines from good years always have greater depth of colour.

Choice of food
Dry whites:
as an apéritif
or with
charcuterie,
cheese soufflé,
white meat,
goats' cheese.
Medium dry:
apéritif;
gourmet fish,
goats' cheese.
Sweet: apéritif;
foie gras.
Sparkling:
apéritif; warm
oysters, poultry,
patisseries.

Nose
Young wines have a fruity and floral nose (verbena, cloves, bitter almonds, bergamot, etc) followed by developing scents of exotic fruits (mango, litchi). Sweet wines that have aged in the bottle for several years have a nose of honey, quince and crystallised fruits. Sparkling wines are reminiscent of apples, brioche or dried fruits.

Palate
Montlouis wines always have a trace of liveliness that makes them fresh and sprightly and gives the sparkling wines their thirst-quenching quality. Rabelais called them 'vins de taffetas' (taffeta wines) – firm and silky.

Serving temperature
Still wines:
10-11°C.
Sparkling wines:
8°C.

Ageing ability
10 years
and more.

Grape variety
Chenin
(or Pineau
de la Loire).

Soil types
Clayey-siliceous.

253

Montrachet

Appellation
Montrachet
AOC
Classification
Grand Cru
Colour
White
Area
8 hectares 7 ares
87 centiares
Production
350 hectolitres

1937

Montrachet first appeared in the Middle Ages and soared to greatness in the 17th century. This magnificent Grand Cru that ranks with the world's greatest white wines is born of light soils rich in active limestone and sodium. The vineyard faces south-southeast on a gently sloping hillside to the south of the Côte de Beaune, facing Chagny and the Côte Chalonnaise, extending over Puligny-Montrachet and Chassagne-Montrachet.

Eye

Classic Montrachet is a brilliant green-gold shimmering with emerald highlights. With age it acquires vivid yellow-gold tones.

Nose

Wines from the Puligny side have nuances of fern. Those from the Chassagne side have buttery, warm-croissant aromas. Other aromas often include citronella, dried fruits, bitter almonds, a suggestion of minerals, spice and honey and sometimes notes of orange.

Palate

Young wines have a honeyed body founded on just the right degree of acidity. Montrachet is a wine of ineffable finesse: smooth yet dry, enveloping and deep, with not a trace of excessive richness or power.

Grape variety
Chardonnay.

Soil types
Gentle slopes of shallow, brown calcareous soils with slope wash.

Ageing ability
10-15 years
(up to 30 years
for good
vintages)

Serving temperature
12-14°C.

Choice of food
Lobster,
rock lobster,
scallops,
poularde with
morels, fish
(bass baked
in a salt crust,
sole, salmon).

Montravel

It was here that the 16th century philosopher Michel Eyquem de Montaigne – one of the most celebrated mayors of Bordeaux and undoubtedly Montravel's most famous child – retired to write his *Essais*. The Montravel AOC, on the right-bank of the Dordogne, between Castillon to the west and Sainte-Foy-la-Grande to the east, produces dry white wines. The Côtes de Montravel and Haut-Montravel appellations are for the sweet wines.

1 9 3 7

Appellations
Montravel AOC
Côtes de Montravel AOC
Haut-Montravel AOC

Colour
White (dry, sweet and rich wines)

Area
Montravel: 299 ha
Côtes de Montravel: 59 ha
Haut-Montravel: 40 ha

Eye

• The dry whites are yellow with green highlights. Montravel wines aged in the wood turn pale gold.
• The sweet wines range from straw-yellow to pale gold depending on the duration of wood ageing.

Nose

• Montravel wines have a typical hint of gunflint followed by notes of boxwood or citrus fruit, mingled with aromas of fruit (pineapple), spice (cloves, pepper), toast and nuts (almonds, hazelnuts).
• The sweet and rich wines reveal aromas of crystallised fruits and honey accompanied by more or less intense 'roasted' aromas.

Palate

• The dry wines have a crisp attack, harmonious balance and medium length, finishing on a slightly acidulous note. Wines vinified in wood are round and full, spicy flavours mingling with aromas of dried fruit and vanilla.
• The sweet wines are gorgeously rich and full, with a harmonious balance and often a hint of nervousness on the finish.

Production
Montravel: 17,120 hl
Côtes de Montravel: 1,090 hl
Haut-Montravel: 3,520 hl

Choice of food
Dry wines: seafood, fish.
Dry wines vinified in wood: fish in a sauce, white meat, poultry à la crème.

Serving temperature
8-10°C.

Ageing ability
Dry wines: 1-3 years.
Sweet wines: 5-10 years (longer for good vintages)

Grape varieties
Sémillon, Sauvignon, Muscadelle.

Soil types
Graves, argillaceous limestone and *boulbènes*.

Morey-Saint-Denis

Appellation
Morey-Saint-Denis AOC
Morey-Saint-Denis Premier Cru AOC

1 9 3 6

Colours
Red
White (3%)

Area
94 hectares
Premier Cru:
27 hectares 74 ares 64 centiares

Production
Red: 4,050 hectolitres
White: 170 hectolitres

Grape varieties
Reds: Pinot Noir.
Whites: Chardonnay and Pinot Blanc.

M orey-Saint-Denis lies between Gevrey-Chambertin and Chambolle-Musigny, and is one of the communes in the Côte de Nuits with the largest number of Grands Crus. The vineyard faces full east and produces mainly red wines. Solid, fleshy reds come from grapes grown at the top or the foot of the hillside, above and below the crus; lighter reds come from the gravel outflow from the valley.

Eye
• Red Morey-Saint-Denis ranges from vivid ruby-red and carmine to intense garnet. Purplish highlights are a sign of well-preserved youth.
• The whites are very light in colour.

Nose
• The reds have a bouquet shared between black berries (blackcurrant, myrtle, blackberries) and pitted red fruits (cherries) plus a wealth of variations (sloe, liquorice, bramble, violets, jasmine, carnations). Aromas of macerated fruits (fruit in eau-de-vie) develop with age.

Ageing ability
Reds: 3-15 years (longer for great vintages and the best Premiers Crus).
Whites: 2-4 years.

Soil types
Clayey-limestone and crinoidal limestone, distinctly more marly towards base of slope.

• The floral notes expressed by the whites are more emphatic than the aromas of spice or butter.

The Premiers Crus
Les Blanchards
La Bussière
Les Chaffots
Les Charrières
Aux Charmes
Aux Cheseaux
Les Chenevery
Clos Baulet
Clos des Ormes
Clos Sorbè
Côte Rôtie
Les Faconnières
Les Genavrières
Les Gruenchers
Les Milandes
Monts Luisants
La Riotte
Les Ruchots
Les Sorbès
Le Village

Palate
• A classic Morey-Saint-Denis red is sustained and well-structured with fruit that matures over the years.
• Morey-Saint-Denis white is a refined wine, perfectly poised between richness and acidity.

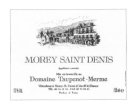

MOREY SAINT DENIS
Appellation contrôlée
Mis en bouteille au
Domaine Taupenot-Merme

Serving temperature
Whites and young reds: 12-14°C.
Older reds: 14-16°C.

Choice of food
Reds: guinea fowl with cabbage, rabbit in mustard sauce, cheese (Epoisses, Munster, Livarot).
Whites: river fish, poultry.

Morgon

People from the Villié-Morgon area use the phrase 'the fruit of a Beaujolais, the charm of a Burgundy' to describe the harmony of these wines. One of the 10 Beaujolais Crus, Morgon takes its time to reveal the subtle characteristics that it inherits from its schistous terroir. A few years' patient cellaring brings rich rewards.

1 9 3 6

Appellations
Morgon AOC
Morgon AOC followed by the name of the *climat* of origin
Colour
Red
Area
1,096 hectares
Production
64,430 hectolitres

Eye
Excellent depth of colour, turning deep garnet red at maturity.

Nose
A highly original wine distinguished by aromas of kirsch, ripe pitted fruit and fruit eau-de-vie which are not to be found in any other Beaujolais cru. Some cuvées reveal characteristic mineral notes.

Palate
Crisp attack, quickly followed by mouth-filling substance that echoes the aromas on the nose. Morgon is a full-bodied, robust wine with a bouquet that grows more refined and intense in the best cuvées.

The particular taste of Morgan has given rise to the French term 'morgonner' which is used in tastings to describe a wine with the characteristics of Morgan together with good ageing potential.

Choice of food
Terrine, leg of lamb, feathered game (pheasant, wild duck), cheese.

Serving temperature
13-15°C.

Morgon's six climats
La Côte de Py
Les Micouds
Les Grands Cras
Les Charmes
Corcelette
Douby

Ageing ability
3-10 years.

Grape variety
Gamay Noir.

Soil types
Schistous, granitic sand, gravely.

Moselle

Appellation
Moselle
AOVDQS
Designation
Name of the
grape varieties
Colour
White
Rosé (vin gris or
blush wine)

1 9 5 1

Red
Area
22 hectares
Production
1,600 hectolitres

Grape varieties
Gamay, Pinot
Noir, Müller-
Thurgau,
Auxerrois,
Pinot Blanc,
Pinot Gris.

The Lorraine vineyard today makes little impression on the overall viticultural map yet a century ago it was a flourishing wine-growing area. Proof of this lies just across the border where vines are everywhere, from the German slopes to the hillsides of the Luxembourg region. The grape varieties in the Moselle bear witness to the Burgundian and Germanic influences: mainly Gamay and Pinot Noir in the communes to the south of the appellation; Riesling, Gewürztraminer and especially Müller-Thurgau in the communes close to the border. The south of the appellation produces predominantly rosé wines. The north is mainly a white-wine region.

Eye
• Young dry whites have yellow-green nuances, becoming more golden after two years' cellaring.
• The rosés are more blush-coloured than pink, except in years of high maturity when they acquire deeper tones
• Red Moselle wines verge on ruby-red.

Nose
• The whites are often aromatic especially when produced from the Auxerrois or Müller-Thurgau varieties.
• The rosés are elegant and very fruity.
• The reds are marked by aromas of red fruit (cherries or raspberries) and a very subtle range of scents.

Palate
• Müller-Thurgau is a cross between Riesling and Sylvaner that gives the whites a nervous, light quality but with good aromatic persistence, finishing on a note of Muscat. Good balance is contributed by the Auxerrois, which is in its element in this particular terroir.
• The rosés have added complexity and length thanks to the blend of Pinot Noir and Gamay – their harmony is excellent.
• The reds are fresh but sufficiently fleshy to accompany a dish of charcuterie.

Choice of food
Entrees,
charcuterie.

**Serving
temperature**
8-10°C.

**Ageing
ability**
2 years.

Soil types
Predominently
clayey limestone.

Moulin-à-Vent

A hilltop windmill is the symbol of this oldest of Beaujolais appellations, which is not a commune but a production area comprising the finest slopes of the Romanèche-Thorins and Chénas AOCs. The vines are bordered to the southwest by the Fleurie cru and to the north by the Chénas appellation. Soils from gore, deriving from decomposed granite, yield robust but refined wines that age well and sometimes stand comparison with their Burgundy cousins in the Côte d'Or.

1 9 3 6

LE VIEUX DOMAINE

Moulin-à-Vent

Appellations
Moulin-à-Vent AOC
Moulin-à-Vent AOC followed by the *climat* of origin
Colour
Red
Area
644 hectares
Production
38,300 hectolitres

Eye

Moulin-à-Vent owes its purplish red colour to the Gamay grape variety and the granite bedrock. With age it turns from dark garnet to deep ruby-red.

Nose

The first scents from the young wines are fruity (well-ripened cherry) and floral (violet). Next to appear are fragrances of faded roses and iris, followed by spicier, more complex notes of truffle, musk, venison and even ambergris. These nuances are always light and discrete, spoiling neither the finesse nor the elegance of the wine.

Palate

This is where the wine is at its most distinctive. There is nothing to compare with the sense of pleasure that is aroused by its perfectly balanced constituents, fine tannins and aromatic persistence. Fleshy, velvety, often mineral, sometimes with a few woody notes remaining from maturation – this is a wine of breeding and class that grows more aristocratic with age.

Choice of food
Red meat, game, cheese (Munster, Epoisses, Camembert).

Serving temperature
15°C.

Ageing ability
4-10 years.

The Moulin-à-Vent *climats*

The Romanèche vineyard is divided into nine *climats*:
Les Carquelins
Les Rouchaux
Champ de Cour
En Morperay
Les Burdelines
La Roche
La Delatte, Les Bois Maréchaux
La Pierre
The best Chénas cuvées come from:
La Rochelle
Les Caves, Rochegrès
Champagne
Les Vérillats and
Les Joies.

Grape variety
Gamay Noir.

Soil types
Granitic sand with seams of manganese.

Moulis-en-Médoc

Appellation
Moulis-en-Médoc AOC

Colour
Red

Area
353 hectares

Production
32,130 hectolitres

1 9 3 8

Grape varieties
Cabernet-Sauvignon, Cabernet Franc, Merlot, Petit Verdot and Malbec.

Soil types
Graves and argillaceous limestone.

Unlike the other communal appellations in the Médoc region, Moulis does not form a block of vineyards but runs in a surprisingly narrow ribbon 12 kilometres (7.5 miles) long and barely 300-400 metres (984-1,312 feet) wide. The appellation is known principally for its large number of Crus Bourgeois, which are in their element in the Moulis terroir. Indeed Moulis and Listrac are the only communal AOC's without a Cru Classé, although their wines are certainly not short of personality. They share good ageing potential, a complex bouquet and great finesse.

Eye
Deep ruby tones with dark highlights promising excellent ageing potential.

Nose
A wealth of delightful fragrances create a bouquet dominated by fruit notes, with modulated aromas that range from ripe fruit to toast, liquorice, roasted aromas and tobacco.

Palate
The palate confirms the complexity of the bouquet with aromas of fresh red fruit, baked fruit, vanilla, cinnamon, liquorice, violets, spices, roasted coffee and the underwood. This is a wine with plump body, sustained by velvety, flavourful tannins.

Ageing ability
7-18 years.

Serving temperature
17-18°C.

Choice of food
Lamb, feathered game (partridge).

Muscadet

One of the unusual features of Muscadet is that it is not named after a geographical or historical area. The name probably dates from the Middle Ages when Muscat wines from Cyprus acquired a reputation at feudal courts. Having being totally wiped out in the great frost of 1709, the vineyard was replanted with a Burgundian grape variety, Melon (or Muscadet). Most of the appellation terroirs are spread back from the coastal zone below the first hills of the Mauges and the Vendée. This is an exceptionally sunny area of low rainfall and Atlantic influences where the vines are planted facing the ocean, producing a lively, thirst-quenching wine. The Muscadets from the sub-regional appellations, aged on lees, are also increasingly interesting.

1936
1937
1994

Grape variety
Melon Blanc.

Maturation on lees (*sur lie*)

'Lees' are the deposit or sediment left at the bottom of the tank after a wine has fermented. Although the gross lees are eliminated, certain Muscadet producers leave the wine on the fine lees that impart aromatic substance and richness. The *sur lie* designation is granted to Muscadet wines that have been kept on lees for more than four months and have not been racked or filtered prior to bottling – which takes place before the last day of June in the year following the vintage.

Soil types
Eocene sand and gravel; brown soils on granite and gneiss mica schist, gabbros (old, dark volcanic rock).

Ageing ability
2-5 years (much longer for some vintages).

Appellations
(each entitled to the *sur lie* designation)
Muscadet AOC (1937)
Muscadet-Sèvre-et-Maine AOC (1936)
Muscadet-Coteaux de la Loire AOC (1936)
Muscadet Côtes de Grand-Lieu AOC (1994)

Colour
White

Area
Muscadet: 1,899 ha
Muscadet-Sèvre-et-Maine: 10,561 ha
Muscadet-Coteaux de la Loire: 328 ha
Muscadet Côtes de Grand-Lieu: 334 ha

Production
Muscadet: 115,207 hl
Muscadet-Sèvre-et-Maine: 541,613 hl
Muscadet-Coteaux de la Loire: 17,1444 hl
Muscadet Côtes de Grand-Lieu: 15,263 hl

Eye

• Muscadet is a very pale green-gold.

• Wines from areas of basic rock, particularly Muscadet-Sèvre-et-Maine from the Vallet and Mouzillon region, sometimes have bronze highlights.

• Muscadet-Coteaux de la Loire often has more pronounced gold-straw highlights.

• Muscadet-Côtes de Grand Lieu shimmers with elegant bronze-gold reflections. It should look very fluid in the glass. Wines bottled on lees have a slightly *perlant* quality.

Nose

• Muscadet wines are dominated in their first year by aromas of fermentation, with mineral or salty nuances to follow. Mature white wines, especially those aged on lees, offer aromas of white flowers and citrus fruit mingled with mineral notes and hints of the sea.

• Muscadet-Sèvre-et-Maine wines are as varied as the terroirs from which they originate. Aromas of fruit and Muscat grapes are occasionally dominant.

• Muscadet-Coteaux de la Loire wines are distinguished by riper aromas reminiscent of violets and exotic fruits.

• Muscadet-Côtes de Grand Lieu wines are enormously elegant and thoroughbred, with complex aromas that testify to the mineral treasures of a remarkable terroir.

Palate

Muscadets are generally low in alcohol (less than 12% proof) with an excellent balance of aromas, acidity and roundness. A beautifully elegant hint of astringency makes them the ideal partners for seafood. Livelier, lighter Muscadets are particularly delicious with shellfish and crustaceans. More robust wines with stronger mineral nuances go better with fish served in a sauce – not forgetting that Muscadet is the perfect accompaniment to dishes prepared with *beurre* blanc, that masterpiece of Loire gourmet cuisine.

Muscadets

The vineyard is divided into three sub-regional appellations:

• Muscadet-Sèvre-et-Maine is the oldest and most important appellation. It covers 23 communes around the Sèvre Nantaise and Maine valleys. Muscadet, Muscadet-Sèvre-et-Maine or Muscadet-Sèvre-et-Maine *sur lie* are all produced within this appellation.

• The Muscadets-Coteaux de la Loire vineyard is spread across the hillsides bordering the Loire, from Ingrandes to Carquefou, centred on the town of Ancenis. Its wines may or may not bear the designation *sur lie*.

• Muscadet-Côtes de Grand-Lieu AOC, the most recent of the sub-regional appellations, is made up of carefully selected terroirs in 19 communes on the borders of the Lac Grand-Lieu. The wines may or may not bear the designation *sur lie*.

Choice of food
Seafood, roasted mussels, grilled fish, goats' cheese, Pont-l'Évêque, Reblochon (with a Muscadet *sur lie*).

Serving temperature
8-12°C.

Muscat de Beaumes-de-Venise

B eaumes-de-Venise is located to the northeast of Avignon, with the Mont Ventoux in the background and the AOCs of Châteauneuf-du-Pape, Vacqueyras and Gigondas to the west. The Muscat terraces of Beaumes-de-Venise, together with selected plots in Aubignan, run from the Salette up to the foot of the Dentelles de Montmirail. The Muscat vines penetrate deep into the heart of the Dentelles, drawing their finesse from the well-oxygenated soils to yield *vins doux naturels* of great elegance.

1 9 4 5

Appellation
Muscat de Beaumes-de-Venise AOC

Colour
White

Area
430 hectares

Production
14,575 hectolitres

Eye

Muscat de Beaumes-de-Venise is generally gold with green highlights. The pink Muscat vines that are still cultivated by some producers yield a pale gold wine with blush-pink highlights.

Nose

Intense and fresh, with aromas of exotic fruits, floral notes, scents of citrus fruit or grapes in eau-de-vie, occasionally mingled with a hint of roses.

Palate

Balance and freshness are key characteristics of the Muscat grape variety. Notes of lime blossom, Muscat fragrances and aromas of crystallised citrus fruits balance the wine's sweet, rich but never cloying substance. There is often a faint hint of menthol on the finish.

Choice of food
Moroccan food (*tajine, pastilla*), lemon tart, walnut cake, crème brûlée.

Serving temperature
9-10°C.

Ageing ability
For early drinking.

Soil types
Sandy, argillaceous-marl; sand.

Grape variety
Muscat Blanc à Petits Grains.

263

Muscat de Frontignan

Appellation
Muscat de
Frontignan or
Frontignan AOC
Colour
White
Area
790 hectares
Production
24,080
hectolitres

1 9 3 6

The Muscat de Frontignan appellation is located between Sète and Mireval, stretching across two communes in the Hérault department: Frontignan and the northwest part of Vic-la-Gardiole. A southeast aspect, protection from the north winds by the Massif de la Gardiole and moist sea breezes blowing from the sea, create a microclimate that encourages Muscat to ripen. The AOC produces two types of *vins doux naturels*: traditional wines, matured in casks that allow controlled oxidation; and modern wines, produced by state-of-the-art technology that protects against oxidation. Frontignan also produces very limited quantities of a rich, sweet wine that contains more than 185 g/l residual sugars.

Eye
Traditional Muscats de Frontignan have a golden hue; modern wines are a paler, brilliant gold.

Nose
The traditional wines reveal aromas of dried raisins and apricots with a fine Muscat fragrance. Modern Muscats have a fresh bouquet of citrus (pink grapefruit) and exotic fruit aromas.

Palate
Traditional Muscat de Frontignan is fat, vinous and long. Wines produced by more elaborate techniques have a palpably viscous quality.

Ageing ability
2 years to
capture the
freshness of
the aromas.
10 years to
develop the
bouquet .

Soil types
Stony, pebbly
molasse
and ancient
alluvia.

Grape variety
Muscat Blanc à
Petits Grains.

**Serving
temperature**
8-10°C.

Choice of food
As an apéritif or
with blue cheese.

Muscat de Lunel

The Muscat de Lunel *vin doux naturel* is produced from a terroir that extends into four communes in the Hérault department: Lunel, Lunel-Viel, Saturargues and Vérargues. The vineyard is planted on gentle slopes, open to the sea and the maritime humidity that allows the grapes to survive the fierce summer heat. Most of the soils are comprised of gravelly moraine contained in a seam of sand and clay. Muscat de Lunel was originally distinguished for its exceptionally sweet palate and is produced to a remarkable standard of quality.

1 9 4 3

Appellation
Muscat de Lunel AOC

Colour
White

Area
317 hectares

Production
10,920 hectolitres

CUVÉE VIEILLES VIGNES
CLOS BELLEVUE
2000
MUSCAT DE LUNEL
APPELLATION MUSCAT DE LUNEL CONTRÔLÉE
MIS EN BOUTEILLE AU DOMAINE
S.C.E.A. MUSCAT DE LUNEL LACOSTE
34400 LUNEL, PRODUCE OF FRANCE
750ml

Eye
Brilliant gold with green highlights.

Nose
Powerful grape aromas combined with a few floral notes.

Palate
Powerfully sweet but tempered by the lightness of the aromas. Lingering persistence with a very clean finish.

Grape variety
Muscat Blanc à Petits Grains.

Soil types
Layers of gravelly moraine, sand and clay.

Choice of food
Foie gras, blue cheese, puddings.

Serving temperature
8-10°C.

Ageing ability
2 years to capture the freshness of the aromas. 10 years to develop the bouquet.

265

Muscat de Mireval

Appellation
Muscat de
Mireval AOC
Colour
White
Area
260 hectares
Production
7,860 hectolitres

1 9 5 9

The Muscat de Mireval appellation lies between Montpellier and Sète, spreading into two communes in the Hérault department: Mireval and part of Vic-la-Gardiole. The vineyard is planted on argillaceous limestone terrain, bordered to the south by the lakes and sea that moderate the fierce summer heat. Mireval was for many years overshadowed by its illustrious neighbour Frontignan but since 1959 has been successfully producing a *vin doux naturel* of its own.

Eye
Brilliant, pale gold.

Nose
Glimpses of floral aromas (white flowers and roses) appear alongside notes of citrus fruit and ripe grapes.

Palate
Muscat de Mireval is smooth but clean, tempered by the freshness of the aromas with a distinctive finesse.

The *vins doux naturels*

It was a 13th century doctor of the University of Montpellier (Arnau de Vilanova) who introduced a method of producing *vins doux naturels* that remains largely unchanged to this day. It was based on what he called *le mutage du vin par son esprit*, or the addition of grape spirit to stop fermentation, so conserving a large part of the residual sugars. The only difference today is that neutral alcohol must be used in place of grape spirit and it is forbidden to add herbs or aromatic substances to the wine.

Grape variety
Muscat Blanc à
Petits Grains.

Soil types
Hard limestone
slope wash;
Jurassic and
Miocene
limestone.

Ageing ability
2 years to
capture the
freshness of
the aromas.
10 years to
develop the
bouquet.

**Serving
temperature**
8-10°C.

Choice of food
As an apéritif or
with melon, foie
gras, fruit tarts.

Muscat de Rivesaltes

For 2,000 years the kingdom of Muscat de Rivesaltes has lain between Corbières to the north, Canigou to the west, the Pyrenees to the south and the Mediterranean to the east. *The vins doux naturels –* mentioned in the writings of Pliny the Elder – are made from Muscat d'Alexandrie and Muscat à Petits Grains that contain a concentrated 252 g/l natural grape sugars thanks to 2,600 hours sunshine per year, less than 600mm (23.5 inches) of rain, near-drought conditions in the summer and the incessant Tramontane wind.

Appellation
Muscat de
Rivesaltes
AOC

Colour
White

Area
4,973 hectares

Production
144,750
hectolitres

Eye

A pale yellow colour with golden highlights indicates a young, elegant wine. Muscat is sensitive to light and oxidation – even in the bottle – and develops orangey, then caramel tints when badly stored.

Nose

Dominantly fruity, ranging from notes of litchi, white peach, apricot and citrus fruit to aromas of pink grapefruit. There are also floral notes reminiscent of orange blossom, eglantine and citronella with just a trace of mint. Next come aromas of citrus fruit, together with notes of grapes in eau-de-vie, honey and crystallised citrus fruit.

Palate

Very powerful from the moment of attack with a melody of fruit that plays on notes of citrus fruit, crystallised fruit and a honeyed bouquet from the *garrigue*. Sweet fruit balances with the natural acidity of the grape: touches of mint or lime blossom modulate the finish. Rounded, mellow, flavoursome and fresh, Muscat goes on forever.

Choice of food
As an apéritif or with foie gras, lemon or orange tart, strawberries, peaches.

Serving temperature
8-10°C.

Grape varieties
Muscat
d'Alexandrie
and Muscat à
Petits Grains
(preferably in
equal quantities).

Ageing ability
Drink early
to capture
the aromatic
freshness
of the wine.

Soil types
Limestone;
granite; gneiss;
schist; sands;
stones (these
varieties prefer
pebbly
terraces and
argillaceous
limestone soils).

Muscat de Saint-Jean-de-Minervois

Appellation
Muscat de
Saint-Jean-de-
Minervois AOC

Colour
White

Area
163 hectares

Production
5,270 hectolitres

1972

The Muscat de Saint-Jean-de-Minervois vineyard is located at the western tip of the Hérault department in the commune of the same name. It stretches from the foot of the southern decline of the Montagne Noire on a limestone plateau at altitudes of 250-280 metres (820-919 feet). The vineyard has increased in size in recent years but production conditions remain unusual because Muscat grapes ripen later here, usually late September or early October, when the temperature drops. The berries concentrate their sugars and develop their aromas at a leisurely rate, imparting distinctive finesse and crispness to the wines.

Grape variety
Muscat Blanc
à Petits Grains.

Soil type
Limestone.

Ageing ability
2 years to
capture the
freshness of
the aromas.
10 years to
develop the
bouquet.

Eye
Brilliant antique gold.

Nose
Muscat de Saint-Jean-de-Minervois offers aromas of citronella, litchis and passion fruit.

Palate
The freshness of the aromas serves to balance the wine's natural sweetness. The best cuvées have a texture of pure laciness.

Serving temperature
8-10°C.

Choice of food
As an apéritif or with blue cheese, puddings (lemon and fruit tarts, sorbets, ice-creams).

Muscat du Cap Corse

The vineyards of the Cap Corse and Nebbio are the oldest on the island, the sweet wines being an ancient speciality. The terroir is as varied as the surrounding scenery and the vines, planted between rocks and scrub, flourish in this arid, wind torn climate. The terrain is predominantly schistous, with granitic terroirs only in the Massif du Tenda in Nebbio. Bands of limestone are to be found in certain communes of the Cap Corse (Rogliano, Tomino) and Nebbio (Patrimonio). Outcrops of green rocks are found here and there on the massifs and escarpments.

1993

Appellation
Muscat du Cap Corse AOC
Colour
White
Area
80 hectares
Production
2,140 hectolitres

Eye
Pale yellow to golden amber.

Nose
A characteristically rich bouquet, with emerging notes of Muscat, aromas of dried fruits (apricot, fig, sultanas), butter, exotic fruits (mangoes, litchi), and hints of spice (cinnamon, white pepper). The range of scents also includes citrus fruit (lemon, citron).

Palate
An initial impression of round, velvety texture is followed by flavours that confirm the aromas identified on the nose. The wine lingers on the palate, often leaving the taster with an impression of having bitten into fresh, juicy grapes. Muscat du Cap Corse *vins doux naturels* vary according to the producer. Those intended as aperitifs will play up the alcohol and play down the sugar; dessert wines on the other hand will emphasise up the sugar.

Choice of food
As an apéritif with Corsican charcuterie or with grilled white meat, puddings (fruit mousse, fruit salad).

Serving temperature
9-10°C.

Soil types
Mainly schist, granite, limestone, green rocks.

Ageing ability
10 years.

Grape variety
Muscat Blanc à Petits Grains.

Musigny

Appellation
Musigny AOC
Classification
Grand Cru
Colours
Red
White (limited
production)
Area
10 hectares 85 ares
55 centiares
Production
Reds: 330 hectolitres
Whites:18 hectolitres

The Musigny AOC is located in the heart of the Côte de Nuits on an east-facing rocky limestone terrace just above the Château du Clos de Vougeot. A path running through the appellation from east to west once divided it into two plots of differing sizes: the Grand Musigny and the Petit Musigny. Then in 1936 the terroir was declared a single appellation with Grand Cru status. Venerable vines that are often more than 40 years old produce a great wine for laying down – one that starts to open after 4-5 years but can develop for much, much longer. Musigny Blanc is very rare and exclusively produced by the Domaine Comte Georges de Vogüé.

Eye
• The reds are a deep shade of raspberry.
• The whites have radiant Chardonnay tones with light golden hues that mature with age to yellow-gold.

Nose
• Musigny red has the fragrance of a garden in the morning dew: roses, eglantine and violets.
• The whites express violets mingled with almonds.

Palate
• Perfectly balanced tannins and finesse are the mark of Musigny red. Body enveloped in roundness – sheer silk.
• The whites have original tones (slightly dense and serious) from the Chardonnay, which is an oddity in the Côte de Nuits.

Grape varieties
Reds:
Pinot Noir.
Whites:
Chardonnay

Ageing ability
10-50 years,
depending
on the vintage.

Soil types
Rocky,
calcareous
terraces with
red clay on the
upper part of
the slope (quite
rare in the Côte
de Nuits).

MUSIGNY
GRAND CRU
APPELLATION MUSIGNY CONTRÔLÉE
DOMAINE JACQUES PRIEUR
Propriétaire à Meursault (Côte-d'Or) France

Serving temperature
Reds: 14-16°C.
Whites: 12-14°C.

Choice of food
Reds:
Duck, roasted
turkey, Bresse
poultry, cheese
(Cîteaux,
Coulommiers).
Whites:
Crayfish, lobster
à l'américaine.

Nuits-Saint-Georges

The Côte de Nuits is named after Nuits-Saint-Georges, between Dijon and Beaune. The AOC extends over the village, abutting Premeaux-Prissey on the Beaune side and Vosne-Romanée to the north. Differences in soil, aspect and geographical situation between the north and south of AOC account for the differences between the wines. What they have in common are solidity and good ageing potential. Plantings are almost entirely dedicated to Pinot Noir with a few Chardonnay vines in the Premiers Crus of Clos Arlot, Les Perrières and Les Porrets Saint-Georges.

1936

Eye

The colour is as nocturnal as the name: Nuits-Saint-Georges is a clear, dark, radiant red, often with deep, dark crimson tones like a fiery sunset, sometimes with a mauve hue.

Choice of food

Ham à la crème, white meat, game, cheese (Epoisses, Langres).

Serving temperature

Whites and young reds: 12-14°C.
Older reds: 15-16°C.

Nose

Frequent nuances of rose and liquorice. Depending on the age of the wine, there may also be youthful fragrances (cherry, strawberry, blackcurrant) or riper aromas (leather, fur, truffle, game, spices). There is often a hint of macerated fruit (prunes).

Palate

Young wines are vigorous, robust and generously tannic, with good body and chewiness. Maturity brings rounded curves and a gorgeous mellowness. Some Premiers Crus are quite tender and accessible from an early stage: for example, Les Damodes, Les Didiers (owned by the Hospices de Nuits), Les Corvées Paget and Les Saint-Georges.

A few Premiers Crus

Aux Boudots
Aux Chaignots
Clos de la Maréchale
Clos des Corvées
Clos des Corvées Paget
Les Damodes
Les Didiers
Les Porrets
Les Pruliers
La Richemone
Les Saint-Georges

Soil types

Communal appellation: quite deep and silty at the base; rather shallow and very calcareous at the top. Premier Cru: fine-grained, brown, pebbly lime-stone and clay (in the middle of the slope).

Appellations

Nuits-Saint-Georges AOC
Nuits-Saint-Georges Premier Cru AOC

Colours

Red
White

Area

307 hectares

Production

Reds: 13,600 hl
Whites: 170 hl

Grape varieties

Reds:
Pinot Noir.
Whites:
Chardonnay.

Ageing ability

5-15 years.

Orléanais

Appellation
Orléanais
AOVDQS
Colours
Red
Rosé
White (17%)
Area
143 hectares

1951

When we think of the Orléans region we think of a land of cereal crops in the vicinity of the Ile-de-France. Yet the same factors (easy access to Paris, urban development, monasteries and river transport) also helped to make the wines of the Orléanais much sought-after in the Middle Ages. In theory the appellation area covers 25 communes but in practice the vineyard is confined to 100 hectares of plateaux bordering the Loire. The main plots are to be found to the south of the river near Notre-Dame-de-Cléry on excellent gravelly siliceous soils. The most original vine variety here is the Pinot Meunier, source of fragrant, highly coloured wines.

Production
5,530 hectolitres

Eye
• The reds are deep in colour.
• The rosés are a vivid salmon pink.
• The whites are a delightful pale yellow with green highlights.

Nose
• The reds are fresh and fragrant with marked notes of redcurrant and blackcurrant, developing a straightforward, balanced palate.
• The rosés express fresh aromas dominated by red berries.
• The whites have all the finesse of the Chardonnay with characteristic aromas of mandarin, lemon and almonds.

Palate
• The reds are sound and balanced, combining finesse with generosity.
• The rosés line the palate, finishing on a fresh and always fruity note.
• The whites have a surprising, agreeable delicacy. They are produced in fairly limited quantities.

Grape varieties
Reds: Pinot Meunier, Cabernet Franc, Cabernet-Sauvignon.
Whites: Chardonnay.

Soil types
Argillaceous-siliceous on tuffeau chalk, erosional sandy soils.

Ageing ability
Reds: 2-4 years.
White and rosés: for early drinking.

Serving temperature
Reds: 12-14°C.
White and *Rosés:* 8-10°C.

Choice of food
Red and rosés: charcuterie.
Whites: grilled fish, goats' cheese.

Pacherenc du Vic-Bihl

The name 'Pacherenc' is of Gascon origin and probably derives from *pachet-en-rènc*, local dialect for 'pickets in rank' which refers to the manner in which the vines are pruned long and trained on individual stakes. This appellation is in the Béarn, overlapping with the Madiran appellation, between Pau, Vic-en-Bigorre and Riscle. Local grape varieties, sometimes blended with Bordeaux varieties, produce a white wine that may be dry or sweet depending on weather conditions. The fruity, dry wines are for early drinking; the sweet wines are best after about ten years.

1975

Appellation
Pacherenc du Vic-Bihl AOC

Colour
White (dry and sweet)

Area
220 hectares

Production
10,020 hectolitres (60% as sweet wines)

Eye
• Dry Pacherenc du Vic-Bilh is a lovely soft golden colour.
• The sweet wines have a glinting gold and copper hue.

Nose
• Dry Pacherenc du Vic-Bilh has the freshness of lemon, pineapple and loquat with a honey coating.
• The sweet wines have a predominantly dried fruit fragrance mingling with notes of exotic fruits, confectionery and honey.

Palate
• The dry wines are very full and as rich as they are vivacious.
• Sweet Pacherenc du Vic-Bilh makes a rich, powerful impression. As it develops, it grows rounder and achieves perfect balance.

Choice of food
Dry wines:
as an apéritif, or with seafood, fish.
Sweet and rich wines: foie gras, fruit puddings, cream puddings.

Serving temperature
Dry wines:
10-12°C.
Sweet and rich wines: 8-9°C.

Soil types
Clayey-limestone, siliceous, calcareous.

Ageing ability
Dry wines:
for early drinking.
Sweet and rich wines: up to 5 years.

Grape varieties
Arrufiat, Petit and Gros Mansengs, Courbu, Sauvignon, Sémillon.

Palette

Appellation
Palette AOC
Colours
Red (40%)
Rosé (30%)
White (30%)
Area
36 hectares
Production
1,460 hectolitres

1 9 4 8

The vines of Palette are planted in a corrie encompassing the hamlets of Troits Sautets, Palette, Basteti and Langesse, 4 kilometres (2.5 miles) southeast of Aix-en-Provence. This distinguished vineyard includes the Clos du Bon Roi René, the 15th century king who introduced the Muscat grape to this area. Palette produces white wines of remarkable aromatic intensity; structured, fruity rosés; and red wines for laying down.

Eye
• The reds are initially ruby-red turning garnet after 18 months' ageing in wood.
• The rosés are made by the *saignée* process and range from salmon pink to peony.
• The whites appear clear and radiant after 18 months' ageing, maturing from yellow with green highlights to straw yellow.

Nose
• The reds offer toasty aromas, animal notes and hints of the underwood, eventually acquiring nuances of cocoa or fresh truffles.
• The rosés have a characteristic fragrance of red fruits (cherry, strawberry).
• The whites combine good intensity with great finesse, developing complex floral notes (acacia and broom) and fruity aromas (citrus fruit, lemon, white peach).

Palate
• The reds are fleshy, robust and full-bodied with plenty of tannins in reserve.
• The rosés are generally structured, rich and round with fruity, sometimes balsamic notes on the finish.
• Palette whites have outstanding ageing potential. These are robust but rounded wines, with plenty of richness and good length. Retro-olfaction reveals notes of nuts (hazelnuts), beeswax, resin and scents of the *garrigue*.

Choice of food
Reds: beef daube, sautéed lamb.
Rosés: Provençale entrees, grilled fish.
Whites: scrambled eggs with truffles, salmon in puff pastry, guinea fowl.

Soil types
Lacustrine limestone from Langesse and Montaiguet; rendzinous soils of limestone slope wash; fairly shallow, stony skeletal soils.

Serving temperature
Reds: 14-16°C.
Rosés and whites: 12-14°C.

Ageing ability
Reds: 10-15 years.
Rosés: 1-5 years.
Whites: 5-10 years.

**Main grape
varieties**

*Principal reds
(at least 50%):*
Mourvèdre
(at least 10%),
Grenache,
Cinsaut or Plant
d'Arles.
Subsidiary reds:
Manosquin,
Durif, Muscats
Noirs (de
Provence,
de Marseille or
d'Aubagne,
de Hambourg),
Petit-Brun,
Tibouren.
*Principal whites
(at least 55%):*
Clairette (à Gros
Grains, à Petits
Grains, de
Trans, Picardan,
Rose).
*Subsidiary
whites:*
Ugni Blanc,
Grenache Blanc,
Muscat Blanc
(Frontignan,
Die, Panse
Muscade or
Panse du Roi
René), Terret,
Piquepoul,
Pascal, Aragnan
and the local
vine variety
known as Tokay.

*Château Simone
and Domaine de
La Crémade are
the two flagship
properties of the
appellation.*

Patrimonio

Appellation
Patrimonio AOC

Colours
Red (52%)
Rosé (34%)
White (14%)

Area
388 hectares

Production
15,640 hectolitres

1968

The Patrimonio appellation is located in an amphitheatre in the north of the island at the foot of Cap Corse. It covers the northern part of the Nebbio region and includes several communes: Saint-Florent and Farinole on the coast; Patrimonio, Barbaggio, Poggio d'Oletta and Oletta at the foot of the mountain; Santo Pietro di Tenda on the edge of the Agriates desert. The vineyard is planted on the hillsides overlooking the Gulf of Saint-Florent where stony soils and a microclimate of mists and breezes provide ideal conditions to produce quality wines from low yields.

Grape varieties
Reds: Niellucciu (90%).
Whites: Vermentinu (or Malvoisie de Corse) (90%).
Subsidiary varieties: Ugni Blanc, Sciacarellu, Grenache.

Soil types
Stony clayey-limestone.

Ageing ability
Reds: 5 years.
Rosés: drink within the year of production.
Whites: 2-3 years.

Choice of food
Reds: beef daube, Corsican cheese, Brocciu tart.
Rosés: summer salads, grilled fish, oriental cuisine.
Whites: as an apéritif or with fish in a sauce, cheese, puddings.

Serving temperature
Reds: 17-19°C.
Whites and rosés: 10-12°C.

Eye

• The reds are a strong, deep ruby-red, promising powerful substance.
• The whites produced from Vermentinu are usually fairly pale.
• The rosés are relatively dark due to the Niellucciu which is a well-coloured grape.

Nose

• The reds have a spicy, almost peppery nose, accompanied by more classic fruit aromas (raspberry, blackcurrant). Animal notes sometimes complete the range.
• The whites are distinguished by their exceptional aromatic intensity, with dominant aromas of flowers and exotic fruits.

• The rosés have spicy notes from the Niellucciu that also imparts aromas of spring fruits such as strawberry or cherry.

Palate

• The reds have good backbone but need 3-4 years' ageing to come into their own.
• Patrimonio rosés are high in alcohol due to the Grenache; fresh, full of flavour and intended for early drinking.
• Patrimonio white wines are soft and silky with a richness that is partly due to the low natural acidity of the Vermentinu grape variety.

Patrimonio was the first Corsican region to receive AOC status. Today it encompasses the largest number of independent producers on the island (about 30).

Pauillac

Appellation
Pauillac AOC
Colour
Red
Area
1,176 hectares
Production
65,420
hectolitres

1936

The small port town of Pauillac is the wine capital of the Médoc and has given its name to an appellation on the left-bank of the Gironde. The remarkably homogeneous terroir consists of a broad plain sloping gently down to the estuary from a high point in the west. The soils are based on very fine outcrops of gravel. Pauillac's terroir boasts 18 Crus Classés, including three Premiers Crus – credit to a historical legacy embodied in the seigneuries and estates of 17th and 18th century parliamentarians. The wines combine finesse and tannic power, giving them outstanding ageing potential.

Main grape varieties
Cabernet-Sauvignon, Cabernet Franc, Merlot.

Soil types
Günz gravel.

Ageing ability
10-25 years and longer for great vintage Premiers Crus.

South and north but above all Pauillac
The appelation is divided into two plateaus that have led some wine tasters to distinguish between two families of Pauillac wines. According to this distinction, 'southern' wines from Saint-Lambert have a finesse that makes them comparable to Saint-Julien; 'northern' wines from Pouyalet place more emphasis on body and structure and are more like Saint-Estèphe. This distinction does not stand the test of tasting however when a northern Premier Cru such as Lafite reveals a distinctive elegance to match that of Latour, a southern Premier Cru. In fact this remarkably homogenous terroir produces wines of authentic personality whatever their north/south origins.

Eye

Pauillac ranges from dark ruby and deep red to garnet, with a depth of colour that is often quite remarkable and consistent with a wine of robust character.

The Crus Classés

Premiers Crus
Château Lafite-Rothschild
Château Latour
Château Mouton-Rothschild
Deuxièmes Crus
Château Pichon
  Longueville Baron
Château Pichon Longueville
  Comtesse de Lalande
Quatrièmes Crus
Château Duhart-
  Milon-Rothschild
Cinquièmes Crus
Château d'Armailhac
Château Batailley
Château Clerc-Milon
Château Croizet Bages
Château Grand-Puy-Ducasse
Château Grand-Puy-Lacoste
Château Haut-Bages-Libéral
Château Haut-Batailley
Château Lynch-Bages
Château Lynch-Moussas
Château Pédesclaux
Château Pontet-Canet

Nose

An alliance of power, complexity and delicacy, with aromas of morello cherries and red berries in perfect harmony with subtle notes of stock, vanilla and leather. A scent of blackcurrant adds the finishing touch, recalling the predominance of the Cabernet-Sauvignon. Ageing brings new riches, introducing notes of roasting, spices, liquorice and vanilla.

Palate

Robust, powerful and well structured: the wines are at their most expressive on the palate. Their character develops with time. In youth they are marked by strong tannins, a quality that can make them appear rather firm but also makes them a match for strong-tasting dishes. Over the years the tannins soften, the aromas open up and the wines quickly lose their aggressiveness to acquire a fine and delicate character with no loss of that great Pauillac power. It is this harmony of body and elegance that invites combinations with strong-tasting but refined dishes such as game or delicate-tasting fish.

Château Latour.

Choice of food
Mushroom fricassee, red meat, game, leg of lamb.

Serving temperature
17-18°C.

Pécharmant

Appellation
Pécharmant
AOC

Colour
Red

Area
375 hectares

Production
17,250
hectolitres

1 9 4 6

The seductively named Pécharmant vineyard in the Dordogne department enjoys a favourable aspect on hillsides to the north of Bergerac. Although threatened by urbanisation and road networks, the hillside vineyard Pécharmant remains faithful to a wine-growing tradition that dates back to the Middle Ages. It produces an exclusively red wine with outstanding ageing potential.

Eye
Dark, dense garnet, acquiring orangey nuances with age but with no loss of depth.

Nose
A bouquet of red, sometimes overripe fruits, and prunes. Notes of the underwood and mushroom emerge when the glass is swirled. Other aromas include a vanilla or roasted fragrance from the wood, sometimes with traces of spice, liquorice or chocolate. Older wines develop animal scents.

Palate
A surprisingly clean and powerful attack. Young wines are often chewy but never rustic. The tannins soften with age, giving good aromatic persistence.

Rosette
The Rosette appellation was delimited in the same year as Pécharmant. It now covers an area of less than 100 hectares in the northwest of Bergerac and produces an airy, mellow sweet wine from Sauvignon, Muscadelle and Sémillon grapes (600 hl).

**Main grape
varieties**
Merlot, Cabernet-Sauvignon, Cabernet Franc, Côt.

Soil types
Argillaceous limestone.

**Ageing
ability**
6-7 years
(10-15 years
for great
vintages).

**Serving
temperature**
18°C.

Choice of food
Game (hare
à la royale),
duck *confit*.

Pernand-Vergelesses

Pernand-Vergelesses nestles into a hillside at the junction of two valleys, back from the main part of the Côte de Beaune. Its vineyard is located on the Montagne de Corton, on the southwestern side of which are the Grands Crus. The vines are planted at the foot of the slope on clay-limestone soils mixed with stones. In 1922 the village of Pernand took the name of its most famous *climat* to become Pernand-Vergelesses. The communal AOC produces excellent white and red wines.

1937

Appellations
Pernand-Vergelesses AOC
Pernand-Vergelesses Premier Cru AOC

Colours
Red
White (30%)

Area
Pernand-Vergelesses: 137 hectares 63 ares 57 centiares
Pernand-Vergelesses Premier Cru: 56 hectares 51 ares 9 centiares

Production
Red: 3,950 hectolitres
White: 1,870 hectolitres

Grape varieties
Reds:
Pinot Noir.
Whites:
Chardonnay.

Eye
• Red Pernand-Vergelesses is a gorgeous deep ruby, dark garnet or intense crimson.
• The whites range from white gold to pale yellow.

Choice of food
Reds: leg of lamb, pigeon with peas, cheese (Reblochon, Tomme de Savoie, Mont d'Or).
Whites: rock lobster, fish, cheese (Comté).

Serving temperature
Reds: 15°C.
Whites: 12-14°C.

Nose
• The reds are centred on aromas of red berries (strawberry, raspberry, cherry) and floral accents (violets). After a few years they develop aromas of ripe and baked fruit, animal notes and scents of musk, leather and spices.
• The whites offer aromas of white flowers (hawthorn, acacia) on a mineral background, within a range of aromas punctuated by nuances of apple and citrus fruit. Age adds notes of amber, honey and spices.

The Premiers Crus
Creux de la Net
En Caradeux
Île des Vergelesses
Les Fichots
Vergelesses

Palate
• Red Pernand-Vergelesses wines have solid tannins and a sound attack. These are robust wines but with a harmony of richness and acidity that promises successful ageing.
• The white wines are dry and vivacious, fairly light and always accessible.

Soil types
Jurassic Oxfordian, argillaceous limestone with pronounced changes further up the slope (marl and limestone strata).
Higher up: pebbly limestone soil.
At the top: marly soil.

Ageing ability
Reds:
5-10 years (up to 15 years).
Whites:
3-8 years.

Pessac-Léognan

Appellation
Pessac-Léognan
AOC

Colours
Red
White (23%)

Area
1,319 hectares

Production
65,360
hectolitres

1 9 8 7

**Main grape
varieties**
Reds: Cabernet-
Sauvignon,
Cabernet Franc,
Merlot, Malbec,
Petit Verdot.
Whites: Sémillon,
Sauvignon,
Muscadelle.

The Pessac-Léognan vineyard, part of which now lies in the suburbs of Bordeaux, used to belong within the Graves AOC. Famous since the Middle Ages, this is one of the oldest vineyards in the region, stretching across the communes of Cadaujac, Canéjean, Gradignan, Léognan, Martillac, Mérignac, Pessac, Saint-Médard-d'Eyrans, Talence and Villenave-d'Ornon. Poor soils, steep gravel ridges and a good hydric system combine to form a homogenous terroir of exceptional quality. Château Haut-Brion, an emblematic cru since the 17th century, ranked alongside the great Médoc châteaux in the Premiers Crus classification of 1855. Other crus however, were not classified until much later: 1953 for the reds and 1959 for the whites (when the classification was established).

Haut-Brion, the prototype wine estate

The Haut-Brion estate, with its manor house dating from the mid-16th century, is the prototype 'wine estate': that is, built on the proceeds of the vineyard. It was also the first Bordeaux Premier Cru to become famous in Great Britain. In the 1660s, Arnaud de Pontac sent his son François-Auguste to London to create a tavern-cum-cellar-cum-grocery store of such luxury that it would attract the nobility – and it did. Arnaud de Pontac was also one of the first growers to produce more powerful and deeply coloured wines by adding press wine to his claret. The Pontac family's greatest achievement however was without a doubt the creation of an exceptional wine-growing terroir from a meticulous selection of the very finest plots – a painstaking task that produced Château Haut-Brion, the only non-Médoc red cru to figure in the 1855 classification.

Eye

• The colour of the reds is an immediate indication of an elegant wine that ages well: deep red with violet highlights, or a black cherry hue.

• The whites are beautifully distinguished, ranging from brilliant golden yellow to almost white or shimmering with green highlights.

Nose

• The reds are powerful and complex, developing fragrances that are dominated by very ripe red fruits and floral notes characteristic of Graves – violets for instance. These are accompanied by agreeable hints of smokiness, toast and especially leather.

• The whites are as complex as the reds, developing deep, delicate aromas ranging from toast and a delicious hint of hazelnuts, to the faintest hint of lemon and exotic fruits.

Palate

• Young Pessac-Léognan reds are robust but beautifully balanced and elegant, asserting their personality with characteristic scents of fruit, the underwood and warm earth. The range of flavours grows richer with age: baked or dried fruits, jam, game, cocoa and coffee.

• The whites are as concentrated as they are complex and exceptionally well balanced. They assert their personality with richness and smoothness, combined with a marked freshness that is characteristic of this appellation.

The Crus Classés

Château Bouscaut (red and white)
Château Carbonnieux (red and white)
Domaine de Chevalier (red and white)
Château Couhins (white)
Château Couhins-Lurton (white)
Château de Fieuzal (red)
Château Haut-Bailly (red)
Château Haut-Brion (red)
Château La Mission Haut-Brion (red)
Château Latour-Haut-Brion (red)
Château La Tour-Martillac (red and white)
Château Laville-Haut-Brion (white)
Château Malartic-Lagravière (red and white)
Château Olivier (red and white)
Château Pape-Clément (red)
Château Smith-Haut-Lafite (red)

Choice of food
Reds: feathered game, red or white meat, mushroom fricassee.
Whites: crustaceans, fish with a sauce, hard cheese.

Soil types
Gravel, clay, sands, limestone (faluns).

Choice of food
Reds:
feathered game, red or white meat, mushroom fricassee.
Whites:
crustaceans, fish in a sauce, hard cheese.

Serving temperature
Red: 17-18°C.
White: 10-12°C.

Petit Chablis

Appellation
Petit Chablis
AOC
Colour
White
Area
535 hectares
Production
29,200
hectolitres

1 9 4 4

The Chablis region, in the northernmost part of Burgundy close to Auxerre, has a long-standing policy of quality production, to the point where the name Chablis is now universally associated with distinctive, dry white wines. Petit Chablis was the first of the four Chablis appellations to be awarded AOC status.

Eye
Silver-gold, with a rather soft, pale gold hue.

Nose
A bouquet of white flowers and citrus fruit aromas plus gunflint and beeswax.

Palate
Robust, fresh and very dry, echoing the hint of minerals on the nose.

Pruning the vines in the Chablis vineyard.

Grape variety
Chardonnay
(once known locally as Beaunois).

Ageing ability
Suitable for drinking in the year following the harvest (rather like a Primeur wine) or after 1-2 years.

Soil types
Brown limestone soils, hard limestone and partly Kimmeridgian marly limestone.

Choice of food
As an apéritif or with seafood (oysters), *andouillette* sausage, Asian cuisine.
Serving temperature
5- 6°C.

Pineau des Charentes

Pineau des Charentes is produced in the Cognac region that runs down towards the Atlantic from east to west. The oceanic climate here is marked by an exceptional degree of sunshine and few extremes of temperature, encouraging a slow ripening process. The vineyard is crossed by the Charente River and planted on hillsides mainly dedicated to the production of Cognac. This is the 'spirit' of Pineau des Charentes, a rich, sweet wine blended from partially fermented grape musts and the world-famous brandy.

1945

Appellation
Pineau des Charentes AOC
Colours
Rosé
White (55%)
Area
83,000 hectares

Eye
• White Pineau des Charentes is straw yellow, glittering with myriad reflections, or antique gold with amber nuances.
• The rosé wines have more of a ruby hue.

Nose
Young Pineau des Charentes releases a bouquet packed with fruit – the rosé wines especially. Age adds characteristic scents of *rancio*.

Palate
• The white wines are powerful, round and impressively long.
• The rosés are rich and long on the palate.

Production
100,000
hectolitres

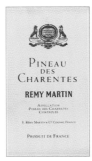

Grape varieties
Rosés: Cabernet Franc, Cabernet-Sauvignon and Merlot.
Whites: Ugni Blanc, Colombard, Montils and Sémillon.

Ageing ability
Drink after two years' ageing.
Old Pineau: more than 5 years.
Very old Pineau: more than 10 years.

Soil types
Principally limestone.

Choice of food
Apéritif; foie gras, *mouclade*, Roquefort, chocolate puddings.

Serving temperature
5-6°C.

Pomerol

Appellation
Pomerol AOC
Colour
Red
Area
802 hectares
Production
36,060
hectolitres

1 9 3 6

Pomerol is a commune without a village, and could have remained a little-known suburb of Libourne were it not for its exceptional terroir located on an extensive terrrace above the Isle River, a tributary of the Dordogne. Today, despite its small size, Pomerol ranks as one of the premier red wine appellations, producing wines of great originality that may be drunk young but are also capable of long periods of ageing. At first sight, the terrain looks quite unremarkable: a prosaic land of dips and mounds, with no buildings of any note, and vines everywhere you look. A closer look reveals the immense accumulations of gravel that underpin the entire terrace.

A few stars
Pomerol is divided into a number of scattered small-holdings that have always resisted official classification – hence the appellation's reputation as a 'village republic' (*république villageoise*). The star crus did not make an appearance until the 20th century with Château Petrus at the top of the list closely followed by other vineyards such as: L'Evangile, Trotanoy, Lafleur, Vieux-Château-Certan, La Conseillante, Petit-Village, Certan de May, Lafleur-Petrus and Beauregard.

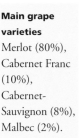

Main grape varieties
Merlot (80%), Cabernet Franc (10%), Cabernet-Sauvignon (8%), Malbec (2%).

Soil types
Gravel terraces, clay, sands.

Ageing ability
7-20 years (longer for certain crus).

Eye

Ruby to dark red with garnet highlights, promising a richly aromatic, well-structured wine.

The Secret of Petrus

Château Petrus is a property of modest size that remained practically unknown until the eve of the Second World War. It was then that the lady owner and a wine merchant became aware of the exceptional quality of this terroir composed of a 'blister' of clay over a layer of gravel. This terrain that no technician would ever regard as suitable for viticulture is in fact rich in clay. When it rains, a small amount of water causes the clay to swell, preventing saturation and encouraging efficient drainage of surface water. When fine weather returns, the clay gradually shrinks,, releasing the water it has absorbed. In this way the vine benefits from regular watering regardless of the climatic conditions.

Nose

A powerful bouquet asserts the wine's personality with pronounced aromas of violets (from the Merlot) and truffles. A distinguishing feature is the very broad spectrum of fragrances ranging from red fruits and animal notes to noble hints of leather.

Choice of food
Nearly all dishes, especially red meat, game, dry cheese.

Serving temperature 17-18°C.

Palate

The wine's aromatic richness and complexity are confirmed on the palate. The young wines are supported by powerful structure and remarkable persistence, developing in strength over the years. Older wines acquire a rich, smooth, silky character in perfect harmony with their aromatic expression. Velvety tannins sustain a structure that is evident from the moment of attack. These are wines of legendary voluptuousness and fleshiness that leave a lingering impression of velvetiness and sappiness.

Pommard

Appellations
Pommard AOC
Pommard
Premier Cru
AOC

Colour
Red

Area
Pommard:
211 hectares
Pommard
Premier Cru:
125 hectares

Production
14,600
hectolitres

1 9 3 6

Grape variety
Pinot Noir.

Pommard, on the road between Beaune and Volnay, marks the spot where the Côte de Beaune branches off in a more southeasterly direction. Its terroir is confined to the commune of Pommard where the hillside vineyard is planted at an elevation of 280 metres (919 feet). Developed by the monasteries in the Middle Ages, Pommard produces exclusively red wines from the Pinot Noir. The village has no Grands Crus but includes 28 Premiers Crus, planted halfway up the slope on rich, argillaceous limestone soils that account for the firmness and excellence of these solid, tannic wines. Certain crus such as Les Rugiens, Les Pézerolles and Les Epenots are especially distinguished.

Soil types
At the base:
ancient alluvia.
Going up the
slope:
Oxfordian marl
that follows the
contours of the
valley towards
the Hautes-
Côtes.
At the top:
brown calcic
soils, then
brown limes-
tone and brown
calcic soils.

**Ageing
ability**
5-10 years.

Choice of food
Saddle of hare
or jugged hare,
rib of beef,
entrecôte wine-
grower style,
game, cheese
(Munster,
Livarot).

**Serving
temperature**
14-15°C.

Eye

Pommard is deep, dark crimson, often nuanced with mauve highlights.

Nose

The aromatic bouquet includes blackberry and myrtle but often tends towards fragrances of redcurrant, concentrated cherry (stone) and even ripe or crystallised plums. Mature aromas evoke leather, pepper or green peppers, chocolate and sometimes fresh crusty bread and liquorice.

Palate

Young Pommard wines are often closed, opening up after 4-5 years to reveal a tender structure, fleshy character, richness and power. Good, chewy fruit.

Château de Pommard.

The Premiers Crus

Les Arvelets
Les Bertins
Les Boucherottes
La Chanière
Les Chanlins-Bas
Les Chaponnières
Les Charmots
Clos Blanc
Clos de la Commaraine
Clos des Epeneaux
Le Clos Micot
Clos de Verger
Les Combes Dessus
Les Croix Noires
Derrière Saint-Jean
Les Fremiers
Les Grands Epenots
Les Jarolières
En Largillière
Les Petits Epenots
Les Pézerolles
La Platière
Les Poutures
La Refène
Les Rugiens-Bas
Les Rugiens-Hauts
Les Saussilles
Le Village

Pouilly-Fuissé

Appellation
Pouilly-Fuissé
Colour
White
Area
756 hectares
Production
43,260
hectolitres

1 9 3 6

The golden vineyards of Pouilly-Fuissé in south Burgundy are overlooked by the prehistoric Solutré cliff, 493 metres high (1,300 feet) and some 200 million years old. Four villages on the outskirts of Mâcon share the Pouilly-Fuissé communal appellation: Fuissé, Solutré-Pouilly, Vergisson and Chaintré. One of the finest examples of Burgundy Chardonnay, Pouilly-Fuissé is a great white wine, highly complex and full of charm.

Eye
Limpid, brilliant gold with good depth of colour and nuances that range from pale gold with blush-pink highlights to pastel yellow.

Nose
The bouquet is a mixture of different groups of aromas: mineral notes, hazelnuts and almonds, citrus fruit (lemon, grapefruit, pineapple), white fruit (peach), fern and lime, honey, fresh breadcrumbs and buttery brioche.

Palate
A full, complete structure supported by good natural alcohol with frequently opulent overtones. Finesse and distinction qualify a palate that frequently reveals a touch of bitterness on the finish – which is by no means a flaw.

Grape variety
Chardonnay.

Soil types
Liassic
reddish marls
covered with
calcareous
slope wash;
Jurassic
limestone
with a
schistous zone.

The best _climats_
The most glorious _climats_ are found mainly around Solutré: Les Boutières, Les Chailloux, Les Chanrues, Les Pras, Les Pelous, Les Rinces.
Climats on Fuissé include: Le Clos, Clos de Varambond, Clos de la Chapelle, Les Chantenets, Les Brûlées, Les Perrières, Les Menestrières, Les Vignes Blanches, Château-Fuissé.

Choice of food
Young wines:
seafood, trout
with sorrel,
turbot with
white butter,
sea bream,
cheese soufflé.
Older wines:
rabbit or chicken
à la crème, fish.

Ageing ability
5-10 years.

Serving temperature
12-14°C.

Pouilly-Fumé

The vineyard of Pouilly-sur-Loire faces south from a limestone promontory on the right-bank of the Loire close to Nevers. It is predominantly planted with Sauvignon or Blanc Fumé (95% of plantings), a remarkably fruity grape variety for which the wines of this appellation are famous. Pouilly wines from flinty soils are structured, with a particular bouquet that is often described as gunflint. Wines from the hard limestone soils (*cris*) that quickly absorb heat are elegant and fragrant. Wines from the impermeable limestone soils of Kimmeridgian marl are full and firm.

1937

Appellation
Pouilly-Fumé AOC

Colour
White

Area
980 hectares

Production
69,360 hectolitres

Eye
Pouilly-Fumé is pale gold.

Nose
The range of aromas reflects all the subtleties of the terroir: blackcurrant or boxwood from the *cris*; notes of tuberose or nuances of narcissus from the marl; more vegetal scents or touches of gunflint from the flint. Common to all of them however are citrus flavours (orange, lemon, grapefruit) delicately mingled with fern and mint.

Palate
Wines from the flint soils are firm and structured with a bouquet that is often described as gunflint. Wines from the *cris* are elegant and fragrant with aromas that develop more quickly. Wines from the marl soils are full and firm and develop more slowly.

Choice of food
Seafood, stuffed tomatoes, smoked fish or fish in a sauce (pike from the Loire), poultry, cheese (Crottin de Chavignol).

Serving temperature
12°C.

Ageing ability
1-5 years.

Grape variety
Sauvignon (or Blanc Fumé).

Soil types
Kimmeridgian marl; hard limestone; flinty clay.

Pouilly-Loché

Appellation
Pouilly-Loché
AOC

Colour
White

Area
29.4 hectares

Production
1,450
hectolitres

1 9 4 0

The Pouilly-Loché vineyard lies to the west of Mâcon at the foot of the rock of Solutré. It is entirely located in the Pouilly-Vinzelles production area, which explains why its wines can also be sold under that label. Pouilly-Loché is quite rare and very similar in style to Pouilly-Fuissé.

Eye
A very subtle shade of yellow with all the nuances of a watercolour painting.

Nose
The range of aromas is similar to those of a Pouilly-Fuissé, sometimes with added hints of peony, pear, apricot, quince, baked apples or beeswax.

Palate
A rather powerful style with a good match of mellowness and acidity, dominated by richness on the finish. Wines from the *climat* of Les Mures have a distinctive quality.

The rock of Solutré.

Grape variety
Chardonnay.

Soil types
Liassic reddish marl covered with argillaceous slope wash; Jurassic argillaceous limestone soil with a schistous zone.

Ageing ability
5-10 years.

Serving temperature
12-14°C.

Choice of food
Young wines:
rock lobster, trout meunière, turbot with white butter, sea bream, pike perch.
Older wines:
Bresse poultry à la crème, quail with grapes.

Pouilly-sur-Loire

The Pouilly-sur-Loire AOC is located in the northeast of the Nièvre department on the banks of the Loire. It extends across Pouilly-sur-Loire and six other satellite communes, in a northern wine-growing area shared by the appellations of Menetou-Salon, Quincy, Reuilly and Sancerre. The Chasselas vine variety continues to take pride of place here, producing light, white wines.

1937

Appellation
Pouilly-sur-Loire
AOC
Colour
White
Area
46 hectares
Production
2,300 hectolitres

Eye
Limpid, even transparent, shimmering with delicately green highlights.

Nose
Modulated mineral notes from the Chasselas are joined by nuances of dried fruits and green apple.

Palate
Pouilly-sur-Loire has a relatively neutral taste but develops subtle hints of white fruits and hazelnuts when produced from some siliceous soils, which are common in the village of Saint-Andelain. As a Primeur wine it is the perfect carafe white, typical of a bistro wine, especially when some of the natural carbon dioxide remains. Pouilly-sur-Loire that has aged on lees of Blanc-Fumé (Sauvignon) may even claim a certain ageing potential.

Choice of food
Fish (skate in brown butter sauce), pike quenelles, cardoon au gratin.

Serving temperature
12°C.

Ageing ability
1-5 years.

Soil types
Kimmeridgian marl; hard limestone; clay with flint.

Grape variety
Chasselas.

Pouilly-Vinzelles

Appellation
Pouilly-Vinzelles

Colour
White

Area
48.8 hectares

Production
2,500 hectolitres

1940

Pouilly-Vinzelles and Pouilly-Loché share a common appellation in the Mâconnais, abutting north Beaujolais. Here the rather steep slopes are arranged in corries that face east and southeast at elevations of 250-350 metres (820-1,148 feet). Pouilly-Vinzelles is a dry, straightforward and agreeable wine that is very similar to Pouilly-Fuissé.

Eye
An eye-catching greenish gold hue.

Nose
Characteristic mineral notes mingle with aromas of hazelnuts and almonds, citrus fruit, peach, lime and brioche. Some wines have noticeable hints of peony, pears, apricots, quince, baked apple or beeswax.

Palate
An impression of finesse and distinction is due to a successful balance of mellowness and acidity, dominated by richness on the finish. The Les Quarts *climat* is especially reputed within this appellation.

Soil Types
Liassic reddish marls covered in limestone scree; Jurassic argillaceous limestone soils with a schistous zone.

Grape variety
Chardonnay.

Ageing ability
5-10 years.

Serving temperature
12-14°C.

Choice of food
Fish (turbot with mousse sauce, filets of sole with lemon butter, salmon in white wine), chicken or rabbit à la crème, *tartiflette au Reblochon*.

Premières Côtes de Bordeaux

This appellation upstream from Bordeaux separates the Entre-Deux-Mers wine-growing region from the right-bank of the Garonne. It forms a narrow strip 60 kilometres (37 miles) long by 5 kilometres (3 miles) wide, comprising some 20 different types of soil. Red wines are produced throughout the region with the name of the commune of production sometimes appearing after the appellation. The sweet whites on the other hand are mainly produced in the south of the AOC that merges with the Cadillac district.

1937

Appellation
Premières Côtes de Bordeaux AOC

Colours
Red (93%)
White (sweet)

Area
3,846 hectares

Production
171,600 hectolitres

Eye
• The reds are an intense, fairly deep ruby-red.
• The whites have those more or less deep golden tones that are characteristic of sweet wines.

Nose
• Young reds are marked by aromas of red- or black-skinned fruit and spices. With age, the bouquet grows more complex and intense, with distinctive notes of stewed prunes, toast, coffee and cinammon.
• Sweet whites made from botritized grapes have fragrances of crystallised fruits, peach and quince.

Palate
• The reds are tannic in their youth but quickly soften and improve with age. After 3-5 years the smoothness grows more pronounced creating a very supple impression on the palate.
• The whites are full-bodied, rich and aromatic.

Choice of food
Reds: red or white meat, game, fish, cheese.
Whites: as an apéritif or with white meat, puddings.

Serving temperature
Reds: 16-17°C.
Whites: 10-12°C.

Ageing ability
4-9 years.

Côtes de Bordeaux Saint-Macaire
The much smaller (46 hectares) Côtes de Bordeaux Saint-Macaire AOC (1937) is a southeastern extension of Cadillac and Premières Côtes. It produces sweet wines with body and fruit which are a good match for foie gras and fruit tarts.

Soil types
Clay, limestone, gravel, argillaceous limestone and clayey gravel.

Grape varieties
Reds: Merlot, Cabernet Franc, Cabernet-Sauvignon and Malbec.
Whites: Sauvignon, Sémillon, Muscadelle.

Puisseguin-Saint-Emilion

Appellation
Puisseguin-Saint-Emilion AOC
Colour
Red
Area
738 hectares
Production
42,530 hectolitres

1936

Puisseguin is not only original for being the most easterly of the St. Emilion satellites. It is also an area shaped by history – often turbulent to judge from the number of underground passageways – and a terroir that is predominantly planted with Merlot. The area is divided between a number of small proprietors who have created an appellation with some delightful surprises in store.

Eye
Somewhere between ruby and topaz with good depth of colour, promising a wine of solid constitution.

Nose
An expressive bouquet is strongly influenced by the Merlot that reveals its presence through well-marked fragrances of ripe red fruits and a few notes of pitted fruit. The range of aromas does not stop there, however. Depending on the cru, the vintage and the bottle, some wines may offer hints of strawberry, cherry or plum. Others have notes of mint or dried fig. The aromas most commonly encountered are scents of blackcurrant, liquorice, leather, the underwood and a rather surprising note of coconut. Barrel-aged wines have a gorgeous vanilla fragrance that harmonises beautifully with this coconut note.

Palate
Smooth, fleshy substance, packed with flavour. The most successful wines have aromas of crystallised fruit blended with a perfectly judged touch of wood and powerful, rounded, lingering tannins.

Choice of food
Red or white meat, game, cheese.

Main grape varieties
Merlot, Cabernet Franc, Cabernet-Sauvignon.

Soil types
Clayey limestone, silty sand and limestone.

Ageing ability
4-9 years.

Serving temperature
16-18°C.

Puligny-Montrachet

Puligny, located between Meursault to the north and Chassagne-Montrachet to the south, became the communal appellation of Puligny-Montrachet in 1879 and the terroir reflects both influences. Wines from sites on the Meursault side are rich and fleshy, those from Chassagne are fragrant and full-bodied. The 'Villages' sites lie at the same elevation as Puligny and a little higher along the same ridge as the Côte. Premier Cru sites face full south along the same ridge, at altitudes of 270-320 metres (886-1,050 feet) and are divided among 24 *lieux-dits* grouped into 14 *climats.* The most famous are: Les Combettes, Les Folatières, Les Pucelles, Clavaillon.

1937

The Premiers Crus
Les Cailleret
Les Chalumaux
Champ Canet
Champ Gain
Clavaillon
Clos de la Garenne
Clos de la Mouchère
Les Combettes
Les Demoiselles
Les Folatières
Les Perrières
Les Pucelles
Les Referts
La Truffière

Soil types
Very varied with brown lime-stone soils, limestone alternating with banks of marly clayey-lime-tone, sometimes deep and loamy, sometimes over hard bedrock.

Ageing ability
Whites:
5-15 years.
Reds:
4-12 years.

Appellation
Puligny-Montrachet AOC
Puligny-Montrachet Premier Cru AOC

Colours
White
Red (limited production)

Area
262 hectares

Production
White: 11,000 hectolitres
Red: 300 hectolitres

Grape varieties
Whites:
Chardonnay.
Reds:
Pinot Noir.

Eye

• The white wines are a lustrous pure gold, with green highlights, growing more intense with age.
• The reds are clear and limpid, with fairly bright crimson tones in their youth that grow darker with age.

Nose

• The whites suggest fern, hawthorn, ripe grapes, marzipan, hazelnuts, amber, citronella and green apple, usually with a honey fragrance, especially after a few years' cellaring. Mineral (gunflint, flint) and lactic aromas (butter) are also frequent.
• The reds offer aromas of strawberry, blackcurrant and red and black berries, tending more towards scents of leather, musk and fur as they age.

Palate

• The whites are exceptionally concentrated, with a bouquet and body that yield with age.
• The reds grow tender, fruity and fleshy after a few years' ageing.

Château de Puligny.

Choice of food
Whites:
vol-au-vent, local fish, pike quenelles, ham à la crème, Bresse poularde with cream and morels.
Reds:
filet mignon, grilled or roasted meat, cheese (Comté, Cîteaux).

Serving temperature
Whites: 12-14°C.
Reds: 14-16°C.

Quarts-de-Chaume

This appellation lies between the Loire and the Layon to the southwest of Angers, nestling at the base of a south-facing hillside, sheltered from the four winds. The hamlet of Chaume is located between Beaulieu-sur-Layon and Saint-Aubin-de-Luigné, but it has remained the property of Rochefort-sur-Loire since the 11th century. The vineyard boasts a high proportion of old, low-yield Chenin vines that give excellent results on the schistous terrain. The AOC produces sweet, rich wines from botrytized grapes picked in batches. Quarts-de-Chaume is named after the medieval Lord of Chaume who retained a quarter of all production from vines on his lands.

1954

Appellation
Quarts-de-Chaume AOC
Colour
White (sweet, rich wines)
Area
33 hectares
Production
690 hectolitres

Eye
Straw gold with blush-pink highlights.

Nose
An agreeable array of fresh fruit aromas – cherry, citrus, peach – plus dried fruits and gingerbread. As is characteristic of wines from this appellation, there is an impression of lightness despite the richness of the bouquet.

Palate
Notes of ripe stewed fruit and dried fruit are well balanced by the naturally high acidity of the Chenin, creating a harmonious, fresh palate.

Choice of food
Foie gras, poultry with cream, fruit tarts, sorbets and ice creams.

Serving temperature
8-10°C.

Ageing ability
5-20 years for wines from average years; great vintage wines are capable of infinite ageing.

Soil types
Shallow soils onweathered Precambrian sandstone schist.

Grape variety
Chenin Blanc (or Pineau de la Loire).

299

Quincy

Appellation
Quincy AOC
Colour
White
Area
169 hectares
Production
10,260
hectolitres

1936

The Quincy vineyard stands midway between the Loire and Burgundy, on a plateau of sand and ancient gravel, on the left bank of the Cher at an elevation of 125 metres (410 feet). Close to Bourges and Mehun-sur-Yèvre, the AOC extends into fairly even terrain, producing white wines made exclusively from Sauvignon that are renowned for the freshness and finesse of their bouquet.

The vineyard extends into the commune of Quincy and part of Brinay.

Eye
Quincy is a distinctive pale gold.

Nose
Sauvignon on these gravelly soils imparts aromas of boxwood, budding blackcurrant and white flowers.

Palate
A wide variety of aromas even for such an aromatic grape as the Sauvignon: spice, ripe apple, budding blackcurrant, honey – the range is vast. The freshness and finesse of the aromas allies with supple structure to create an impression of matchless harmony.

Grape variety
Sauvignon.

Soil types
Gravelly-sandy alluvia; lacustrine limestone.

Ageing ability
2 years.

Choice of food
Seafood, fish (grilled sole, salmon with sorrel), *mouclade* (mussel stew), goats' cheese (Crottin de Chavignol, Pyramide de Valençay).

Serving temperature
12°C.

Rasteau

The Rasteau AOC vineyard is located to the north of Avignon, between Aygues and Ouvèze, separated from Beaumes-de-Venise by Gigondas. It enjoys a sheltered position among the last foothills of the Massif des Baronnies at an altitude of 300 metres (984 feet). The only vines suitable for the production of Rasteau *vins doux naturels* are ideally exposed, low-yield Grenache vines of more than 30 years of age.

1944

Appellation
Rasteau AOC
Colours
Red
White
(*vin doux naturel*)
Area
43 hectares
Production
3,030 hectolitres

Eye
• Red Rasteau wines develop nuances of ruby or dark garnet.
• The white wines are amber coloured with copper highlights.

Nose
• The reds give pride of place to scents of red fruits dominated by cherry and blackberry.
• The whites are more complex, evoking crystallised or dried fruit and, depending on the stage of development, scents of honey, the *garrigue*, traces of toast and a hint of caramel.

Palate
• The magic of Rasteau red lies in the fruit sensation cushioned by silky, delightfully spicy tannins.
• The white wines have fruity palate aromas developing from crystallised to dried fruit, quince to sultanas, accompanied by vanilla, spices and roasted scents. These are smooth, creamy, viscous wines: rich and honeyed with well-blended tannins.

Choice of food
Reds: apéritif.
Vins doux naturels: blue cheese, myrtle tart, red fruit soup.

Serving temperature
Reds: 17°C.
Whites: 12°C.

Ageing ability
10 years.

Soil types
Marl; Riss terraces.

Grape variety
Grenache Noir (mainly), Blanc or Gris.

Régnié

Appellation
Régnié AOC
Colour
Red
Area
553 hectares
Production
33,880
hectolitres

1988

The commune of Régnié-Durette became the tenth Beaujolais cru in 1988. Régnié is located on the road from Belleville-sur-Saône to Beaujeu, overlooking the Briare canal that helped Beaujolais wines to become known in Paris in the 17th century. The vineyard is planted on a series of granite hilltops, facing the Brouilly mountain. It produces early maturing, fruity wines of good constitution.

Eye
In their first few months, young Regniés have the purplish tones consistent with wines from granite terroirs. They then become bright red, like a perfectly ripe cherry.

Nose
Régnié offers the full range of red fruit aromas, especially redcurrant and raspberry. Some very delicate cuvées develop fragrances of violet.

Palate
Solid tannic structure coupled with a sense of lingering fruitiness at the back of the palate. Côte de Durette wines were previously vinified as Primeur Villages Nouveaux wines that excited fierce competition between the greatest regional wine merchants. Today, Regnié is a wine for laying down that is vinified in the Beaujolais manner for especially long periods (8-12 days' fermentation on skins).

Grape variety
Gamay Noir.

Soil types
Granitic sands.

Ageing ability
3-5 years.

Serving temperature
14°C.

Choice of food
Terrine, charcuterie, white meat.

Reuilly

The Reuilly AOC lies on the border of the Indre and Cher departments, 30 kilometres (18.5 miles) to the south of Vierzon. It is divided into two viticultural zones about 10 kilometres apart (6.2 miles) separated by a plateau of agricultural land. The vines are planted on sunny slopes on the banks of the Arnon and La Théols, producing dry, fruity whites, light, distinctively fruity reds and original blush rosés (*vins gris*).

 1 9 3 7

Appellation
Reuilly AOC

Colours
Red
Rosé (*vin gris* or blush wine)
White (61%)

Area
130 hectares

Eye
• The whites are distinguished by their pale gold tones.
• The reds are a very pretty ruby red.
• The rosés are a shade of salmon pink.

Nose
• The whites modulate lemony notes mingled with white fruit.
• The reds give pride of place to red fruits (especially cherries).
• The rosés are dominated by scents of peach and apricot.

Palate
• The whites are exceptionally full-bodied with long, lingering fruitiness.
• The reds and rosés are packed with scents of cherry and peach that explode on the palate. They have characteristically supple tannins.

Choice of food
Whites:
fish, fricassee of veal, rabbit with cream, goats' cheese.
Reds and rosés:
charcuterie, poultry, goats' cheese.

Serving temperature
Whites and rosés: 12°C.
Reds: 17°C.

Ageing ability
Whites and rosés: 2 years.
Reds: 4 years.

Production
8,625 hectolitres

Grape varieties
Whites:
Sauvignon.
Reds: Pinot Noir and Pinot Gris.

Soil types
Kimmeridgian marl.

303

Richebourg

Appellation
Richebourg AOC

Classement
Grand Cru

Colour
Red

Area
8 hectares 3 ares
43 centiares

Production
275 hectolitres

1 9 3 6

Soil types
Brown limestone and rendzina, more or less clayey depending on the slope and decline, on hard Prémeaux limestone mixed with fine slope wash.

Richebourg wines are produced in two *climats* on the Vosne-Romanée hillside: one is in the village of Les Richebourg itself; the other is in Les Véroilles. In France therefore *les Richebourgs* (plural) refers to the vineyards and *le Richebourg* (singular) to the wine. Only a footpath separates La Romanée-Conti from Richebourg, where fine-particled slope wash, perfect microclimates and east and east-northeast aspects together create an exceptionally favourable growing environment for one of the greatest Burgundy wines.

Eye
Whether light ruby, velvety red or dark red verging on crimson, Richebourg is nearly always dense, intense and radiant, shimmering with carmine highlights.

Nose
Young wines reveal aromas of musk, Russia leather and sandalwood. Maturity brings aromas of hawthorn and peach blossom, followed by two different families of aroma that are perceived through nuances of lichen, the underwood, mushrooms and notes of cherry, blackcurrant and cooked or crystallised fruit.

Grape variety
Pinot Noir.

Palate
Young Richebourg is intense and violent. This is a wine that needs time to establish its power and find its balance. In great years it becomes elegant and thoroughbred, very concentrated and capable of prolonged ageing.

Ageing ability
5-15 years (often much longer).

Choice of food
Charollais beef, young pigeon, capon with truffles, pheasant with celery, venison with grapes, hare à la Royale.

Serving temperature
Young wines:
14-15°C.
Aged wines:
15-16°C.

Rivesaltes

The Rivesaltes vineyard is the largest and most important of the *vins doux naturels* appellations. It is located in the departments of the Pyrenees-Orientales and the Aude where the hot, dry climate and windy summers produce naturally concentrated grapes. The wines are mainly from Grenache, Muscat, Macabeu and Malvoisie. Red Rivesaltes are macerated for different lengths of time and it is up to the wine grower to judge the moment of *mutage* and whether to add the spirit to the free-run juice or the berries. The whites may or may not be macerated and are mainly formed by maturation.

1936

DOMAINE
CAZES
1975
Cuvée Aimé Cazes
RIVESALTES

Appellation
Rivesaltes AOC
Colours
White (amber-coloured - 85%)
Red (reddish-brown)
Area
8,121 hectares
Production
110,000 hectolitres

Eye

• The whites quickly lose their golden tones to take on an amber hue, verging on shades of walnut in the case of very old wines.
• Young reds are deep garnet-coloured, maturing to mahogany tones similar to the walnut shades of the old whites.

Choice of food
As an apéritif or with warm duck foie gras with apples, red fruit soup, aniseed bread.

Nose

• The whites soon abandon notes of acacia and aniseed or fennel fragrances in favour of aromas of honey, broom, cistus and beeswax. After long periods of ageing, they develop scents of dried fruits plus hints of toastiness when aged in old barrels.
• Young reds are packed with scents of red fruit, notes of cherry, blackberry and a touch of spice. The range of fruit aromas mingles with nuances of the underwood, preserved meat and leather. Oxidation changes the colour to reddish brown and brings out aromas of cooked fruit, prunes and crystallised fruit, followed by empyremeutic scents (dried fruits, cocoa and coffee).

Serving temperature
Whites: 10°C.
Reds: 15°C.

Palate

• Freshness is the quality required in young white Rivesaltes. Maturity adds fullness, finesse, richness and subtle aromas. Orange peel, crystallised fruits, apricot, honey, hazelnut, almond, toast and finally walnut in *rancio* wines: Rivesaltes wines create a universe of fragrance, always signing off with a finish of astonishing length.
• The reds are dominated by strong tannins and fresh fruit. Time and maturation add smoothness, creaminess and silky tannins. Retro-olfaction reveals scents of prunes, cooked fruits, tobacco, spices and roasted aromas.

Ageing ability
30 years and upwards.

Main grape varieties
Grenache Noir, Grenache Blanc and Gris, Macabeu, Malvoisie (rare) and Muscats.

Soil types
Schist, clayey limestone, sand, terraces.

La Romanée

Appellation
La Romanée
AOC

Classification
Grand Cru

Colour
Red

Area
84 ares 54
centiares

Production
31 hectolitres

1936

La Romanée is the smallest appellation in France and overlooks Romanée-Conti from which it is separated by a path running above the village of Vosne. Since 1833, this Grand Cru has been in the hands of the Liger-Belair family, a famous Burgundian wine-growing dynasty founded by a general of the Napoleonic era who planted a celebrated vineyard in the Côte de Nuits.

Eye
Young wines are deeply coloured, growing vivacious and intense after around 15 years' cellaring.

Nose
Young wines have black-skinned fruit on the first nose (blackcurrant and blackberry) and remain fairly closed for the first 5-6 years. With time they develop aromas of

figs, dates, plums and crystallised fruit that take on animal nuances (musk, leather, fur) on contact with the air.

Palate
Packed with fresh cherry aromas and either fruity or full-bodied depending on the vintage. Young wines are somewhat hard in youth, later becoming velvety.

Grape variety
Pinot Noir.

Ageing ability
20 years
(more than
50 years
for great
vintages).

Soil types
Rendzina
on Premeaux
limestone
and oolite,
not very
argillaceous
in texture and
rich in slope
wash. Thicker
and verging
on brown
limestone
towards
the top.

**Serving
temperature**
15°C.

Choice of food
Feathered game
(pheasant,
partridge) or
animal game
(medallions
of venison with
grapes), capon
with truffles,
leg or saddle
of lamb, cheese
(Epoisses or
Cîteaux).

Romanée-Conti

There are three Grand Crus in the Vosne-Romanée area which bear the name of Romanée: Romanée-Saint-Vivant and two wholly-owned crus, La Romanée and Romanée-Conti. The latter is home to one of the most celebrated and expensive wines in the world: 6,000 bottles at most, each one individually numbered. The history of Romanée-Conti symbolises Burgundian wine growing. Owned by the monks until 1584, it was bought for a small fortune in 1760 by Louis-François de Bourbon, Prince de Conti, who lent the estate his name and his status. The area and boundaries have remained virtually unchanged since the early 16th century.

_1936_

Appellation
Romanée-Conti AOC
Classification
Grand Cru
Colour
Red
Area
1 hectare 80 ares 50 centiares
Production
50 hectolitres

Eye
Bright, lustrous red indicates a young wine – it will be 5-10 years before it develops those carmine tints with nuances of bronze mahogany indicating more mature wines.

Choice of food
Loin of mutton, hare à la Royale, leveret filets with truffles, roast beef, cheese (Cîteaux, Saint-Nectaire, Coulommiers, Brillat-Savarin, Reblochon).

Nose
Mature wines have a bouquet as subtle as it is complex, mingling barely wilting rose with grape blossom, blackberry, violet, wet earth, cherry stone, heather, cep mushroom, truffle and sometimes walnut, musk and leather.

Palate
In youth, particularly discreet but already perfectly structured, being supple but restrained and supported by elegant acidity. A wine of monumental constitution and ineffable finesse, slowly revealing a personality of unfathomable complexity.

Serving temperature
15-16°C.

Grape variety
Pinot Noir.

Soil types
Fairly shallow brown limestone.

Ageing ability
10-20 years (more than 50 years for great vintages).

Romanée-Saint-Vivant

Appellation
Romanée-Saint-
Vivant AOC

Classification
Grand Cru

Colour
Red

Area
9 hectares 43 ares
74 centiares

Production
300 hectolitres

1 9 3 6

Romanée-Saint-Vivant was founded and named by the monastery of the Grand Prieuré de Cluny. The vineyard became famous at the end of the 18th century when the Prince de Conti decided to withdraw his Romanée wines from the market and keep them for himself. The appellation lies on marl soils on the upper slopes, producing approximately 40,000 bottles a year of a very great red wine made from Pinot Noir and capable of substantial ageing. The abbey of Saint-Vivant, part of Romanée-Conti, is currently being restored by the owner who is the most important producer in this AOC.

Eye
Crimson with impressive depth of colour that loses none of its brightness with age. With age, the colour takes on a bronze or mahogany hue.

Nose
Whiffs of wildfowl and peppermint underlie a bouquet that frequently evokes rose, cherry, sometimes resin, pistachio and incense.

Palate
Exquisitely feminine, often with a flavour of freshly picked cherries. A gracious wine, with an underlying texture of great finesse – the mark of Pinot Noir – and mouth-filling richness. A wine to be lovingly set aside.

Soil types
Brown limestone with a high proportion of active limestone and rich in marly clay; slope wash.

Grape variety
Pinot Noir.

Ageing potential
Up to 50 years (not to be opened for at least 5-10 years).

Serving temperature
15-16°C.

Choice of food
Game, hare à la Royale, coq au vin, cheese (Cîteaux).

Rosé d'Anjou

Rosé d'Anjou wines first appeared at the end of the 19th century and currently account for a third of the wines produced in this region. Various factors have contributed to their success: a vineyard that was entirely replanted after the phylloxera crisis; the emergence of new vine varieties; the shift from traditional grape varieties to red varieties; and the development of rosé wines in response to increased demand for everyday wines. Rosé d'Anjou is fresh, fruity, light and agreeably refreshing and should be drunk within the year. It is made by direct pressing, sometimes after periods of maceration lasting just a few hours.

1952

Appellation
Rosé d'anjou AOC

Colour
Rosé

Area
2,370 hectares

Production
150,000 hectolitres

Eye
The first thing that strikes you about this wine is its delicacy.The colour ranges from pale to intense pink, with occasional glints of orange.

Nose
A flurry of delightful scents of small, ripe fruit (peach, pomegranate, cherry) plus a scattering of amyl notes (banana, strawberry, fruit drops). Wafting aromas of rose petals accompany a fresh and fragrant range of aromas.

Palate
Supple and harmonious, as though biting into ripe fruit and remaining fruity right through to the finish.

Grape varieties
Cabernet Franc, Cabernet-Sauvignon, Pineau d'Aunis, Gamay, Côt, Grolleau.

Choice of food
Terrine, quiche Lorraine, red fruit soup.

Serving temperature
8-10°C.

Ageing ability
For early drinking.

Soil types
All the terroirs in the AOC.

Rosé de Loire

Appellation
Rosé de Loire
AOC

Colour
Rosé

Area
782 hectares

Production
53,400
hectolitres

1974

Rosé de Loire wines can be produced within the regional appellation boundaries of Anjou, Saumur and Touraine. These wines are strongly characteristic of their native terroir and of the grape variety from which they are made. They range from light to more robust.

Eye
Pale pink with salmon highlights.

Nose
Charming, powerful and complex, with marked aromas of red berries (raspberry, cherry) but also scents of flowers and fruit drops.

Palate
The wine makes an elegant, balanced impression, finishing with a sense of freshness and lightness.

The Rosé de Loire appellation is divided between Anjou-Saumur and Touraine.

Grape varieties
Cabernet Franc,
Cabernet-
Sauvignon,
Pineau d'Aunis,
Grolleau.

Soil types
Schist and
tuffeau.

Ageing ability
For early
drinking.

Choice of food
Summer dishes,
quiche Lorraine,
savoury tarts,
white meat,
cold fish,
fruit salad.

Serving temperature
8-10°C.

Rosé des Riceys

Les Riceys and its three villages are in the south of the Champagne appellation, in the Aube department. Only the best plots planted with old Pinot Noir vines are capable of producing grapes sufficiently rich in sugar to be suitable for vinification as Rosé des Riceys – a wine of such distinctive taste that is has given rise to the French expression *goût des Riceys* (Ricey taste). There are two types of Rosé des Riceys: either aged in tanks and intended for early drinking (the bouquet fades after three years); or matured in the wood for 1-2 years, with better ageing potential.

1947

Appellation
Rosé des Riceys AOC
Colour
Rosé
Area
100 hectares
Production
470 hectolitres

Eye
The colour ranges from pale to very dark pink and red. Purplish nuances are a sign of wines aged in vats.

Nose
Complex, rich and difficult to define. Notable scents are ripe cherry and red and black berries, ranging from a hint of raspberry to just a trace of blackcurrant. The famous 'Ricey taste' includes a touch of vanilla-flavoured almonds and grenadine, underscored by Bergamot.

Palate
A great vintage Rosé des Riceys is round, full-bodied and generous, with a richness of texture and tightly woven palate that makes it more like a red than a rosé. Wines of lesser vintage tend to be more suitable for easy drinking.

Choice of food
White meat, poultry, lean fish, cheese (Cendré des Riceys).

Serving temperature
Wines aged in tanks: 8-9°C.
Wines aged in barrels: 10-12°C.

Ageing ability
Wines aged in tanks: 3 years at most.
Wines aged in barrels: 3-8 years.

Grape variety
Pinot Noir.

Soil types
Clayey-limestone and Kimmeridgian marl.

311

Roussette de Savoie

Appellation
Roussette de
Savoie AOC
Colour
White
Area
145 hectares
Production
1,880 hectolitres

1 9 7 3

The Roussette de Savoie appellation applies to a dry white wine produced from a regional white grape variety, Altesse, otherwise known as Roussette. The vineyard lies mainly in Frangy, along the Usses River, in Monthoux and in Marestel on the edge of Lake Bourget. In contrast to most of the other regional crus which are for early drinking, Roussette de Savoie wines have great finesse and improve after a few years' cellaring.

The Altesse grape variety (or Roussette) is in its element on the slopes of Jongieux, producing richly fragrant wines.

Eye
A pretty straw gold colour.

Nose
Fresh and open revealing toasty notes and nutty aromas reminiscent of hazelnuts and walnut.

Palate
A clean, sprightly attack precedes a fairly long palate flavoured with nuts and fresh walnut.

Grape variety
Altesse.

Soil types
Argillaceous
limestone,
slope wash
from Jurassic
ridges.

Ageing ability
2-5 years.

**Serving
temperature**
10-12°C.

Choice of food
Fish, crayfish,
white meat
(veal escalope
pané),
cheese
(Beaufort,
Reblochon).

Ruchottes-Chambertin

Ruchotte-Chambertin stands just above Mazis in the Côte de Nuits, occupying the untidiest area of land in the Chambertin vineyard, littered with piles of stones, old walls and brambles. The word ruchotte first appeared in 1508 and is derived from *rochers à fleur de terre* meaning 'rocks at the surface of the earth'. This small appellation with its shallow, stony soil produces wonderfully distinguished wines. Le Clos des Ruchottes (one third of the Grand Cru) is wholly-owned by the Domaine Armand Rousseau.

1 9 3 7

Appellation
Ruchottes-Chambertin AOC

Classification
Red

Colour
Rouge

Area
3 hectares 30 ares 37 centiares

Production
110 hectolitres

Eye
Bright ruby-red with a multitude of highlights.

Nose
Discreet, fruity (blackcurrant, redcurrant, raspberry) and floral (rose, jasmin).

Palate
Vigourous with plenty of bite, rich tannins and substantial alcohol – characteristic features of this wine that is both rich and smooth.

Choice of food
Fish (trout, Saône fish stew, pike poached in Chambertin), game, beef casserole, cheese (Ami du Chambertin).

Serving temperature
Young wines: 12-14°C.
Older wines: 15-16°C.

Grape variety
Pinot Noir.

Soil types
Limestone and pebbles.

Ageing ability
10-15 years (up to 30-50 years for great vintages).

Rully

Appellations
Rully AOC
Rully Premier
Cru AOC

Colours
Red (35%)
White

Area
329.1 hectares

Production
15,270
hectolitres

1939

The Rully AOC lies next to Chagny, between Bouzeron to the north and Mercurey to the south. It is evenly divided between Chardonnay and Pinot Noir vine stock, on what is probably the finest face of the slope, looking out over the Saône plain at altitudes of 230-300 metres (755-984 feet). Pinot Noir here yields straightforward, full, fleshy wines. Twenty-three sites rank as Premiers Crus, some of the most distinguished being Clos Saint-Jacques, Grésigny, Chapitre and Les Cloux. They are all located at favourable altitudes of 240-300 metres (787-984 feet) with east and southeast aspects. White wines were traditionally produced from vines at the top of the slope, reds from the *climats* lower down.

Grape varieties
Reds:
Pinot Noir.
Whites:
Chardonnay.

Soil types
Mainly
argillaceous-
calcareous
(suitable for
Chardonnay);
brown or calcic,
less argillaceous
in texture
(suitable for
Pinot Noir).

**Ageing
ability**
Reds: 4-5 years.
Whites: 3 years.

**Serving
temperature**
Reds: 14-16°C.
Whites: 12-14°C.

Eye

• The reds are ruby-red or deep garnet.
• The colour of the whites – golden with green highlights – often becomes more pronounced with age, acquiring strong buttercup-yellow tones.

Château de Rully was built in the 12th century.

Nose

• The reds lead with notes of black (ripe blackcurrant) and red berries (bigarreau cherry) accompanied by aromas of liquorice, lilac and rose petal. As it matures, the bouquet tends towards aromas of cooked fruit and impressions halfway between kirsch and pepper.
• The whites offer notes of hedgerow flowers or acacia, honeysuckle, very delicate elderberry, violet, white peach, lemon and gunflint, often mixed with honey and buttered toast. Nuances of quince and dried fruit develop with age.

Palate

• The tannic substance of the reds is not enough to crush their fruitiness and texture but they do take a little while to mellow. After short periods of ageing, their mildly astringent quality and chewiness blend exquisitely on the palate to create a long, lingering finish.
• The whites are characteristically fruity, but also rounded, firm, fleshy and long.

Choice of food

Reds: feathered game, duck à l'orange, cheese (Reblochon).
Whites: andouillette sausage, frogs' legs, pike with white butter, mussels and scallops, poultry with cream.

The Premiers Crus
Agneux
La Bressande
Champs Cloux
Chapitre
Clos du Chaigne
Clos Saint-Jacques
Cloux
La Fosse
Grésigny
Margotés
Marissou
Le Meix-Cadot
Le Meix Caillet
Molesme
Mont-Palais
Les Pierres
Pillot
Préaux
La Pucelle
Rabourcé
Raclot
La Renarde
Vauvry

Saint-Amour

Appellations
Saint-Amour
AOC
Saint-Amour
followed by the
climat of origin
AOC

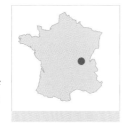

1 9 4 6

Colour
Red

Area
313 hectares

Production
18,120
hectolitres

Grape varieties
Gamay Noir.

Soil types
Slopes of
granitic sand;
argillaceous-
siliceous colluvia
and gravelly
moraine.

Ageing ability
2-5 years.

This delightfully named cru is located in Saint-Amour-Bellevue at the northernmost tip of Beaujolais, 15 kilometres (9 miles) from Mâcon. Most of the vines grow at an altitude of 250 metres (820 feet) on granite and argillaceous clay, shingle and layers of schist. The wines they produce are crimson-coloured, elegant and charming.

Eye
Usually deep ruby-red with dark purple highlights.

Nose
Fragrances of peach and apricot that can be very marked (especially in the first year) combine with scents of red berries (blackcurrant and raspberry). The aromas grow more spicy after 2-3 years' cellaring.

Palate
Short periods of fermentation on skins (8-10 days) produce tender, fruity and floral wines that are accessible within barely 18 months of the harvest – much to the delight of impatient wine lovers. Longer periods of maceration produce more solid wines that seem somewhat harsh at first but come into their own after 3-4 years and still have a good few years ahead of them.

Choice of food
Feathered game,
red meat.

**Serving
temperature**
14°C.

Heavenly juice
Paradis, the name of a famous Saint-Amour *climat* also refers to the exquisite juice that flows off the presses in Beaujolais. Press wines made by traditional methods of vinifying red wines have an acrid, unpleasant taste. Not so in Beaujolais where a special whole-grape vinfication process produces deeply coloured, fruity, fragrant press wines that remain high in natural sugars. After each pressing, the wine grower picks the right moment to draw off a few litres of Paradis. Visitors are treated to a glass of this heavenly juice that is then left to ferment and very quickly loses its initial sweetness.

Saint-Aubin

The tiny village of Saint-Aubin is tucked away at the back of the Côte in the immediate vicinity of Montrachet. Its vineyard is planted on some fairly steep hillsides, especially around Puligny-Montrachet where the terroir is composed of clayey *terres blanches* and the climate is dry and rather cold due to the altitude. These conditions produce fleshy, opulent wines.

1937

Appellations
Saint-Aubin AOC
Saint Aubin Premier Cru AOC

Colours
Red (38%)
White

Area
149 hectares (planted)

Ageing ability
Reds: 4-6 years (up to 10-15 years for good vintages).
Whites: 6-10 years (up to 15 years for good vintages).

Soil types
Fairly argillaceous *terres blanches*, (white wine). Reddish-brown, more clayey, stony soil (red wine). White rendzinas on marl, red rendzinas on brown calcareous soils.

Production
Whites: 4,750 hectolitres
Reds: 2,870 hectolitres

Grape varieties
Reds:
Pinot Noir.
Whites:
Chardonnay.

317

Eye
• The reds are dark garnet or carmine, usually intense, twinkling with raspberry-coloured highlights.
• The whites are pale gold or buttercup, with an infinite range of nuances depending on the method of vinification and the vintage.

The Premiers Crus
There are 15 Premiers Crus divided into several groups: Les Murgers des Dents de Chien (around Puligny-Montrachet and Chassagne-Montrachet); En Remilly, Les Combes, Le Charmois (in the valley going up to Saint-Aubin); Sur Gamay, La Châtenière, Les Champlots (higher up the slope, in the Gamay hamlet area and close to Blagny); Derrière la Tour, En Créot (further west); Bas de Vermarain (to the east); Sur le Sentier du Clou, Les Frionnes, Le Puits, Derrière chez Edouard and Les Castets (on the hillside on the road to La Rochepot). The best Chardonnays are mainly found in the vicinity of the Grande Côte des Blancs, or in the *lieu-dit* of Le Charmois. Pinot Noir does well in the *climats* of En Créot, Les Castets, Sur le Sentier du Clou (or *clos*) and Les Frionnes.

Nose
• The reds reveal aromas of blackberry, crème de cassis, morello cherry and kirsch – like a pot of red jam held under your nose. Scents of the underwood, humus and mushroom complete this range of aromas. More mature wines tend towards spice (cloves), prunes, animal aromas and leather.
• Young whites have a bouquet of white flowers, gunflint, green almond, orange blossom, fern and lemony floral notes. With age they evoke beeswax and honey, marzipan, amber and spices (pepper, cinnamon).

Palate
• Red Saint-Aubin wines are fleshy from an early stage, with good chewiness supported by palpable tannins. As they mature, they become tender, supple and warm and the taste they leave behind is often very persistent.
• The whites are dry and unctuous, firm and caressing. Saint-Aubin is occasionally somewhat sharp and lively in adolescence, becoming mellow after 2-3 years maturation to reveal a deliciously honeyed palate. Mature wines are rich, fat and complete, supported by good acidity.

Choice of food
Reds: hare paté, baked lamb, Charollais beef, roasted poultry, cheese.
Whites: crustaceans, trout with almonds, fish à la crème, foie gras, savoury puffs, white meat, cheese.

Serving temperature
Reds: 15-16°C.
Whites: 12-14°C.

Saint-Chinian

The Saint-Chinian appellation is located in the northwest of the Hérault department, either side of the Orb and its tributary the Vernazobre. It encompasses 20 communes between the appellations of Minervois to the southwest and Faugères to the northeast. The vines are planted on the south-southeast-facing slopes of the Montagne Noire, from the Monts de Pardailhan to the Monts de Faugères, extending southwards as far as the Biterrois plain. The terrain to the north of the Vernazobre is predominantly schistous, with very varied, mainly argillaceous limestone to the south, producing two categories of red wines plus a small quantity of rosé wines.

1982

Appellation
Saint-Chinian
AOC
Colours
Red
Rosé (5%)
Area
2,800 hectares
Production
130,120 hectolitres

Choice of food
Reds: meat and game in a sauce or spit-roasted (with more robust wines); red meat and poultry (with lighter, more quaffable wines).
Rosés: salads, charcuteries (including smoked meats).

Serving temperature
Reds: 16-18°C.
Rosés: 11-13°C.

Soil types
Schist, argillaceous-limestone.

Ageing ability
Reds: 4-5 years.
Rosés: for early drinking.

Grape varieties
Grenache, Syrah, Mourvèdre, Carignan, Cinsaut.

Eye

• The red wines from schistous terrain have deep, dense tones when richly pigmented due to high levels of colour extraction.

• The red wines from the argillaceous-limestone terrain are characterised by their gorgeous red tones – young wines shimmer with light violet highlights.

• The colour of the rosés varies from bright pink to pale pink.

A vineyard in the vicinity of Cessenon-sur-Orbe.

Nose

• The red wines from schistous terrain have empyreumatic aromas, ranging from mildly smoky notes to unmistakable scents of roasted coffee and even cocoa in certain vintages.

• The red wines from the argillaceous-limestone terrain are marked by notes of fresh fruit, sometimes with a floral hint of violets. Wines made from perfectly ripe grapes have distinct notes of crystallised fruit. As it develops, the bouquet takes on notes of the *garrigue*, bay leaf, cistus and spice plus traces of vanilla and liquorice in wines that have aged in the wood.

• The rosés are discreet but elegant with a characteristic fruitiness that sometimes includes a hint of fruit drops.

Palate

• The red wines from the schistous terrain have weak acidity linked to a high pH value (often more than 4). Their tannins are quick to develop, usually within the first two years, becoming remarkably velvety with a smoothness that lasts for five years.

• The red wines from the argillaceous-limestone terrain create an impression of richness and roundness but with a strong sense of underlying tannic character. These tannins are slow to develop. The finest cuvées may be aside for up to 10 years.

• The rosés are impressively rounded with good acid balance and should be drunk within two years to enjoy them at their freshest.

Sainte-Croix-du-Mont

Seen from the sky, the strange stronghold just next to the church in Sainte-Croix-du-Mont seems to balance at the top of the steep slope. This appellation lies on the right-bank of the Garonne opposite Sauternes, benefitting from a local microclimate created by the fogs that form at the confluence of the Ciron and the Garonne. These, together with an excellent terroir founded on thick layers of limestone, create suitable conditions for the production of fragrant sweet wines that age well.

 1 9 3 6

Appellation
Saint-Croix-du-Mont AOC
Colour
White (sweet)
Area
463 hectares
Production
16,440 hectolitres

Eye
Young wines are pale gold turning amber with age.

Nose
The dominant note is fruity within a melody of aromas that evoke raisins, flowers (acacia or honeysuckle) and ripe fruit (apricot, peach) plus the merest trace of honey to whet the taster's curiosity.

Palate
Sainte-Croix-du-Mont may be drunk young or laid down for many years. Fruity and nervous in the early years, these wines have an explosive character that makes them highly seductive. With increasing age, they grow progressively more unctuous and thoroughbred but with no loss of body.

Choice of food
Apéritif; foie gras, gourmet fish, poultry, puddings (tarts, fruits, sorbets).

Serving temperature
8-10°C.

Ageing ability
8-10 years (25 years and more for certain crus).

Main grape varieties
Sémillon, Sauvignon, Muscadelle.

Soil types
Limestone and argillaceous limestone.

Sainte-Foy-Bordeaux

Appellation
Sainte-Foy-
Bordeaux AOC
Colours
Red
White (dry
and sweet)
Area
170 hectares
Production
12,290
hectolitres

1937

Sainte-Foy is an ancient medieval city and a centre of humanism and learning, located between the regions of Bordeaux, the Périgord and Agen. This enclave of the Gironde between the Lot-et-Garonne and the Dordogne looks similar to the eastern part of Entre-Deux-Mers: vines on the plateaux, orchards concentrated in the valleys. For many years the Sainte-Foy-Bordeaux AOC was mainly known for its sweet wines but reds and dry whites these days account for the lion's share of production.

Eye
• The reds have intense ruby or cherry tones.
• The dry whites are an attractive pale yellow; the sweet whites have a more golden hue.

Nose
• The reds offer a bouquet marked by the Merlot, with a charming freshness arising from a delicate fruitiness, also developing toasty notes and hints of ripe or crystallised fruit.
• The dry whites are also delicately fruity, with aromas that are often marked by the Sauvignon. The sweet whites mingle notes of beeswax and apricot with floral scents of lime blossom.

Palate
• The reds are robust and fleshy and characteristic of their terroir. Those from argillaceous limestone slopes have solid backbone.
• The dry whites are crisp and lively but also supple and rich and as fruity on the palate as on the nose. The sweet whites achieve a perfect balance of richness and acidity.

Main grape varieties
Reds: Merlot,
Cabernet-
Sauvignon,
Cabernet Franc.
Whites: Sémil-
lon, Sauvignon,
Muscadelle.

Soil types
Gravel and sand.

Ageing ability
Reds: 3-7 years.
Whites:
1-5 years.

Serving temperature
Reds: 16-17°C.
Whites: 8-10°C.

Choice of food
Reds:
white meat,
poultry,
cheese.
Whites: entrees,
seafood.

Saint-Emilion

Saint-Emilion is a delightful medieval city in the Libourne region and part of Unesco world heritage. It has given its name to two appellations: Saint-Emilion and Saint-Emilion Grand Cru. The vineyard encompasses eight communes that replace the parishes traditionally administered by the Jurade. This is a land of small-scale properties and very varied terroirs producing wines of highly distinctive character. The *Union des Producteurs de Saint-Emilion* (the local wine growers' co-operative) has played a leading role in the development of Saint-Emilion wines.

1936

Appellation
Saint-Emilion AOC

Colour
Red

Area
2,260 hectares

Production
131,350 hectolitres

Eye
Young wines have ruby tones, acquiring deeper garnet shades after a few years' cellaring.

Nose
Wines from grapes of peak maturity have fresh, fruity aromas (redcurrant, wild strawberry) developing spicy notes and a trace of vanilla after maturation in wood. Ideally, the initially floral bouquet should take on a wealth of different nuances associated with ageing: flowers, cocoa, smoke, leather and toasty notes.

Palate
These are textured wines that are generous but very diverse depending on the terroir of origin. Solid tannins support the structure that softens with age and puts on a gorgeous fleshiness in good vintages.

Choice of food
Charcuterie, saddle of lamb Provençale, young guinea fowl with chanterelles, haunch of venison Grand Veneur, escalopes Bordeaux style.

Serving temperature
16-17°C.

Ageing ability
2-6 years.

Main grape varieties
Merlot (60%), Cabernet Franc, Cabernet-Sauvignon.

Soil types
Limestone, gravelly, sandy, argillaceous limestone.

323

Saint-Emilion Grand Cru

Appellation
Saint-Émilion
Grand Cru AOC

Colour
Red

Area
3,420 hectares

Production
156,500
hectolitres

1 9 3 6

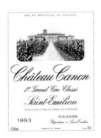

**Main grape
varieties**
Merlot, Cabern-
et Franc, Cabern-
et-Sauvignon.

**Ageing
ability**
6-18 years
(much longer
for the
Crus Classés).

This appellation that overlaps with the Saint-Emilion AOC relates to no specific terroir or even a specific grape variety but to a selection of the very best wines. Most are from the edge of the limestone plateau and the argillaceous limestone slope. They must be estate bottled and vetted in two separate tastings. The 1955 Grand Crus classification system is unusual in that it requires the classed châteaux to be reviewed every ten years. It distinguishes between two categories of crus. The first category are the Premiers Grand Crus Classés, subdivided into two A-class crus (Ausone and Cheval-Blanc) and 11 B-class crus, representing less than 3% of production. The second category are the Grands Crus Classés: 55 châteaux accounting for slightly more than 12% of AOC production.

Château Cheval-Blanc

Cheval-Blanc is one of the most extensive crus in the appellation. It emerged from obscurity in the Second Empire after its then owner, Jean Laussac-Courcaud, ordered the land to be drained and planted with Médoc grape varieties that suited the terroir of gravel and ancient sands. Cheval-Blanc wines are made from 57% Cabernet Franc (a Médoc grape). They possess a finesse and elegance that are almost eternal.

Eye

Young Saint-Emilion Grands Crus are bright ruby with garnet highlights, developing lustrous crimson nuances.

Nose

An overture of deeply concentrated, dominant notes of red berries is followed by a wide range of developing aromas: from vanilla arising from ageing in new wood, to flowers, roasted almonds, fig and cooked prunes.

The 1996 Saint-Emilion Premiers Grands Crus Classés classification

Premiers Grands Crus Classés

A Château Ausone   Château Cheval-Blanc

B Château Angelus   Château Figeac
  Château Beauséjour   Clos Fourtet
    (Duffau-Lagarrosse)   Château La Gaffelière
  Château Beauséjour (Bécot)   Château Magdelaine
  Château Belair   Château Pavie
  Château Canon   Château Trottevieille

Grands Crus Classés

Château Balestard La Tonnelle	Château La Couspaude
Château Bellevue	Château La Dominique
Château Bergat	Château La Marzelle
Château Berliquet	Château Laniote
Château Cadet-Bon	Château Larcis-Ducasse
Château Cadet-Piola	Château Larmande
Château Canon-La Gaffelière	Château Laroque
Château Cap de Mourlin	Château Laroze
Château Chauvin	Château L'Arrosée
Clos des Jabobins	Château La Serre
Clos de l'Oratoire	Château La Tour du Pin-Figeac
Clos Saint-Martin	(Giraud-Belivier)
Château Corbin	Château La Tour du Pin-Figeac
Château Corbin-Michotte	Château La Tour du Pin-Figeac
Château Couvent des Jacobins	(Moueix)
Château Curé Bon La Madeleine	Château Le Prieuré
Château Dassault	Château Matras
Château Faurie de Souchard	Château Moulin du Cadet
Château Fonplégade	Château Pavie-Decesse
Château Fonroque	Château Pavie-Macquin
Château Franc-Mayne	Château Petit Faurie de Soutard
Château Grandes Murailles	Château Ripeau
Château Grand Mayne	Château Saint-Georges
Château Grand Pontet	Côte Pavie
Château Guadet Saint-Julien	Château Soutard
Château Haut Corbin	Château Tertre Daugay
Château Haut Sarpe	Château Troplong Mondot
Château La Clotte	Château Villemaurine
Château La Clusière	Château Yon-Figeac

Palate

There is the same aromatic richness on the palate as on the nose. Saint-Emilion Grand Cru wines are enormously generous and robust with plenty of backbone. The presence of the tannins is very marked for the first few years, making the wines firm but not unpleasant thanks to a certain suppleness and fleshiness – in contrast to the wines of the left-bank that remain austere for much longer. Maturity comes relatively quickly to Saint-Emilion Grands Crus but lasts for a very long time.

Château Ausone

Château Ausone is located at the top of the *Grande Côte* on a near-perfect terroir: steeply sloping shallow argillaceous limestone soils facing east or southeast depending on the area. Vinification and maturation are particularly rigorous, producing a wine that makes no concessions to fashion.

Choice of food
Red meat, pheasant with grapes, young pigeon and other feathered game.

Serving temperature
16-18°C.

Soil types
Limestone, gravelly, sandy, argillaceous limestone.

Saint-Estèphe

Appellation
Saint-Estèphe
AOC
Colour
Red
Area
1,234 hectares
Production
68,950
hectolitres

1936

This proud wine-growing area at the northernmost tip of the Haut-Médoc stands on a plateau overlooking the Gironde, separated from the Pauillac appellation by a stream. Three of its châteaux have left their mark on its history. The most ancient is a Troisième Cru Classé of the 1855 classification, Calon-Ségur, originally a fief of the noble house of Calon. The second is a Deuxième Cru Classé, Cos d'Estournel, famous for the oriental architecture of its chais. The third, also a Deuxième Cru Classé, is Montrose dating from 1815. The gravels here contain slightly more clay than in the Médoc AOCs further south, giving Saint-Estèphe wines solid character in youth plus the ability to age well over long periods.

**Main grape
varieties**
Cabernet-Sauvignon, Merlot,
Cabernet Franc,
Petit-Verdot.

Soil types
Gravelly alluvia
on limestone
bedrock or oyster
marl (*marnes à
huîtres*).

Ageing ability
10-20 years
(30 years
for great
vintages).

The Crus Classés
Château Cos d'Estournel
  (Deuxième Cru Classé)
Château Montrose
  (Deuxième Cru Classé)
Château Calon-Ségur
  (Troisième Cru Classé)
Château Lafon-Rochet
  (Quatrième Cru Classé)
Château Cos-Labory
  (Cinquième Cru Classé)

Eye

Intense colour somewhere between carmine-ruby and crimson with black highlights, turning every shade of deep red in the course of ageing.

Nose

A rich, strong bouquet with aromas of maturation that vary with the proportion of new wood used (roasted aromas, spices, liquorice) accompanied by notes of ripe fruits (blackcurrant) from the Cabernet and floral notes (violets) from the Merlot.

Palate

Powerful structure plus exceptional length due to the wine's constitution. A period of 10 years' cellaring brings out the complexity of the bouquet, allowing the tannins to blend and create a sense of perfect harmony.

Choice of food

Jugged hare, feathered game (pheasant, pigeon).

Serving temperature

17-18°C.

The Oriental Folly of Louis Gaspard d'Estournel

Louis Gaspard d'Estournel, the owner of Cos in the early 19th century, had three great passions: Arabian horses, sailing and wine. He decided to build not the customary château but vast *chais* in a mixture of classical and oriental styles inspired by his travels in the Indian Ocean. Stendhal described them as 'a most elegant construction, bright, light yellow in colour and of no particular style; neither Greek nor Gothic, but very cheerful to look at in what I suppose to be the Chinese fashion'.

Saint-Georges-Saint-Emilion

Appellation
Saint-Georges-
Saint-Emilion
AOC

Colour
Red

Area
170 hectares

Production
10,120
hectolitres

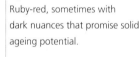

1 9 3 6

Producers in this part of the Libournais are entitled to both the Montagne and Saint-Georges-Saint-Emilion appellations. Some have however remained faithful to the Saint-Georges appellation out of a sense of attachment to the terroir: an area of very homogeneous terrain separated from the Saint-Emilion plateau by the Barbanne River. Soils of almost exclusively argillaceous limestone on uniform, south-facing slopes provide good drainage and excellent ripening conditions for the vines. The vineyard is overlooked by Château Saint-Georges, one of the finest examples of 18th century architecture.

Eye

Ruby-red, sometimes with dark nuances that promise solid ageing potential.

Nose

The bouquet has two distinguishing characteristics: pronounced spiciness and marked complexity. Of these, the most striking quality is spiciness. A wide range of aromas comes into play: blackcurrant, leather, prune, cherry, the underwood, green peppers, blackberry, liquorice and game.

Palate

Saint-Georges-Saint-Emilion is a forceful wine with solid tannic constitution, admittedly a little austere in youth but sufficiently rich, smooth and powerful to continue improving for many years.

Main grape varieties
Merlot, Cabernet Franc, Cebernet-Sauvignon.

Soil types
Clayey lime-stone, silty-clayey and gravel.

Ageing ability
5-10 years.

Serving temperature
16-18°C.

Choice of food
Red or white meat, rabbit.

Saint-Joseph

The Saint-Joseph AOC extends over 26 communes on the right-bank of the Rhône on a narrow strip of land some 60 kilometres (37 miles) long, linking the AOCs of Condrieu and Côte Rôtie in the north with Cornas in the south. It comes as no surprise therefore to find that Saint-Joseph wines reflect certain differences in style. The vineyard faces the hill of L'Hermitage, on slopes of granite, gneiss and mica schist where the soils are often retained by low walls. It produces red wines that may be tender, or solid and powerful depending on origin. It also produces thoroughbred whites.

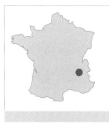

1956

Appellation
Saint-Joseph
AOC

Colours
Red
White

Area
946 hectares

Production
23,580
hectolitres

Ageing ability
3-10 years,
depending on
the terroir and
the vintage.

Soil types
Mainly
granitic
sand.

Grape varieties
Reds: Syrah.
Whites:
Marsanne,
Roussanne.

329

Eye

• The reds are fairly deep in colour, with garnet tones in their youth that verge on more orangey nuances after a few years ageing.
• The whites are light with green highlights at first, developing more or less golden highlights as they mature.

Nose

• The reds are very rich and refined with characteristic aromas of fresh red fruits when young, plus a blackcurrant fragrance that can be quite pronounced. The fruitiness remains with age but becomes more suggestive of very ripe or even cooked fruit, combined with spicy sensations, notably pepper.
• The whites are distinguished by an elegant, subtle bouquet fragrant with mellifluous floral notes such as hawthorn. Age adds spicy aromas that are more pronounced in wines aged in wood.

Palate

• The reds have the advantage of elegant, fine tannins. The overriding impression is of roundness and richness: a gorgeous, rich wine that is velvety on the palate and tends to play down its acidity.
• The whites have an astonishing balance of acidity and sweetness. Those from the best terroirs are rich and round more than vivacious, especially when vinified in the traditional manner using malo-lactic fermentation. Retro-olfaction reveals the same aromas as those perceived directly on the nose.

The towns of Tournon and Tain-l'Hermitage are located on either side of the Rhône. Tournon wines (dating from the Middle Ages) became entitled to Saint-Joseph appellation in 1956.

Choice of food
Reds: grilled white or red meat, hare à la Royale. *Whites:* fish in a sauce.

Serving temperature
Reds: 16-18°C. *Whites:* 12-14°C.

Saint-Julien

The commune of Saint-Julien-Beychevelle has two exceptional terroirs, characterised by small valleys plus gravel soils that together provide good natural drainage for the vines. This as you might expect, is the home of some of the most famous crus in the world, including Châteaux Beychevelle, Talbot and Ducru-Beaucaillou. Saint-Julien's geographical situation puts it at the centre of the Médoc viticultural district, halfway between Margaux and Saint-Estèphe, between Blanquefort and Jau. Saint-Julien wines have remarkable ageing potential and are renowned for qualities that combine the power and sappiness of wines from the communal appellations in the north (Saint-Estèphe and Pauillac) with the finesse of Margaux.

1 9 3 6

Appellation
Saint-Julien AOC
Colour
Red
Area
902 hectares
Production
48,200 hectolitres

Ageing ability
10-20 years (longer for certain crus and certain vintages).

Soil types
Günz gravel .

Main grape varieties
Cabernet-Sauvignon, Cabernet Franc, Merlot, Petit-Verdot, Malbec.

331

Eye

Dark tones that start out as deep ruby in young wines remain surprisingly dark, almost black for a long time – even 10-12 years after the vintage.

Nose

Saint-Julien wines have an enormously complex bouquet. Scents of violet mingled with empyreumatic aromas are surrounded by a flurry of notes including: myrtle, blackberry, black tobacco, morello cherry, cocoa, prune, vanilla, caramel… Nuances of game, truffle or Russia leather emerge with age.

Palate

Rich, sappy and immensely elegant with firm, powerful tannins that promise excellent ageing. This is a tightly woven, highly concentrated wine but with a charming velvetiness supported by good-quality woodiness. The impression of harmony conveyed by young wines grows more pronounced with age. Saint-Julien is best left untouched in the cellar, to be rediscovered 10, 12, or even 15-20 years later, by which time the entire fabric of the wine will have changed to become delicate, occasionally floral and deliciously plump. Age causes no loss of tannic structure but brings out the wine's fullness and richness without the smallest trace of aggression. With time, the finish grows even more complex and elegant to achieve a remarkable degree of aromatic subtlety.

The Crus Classés

Château Ducru-Beaucaillou
 (Deuxième Cru Classé)
Château Gruaud-Larose
 (Deuxième Cru Classé)
Château Léoville Las Cases
 (Deuxième Cru Classé)
Château Léoville-Poyferré
 (Deuxième Cru Classé)
Château Léoville-Barton
 (Deuxième Cru Classé)
Château Lagrange
 (Troisième Cru Classé)
Château Langoa
 (Troisième Cru Classé)
Château Beychevelle
 (Quatrième Cru Classé)
Château Branaire-Ducru
 (Quatrième Cru Classé)
Château Saint-Pierre
 (Quatrième Cru Classé
Château Talbot
 (Quatrième Cru Classé)

Beychevelle

An imposing stronghold originally stood where Beychevelle stands today, watching over the point where the ships lowered their sails and floated up to Bordeaux on the tide dragging their anchors. The name 'Beychevelle' comes from Gascon dialect for *baisse voile* ('lower sails'). The stronghold was demolished towards the mid-18th century and replaced by the beautiful neoclassial residence that we see today. In the 17th century, the estate was owned by the Duke of Epernon, French Admiral and Governor of French Guyana. Then from 1874-1984 it was owned by the Fould family, several of whom became ministers.

Serving temperature
17-18°C.

Choice of food
Red or white meat, poultry, feathered game, cheese.

Saint-Nicolas-de-Bourgueil

Saint-Nicolas-de-Bourgueil stands halfway between Langeais and Saumur. It has given its name to a terraced vineyard on the right-bank of the Loire that is almost exclusively planted with Cabernet Franc (or Breton). Here soils from tuffeau and gravels yield richly aromatic wines that take 4-5 years to come into their own but are well worth waiting for.

1937

Appellation
Saint-Nicolas-de-Bourgueil AOC
Colours
Red
Rosé (3%)
Area
930 hectares
Production
53,570 hectolitres

Eye
Dark, almost black colour with violet nuances, turning dark garnet with age, shimmering with light reddish-brick nuances.

Nose
An intense bouquet with aromas of ripe red fruits underscored by a hint of green pepper or liquorice – these wines are said to *bretonner* (see page 72). Wood-ageing sometimes leaves a spicy sensation.

Palate
Young wines have good, palpable tannins and a vivid attack, promising a wine with a future. With time, the tannic fabric becomes surrounded by aromatic substance of remarkable persistence.

Choice of food
Young reds: charcuterie, white meat, grillage, pot-au-feu, goats' cheese.
More aged reds: red meat, game, cheese (Tomme de Savoie, Gouda, Saint-Paulin).

Serving temperature
14-16°C.

Ageing ability
5-10 years.

Soil types
Tuffeau (clayey limestone); gravel (silico-clayey or siliceous) on the Loire terraces.

Grape varieties
Cabernet Franc (with maximum of 10% Cabernet-Sauvignon).

Saint-Péray

Appellations
Saint-Péray AOC
Saint-Péray
Mousseux AOC

Colour
White

Area
61 hectares

Production
1,500 hectolitres

1 9 3 6

The Saint-Péray vineyard is the last one in the Northern Rhône Valley, at the southernmost tip of the region, protected from the north winds – unlike the Mialan valley that is open to the north and tends to be very windswept. Saint-Péray produces white, predominantly sparkling wines (70% of production) that owe much of their originality to the granitic subsoil, being vinous and less acid than other French sparkling wines.

Eye
• Still Saint-Péray is pale with green highlights, acquiring straw-gold hues with time.
• Sparkling Saint-Péray is also pale with green highlights, plus an abundance of very fine bubbles.

Nose
Sparkling and still wines alike have subtle aromas of hawthorn, violets and acacia that take on mineral and honeyed notes over the years.

Palate
• Depending on the ripeness of the harvest, the still wines may be lightly acidic or marked by richness and roundness.
• Sparkling Saint-Péray wines display a rather original balance. Unlike other wines of this type, they are not necessarily dominated by acidity and reveal a marked vinosity.

Grape varieties
Marsanne,
Roussanne.

Soil types
Granitic sand,
argillaceous-
limestone silt.

Ageing ability
Still wines: 2-10 years depending on the vintage.
Sparkling wines: for early drinking.

Serving temperature
Still wines: 10-12°C.
Sparkling wines: 8-10°C.

Choice of food
Still wines: crustaceans, fish.
Sparkling wines: apéritif; puddings.

Saint-Pourçain

A barrel and a fleur-de-lis have formed the coat of arms of Saint-Pourçain-sur-Sioule since the 13th century: two highly symbolic motifs for this Bourbon city that gave its name to one of the favourite wines of the kings of France. The vineyard spreads along the left-bank of the rivers Allier, Sioule and the Bouble. Traditionally renowned for its white wines, Saint-Pourçain today also produces reds and rosés.

1951

Appellation
Saint-Pourçain
AOVDQS
Colours
Red
Rosé
White (23%)
Area
530 hectares

Eye
• The reds are ruby with vivid highlights.
• The rosés are pale with orangey-yellow nuances.
• The whites are pale yellow gold with green highlights.

Serving temperature
Reds: 14°C.
Whites and rosés: 10°C.

Choice of food
Reds: charcuterie, barbecues, cheese.
Rosés: apéritif salads.
Whites: pompe aux grattons (brioche-type bread with bacon pieces), fish.

Nose
• The reds have a surprisingly mineral range of aromas, mingled with spices, redcurrant and scents of the underwood.
• The rosés reveal aromas of pear and white pepper.
• The whites have floral (acacia) and fruity notes (grapefruit, peach).

Palate
• The reds are pleasantly tannic with a peppery finish.
• The rosés have a fruity fleshiness rather like pear.
• The whites are crisp and fruity.

Ageing ability
Reds: 2-3 years (up to 5-6 years).
Whites and rosés: for early drinking.

Soil types
North: Bourbon sands. Centre: argillaceous-limestone ridge. From east to west: crystalline (schist), Tertiary outwash.

Production
26,800 hectolitres

Grape varieties
Reds: mainly Gamay and Pinot Noir.
Rosés: Gamay.
Whites: Chardonnay, Tressallier, Sauvignon.

335

Saint-Romain

Appellation
Saint-Romain
AOC

Colour
Red
White

Area
88 hectares

Production
White: 2,330
hectolitres
Red: 1,760
hectolitres

1 9 4 7

Grape varieties
Reds:
Pinot Noir.
Whites:
Chardonnay.

The landscape in this part of the Côte de Beaune, to the west of Meursault, is centred on a deep, broad fault that extends all the way to Auxey-Duresses. The view from the top of the cliff at an altitude of 450 metres (1,476 feet) is one of the most spectacular in all of the region. Sheltered by the cliff, the vines face south-southeast and north-northeast on the slopes of a trench cut deep into the Côté, where clay beds and a marl-limestone environment provide ideal conditions for the production of white wines.

The Saint-Romain *climats*
There are no Premiers Crus in Saint-Romain but some of its *climats* need no introduction especially Sous-le-Château and Sous-la-Velle, open to the east at the foot of Saint-Romain-le-Haut. Other crus with a certain reputation are: Sous Roche and La Combe Bazin, opposite the hillside of Saint-Romain-le-Haut; Le Jarron, close to Auxey-Duresses and La Perrière; and En Poillange close to the hamlet of Melin.

Soil types
Marl limestone with clay beds favouring the production of white wines.

Ageing ability
Reds:
6-12 years.
Whites:
5-10 years.

Choice of food
Reds: poached eggs in red wine, meat pastries, roasted poultry, blanquette de veau, stewed lamb, cheese (Cîteaux, Brillat-Savarin).
Whites: crustaceans, fish (especially smoked), frogs' legs, jellied trout, goat's cheese.

Eye

• Red Saint-Romain wines have black cherry tones that mature to carmine.

• The whites are pale gold with green highlights, growing slightly darker with age.

The vineyards below the Saint-Romain cliff are divided between the Côte and Hautes-Côtes de Beaune. The caves here were lived in from the Neolithic period to the start of the first Millennium.

Nose

• The reds offer a bouquet of sour cherry, redcurrant, budding blackcurrant and the underwood. After 4-5 years, they develop nuances of fruit macerated in alcohol, spices or smokiness.

• The whites have the full range of white flower aromas, with distinct nuances of lime blossom, citronella and boxwood underpinning frequently mineral notes. There is sometimes a fragrance of rose-essence or quince. After 3-4 years' ageing, scents of ripe yellow fruit emerge (plums and mirabelle plums) plus the merest trace of honey.

Palate

• Saint-Romain reds tend to be slightly severe in their youth and need a few years cellaring to perfect their qualities and reach their prime. But provided they are well supported by acidity and the tannins remain discreet, these wines soon develop a firm, elegant body with just enough flesh to make an impression.

• Saint-Romain whites bear the mark of the fairly crisp Chardonnay, appearing sappy and spirited from their early years. Four to five years' ageing adds a mellowness that caresses the palate and echoes the early fruit qualities.

Serving temperature
Reds: 12-15°C (or lightly chill-ed when young). *Whites:* 12-14°C (chilled when young).

Saint-Véran

Appellation
Saint-Véran AOC
Colour
White
Area
553 hectares
Production
36,230
hectolitres

1 9 7 1

The Arlois valley is in the southernmost part of the Saône-et-Loire department on the boundary with Beaujolais, marking a geological dividing line between the Mâconnais and its southerly neighbour. The northern part of Saint-Véran close to Pouilly-Fuissé includes Prissé and Davayé. The southern part encompasses Chasselas, Leynes, Chânes, Saint-Vérand and a few plots in Solutré-Pouilly and Saint-Amour-Bellevue. Here the Chardonnay imparts generosity and subtlety to a white wine that was once better known as 'White Beaujolais'.

Eye

A crystalline, pale gold wine, shimmering with green highlights. Wines that have aged in the wood develop buttercup tones.

Nose

Fruit aromas (peach, pear) mingle with acacia, fern and honeysuckle. Notes of fresh almonds, hazelnuts and butter are also quite frequent although scents of honey, exotic fruits and citrus (orange peel) are only noticeable in more mature wines.

Palate

A dry, round, often mineral wine (gunflint, that glorious flint from the region of Solutré). Fiery on the palate, with a good balance of richness and acidity and sometimes a Muscat-like sensation on the finish.

Grape variety
Chardonnay.

Soil types
At the limit of granitic terrain in the south, calcareous and marly-calcareous in the north.

Choice of food
Oysters au gratin, *andouillette* sausage cooked in white wine, blanquette de veau, veal fricassee with chanterelles, goats' cheese (Saint-Marcellin, Bouton de Culotte, Crottin).

Ageing ability
5-7 years.

Serving temperature
11-13°C.

Sancerre

Sancerre perches on a hilltop on the left-bank of the Loire, overlooking a historic vineyard whose wines were praised by poets back in the reign of Philippe Auguste. Such a site epitomises the inter-relationship of a terroir and its grape variety. The Sauvignon vines planted on these river-carved hillsides impart a wealth of aromatic nuances that make Sancerre a wine of breeding and elegance. Red Sancerre is a gorgeous but recent addition to the vineyard and already very popular.

1 9 3 6
1 9 5 9

Appellation
Sancerre AOC (1936, Sancerre white; 1959, Sancerre red and rosé)

Colours
Red
Rosé
White (75%)

Choice of food
Reds:
poultry, cheese (Crottin de Chavignol, Salers).
Whites:
seafood, fish in sauce (pike), cheese (Crottin de Chavignol).
Rosés:
charcuterie, entrees.

Serving temperature
Reds: 14°C.
Whites and rosés: 12°C.

Soil types
Terres blanches (calcareous marl rich in shells), hard limestone (*caillottes*), flinty clay.

Ageing ability
1-5 years.

Area
2,400 hectares
Production
158,000 hectolitres

Grape varieties
Reds:
Pinot Noir.
Whites:
Sauvignon.

Eye
• The whites are light gold.
• The reds have ebullient ruby tones.
• The rosés, from Pinot Noir, verge on blush-pink.

Nose
• The whites reflect the qualities of the Sauvignon that is in its element in Sancerre: notes of citrus, orange, grapefruit and lemon mingle gracefully with mint, fern or acacia. Wines from the *caillottes* have dominant aromas of blackcurrant or boxwood; those from the *terres blanches* have developing notes of tuberose or narcissus; wines from flinty soils inherit scents of acacia, broom or gunflint.
• The reds from Pinot Noir express notes of cherry (ranging from morello cherry to cherry stalk or lush, ripe bigarreau cherry) and venison. Some wine growers mature their red wines in oak casks.
• The rosés have a delicate peach fragrance.

Palate
• The whites are marked by the fragrance of the Sauvignon, a naturally very aromatic grape variety and highly sensitive to its terroir. Here it lines the palate with flavours of orange or orange blossom, quince, blackcurrant, apple, mint, honey and spices. There are marked differences in the aromas depending on the terroir. The aromas develop quite slowly in the full-bodied, robust wines from the white argillaceous limestone soils, and much faster in the elegant, light wines from the very stony *caillottes*. Flinty soils yield firm, structured wines with a characteristic bouquet that is often referred to as 'gunflint'.
• The reds have supple structure thanks to well-blended tannins. Retro-olfaction reveals the scents of cherry and violet noticed on the nose.
• The rosés are fresh and fruity.

Santenay

Santenay is located at the southern end of the Côte de Beaune, on the borders of the Côte-d'Or and the Saône-et-Loire department. The vineyard lies either side of the gently flowing Dheune River, separated from Maranges by the departmental boundaries that were fixed at random in the French Revolution. Previously known as Santenay-les-Bains and better known for its hot springs than its wines, Santenay is now entirely devoted to the cult of Bacchus and wines that include reds 'with the soul of Volnay and the body of Pommard'.

1937

Appellation
Santenay AOC
Santenay Premier Cru AOC

Colours
Red
White (10%)

Area
265 hectares

Production
Reds: 14,300 hectolitres
Whites: 1,700 hectolitres

The Premiers Crus
Beauregard
Beaurepaire
Clos de Tavannes
Clos des Mouches
Clos Faubard
Clos Rousseau
Grand Clos Rousseau
La Comme
La Maladière
Les Gravières
Les Gravières – Clos de Tavannes
Passetemps

Domaine Vincent Girardin
1993
SANTENAY 1ᵉʳ CRU
"LES GRAVIÈRES"
APPELLATION CONTRÔLÉE
12.5% vol.   750 ml e

Soil types
Hard limestone reinforced with marl; brown limestone or marly soil, more or less stony depending on the slope (the best terroirs are on magnesium limestone of the great Oolitic formation).

Ageing ability
5-10 years (20- 25 years for the best vintages).

Grape varieties
Reds:
Pinot Noir.
Whites:
Chardonnay.

341

Eye

• The colour of the reds lives up to the name of one of the Santenay *climats*, 'Beauregard', meaning 'beautiful looking'. These are dark, almost black wines – cherry- or tulip-black – or sometimes very deep peony or purplish ruby.

• The whites are light yellow, developing gold and emerald hues.

Nose

• Santenay reds have classically Pinot Noir aromas: red berries (raspberry, redcurrant, myrtle), spices (pepper, cinnamon), violet nuances, mint, liquorice or even balsam (pine resin). A scent of mushrooms is not uncommon. With age, the wine takes on aromas of leather and macerated, crystallised fruits, especially fruits with stones (prunes).

• The whites offer hints of white flowers, citrus, sweet almonds and toast.

Palate

• Santenay reds are robust, serious, accomplished and definitely for cellaring, but they can also be smooth, tender and round at a young age, with a pretty flurry of fruity palate aromas.

• Santenay whites are clearly related to their neighbour, Chassagne-Montrachet. They are vigorous and robust, with a very fragrant expression (hazelnut, fern).

The village of Santenay.

Choice of food

Reds: roast veal, duck with green pepper spice, game, cheese (Morbier, Pont-l'Evêque, Chaource). *Whites:* seafood, fish (trout with almonds).

Serving temperature

Whites and young reds: 12-14°C. *More mature reds:* 14-15°C.

Saumur

Saumur, the viticultural centre of the Anjou region, became the focus of the Loire wine trade in the 17th century. The vines are arranged in small islands on the famous subsoils of tuffeau or white chalk of white Anjou, in sharp contrast to the dark terrain of black Anjou. Renowned for its white wines since the Middle Ages, the Saumur region today is increasingly noted for its reds. But whatever the colour or style, all Saumur wines are supple and fresh with the delicacy you would expect of wines from a region famous for the good things in life.

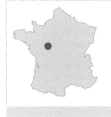

1957
1976

Appellation
Saumur AOC
Saumur Mousseux
(1976)

Colours
Red
White
(sparkling - 30%)

Area
Red: 887 hectares
White: 437 hectares
Sparkling:
848 hectares

Coteaux de Saumur

Coteaux de Saumur wines are to the Saumur area what Coteaux du Layon wines are to Anjou. This small 32-hectare area produces sweet wines from exclusively Chenin grapes planted on tuffeau chalk. Ideal with foie gras or puddings, these delicious sweet wines deserve to be set aside for 10-30 years.

Grape varieties
Reds: Cabernet Franc, Cabernet-Sauvignon, Pineau d'Aunis.
Whites: Chenin (or Pineau de la Loire, 80%), Chardonnay, Sauvignon.
Sparkling wines: Chenin Blanc, Chardonnay, Sauvignon, Cabernet Franc, Cabernet-Sauvignon, Côt, Gamay Noir, Grolleau, Pineau d'Aunis and Pinot Noir.

Soil types
Argillaceous limestone on tuffeau; sandy soils on Sénonian sand at the top of the slope.

Production
78,760 hectolitres
Sparkling: 78,970 hectolitres

Ageing ability
3-5 years (up to 10 years for great vintages).

343

Eye

- The reds are an intense shade of ruby reminiscent of very ripe cherry.
- The whites are pale with attractive green highlights. The sparkling wines have delicate, persistent bubbles.

Nose

- The reds are powerfully evocative of red fruits (raspberry) with accompanying floral (violets) and spicy scents or hints of black-skinned fruits. Vegetal aromas of green peppers indicate a lack of maturity.
- The whites (still and sparkling) unite mineral aromas with notes of white or yellow flowers (acacia or lime blossom). Fruity hints of peach, pear and prune complete a bouquet that leaves an impression of freshness.

Palate

- The reds seem rounded and entirely free of harshness, with a balance that is dominated by mellowness and a simple tannic structure based on well-blended tannins. The palate aromas follow through from the nose, echoing that delightful sensation of biting into lush red fruits.
- The whites (still and sparkling) are refreshing. The sparkling wines create an overriding impression of lightness and finesse as the carbon dioxide titillates the taste buds.

The Saumur district encompasses 29 communes in the Maine-et-Loire department, nine in the Vienne department and two in the Deux-Sèvres department. It is bordered to the north by the Loire and crossed by the Thouet river valley and the Dive that feeds into it.

Serving temperature
Reds: 16°C.
Whites: 14°C.
Sparkling wines: 12°C.

Choice of food
Reds: beef grills, veal escalope pané, cheese (Cantal, Salers, Coulommiers). *Whites:* scallops, fish, cheese. *Sparkling wines:* as an apéritif or with puddings (*clafoutis*, fruit tarts, sorbets).

Saumur-Champigny

Saumur-Champigny is in the Maine-et-Loire department, not far from Chinon, Bourgueil and Saint-Nicolas-de-Bourgueil. The vineyard spreads across the limestone hillsides of the left-bank of the Loire around the town of Saumur. The Cabernet Franc grape variety (known locally as Breton) is the source of dense and elegant red wines with intense but supple tannins that express all the originality of this terroir.

1957

Appellation
Saumur-Champigny AOC

Colour
Red

Area
1,332 hectares

Production
78,175 hectolitres

Eye
A vivid, intense, brilliant ruby, developing dark highlights as the ruby turns garnet over the years.

Nose
Young wines have dominant aromas of red- and black-skinned fruits (raspberry, blackberry, blackcurrant, redcurrant, etc) filled out by notes of spice (nutmeg, tobacco, liquorice) and vegetal fragrances (mint, fern, budding blackcurrant). Nuances of green pepper are sometimes noticeable. With age, the spicy and smoky, toasty notes grow more pronounced, tending towards more pungent scents (belly of hare, fresh leather, a tuffeau cellar).

Palate
Saumur-Champigny wines are often drunk young and undoubtedly owe their success to their supple tannins. This framework serves to bolster the persistency of aromas identified on the nose. Quality tannins are also an advantage where long ageing is concerned.

Choice of food
Grilled *andouillette* sausage, lamb, beef Bourguignon, fish (young wines), cheese soufflé, red fruit puddings and sometimes chocolate.

Serving temperature
12-14°C.

Ageing ability
10 years.

Grape varieties
Cabernet Franc, Cabernet-Sauvignon.

Soil types
Sandy-gravelly to sandy-clayey on tuffeau chalk; green sand with glauconite on upper Turonian chalk.

CHATEAU DU HUREAU
SAUMUR-CHAMPIGNY
APPELLATION SAUMUR-CHAMPIGNY CONTROLEE
1994
Philippe et Georges VATAN

Saussignac

Appellation
Saussignac AOC

Colour
White (sweet
and rich wines)

Area
49 hectares

Production
1,520 hectolitres

1 9 8 2

Saussignac, that other great sweet wine of the Bergerac region, has been famous for centuries. Vines have been cultivated in Saussignac since the beginning of the 11th century and François Rabelais in his 16th century novel *Pantagruel* refers to 'the monks who were the pioneers of Monestier and great drinkers of Saussignac'. The vineyard lies on the left bank of the Dordogne in a superb setting of plateaux and hillsides, producing wines that combine finesse with opulence.

Eye
Deep yellow turning antique gold with age.

Nose
The bouquet mingles white flowers and fruity notes, including distinct notes of apricot and quince plus characteristic scents of nobly rotted grapes: crystallised fruits, honey and roasted aromas. Barrel-ageing imparts nuances of toastiness and liquorice.

Palate
A sensation of fresh fruit precedes flavours of crystallised fruit, beeswax, honey and intense roasted aromas. Next come scents of toastiness, vanilla and liquorice. The palate is rich, full-bodied and fleshy, without a trace of heaviness despite the high sugar content. The persistent finish leaves an impression of completeness.

Main grape varieties
Sémillon, Sauvignon, Muscadelle.

Soil types
Clayey lime-stone, *boulbènes*.

Ageing ability
5-10 years (good vintages are capable of longer ageing).

Serving temperature
8-10°C.

Choice of food
As an apéritif or with veined cheeses, creamy puddings.

Sauternes

Appellation
Sauternes AOC
Colour
White (sweet,
rich wine)
Area
1,623 hectares
Production
36,200
hectolitres

1 9 3 6

U nlike the left-bank of the Garonne that appears mainly forested, the landscape either side of the Ciron is interrupted by vines. The Ciron is a small, cool river that flows from the Landes into the warmer waters of the Garonne. Hence those special morning mists in the Sauternes region that are so favourable to the development of *Botrytis cinerea*, that magical fungus that shrivels the grapes, concentrating the sugars and aromas. The 'nobly rotted' or 'botrytized' grapes are then picked by hand in batches. Sauternes, Bommes, Fargues, Preignac and Barsac are home to the most famous sweet wines in the world. As well as enjoying ideal weather, Sauternes has very favourable soils on the gravelly hills around Yquem – site of the greatest Grands Crus Classés of the 1855 classification. Château d'Yquem itself played an essential role in the development of the Sauternes vineyard. Thomas Jefferson on a visit to Bordeaux in 1784 ranked it as the region's greatest cru.

**Ageing
ability**
20-100 years.

Soil types
Gravelly, clayey
limestone or
limestone.

Grape varieties
Sémillon
(70-80%),
Sauvignon
(20-30%),
Muscadelle.

347

Eye

Pure gold: antique gold at first, turning amber then tea-coloured after a few decades.

Nose

That famous, subtle, delicate 'roasted' scent typical of nobly rotted grapes is experienced here in perfect harmony with the wine, enhancing aromas of almond, quince, citrus, sloe, apricot, peach, etc. No other French wine can match the aromatic complexity of a Sauternes.

Palate

Full, rich, unctuous and powerful, mingling notes of crystallised fruit and roasted aromas with scents of honey, beeswax, white flowers and white and yellow fruits (apricot). The greatest Sauternes have an added elegance due to the toasty notes contributed by the wood.

The 1855 Crus Classés

Premier Cru Supérieur

Château d'Yquem

Premiers Crus

Château Climens
Château Coutet
Château Guiraud
Château Lafaurie-Peyraguey
Clos Haut-Peyraguey
Château Rayne-Vigneau
Château Rabaud-Promis
Château Sigalas-Rabaud
Château Rieussec
Château Suduiraut
Château La Tour Blanche

Deuxièmes Crus

Château d'Arche
Château Brousset
Château Caillou
Château Doisy-Daëne
Château Doisy-Dubroca
Château Doisy-Védrines
Château Filhot
Château Lamothe (Despujols)
Château Lamothe-Guignard
Château de Malle
Château Myrat
Château Nairac
Château Romer
Château Romer du Hayot
Château Suau

Château d'Yquem.

Choice of food

Foie gras (terrine or lightly sautéed), roasted chicken, white meat à la crème, duck with peaches, gourmet fish with cream, cheese (Roquefort), puddings (fruit salad, apple charlotte, pineapple tart).

Serving temperature
8-9°C.

A golden legend

Was Sauternes invented in Suduiraut or in Yquem? Although every château has its own version of the legend, everyone agrees that the owner was away at the time of the harvest and had ordered nothing to be harvested in his absence. The grapes withered on the vine, turned a deep plum colour and shrivelled, but they had an inimitably sweet, crystallised taste and the owner decided to vinify them anyway. The result was quite exceptional.

Sauvignon de Saint-Bris

The Sauvignon grape variety, originally from the Loire, was introduced to the Auxerre region at the start of the 20th century following the phylloxera crisis. Now established in this part of Burgundy, moments from the Chablis region and close to Sancerre, it yields early-maturing, aromatic wines that express the originality of the terroir. The vineyard is planted on the limestone plateaux of the Yonne River valley.

1 9 7 4

Appellation
Sauvignon de
Saint-Bris AOC

Colour
White

Area
98 hectares

Production
6,900 hectolitres

Eye
Saint-Bris Sauvignon is often mat white with a light golden hue; some wines are a deeper shade of yellow.

Nose
Mineral aromas of flint and gunflint plus nuances of mushroom and the underwood that reveal the wine's Chablisian side. Leather and spice are also noticeable. Some wines are even more aromatic, revealing scents of citrus – especially grapefruit – white flowers, rosewood, blackcurrant leaf, apple, bitter almond and sometimes even raspberry.

Palate
Very dry, with an impression of liveliness from acidulous notes of green apple. After This youthful greeness disappears after 2-3 year's cellaring, leaving a much sappier, floral and tender wine.

Choice of food
Young wines:
as an apéritif.
More mature wines:
seafood, quiche Lorraine, Burgundy snails, saltwater fish, cheese (Crottin de Chavignol).

Serving temperature
12-13°C.

Ageing ability
5-6 years.

Grape variety
Sauvignon.

Soil types
Lower Kimmeridgian limestone (*calcaire à astartes*) on the border of Yonne alluvia and at the foot of marly-calcareous slopes. Best sites: tops of north-facing slopes.

Savennières

Appellation
Savennières AOC

Colour
White (dry and sweet)

Area
126 hectares

Production
3,880 hectolitres

1952

Savennières has a special place in the history of great white wine production in Anjou: since the Middle Age, it has been producing a dry white wine in a sweet wine region that only became established in the 17th century under the influence of the Dutch wine trade. The AOC lies on the right-bank of the Loire, some 15 kilometres (9 miles) to the south-southwest of Angers, on sheltered hillsides of schist soils.

Eye
Pale yellow with a wealth of nuances, from youthful green highlights to golden hues in wines produced in warm years.

Nose
The first nose is often reminiscent of white flowers, especially acacia, with accompanying mineral notes and sometimes nuances of lime and camomile. Airing brings out the aromas of ripe or dried fruits.

Palate
Harmonious, with that balance of smoothness and freshness, structure and delicacy that is the signature of the great Val de Loire wines.

Choice of food
As an apéritif or with fish, white meat (chicken Anjou-style).

Grape variety
Chenin Blanc (Pineau de la Loire).

Soil types
Shallow soils on schist or sandy schist.

Ageing ability
10-20 years.

Serving temperature
10-12°C.

Savennières Coulée-de-Serrant

Coulée-de-Serrant, in the heart of the Savennières vineyard, is the most renowned cru of the Anjou area. The AOC is located on a rocky spur that juts out over the Loire, overlooking a fortress at the base that dates from the Middle Ages. The terroir comprises three plots: the Grand Clos de la Coulée on the western flank of the Coteau de Chambourreau; the Clos du Château on slopes that are symmetrical with the Grand Clos; and Les Plantes. Coulée-de-Serrant produces single-estate, biodynamic white wines that may be laid down for many years.

1952

Appellation
Savennières Coulée-de-Serrant AOC

Colour
White

Area
19 hectares

Production
210 hectolitres

Eye
Delicate pale yellow with distinctive green highlights plus a wealth of other nuances.

Nose
Each of the aromatic notes stands out clearly as scents of white flowers and lime blossom unite with mineral notes, then with accents of ripe or dried fruits.

Palate
The balance achieves finesse within an overall complexity that is linked to the aspect – east, west, south – of each of the three different Coulée de Serrant plots. The expression of the grapes varies with the terroir.

CLOS DE LA
Coulée de Serrant
APPELLATION SAVENNIÈRES · COULÉE DE SERRANT CONTROLÉE
1990 Joly
Vin issu d'agriculture biodynamique - Demeter
Nicolas JOLY, Propriétaire-Viticulteur
au Château de la Roche-aux-Moines - 49170 SAVENNIÈRES
Mise en bouteilles au Château
PRODUCT OF FRANCE   NET CONTENTS : 750 ML.   ALC. : 12,5 %/VOL.   L1

Choice of food
Pike quenelles, salmon with sorrel.

Serving temperature
10-12°C.

Ageing ability
10-20 years.

Soil types
Shallow soils on schist or sandy schist.

Grape variety
Chenin Blanc (Pineau de la Loire).

Savennières Roche-aux-Moines

Appellation
Savennières
Roche-aux-
Moines AOC

Colour
White

Area
6.85 hectares

Production
600 hectolitres

1 9 8 4

This celebrated *lieu-dit* within the Savennières area was named Roche-aux-Moines after the monks of Saint-Nicholas to whom it was given in 1285. At other times in its history, it was named Roche-au-Duc following its acquisition by Duke Louis II of Anjou in 1370; then Roche de Serrant in 1481 when Louis XI gave it to his chamberlain, Perthus de Brie, Lord of Serrant; and Roche Vineuse during the French Revolution. The underground passages upon which the château is built are used today to store the wines.

Eye
Pale gold, shimmering with green highlights.

Nose
Savennières Roche-aux-Moines is fresh and intense, revealing aromas of acacia and honey, notes of hazelnuts and crystallised fruits plus a trace of minerals.

Palate
Freshness, fullness and length make Savennières Roche-aux-Moines a very harmonious wine.

Château de la Roche-aux-Moines.

Main grape variety
Chenin (Pineau de la Loire).

Soil types
Shallow soils on schist and sandy schist.

Ageing ability
10-20 years.

Choice of food
Crayfish, grilled fish, *andouillette* sausage or rabbit in white wine, veal chop à la crème.

Serving temperature
10-12°C.

Savigny-lès-Beaune

The village of Savigny-lès-Beaune nestles in the hollow of a small river valley, the Rhoin, just to the north of Beaune. The Dukes of Burgundy, the abbeys and the knights of Malta are among the former owners of this celebrated vineyard that comprises two fairly distinct areas: one facing full south not far from Pernand-Vergelesses; the other located beneath the Mont Battois, on the Beaune side. The soils are quite sandy and the vines face east and northeast. Savigny-lès-Beaune is essentially a red wine although white wines account for an increasing share of production.

1937

Appellation
Savigny-lès-Beaune AOC
Savigny-lès-Beaune Premier Cru AOC

Colours
Red
White (10%)

Area
348 hectares

Production
Red: 14,600 hectolitres
White: 1,700 hectolitres

Eye
• The reds are intense garnet, sometimes verging on black tulip.
• The whites are pale gold with green highlights.

Nose
• The reds release aromas of red berries (cherry, raspberry) and black berries (blackcurrant, blackberry), flowers (violets), pitted fruit macerated in alcohol and liquorice nuances. With age, these wines often express animal notes and accents of humus and the underwood mingled with spices.
• The whites offer scents of hawthorn, fresh almonds, mint, lemon, pear, blackcurrant leaf, rose, nutmeg, fresh breadcrumbs and hazelnuts.

Palate
• The reds sometimes taste of blackberries and liquorice. They have a robust framework built on palpable tannins.
• The whites have all the fruit and floral qualities of the Chardonnay. They tend to be fairly lively but settle down with time to reveal a rich, voluptuous character.

Serving temperature
Reds: 14-16°C.
Whites: 12-14°C.

Choice of food
Reds: parsley ham, poultry or venison with sauce, cheese (Epoisses, Soumaintrain, Langres, Munster).
Whites: Quiche Lorraine, *andouillette* sausage, Burgundy snails, filets of sole, turbot, bass, cheese (Comté, Saint-Nectaire).

Soil types
Towards Pernand-Vergelesses: gravelly, sprinkled with ferruginous oolite; down the slope, more clayey, stony terrain, related to the same reddish-brown limestone. Towards Beaune: clayey limestone, but sandier.

Grape varieties
Reds:
Pinot Noir.
Whites:
Chardonnay.

Ageing ability
Reds:
5-15 years.
Whites:
4-12 years.

Seyssel

Appellation
Seyssel AOC
Seyssel Mousseux
AOC

Colour
White

Area
82 hectares

Production
Still wines: 2,600
hectolitres
Sparkling wines:
575 hectolitres

1 9 4 2

The ancient vineyard of Seyssel is wedged between the northern pre-Alps and the southern tip of the Jura massif, between the departments of Haute-Savoie and Ain, in the communes of Corbonod and Seyssel. The vines are planted on softly undulating slopes on both sides of the Rhône, just before the river flows into the Bugey AOC. The wines are essentially produced from glacial moraine backing on to the secondary Jurassic range. They owe their impressive finesse to the Altesse and Molette grape varieties. Expect these wines to be spirited and reserved rather than powerful or opulent.

Eye

• The dry whites are straw coloured with green highlights.
• The sparkling wines are paler with a cordon of fine persistent bubbles.

Nose

Still and sparkling wines offer floral and fruity aromas, plus a distinct hint of violets often accompanied by white fruits.

Palate

Discreet on the attack with an assertive balance of freshness and roundness and generous, mouth-filling palate aromas.

The village of Seyssel on the banks of the Rhône.

Grape varieties
Altesse and
Molette.

Soil types
Tertiary basin
with substratum
of waste rock.

**Ageing
ability**
2 years.

Choice of food
Still wines: fish
with sauce,
crustaceans.
Sparkling wines:
as an apéritif.

**Serving
temperature**
10-12°C.

La Tâche

La Tâche is one of several remarkable Grands Crus in Vosne-Romanée. It is located south of La Grande Rue and its name comes from an old Burgundian expression, *'faire une tâche'*, meaning to perform a task – in this case, to cultivate vines in exchange for a lump sum. Wholly owned by the Domaine de La Romanée-Conti since 1933, La Tâche has known only four owners since the 17th century. Grafts from its vineyards were used to rebuild the vineyard of La Romanée-Conti between 1947 and 1948, thus creating 'family' ties between these two flamboyant wines.

1 9 3 6

Appellation
La Tâche AOC
Classification
Grand Cru
Colour
Red
Area
6 hectares
Production
170 hectolitres

Eye
Ruby, glinting with dark highlights.

Nose
Rich and concentrated with a liquorice range of aromas, mingling wild herbs, spices, mushrooms and fruits in alcohol.

Palate
La Tâche may seem reserved for the first two years but it subsequently achieves elegant expression thanks to a long, full-bodied structure.

SOCIÉTÉ CIVILE DU DOMAINE DE LA ROMANÉE-CONTI
PROPRIÉTAIRE A VOSNE-ROMANÉE (COTE-D'OR) FRANCE

LA TÂCHE
APPELLATION LA TÂCHE CONTROLÉE
17.971 Bouteilles Récoltées
BOUTEILLE N° 00000 LES ASSOCIÉS-GÉRANTS
ANNÉE 1993
Mise en bouteille au domaine

Choice of food
Hen pheasant, Bresse poularde, truffle, cheese (Coulommiers, Cîteaux).

Serving temperature
14-15°C.

Ageing ability
15-20 years.

Soil types
Brown limestone soils, rather rendzina-like, fairly shallow at the top, deeper at the botttom.

Grape variety
Pinot Noir.

Tavel

Appellation
Tavel AOC
Colour
Rosé
Area
933 hectares
Production
43,370 hectolitres

1 9 3 6

The village of Tavel is in the Gard, backing onto a limestone plateau covered with *garrigue* on the right-bank of the Rhône opposite Châteauneuf-du-Pape. This is the only Rhône appellation to produce exclusively rosé wines, for which it has been famous since the days of the popes of Avignon. The vines are planted on soils of fine sand, argillaceous alluvia or rounded pebbles. Tavel rosé is one of the most celebrated French rosé wines and is easily recognisable by its slender bottle engraved with a coat-of-arms.

Main grape varieties
Grenache, Cinsaut, Syrah, Clairette Blanche and Rose, Piquepoul, Calitor, Bourboulenc, Mourvèdre, Carignan.

Soil types
Sandy soils; rounded pebbles on ancient terraces; meagre soils on limestone splinters.

Eye

The young wines have light, luminous, pure pink tones that take on a pale gold hue after a year, gradually turning copper coloured and amber as they mature.

Nose

Tavel offers a bouquet of flowers, red berries, pitted fruits, sometimes underscored by a hint of fresh almond. A year's cellaring produces aromas of ripe fruits, grilled almond and spices. Wines that have aged for longer periods have dominant scents of Maderia and liquorice.

Palate

An overall impression of warmth, with aromas of pitted fruit, almonds, spices and toast that echo the aromas on the nose. The wine's roundness and fullness are due to the grape varieties of the appellation and the practice of cold macerating the grapes for periods of 12-48 hours. The sensations on the palate are long and lingering.

Ageing ability
2-3 years
(and longer depending on the vintage).

Serving temperature
10°C.

Choice of food
Apéritif; charcuterie, artichokes, barbecues, ham soufflé.

Touraine

The Loire River flows through the Touraine region for almost 100 kilometres (62 miles), joined by the Cher, Indre and Vienne rivers in the south and the Cisse and Brenne in the north. On the slopes of these river valleys are the grape varieties of the Touraine appellation that differ depending on the terroir but share a great freshness and fruit. Maritime influences are felt in the far west where fine autumn days favour the ripening of late-maturing vine varieties such as Cabernet Franc. To the east the climate becomes definitely continental, imparting distinctive expression to the Sauvignon in the dry white wines. Touraine Primeur wines, made primarily from Gamay Noir, were awarded appellation status in their own right in 1979.

1939

Appellation
AOC Touraine

Colours
Red (51%)
Rosé (4%)
White (dry and sparkling)

Area
5,282 hectares

Choice of food
Reds:
red or white meat, cheese.
Whites:
charcuterie, seafood, fish.
Sparkling:
as an apéritif.

Serving temperature
Reds:
12-14°C.
Still and sparkling whites:
8-10°C.

Grape varieties
Reds: Gamay Noir, Cabernet Franc, Cabernet-Sauvignon, Côt.
Rosés: Gamay Noir (sometimes with Cabernet and Côt), Pineau d'Aunis.
Whites: Sauvignon, Chenin Blanc (Pineau de la Loire).

Ageing ability
Gamay and Sauvignon:
for early drinking.
Cabernet Franc, Cabernet-Sauvignon and Côt: 2-4 years.
Chenin:
5-15 years.

Production
353,100 hectolitres

Soil types
Argillaceous limestone and sands on clay.

Eye

• Gamay or Cabernet wines are a cherry colour.

• Touraine wines from Sauvignon are straw-yellow with green highlights. Pineau de la Loire imparts tones that turn golden in old wines.

• Touraine rosé is usually thinly coloured when made from Gamay or Cabernet, and blush-pink when made from Pineau d'Aunis.

Nose

• Gamay reds have a strawberry or cherry fragrance; Cabernet reds recall raspberry, green peppers and liquorice. Blended wines are dominated by aromas of tobacco or leather from the Cabernet. Côt adds scents of red fruits that acquire animal nuances with time. Touraine Primeur wines evoke fruit-drops and banana.

A meeting place of grape varieties

Sauvignon white wine, produced mainly in the Cher valley upstream from Montrichard, is a very fragrant wine that should be drunk young. Pineau de la Loire is the source of still, mainly dry wines and sparkling wine made by the *Méthode Traditionnelle*. It is a rule of this appellation that Chardonnay (which is in any case rare in the Touraine) must be blended with Pineau de la Loire.

• Whites made from Sauvignon may be floral with a touch of gooseberry or budding blackcurrant, mingled with traces of musk and spices. They often have a mineral side to them. Whites made from Pineau de la Loire have agreeable aromas of acacia, quince, dried fruits, honey or citrus.

Palate

• Gamay reds have discreet tannins and dominant fruitiness and should be drunk within two years. Reds made from Cabernet and Côt may be laid down for 2-4 years thanks to their good tannic support.

• The rosés based on Pineau d'Aunis are always dry and fresh, bringing to mind spices and cloves.

• Whites from Sauvignon are delicately lively. Pineau de la Loire whites are also lively with a rich and elegant bouquet. The sparkling wines made by the *Méthode Traditionnelle* have mouth-filling flavours of brioche and apple.

Vineyards around Châteauvieux.

Touraine Amboise

The Amboise vineyard is located between Tours and Blois, extending along both banks of the Loire on the classical clay-with-flint soils of the Touraine. Although the Atlantic influences are much less marked here, the climate remains favourable to late-ripening grape varieties. Chenin Blanc gives dry, medium dry and sweet white wines; Gamay is usually the basis of red and rosé wines. The AOC also produces blended wines of moderate ageing potential containing a high proportion of Cabernet and Côt.

1939

Appellation
Touraine
Amboise AOC

Colours
Red (55%)
Rosé (25%)
White (20%)

Area
236 hectares

Eye
- Reds produced from a blend of Gamay Noir and Cabernet are a vivid cherry colour.
- The rosés are light in colour.
- The whites are straw-yellow in their youth, turning gold after 3-4 years' cellaring.

Nose
- The reds modulate scents of red fruits and develop aromas of game as they age.
- The rosés bring to mind a bouquet of roses and lilac underscored by almond notes.
- The whites are all quince and honey.

Palate
- The reds are solid and full.
- The rosés have a refreshing quality.
- The whites have a certain suppleness due to the influence of the more continental climate.

Production
11,900
hectolitres

Choice of food
Reds: red or white meat, cheese.
Rosés: charcuterie, grilled foods.
Dry whites: charcuterie, seafood, fish, poultry with cream, puddings.

TOURAINE AMBOISE

Serving temperature
Reds: 12-14°C.
Whites and rosés: 8-10°C.

Ageing ability
Reds: 2-5 years.
Rosés: for early drinking.
Whites: 5-15 years.

Soil types
Siliceous clay, clayey-calcareous.

Grape varieties
Reds and rosés: Gamay, Cabernet Franc, Côt.
Whites: Chenin Blanc.

359

Touraine Azay-le-Rideau

Appellation
Touraine Azay-le-Rideau AOC
Colours
Rosé
White (38%)
Area
45 hectares
Production
2,500 hectolitres

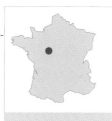

1 9 3 9

The small wine-producing region of Azay-le-Rideau stretches along the Indre valley between Montbazon and the Loire, on clay-with-flint soils. The especially mild climate here at the confluence of the Indre and Loire rivers favours the ripening of late-maturing grape varieties. The AOC produces refined and elegant rosés, and dry and medium dry white wines.

Eye
• The rosés fill the glass with lightness.
• The whites are never very deeply coloured and retain their straw-yellow tones for many years.

Nose
• The rosés are dainty, bringing to mind roses, marsh mallow, lilac and almond.
• The whites are rich in floral and fruit aromas (acacia, dog rose, white peach, apricot, green apple) but also have a mineral edge inherited from the erosional soils of the Indre hillsides. After a few years' cellaring, Touraine Azay-le-Rideau wines evoke honey and quince.

Palate
• The rosés have a well-behaved liveliness that makes them especially agreeable in summer.
• The freshness of the whites is emphasised by mineral aromas, notes of gunflint reflecting the influence of the terroir.

Grape varieties
Rosés: Grolleau de Cinq-Mars, Gamay Noir, Côt, Cabernet Franc and Cabernet-Sauvignon.
Whites: Chenin Blanc (or Pineau de la Loire).

Soil types
Siliceous-clay, clayey-calcareous.

Ageing ability
Rosés:
for early drinking.
Whites:
5 to 15 years.

Serving temperature
8-10°C.

Choice of food
Rosés:
charcuterie, grills.
Dry whites:
charcuterie, seafood, fish.
Medium dry wines: apéritif poultry à la crème, puddings.

Touraine Mesland

The Mesland vineyard is situated west of Blois, planted on the slopes of the right-bank of the Loire facing the Château de Chaumont, a Gothic and Renaissance building set in grounds planted with rare species of plants. Gamay Noir replaced plantings of Côt here in the 1840s and has adapted perfectly to the local clay-with-flint soils mixed with sands and granite. Terroir, a continental climate and low yields all contribute to the production of full-bodied wines that age well.

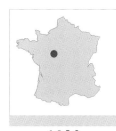

1939

Appellation
Touraine Mesland AOC

Colours
Red
Rosé
White (10%)

Area
85 hectares

Production
6,400 hectolitres

Choice of food
Reds: salted pork with lentils, roast pork, rabbit with mustard, cheese (Cantal, Tomme de Savoie), clafoutis.
Rosés: charcuterie, grills, lamb kebab.
Whites: seafood, fish (grilled trout, salmon with sorrel), poultry à la crème, white pudding.

Eye
• The reds are reminiscent of a well-ripened cherry.
• The rosés sparkle with salmon highlights.
• The whites reveal straw-yellow tones.

Nose
• The reds reveal complex aromas of very ripe fruits.
• The rosés display fresh, delicate aromas of spices and red fruits.
• The whites have a fragrance of white fruits (pear) and spices.

Palate
• The Gamay wines are substantial, imbued with aromas of well-ripened red fruit and prunes.
• The rosés have a definite, solid structure that makes them suitable to accompany an entire meal.
• The whites are lively from the moment of attack and benefit from the roundness of the Sauvignon.

Serving temperature
Reds: 12-14°C.
Whites and rosés: 8-10°C.

Ageing ability
Reds: 2-5 years.
Rosés: for early drinking.
Chenin whites: 5-15 years.

Soil types
Siliceous clay, argillaceous-calcareous; rich in granitic sand.

Grape varieties
Reds and rosés: Gamay Noir, Cabernet Franc (or Breton), Côt.
Whites: Chenin Blanc (or Pineau de la Loire), Sauvignon, Chardonnay.

361

Touraine Noble-Joué

Appellation
Touraine Noble-Joué AOC

Colour
Rosé

Area
25 hectares

Production
1,200 hectolitres

2 0 0 1

Following many years under the aegis of the Touraine AOC, the Noble-Joué vineyard now once again enjoys appellation status in recognition of its characteristic rosé wines. Vines were cultivated in this area well before the 15th century and are part of the viticultural heritage of the Touraine region. At the end of the 19th century, Noble-Joué was one of the largest vineyards in the region, but fluctuations in the climate and creeping urbanisation eventually brought about its disappearance after the First World War. In 1970, the former terroir was restored to life by local wine growers who confined plantings to the most favourably exposed slopes east of Tours, between the Cher and Indre rivers.

Eye
Rather blush tones maturing to shades of partridge eye.

Nose
Aromas of flowers (peony, hyacinth) on the first nose, followed by notes of red fruits (redcurrant, cherry, morello cherry) or white-fleshed fruit (ripe pear).

Palate
Marked flavours of morello cherry, with the merest trace of spiciness due to a nuance of cloves. The wine is never tannic and leaves an impression of roundness. The Malvoisie gives it good body together with aromas of ripe pear on the finish; the Pinot Meunier provides fruitiness and freshness; the Pinot Noir imparts aromatic finesse.

Grape varieties
Pinot Meunier (50-60%), Pinot Gris or Malvoisie (30-40%), Pinot Noir (10-20%).

Soil types
Clay-with-flint, stony.

Ageing ability
For early drinking (up to 5 years for good vintages).

Serving temperature
10-12°C.

Choice of food
Apéritif; charcuterie, fish, white meat, North African cuisine.

Tursan

This former property of Alienor d'Aquitaine, extends from Madiran across the hillsides of east Chalosse, in the cantons of Aire-sur-Adour and Geaune. Like all the vineyards of the region, Tursan has a long history of export. In the 12th century, Tursan wines were sold in London, Cordoba and Seville. From the 15th to the 18th centuries, they became established in the Hanseatic markets. The white wines owe their originality to a local grape variety called Baroque, but the reds and rosés are also full of character.

1958

Appellation
Tursan AOVDQS
Colours
Red
White (35%)
Rosé
Area
239 hectares
Production
13,400 hectolitres

Eye
• The reds range from dark crimson and garnet to almost black – sign of a powerful palate.
• The rosés are fairly pale in colour.
• The whites are a very typical, rather pale, straw-yellow.

Nose
• The reds reveal aromas of red fruits in their youth, maturing to scents of prunes, game and old leather.
• The rosés offer fruit aromas that develop with extreme finesse.
• The whites are fragrant with scents of white fruits, verbena and lime blossom.

Palate
• The reds are tannic, robust and foursquare – they need short periods of ageing.
• The rosés assert their character and freshness with mineral notes (gunflint).
• The whites are dry, nervous and very fragrant.

Choice of food
Reds: grills, *confit, magret* and *garbure.*
Rosés: charcuterie, grills.
Whites: shad, young eels, grilled fish.

Serving temperature
Reds: 15-17°C.
Whites and rosés: 8-10°C.

Ageing ability
Reds: 4-8 years.
Whites and rosés: for early drinking.

Soil types
Gravel, marl and limestone.

Grape varieties
Reds: Tannat, Cabernet-Sauvignon, Cabernet Franc and Pinenc.
Whites: Baroque (main variety).

Vacqueyras

Appellation
Vacqueyras AOC
Colours
Red (95%)
Rosé (4%)
White (1%)
Area
1,050 hectares
Production
39,700 hectolitres

1990

V acqueyras, the most recent of the Rhône valley communal appellations, derives its name from the Latin *Vallea quadreria*, meaning 'valley of stones'. The AOC extends over the communes of Vacqueyras and Sarians, in the Vaucluse department, at the foot of the Dentelles de Montmirail. In the Quaternary period, the river Ouvèze deposited layers of rounded stones here that temper the summer heat. The wine growers of Vacqueyras have acquired a certain reputation, based mainly on complex and concentrated red wines.

Eye
• Young reds are ruby, turning darker with age.
• The rosés are deep pink.
• The whites fill the glass with glistening pale gold tones, twinkling with green highlights.

Nose
• One-year-old reds release aromas of red fruit (blackcurrant, cherry). Bottle-aged wines offer notes of cooked or crystallised fruit (figs) accompanied by spicy nuances (pepper and the *garrigue*), empyreumatic notes (smoke) and sometimes touches of leather and game.
• The rosés develop a citrus theme with dominant notes of grapefruit.
• The whites have a floral bouquet with aromas of acacia and broom to the fore backed by a sudden gushing hint of citrus (grapefruit).

Palate
• The reds are powerful and rich but remain delicate, with a tannic structure that can survive years of ageing.
• The rosés are fragrant with notes of the terroir and the *garrigue*.
• The whites have sufficient richness and freshness to achieve good balance. They also have good aromatic persistence.

Main grape varieties
Reds: Grenache Noir, Syrah, Mourvèdre, Cinsaut.
Whites: Clairette, Grenache Blanc, Bourboulenc, Roussanne.

Soil types
Limestone, rounded pebbles.

Ageing ability
1-5 years.

Serving temperature
Reds: 14-16°C.
Rosés and whites: 10-12°C.

Choice of food
Reds: lamb, grilled red meat.
Rosés: fish.
Whites: charcuterie.

Valençay

The Valençay vineyard at the northwest gateway to the Berry region, extends from the Val de Loire across 14 communes in the Indre department and one in the department of Loir-et-Cher (Selles-sur-Cher), on the south bank of the Cher. The vines line the hillsides formed by the network of rivers that criss-cross the plateaux. The wines they produce are fresh and fragrant, marked by aromas of gunflint.

1970

Appellation
Valençay AOVDQS
Colours
Red
Rosé
White (dry)
Area
129 hectares
Production
7,850 hectolitres

Eye
• The reds are light in colour with a scattering of violet nuances.
• The rosés have pale tones.
• The whites are pale yellow with green highlights.

Nose
• The reds mingle scents of red fruit (blackcurrant) with spices.
• The rosés have fruit aromas to the fore.
• The fragrant whites bear the mark of Sauvignon with powerful aromas of blackcurrant and broom that balances with the finesse of the Chardonnay.

Palate
• The structure of the reds is influenced by the grape varieties that make up the blend: Gamay sets the overall tone, Côt reinforces tannic structure and Pinot Noir increases finesse.
• The rosés are crisp and delicate.
• The whites are vivacious, and supple and seductively crisp, developing a silky, enveloping structure.

Grape varieties
Reds: Gamay and Pinot Noir, Côt, Cabernet Franc and Sauvignon.
Whites: Sauvignon, Chardonnay.

Ageing ability
Reds: 2-4 years.
Whites and rosés: for early drinking.

Soil types
Clayey-silliceous on tuffeau chalk, erosional sandy soils.

Choice of food
Reds and rosés: charcuterie.
Whites: grilled fish, goats' cheese.

Serving temperature
Reds: 12-14°C.
Whites and rosés: 8-10°C.

VALENÇAY
APPELLATION D'ORIGINE
VIN DÉLIMITÉ DE QUALITÉ SUPÉRIEUR
MISE EN BOUTEILLE A LA PROPRIÉTÉ

Vin de Corse

Appellation
Vin de Corse
AOC
followed by one
of the following
denominations:
Coteaux du Cap
Corse, Calvi,
Figari, Porto-
Vecchio, Sartène.

1976

This ancient vineyard, overshadowed by the monolithic statues of Filitosa, was first planted by the Genoese in the 16th century, testifying to a wine-growing tradition that dates back to 570 BC when the Phœnicians planted vines on what they called this 'mountain in the sea'. The vines are concentrated near the coast, mostly in the eastern sector from Bastia to Ghisonaccia. It is here that the largest co-operatives and private estates are to be found. Corsican wines belong to the same broad family as southern French wines but with distinctive characteristics of their own linked to the powerfully aromatic, local grape varieties.

Colours
Red (60%)
Rosé (30%)
White (10%)
Area
1,785 hectares
Production
76,210
hectolitres

**Main grape
varieties**
Vermentinu
(Malvoisie
de Corse),
Niellucciu
(or Nielluccio),
Sciacarellu
(or Sciacarello),
Grenache,
Mourvèdre.

Soil types
Siliceous-clay,
schists, granitic
sand, clayey
limestone,
tuffeau.

Ageing ability
Reds:
4-5 years.
Rosés and whites:
2 years.

Choice of food
Reds: civet and
stews, grilled
meat, mild
sheep's cheese.
Rosés: summer
salads, grilled
fish, oriental
cuisine.
Whites: apéritif;
fish in sauces,
goats' cheese,
brocciu,
puddings.

Eye

• The reds are made mainly from Nielluccio and Sciacarellu blended with Grenache and Syrah, and are quite deep in colour.

• The rosés, made mainly from Sciacarrelu, Niellucciu and Grenache, range from deep to diaphanous pink.

• The whites are made principally from Vermentinu (also known locally as Malvoisie de Corse). They have light tones with golden highlights.

Nose

• The reds offer fruit aromas coupled with notes of liquorice and leather.

• The rosés are straightforward and crisp, with fragrances of dog rose, honeysuckle and heather, punctuated with peppery touches.

• The whites are floral, fresh and generous with a winning combination of hints of citrus and exotic fruits.

Palate

• The reds leave a silky sensation on the palate and are surprisingly long.

• After an acidulous attack that creates an impression of freshness, the rosés are rounded and supple on the mid palate and respectably long on the finish.

• The whites have subtly spicy palate aromas, good structure but without a trace of aggression, and good persistence.

The Sartène vineyard.

Serving temperature
Reds: 16-18°C.
Rosé and whites: 7-10°C.

Vin de Savoie

1973

Appellation
Vin de Savoie
AOC
Colours
Red
White (70%)
Area
1,725 hectares
Production
123,230
hectolitres

Main grape varieties
Reds: Mondeuse,
Gamay Noir,
Pinot Noir.
Whites:
Chasselas,
Jacquère, Altesse,
Roussanne.

The valleys of Savoie and the Haute-Savoie are punctuated by small islands of south-facing vines that extend from Lake Geneva to the right-bank of the Isère River. The climate on these lower slopes of the Alps is moderated by the proximity of the lakes and the wines are as crisp as the mountain air. They include: white wines made predominantly from a local grape variety called Jacquère; red wines based on Mondeuse, Gamay (imported from Beaujolais) or even Pinot Noir (imported from Burgundy); rosés based on Gamay; and sparkling wines made in Ayze.

Eye
• The reds based on Mondeuse have characteristic crimson tones. Arbin wines, the most typical of the region, have black cherry highlights.
• The whites shimmer with straw highlights.

Choice of food
Reds:
air-dried beef,
game, chicken
with
chanterelles,
pork grill,
Savoie cheese
(Beaufort,
Tomme,
Reblochon).
Whites:
fish (trout,
char), frogs'
legs, snails.

Soil types
Argillaceous
limestone, slope
wash from
Jurassic ranges.

Ageing ability
Reds: 2-6 years.
Whites: 2 years.

Serving temperature
Reds: 16-18°C.
Whites: 10-12°C.

Nose

• The reds made from Mondeuse are reminiscent of strawberry, raspberry and blackcurrant, with floral nuances (violet, iris) and spicy tones that became highly developed in the course of ageing.

• The whites are marked by white flowers, aromas of exotic fruits and mirabelle plums.

Palate

• The reds are based on Mondeuse, the predominant grape variety in this region before the phylloxera epidemic. They are robust with silky tannins and intense palate aromas.

• The Jacquère-based whites are light, crisp and appealing from an early age. Those based on Altesse – or Roussette de Savoie – are very delicate and improved by short periods of ageing. Those made from Roussanne – known locally as Bergeron – have a well-balanced, refreshing palate.

The vines of the Domaine de Ripaille, on the borders of Lake Geneva.

Vins d'Entraygues-et-du-Fel

Appellation
Vins d'Entraygues-et-du-Fel AOVDQS

Colours
Red
White
Rosé

Area
18 hectares

1965

Production
985 hectolitres

Grape varieties
Reds: Cabernet-Sauvignon, Cabernet Franc, Fer-Servadou (plus eight others including Gamay and Mouyssaguès).
Whites: Chenin, Mauzac.

Estaing wines
The village of Estaing is on one of the routes to Santiago de Compostela and used to cultivate as many as 1,200 hectares of vines in this part of the upper Lot valley. The VDQS appellation area (12 hectares) encompasses three communes of astonishingly different geology: schists, limestone and even the so-called *rougiers de Marcillac.* The grape varieties are as varied as the soils, producing characterful wines: fresh, fragrant red wines based on Fer-Servadou and Gamay; and white wines blended from Chenin, Mauzac and Roussellou.

Soil types
Schist in Fel, granitic in Entraygues, red *rougiers* Marcillac soils.

Ageing ability
3-5 years.

The vineyards of Entraygues-et-du-Fel cling to the steep hillsides of the first foothills of the Cantal and Aubrac massifs. The village of Entraygues (meaning 'between two waters') is located at the confluence of the Lot and Truyère rivers, in the centre of an appellation that encompasses six communes. The vines grow on narrow terraces where the soils determine the type of wine produced: robust reds from the schistous soils of Fel; crisp, fragrant whites from the granitic soils of Entraygues (that suit the Chenin).

Eye
• The reds are ruby with violet highlights.
• The whites are brilliant pale gold with green highlights.

Nose
• The reds are marked by aromas of red fruit (blackcurrant, raspberry).
• The whites release a melody of fresh aromas, first floral (broom, acacia, lime), then fruity (citrus) and mineral (notes of gunflint).

Palate
• The reds are delicious, with a rather solid, rural character.
• The crisp whites have a delicately *perlant* quality and leave behind an acidulous impression.

Serving temperature
Reds: 15-16°C.
Whites: 10-12°C.

Choice of food
Reds: charcuterie, *tripoux Rouergats* (sheep's offal and sheep's feet), Auvergne hotpot, Causses lamb. *Whites:* seafood, river fish (trout), mild cheese.

Viré-Clessé

The villages of Viré and Clessé, between Tournus and Mâcon, were the first to be granted Mâcon-Villages communal appellation. The Viré-Clessé AOC is a distinctive presence at the heart of the vineyard, producing exclusively white wines from Chardonnay that are well structured and richly aromatic. The designation Grand Vin de Macon (or de Bourgogne) may figure on the label.

1 9 9 8

Appellation
Viré-Clessé AOC
Colour
White
Area
552 hectares
Production
22,000 hectolitres

Eye

Brilliant pale gold, neither white nor yellow but ash-gold, often shimmering with delicate green highlights.

Nose

Aromas reminiscent of hawthorn or acacia, honeysuckle and even broom are joined by scents of white peach and mentholated notes, sometimes with a hint of pine and quince jam. Verbena, fern and almond complete the bouquet.

Palate

Crisp and vivacious but still very rounded and charming. Chardonnay comes into its own here with particularly good results.

Choice of food
Frogs' legs, snails, *andouillette* sausage cooked in white wine, parsley ham, Bresse poultry à la crème, goats' cheese.

Serving temperature
11-13°C.

Ageing ability
About 5-6 years.

Soil types
Bajocian crinoidal limestone, Oxfordian marly-calcareous layers, clay with sandstone pebbles.

Grape variety
Chardonnay.

Volnay

Appellations
Volnay AOC
Volnay Premier
Cru AOC
Colour
Red
Superficie
Volnay:
98 hectares
Volnay Premier
Cru: 115 hectares
Volnay-
Santenots:
29 hectares
Production
10,120
hectolitres

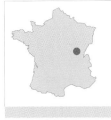

1984

Volnay is a steep narrow village perched quite high up in the Côte de Beaune at an altitude of 275 metres (902 feet). To the north is Pommard, to the south Meursault. The vineyard huddles against the side of the Chaignot hill, facing southeast on limestone soils. It produces a fairly precocious, smooth and subtle wine that is generally regarded as rather feminine – the most refined red wine in the Côte de Beaune.

A first choice
Premier Cru
Volnay-Santenots (29 hectares) is a red Premier Cru produced in the village of Meursault on the border with Volnay. Plainly a Volnay by its style and colour, Volnay-Santenots has a silky framework and fetches top price at the Hospices de Beaune wine auction. The *climat* of Les Santenots du Milieu is generally classified as the *tête de cuvée* (source of the best wines) though the differences with the Clos de Santenots and Les Santenots are only minor.

Soil types
White Argovian limestone at the top of the slope; limestone and reddish ferruginous soil in the middle; schistous beds; deeper gravelly soil at the base.

Choice of food
Roast meat, poultry (roasted duck, stuffed quail), filet mignon; also red meat, cheese (Chaource, Brie, Reblochon) with the more robust crus.

Serving temperature
15-16°C.

Grape variety
Pinot Noir.

Ageing ability
3-8 years.

Eye

Lustrous vivid red, sometimes verging on dark garnet, often with flickering glints of ruby.

Premiers Crus

The 36 Volnay Premiers Crus are divided into four groups, each with markedly different characteristics.

• The upper sector on the Pommard side soft, produces soft, sensual wines from crus such as Clos des Ducs, Pitures Dessus, Chanlins, Fremiets, Bousse d'Or, la Barre and Clos de la Barre.

• The middle sector, still on the Pommard side, is characterised by crus such as Les Mitans.

• The middle sector on the Meursault side produces harmoniously fleshy wines of exquisite finesse. Famous *climats* include Carelles, Caillerets and Champans.

• The upper sector on the Monthélie side, notably Clos des Chênes and Taillepieds, is the source of seductive, rather bracing and powerful wines. Lyrically breathy, even a little wild, these are the least feminine wines of the appellation.

Many former *climats* are now 'clos' including: Clos de la Rougeotte, du Verseuil, de l'Audignac, de la Chapelle, de la Cave, de la Barre, de la Bousse d'Or and des Soixante Ouvrées.

Nose

Fresh, light aromas tending towards vegetal and floral notes (violets, the classical fragrance of Burgundy red, and sometimes roses) plus traces of red berries (raspberry, redcurrant) or black berries (blackberry).

Clos de la Bousse d'Or.

Palate

A powerfully seductive, light and fruity palate. Volnay Premier Cru is frequently more concentrated and elegant than Volnay although the degree of difference depends largely on the estate and the vintage.

Vosne-Romanée

Appellations
Vosne-Romanée
AOC
Vosne-Romanée
Premier Cru
AOC

Colour
Red

Area
Vosne-Romanée:
98 hectares 56
ares 78 centiares
Vosne-Romanée
Premier Cru: 57
hectares 18 ares
58 centiares

Production
6,950 hectolitres

1 9 3 6

1993

VOSNE~ROMANÉE
AUX RÉAS
APPELLATION VOSNE-ROMANÉE CONTRÔLÉE
Mis en bouteille par
BERTRAND MACHARD DE GRAMONT
PROPRIÉTAIRE A NUITS-ST-GEORGES (COTE-D'OR) FRANCE
Tél. 80 61 16 96

Grape variety
Pinot Noir.

Romanée became Vosne-Romanée in 1866. The vineyard extends across some 100 hectares in the communes of Vosne-Romanée and Flagey-Echézeaux, abutting such famous names as Romanée-Conti, La Romanée, Romanée-Saint-Vivant, La Tâche, Echézeaux, Grands-Echézeaux, Les Richbourgs – magnificent Grands Crus yielding a Pinot Noir wine of matchless complexity. For all their undeniable excellence however, they are often closely rivalled by the excellent Premiers Crus and Villages wines.

Soil types
The communal appellation is situated at the top of the slope or at the beginning of the piedmont, either side of the Grands Crus and sometimes beyond: limestone mixed with argillaceous marl of varying depth (from a few dozen centimetres to a metre).

The Premiers Crus
Flagey-Echézeaux: Les Beaux Monts, Les Rouges and En Orveaux – three *climats* close to Les Echézeaux and very similar in quality. Vosne-Romanée, to the north and on the Flagey side: Les Suchots, surrounded by Romanée-Saint-Vivant and Les Richebourgs, two *climats* that are often superior to Les Echézeaux and equivalent to a Premier Cru; Les Beaux Monts at the top of the slope; Aux Brûlées in the vicinity of Les Richebourgs. Above La Romanée and Les Richebourgs: Cros Parantou, Les Petits Monts and Les Reignots continue from La Romanée along the top of the hillside and age well. On the Nuits side and southwards: Les Malconsorts and Dessus des Malconsorts abutting La Tâche; Les Chaumes, le Clos des Réas and La Croix Rameau.

Ageing ability
5-15 years.

Eye

Intense crimson, fiery red,
sometimes tending towards garnet.

The Vosne-Romanée vineyard abuts
the Echézeaux vineyard in the north.

Nose

Dominated by aromas of lush ripe
fruit on a spicy background. Refined,
well-blended aromas of red berries
(strawberry and raspberry) and black
berries (blackberry, bilberry and
blackcurrant) evolve with age to
scents of cherries in brandy,
preserved meats, leather and fur,
sometimes with roasted notes
from barrel-ageing.

Palate

Velvety distinction, the epitome
of Pinot Noir. Vosne-Romanée is
slightly austere and firm in youth
and needs time to flesh out its
tannins. This is a wine for laying-
down that takes many years to
reach maturity. The finish is
remarkably long.

Choice of food

Eggs poached in
red wine,
feathered game,
duck with
turnips, Bresse
chicken, fricassee
of mushrooms,
cheese (Brie,
Saint-Nectaire,
Coulommiers).

Serving
temperature

Young wines:
13-14°C.
More mature
wines: 14-16°C.

Vougeot

Appellations
Vougeot AOC
Vougeot Premier
Cru AOC

Colours
Red
White (13%)

Area
16.5 hectares

Production
Reds:
525 hectolitres
Whites:
150 hectolitres

1 9 3 6

The Premiers Crus
Clos de la Perrière
Le Clos Blanc
Les Crâs
Les Petits Vougeots

The village of
Vougeot.

Soil types
Shallow, brown
limestone at the
top; limestone
and fine-
textured marl
with clay further
down in the
piedmont (site
of the 'Village'
appellation).

Grape varieties
Reds:
Pinot Noir.
Whites:
Chardonnay.

**Ageing
ability**
5-15 years.

The village of Vougeot, in the heart of the Côte de Nuits between Chambolle-Musigny and Flagey-Echézeaux, is named after the little river Vouge that flows into the Saône. The Vougeot appellation is tiny and, being sandwiched between two such heavyweights as Clos de Vougeot and Musigny, is unlikely to get any bigger. Two-thirds of the vineyard consists of Premiers Crus planted with Pinot Noir and Chardonnay. In this area dedicated to red wines, Vougeot's originality lies in its historic white wines that originated in Clos Blanc.

Choice of food
Reds: grilled or
roasted red meat,
game (pheasant,
venison), cheese
(Cîteaux,
Brillat-Savarin,
Reblochon,
Vacherin,
Mont-d'Or).
Whites: grilled
or baked fish,
cheese (Comté,
goats' cheese).

**Serving
temperature**
Reds: 16-17°C.
Whites: 8-10°C.

Eye

• The reds are deeply luminous with crimson tones.

• The whites are refined and delicate, acquiring deeper golden tones after a decade.

Nose

• The reds evoke flowers (violets) and red or black berries (raspberry, morello cherry, blackcurrant). Matures wines develop notes of the underwood, dead leaves and truffle, together with animal aromas.

• The whites offer accessible aromas of hawthorn and acacia, followed by a mineral nuance derived from the stony, very calcareous soils of Vougeot. Some wines reveal apple or citrus scents; older wines develop fragrances of amber and spice.

Palate

• The whites are dry and sharp with that nuance of robustness that tends to be a particular feature of Chardonnay from the Côte des Nuits.

• The reds have a harmony built on richness and acidity, with noticeable but delicately fleshy tannins and a not infrequent touch of liquorice.

There are a dozen or so producers in the Vougeot appellation, with an output of approximately 41,000 bottles.

Vouvray

Appellation
Vouvray AOC
Colour
White (dry,
sweet and
sparkling)
Area
2,050 hectares
Production
Still wines:
46,913 hectolitres
Sparkling wines:
72,159 hectolitres

1 9 4 6

The Vouvray vineyard is in the heart of the Touraine region, carpeting the slopes that border the right-bank of the Loire and the valleys that criss-cross the plateau east of Tours. Well-drained soils that warm up easily favour maturation of the Chenin grape variety. Vouvray never experiences extreme weather but marked variations in sunshine and rainfall from one year to the next make the concept of the vintage all the more important. Grapes harvested late in good years produce medium dry or sweet wines; grapes harvested earlier yield dry wines. Sparkling wines, which first appeared at the end of the 19th-century, complete the range.

Grape variety
Chenin Blanc
(or Pineau de
la Loire).

**Ageing
ability**
Still wines:
5 years.
Sweet wines:
10 years
(longer for
great vintages).
Sparkling wines:
for early
drinking.

Soil types
Siliceous-clay
(high in flint);
argillaceous
limestone
(clay on
tuffeau chalk).

Choice of food
Dry wines:
charcuterie,
andouillete
sausage cooked
in Vouvray,
blanquette de
veau, Vouvray
cake, Tarte Tatin.
*Medium dry or
sweet wines:*
puddings.
**Serving
temperature**
10-11°C.

Eye

• Dry Vouvray wines are pale with green highlights.

• The young sweet wines are a clear straw-yellow, acquiring deeper, almost amber tones with age. Wines from certain years when the grapes have reached a high level of maturity are a gorgeous golden colour.

• Sparkling Vouvray is deep yellow with very fine bubbles.

Nose

• Dry Vouvray evokes citrus and white fruits (apple, peach). Wines from very ripe harvests develop aromas of ripe fruit, almonds and hazelnut.

• The young sweet wines reveal scents of acacia, cloves and rose mingled with notes of fresh fruit – apple, pear and sometimes citrus. Honey, beeswax, Virginia tobacco and nuances of ripe quince are signs of concentrated grapes. With age, the nose is more reminiscent of apricot or quince jam.

• Sparkling Vouvray has a surprisingly brioche-like quality, with notes of hazelnuts or almonds and often the fragrance of green apples. Wines of character are comparable to still Vouvray.

Palate

• Dry Vouvray wines always have a touch of well-behaved liveliness (due to the absence of malo-lactic fermentation) that gives them an agreeably fresh quality.

• The medium dry or sweet wines achieve a delicate balance of sweetness and liveliness that persists throughout the long, lingering finish.

• Sparkling Vouvray wines balance liveliness with a certain roundness, and give an impression of elegance and freshness.

Mousseux or *pétillant*?

Sparkling Vouvray wines are produced by the *Méthode Traditionnelle* based on second fermentation in the bottle. They are said to be *pétillant* when the pressure in the bottle reaches 2.5 kg/cm2 and *mousseux* when it is more than 5 kg. By law, the wines must remain at least nine months *sur* lattes (on slats) but many producers allow longer periods of bottle fermentation.

The wines age well in the tuffeau cellars.

Alsace

Beaujolais

Bordeaux Region

Burgundy

Bugey

Champagne

Charente

Corsica

Eastern France

The Jura

Languedoc

The Loire Valley

Provence